T0345580

IBERIAN AND LATIN AMERICAN STUDIES

'Los Invisibles'

IBERIAN AND LATIN AMERICAN STUDIES

'Los Invisibles'

A History of Male Homosexuality in Spain, 1850–1939

RICHARD CLEMINSON
AND
FRANCISCO VÁZQUEZ GARCÍA

UNIVERSITY OF WALES PRESS
CARDIFF
2007

British Library Cataloguing-in-Publication Data
A catalogue record for this book is available from the British Library.

ISBN 978–0–7083–2012–9

Typeset by Columns Design Ltd, Reading
Printed in Great Britain by Antony Rowe Ltd, Chippenham, Wiltshire

Contents

Series Editors' Foreword

Over recent decades, the traditional 'languages and literatures' model in Spanish departments in universities in the United Kingdom has been superceded by a contextual, interdisciplinary and 'area studies' approach to the study of the culture, history, society and politics of the Hispanic and Lusophone worlds – categories which extend far beyond the confines of the Iberian Peninsula, not only to Latin America but also to Spanish-speaking and Lusophone Africa.

In response to these dynamic trends in research priorities and curriculum development, this series is designed to present both disciplinary and interdisciplinary research within the general field of Iberian and Latin American Studies, particularly studies which explore all aspects of **Cultural Production** (*inter alia* literature, film, music, dance, sport) in Spanish, Portuguese, Basque, Catalan, Galician and the indigenous languages of Latin America. The series also aims to publish research on the **History and Politics** of Hispanic and Lusophone worlds, both at the level of region and that of the nation-state, as well as on **Cultural Studies** which explore the shifting terrains of gender, sexual, racial and postcolonial identities in those same regions.

Acknowledgements

Francisco Vázquez would like to acknowledge the part played in this book by two people who are no longer with us: Jean-Louis Flandrin and Mariano Peñalver. What is of value in his contribution to this book stems from the guidance of these two figures. J. L. Flandrin inspired his interest in the history of sexuality. M. Peñalver has been his intellectual mentor in all his undertakings. He would also like to mention his friend Andrés Moreno, who has accompanied his exploration of the sexual history of Spain, and Raphael Carrasco, of the University of Montpellier, a pioneer in the history of homosexuality in Spain. He would like to thank the librarians Ana Remón y Charo Gestido for their kindness and assistance when consulting the wonderful special collections of the Faculty of Medicine, University of Cadiz. His colleagues José Luis, Juan, Ramón, Rafael, Antonio, Cándido, Carlos and Cinta have provided a pleasant and stimulating place to work in and his development of a researcher would not have been possible without them. He has learned more from his doctoral students Pepe Moreno Pestaña, José Benito, Alfonso Marqués, Antonio Polo and Alejandro Estrella than he could ever have taught them. Finally, he would like to thank Oliva – without her love and support he would not have managed to summon the strength to finish this project.

Richard Cleminson, for his part, would like to acknowledge the encouragement to research and write this book at different stages of this project, from a mere idea to completion, from Chris Perriam, Alison Sinclair, Julia Varela, Fernando Álvarez-Uría, Ángel Gordo López, Rosa María Medina Doménech, Paul Julian Smith and Jorge Uría. Colleagues at the University of Leeds and his previous institution have provided a stimulating background at different stages. His research into the medicalization of male homosexuality in Spain was made possible by a generous Award in the History of Medicine from the Wellcome Trust in 2002–3 and by being given an academic home in the Department of Pathological Anatomy and the History of Medicine, University of Granada, from 2003 to 2004. His invitation to speak at the

University of Oviedo in 2002 turned out to be a life-changing event, as did his longer sojourn in Granada from 2002 to 2004. Many of the challenges and joyous moments of these places were faced accompanied by Fredy – to him my greatest thanks of all.

Both authors would like to thank Sarah Lewis, of the University of Wales Press, for her encouragement and patience in the final stages of the delivery of the manuscript.

Chapter One

Introduction

In *Alexis o el significado del temperamento urano*, published in 1932 in Madrid, the Uruguayan literary critic and homosexual rights advocate Alberto Nin Frías wrote that in his day like no other, the individual's sexual life had gained a significance far above any other aspect of their existence.[1] Nin Frías, whose book *Homosexualismo creador* was also published by the well-known Morata house,[2] reflected the realities of a time which, despite considerable differences, strikes a chord in today's world where sexuality is still claimed to be the driving force behind one's character, feelings and actions. It is true that Nin Frías wrote his two books on the 'homosexual question' in a period that was in many senses exceptional. It cannot be denied that his books would have been published with difficulty even five years earlier, under the dictatorship of General Miguel Primo de Rivera (1923–30). The Spanish Republic (1931–6), emblem of modernity, opened up a political and cultural space which was, apart from the period from 1975 onwards, unrivalled in Spain's contemporary history for its degree of openness and spirit of cultural experimentation.[3] The homosexual question flourished under its aegis.

However, despite certain parallels that can be drawn between the 1930s and the present day it is noteworthy that, in contrast to some other European countries, most of the now extensive work on sexuality and gender in Spain has been confined either to the Inquisition period or to more literary or sociological accounts of post-Franco times.[4] Save the more accessible subjects of study from the early twentieth century such as the poet and playwright Federico García Lorca and literary figures in more present times such as Juan Goytisolo, Luis Antonio de Villena and Terenci Moix, work on the contemporary history of male homosexuality in Spain has been minimal (it is even more sparse on female homosexuality), despite the large, although disparate, variety of sources readily available to the historian.[5] It is, therefore, not surprising that in recent publications related to male homosexuality in literature or culture, to name two areas, the past really does seem to be a 'foreign country', with accounts rarely touching upon the pre-Transition period.[6] There may well be, nevertheless, good reasons for this lack of historical emphasis. The conception that homosexuality was 'repressed' and therefore invisible before the 'transition to democracy' is a strong motif which still holds sway. The aura around famous homosexual figures, such as García Lorca, may have, paradoxically, obscured the very nature of homosexual subcultures in the 1920s and 1930s as well as their historical investigation. The fact that homosexuality is, to a considerable degree, still taboo in Spain, is a third historically potent explanation.[7]

Eric Hobsbawm, in his recent book on the 'short twentieth century', wrote that one of the most eerie developments in recent years has been the tendency to forget history, to have one's past erased.[8] In the context of the recuperation of all kinds of people's history – from that of the persecutions of the Nazi period, the recent attempts to 'recover' historical memory from the Franco period, and that of the multiple directions that social history has moved into – a history of male homosexuality in the contemporary period is, we feel, justified and necessary on numerous grounds. The increasingly sophisticated arguments that sexual history cannot be divorced from wider social and historical processes has been championed convincingly by too many historians to list.[9] That Spain's sexual history is still largely to be explored suggests that there are multiple insights to be drawn from an analysis of the workings of sexuality in its broader historical context. Furthermore, the study of similarities and differences between different national sexual histories can only enrich our historical understanding of all societies concerned.[10]

The methods of research employed here and the conceptualization of what material is relevant to this history will reflect, to some degree, the authors' own quests and concerns, not to speak of the availability of archive material. Instead of an extensive exposition of our theoretical framework, apart from some necessary considerations which follow, we have tried to let theoretical insights inform our writing implicitly. Our book is guided by a number of questions such as the following: how far are existing models for the history of homosexuality both in Spain and wider afield adequate for Spain? Are the discourses on the configuration of the history of male homosexuality in Spain as specific as, say, the Spanish nineteenth century with its battles between absolutism and liberalism and the rise of political movements such as Carlism or anarchism? How peculiar, in a word, is the history of Spanish homosexuality?

These questions necessarily invite some kind of methodological and theoretical positioning. The pages of this book are devoted to presenting a history – not *the* history, as if there were such a thing – of male homosexuality in Spain in the period from 1850 up to the years of the Civil War (1936–9). The concentration on a relatively short period of time requires some justification. We do not focus on this period because there is somehow 'more' history to be written about but rather because we feel that, in accordance with much historical writing about the history of male (and female) homosexuality in Europe and elsewhere, the late nineteenth and early twentieth centuries were the formative years of what became crystallized as 'homosexuality' in the contemporary period.[11]

If we believe that 'homosexuality' more or less as it exists, is represented and lived today has more in common with the mid to late nineteenth century and early twentieth century than it does with, say, the early eighteenth century, such an impression responds to the fact that we take as the 'creation' of European homosexuality the latter years of the nineteenth century. The concept of homosexuality having been 'created' in this period (it was named thus in 1869), however, is often employed as a shorthand which is just too brief and uncritical.[12] The assertion begs the question who or what created it and for what purpose, if any? We also may ask, if homosexuality was thus created or 'invented' in Europe, was its path the same in all European countries? Is this framework valid for Spain?

Our assertion that 'homosexuality' describes a recent phenomenon inevitably touches upon a historiographical nerve that is often seen to be articulated around what has been too rigidly interpreted as a basic divide in the way in which homosexual history can be written. While John Addington Symonds in England at the end of the nineteenth century or Nin Frías in Spain in the third decade of the twentieth, in their bid to argue that homosexuals should be treated more justly, marshalled for their arguments a historical train of 'homosexual' individuals from Greek times through to their own present, historians in the 1980s, particularly in the United States and Britain, began to question the essential historical links of continuity between individuals in vastly different societies over long periods of historical time. Instead of such continuities, which these latter authors believed to be more imaginary than real, historical inquiry focused on how similar or identical acts could represent or mean different things in different places and times.[13]

The two positions thus described enjoyed theoretical dominance principally in the 1980s and 1990s in the context of the upsurge of Lesbian and Gay Studies and, later, Queer Studies and have been labelled, respectively, essentialism and social constructionism.[14] While some English-language historiographical circles now consider the debate to have exhausted itself, it is perhaps too early to assume the same for Spain.[15]

The possibilities and limitations afforded by both positions have recently been analysed by Eve K. Sedgwick. For the purposes of individual or even collective biographies, in terms of constructing or affirming identity or for the demanding of political rights, the essentialist perspective holds much attraction. On an individual biographical level, it is common to see how essentialism is used to buttress a claim or justify a historical identity. Historically, this has relied on the notion of a special nature for homosexuals, either anatomical in some way or psychological, which is read as fuel for affirming rights. Often, as a result, the essentialism versus social constructionism battle tends to be reduced to the nature/nurture or innatism/environmentalism supposed dichotomy.[16] Such an essentialist narrative would allow for the affirmative construction of identity and effectively resists other epistemologies which argue that such an identity is socially produced, learned or fleeting. But the inverse 'everything is constructed' and therefore fictive, denies personal experience and, for some, destroys any political basis from which to claim rights.

On the political front, both positions can be productive[17] but there is nothing necessarily progressive about either. Essentialist positions which generally emphasized the congenital nature of homosexuality, in the writings of past advocates of homosexual

equality such as Ulrichs, Hirschfeld and Ellis, may have functioned as a weapon against persecution in the late nineteenth and
early twentieth centuries; one must recall that many Nazi commentators viewed homosexuality as contagious at least in the
'Aryan' population and not something which was congenital.[18]
While essentialism may have something to offer in terms of
individual biographies or even as a political tactic, it must be less
effective in the writing of gay history as it tends to project back
into the past a more or less stable homosexual subject or identity,
with less emphasis on the formation of that subject in relation to
medical, psychiatric or political discourses. In the light of social
constructionists' criticism, some accounts that rely explicitly on
essentialism have adapted the latter to form a more sophisticated
form of this position. Rictor Norton, for example, proposes the
use of 'queer cultural essentialism', which considers there is a
nucleus of 'queer' desire that is transcultural, transnational and
transhistorical, a 'queer essence' that is innate, congenital and
constitutional. The key, for Norton, is 'not to confuse the constancy of the desire with the variability of its expression'.[19]

One of the many problems with such concessions, however, is
the category 'desire'. Here, the notion of desire is too static,
primitive and naturalized. Desire, we would argue, changes in its
expression, in its very 'being', according to the historical circumstances in which it is realized. It does not just mean the same
regardless and therefore is with difficulty 'transhistorical'. In this
book, we prefer to take a leaf from John Searle's recent account of
the construction of social reality according to which it could be
argued that 'homosexuality' should not be taken as a 'natural
fact' but as an 'institutional fact', a kind of subjectivity forged
from language and human action in a specific historical circumstance.[20] Or, as Ian Hacking has argued with respect to his
thoughts on the history of homosexuality in terms that he calls
'dynamic nominalism':

> The claim of dynamic nominalism is not that there was a kind of
> person who came increasingly to be recognized by bureaucrats or
> by students of human nature but rather that a kind of person came
> into being at the same time the kind itself was being invented. In
> some cases, that is, our classifications and our classes conspire to
> emerge hand in hand, each egging the other on.[21]

Such an argument allows for a dynamic interpretation of the relationship between subjectivity, discourse and control and denies the merely discursive form of social constructionism that appears to suggest that homosexuality is no more than a myth, a fiction, thus not taking into account the material effects and the consequences for the lived reality of those who identified as 'homosexual' and those who did not. To be homosexual is not just to fill a discursive space or to take on a cultural role but (still) to suffer the consequences of being labelled and labelling oneself as such an individual.

As we have noted above, the 'nineteenth-century' thesis, which placed emphasis on the medical and psychiatric discourse as the principal creator of 'homosexuality', deriving in the first instance from Foucault and substantiated by many historical studies across different countries,[22] is now broadly accepted in the field of gay history. One of Foucault's most renowned allocutions on the development or 'creation' of the homosexual from earlier states such as 'sodomy' reads as follows:

> As defined by the ancient civil or canonical codes, sodomy was a category of forbidden acts; their perpetrator was nothing more than the juridical subject of them. The nineteenth-century homosexual became a personage, a past, a case history, and a childhood, in addition to being a type of life, a life form, and a morphology, with an indiscreet anatomy and possibly a mysterious physiology. Nothing that went into his total composition was unaffected by his sexuality . . . Homosexuality appeared as one of the forms of sexuality when it was transposed from the practice of sodomy onto a kind of interior androgyny, a hermaphrodism of the soul. The sodomite had been a temporary aberration; the homosexual was now a species.[23]

Perhaps as a result of what could be understood as a quasi-teleological mode of thinking here (the sodomite was a '*temporary aberration*' as though something else *had* to follow) some authors have adopted the Foucauldian model too closely and have presented a rather schematic and over-determined shift from sodomite to invert through to homosexual. In fact, Foucault discusses the invert only in passing, as an auxiliary in the movement towards the 'homosexual'. In this sense, the 'creation' of the homosexual has come to adopt the status of a near universal or natural end product which was never intended by the original author as the steps towards his creation are remorselessly traced from one period or country to the next.[24]

This 'vulgarized' model of Foucauldian thought would correspond to the following steps. The homosexual is viewed as a personage who was created essentially by late nineteenth-century psychiatry. Before this time, in the medieval and modern period, 'sodomites' and 'sodomy' were referred to in law, theology and literature but these labels designated not a psychic state, or special character, but a practice or a vice 'against nature', which could potentially befall anyone. The sodomite disrupted the natural order ordained by God, in which humans should propagate their faith by means of their own reproduction.[25]

Nevertheless, the Greco-Roman sexual ethic was also devoid of any strict division between hetero and homosexual in the terms we appreciate them today. What counted, according to Foucault's volumes two and three of *The History of Sexuality* were other matters such as age, status and who adopted the 'active' or 'passive' role in anal intercourse between men. The active role was associated with older men, virility, the status conferred on 'citizens' and the ability to control one's passions. The passive position was fulfilled by younger men, slaves, or women, and was characterized by effeminacy and lack of self control. Social judgement transpired around what was done sexually with whom, not necessarily the sex of the person.

This kind of categorization would hold until the time of the medieval sodomite, who indulged in 'vice' with individuals of the same sex, with women or with animals, that is, those who achieved the emission of semen in the incorrect 'vessel'. While recent work has suggested that there was a shift from this kind of sodomite to a more effeminate variety as an intermediate category before the modern homosexual,[26] in some accounts there has been too much concession to a teleological shift from sodomite, to pederast to invert to homosexual, all carefully graded steps on the way to the modern 'gay'.[27]

Rather than follow such a linear, unitary, although discontinuous historical model, which evokes the progressive resolution of old categories and mentalities in favour of innovation and change, what we suggest here is an analysis that is conscious of the possible multiplicity of terms, personages and representations of 'homosexuality' at one time. If George Chauncey has acknowledged that the shift from inversion to homosexuality in American medical doctors' minds was not as unanimously produced and did not take place as early as he had previously thought (the 1910s and 1920s) such lessons must be taken into consideration in other countries' histories of homosexuality.[28] This multiplicity of personages – sodomites, inverts and homosexuals – may have coexisted in the same society at one time or even within a particular 'field' such as medicine, psychiatry or at large in the public conceptualization.[29] It is possible, of course, that it took years for a particular categorization to 'filter through' to other areas of society, with some individuals thus named by science continuing in blissful ignorance of their 'condition'.[30] Older categorizations do not necessarily disappear from view; they may continue in uneasy cohabitation or be 'resignified', to use one of Judith Butler's concepts, in response to new representations.[31]

We have encountered this multiplicity or coexistence of old and new figures, of old and new models of subjectivity, in many instances in the history of homosexuality in Spain. There is a marked contrast between, for example, the slow transformations wrought in the Spanish legal field – homosexuality in some quarters of jurisprudence was still referred to as 'sodomy' well into the 1950s and 1960s – and the more dynamic field of psychiatry which was one of the principal sites for the dissemination of new knowledge on the 'sexual perversions' from the late nineteenth century. This diversity of subject positions – of subcultural expressions of homosexuality – can be found in Spain in literary representations during the same period. The protagonist of A. Hernández-Catá's novel, *El Ángel de Sodoma* (1929),[32] shies away in horror at the sight of a rouged fairy, the publicly visible working-class homosexual, a figure that coexisted, often in the same space, with aristocratic dandies who sought sexual adventures.[33]

The above points invite a reconsideration of the linear progress from sodomite to homosexual in favour of a more historically informed account which emphasizes multivocality and multiplicity in respect of the subjectivities created from 1850 to the late 1930s. The methodological suggestions offered by David Halperin are in this sense useful.[34] Five categories or principal ideal types, which would be distributed not in linear fashion but, potentially, through the whole narrative time scale, can be drawn upon to account for the multiple subject positions produced by the juxta-position of medicine and existing subcultures or those in forma-tion. The categories, variants or subject positions are: active sodomy, sexual inversion, effeminacy, homosexuality and homoso-ciality. While a certain general chronological shift may be observed in some of these cases, with an undeniable move towards the use of the term 'homosexual' as the latest in a number of designations, what we emphasize is the coexistence of such categorizations. Crucial to the understanding of any coun-try's history of homosexuality is not only the overlapping or replacement of one 'new species' by another but, something which Foucault observed less acutely, changes in gender expecta-tions for each sex, and the pervasive instability of boundaries between what were held culturally to be masculinity and feminin-ity.[35] Indeed, as Chauncey has observed, 'the intellectual history of homosexuality throughout the twentieth century has to some extent been concerned with the working out of the boundaries and relationship between "sexuality" and "gender"'.[36]

If 'sex' is a category that has been denaturalized through deconstruction, 'gender' has followed the same fate. If, in the words of some feminist analysts, sex as a supposed biological category has not created gender as a set of cultural scripts of masculinity and femininity, but the reverse, the cultural expecta-tion that one conforms to the sexual practices in accordance with one's biological sex becomes a heuristic device which allows us to draw up renovated epistemologies of 'homosexuality'.

The five types referred to by Halperin above exist in a variable relationship with the categories of sex, gender and hence sexual-ity. Sexual categories that emerge in particular time periods can be understood in accordance with changing associations between sex, gender and sexuality. Óscar Guasch has argued that there existed a 'pre-gay' model in Spain whose members were not conscious of themselves as a separate category of human beings.[37] The two figures that populated this model were the specifically Spanish *marica* (effeminate fairy) and *maricón* (active 'homo-sexual');[38] not homosexuals, but types, distinguished by their penchant for the active or passive role in sex and by their degree of effeminacy and who were used by the heterosexual world to draw the boundaries between acceptable and non-acceptable masculinities. This 'Mediterranean model' of sexuality,[39] predi-cated on the active/passive divide rather than on sexual identities according to sex preference per se, would decline in the face of the nineteenth-century medical process of transformation of the sodomite into the homosexual. Such a process entailed that the 'pre-gay' figures entered into decline as the homosexual became aware of his own condition. Instead of such a decline, however, it seems more likely that various figures occupied the same temporal space and it is possible that the old model of the active/passive sodomite held strong in Spain well into the twentieth century.[40]

Instead of the disappearance of these figures, then, our task is to trace their resignification and reincorporation into new economies of the sexuality/gender system.[41] Personages such as the *marica* could be considered as figures who have some correspondence with the 'invert' and the 'homosexual' respectively in terms of their significance with regards to gender and sexuality in the ways in which their characteristics were incorporated into new medical and psychiatric typologies in Spain.[42]

These variations on the theme of gender and sexuality could be represented thus, according to the relative importance of the gender or sexuality elements:

	Gender	Sexuality
Active sodomy	–	+
Inversion	+	–
Effeminacy	+	
Homosexuality		+
Homosociality	+	

The category 'active sodomy' would describe the sexual relation between an adult male with another male, in which the former penetrates the latter anally, often in a dominant/dominated equation. 'Socratic love' or pederasty is the classic version of the active sodomite, although more recent examples can be found across the globe, as in some North African societies and some countries of Latin America. As this act is primarily related to the field of sexuality, but is not without certain gender attributes, it is designated with a '+' and a '–' respectively.

Almost the mirror image of the active sodomite is the 'invert', who was believed to have inverted the roles of the sexes in terms of comportment, dress and voice, to name some characteristics. The sexual aspect of the invert, at least at first, was given less importance and it was only as the twentieth century wore on that the invert came to express a sexual aspect too. The invert was a person whose body and soul did not match up according to cultural assumptions of gender and sex, such as a male desire to play with dolls or cook; her or his typology and characteristics were further complicated when it was admitted that sexual practices were engaged in.[43] This type has included a huge range of gender-deviant individuals and types, from the 'psychic hermaphrodite', the 'third sex' and the 'Uranian', each with varying relative associations between gender and sexuality.

The category of the 'effeminate', at least until the end of the nineteenth century, is limited to the field of gender. Effeminacy, in its various forms and expressions, appears in many cultures as a designation for the female sphere, domestic tasks or dress, in contrast to the male world of hunting, war-making or political decision-making. The association between effeminacy and the passive sodomite is relatively late and forms part of a number of scorned practices under the rubric of 'mollities', softness or overly indulgent behaviour. The fop, for example, was deemed 'effeminate' but this was partly because of his desire to attract women through his overly sophisticated dress, speech or behaviour. While there are examples of effeminacy in men being related to the desire for sex with other males in previous periods,[44] it seems that, in England at least, effeminacy only became synonymous with the charge of homosexuality from the time of the Oscar Wilde trials of 1895.[45] In Spain, effeminacy had been associated with excess and possible homosexuality in the figure of Don Juan (see Chapter Three) and certainly by the 1920s in the pages of the psychiatry-inspired review *Sexualidad*.[46]

The term 'homosociality' is more suggestive of possible deviance, both gender and sexual, rather than any acts in themselves. It refers to the preference for the company and friendship of members of the same sex but, as such, is a border concept which may respond to the desire to exclude all things connected to women, and hence responds most likely to an aggressive expression of heterosexuality in which women would be conceived mainly as sexual beings, or may, and here lies the 'danger', respond to a desire to be among company of the same sex because of erotic preferences. Because of its inherent fragility, some writers prefer to see homosociality as something not clearly defined but as part of a continuum which allows for the structuring of men's relations with other men. Homosociality, like the shifting parameters of masculinity and femininity, is integral to what is deemed acceptable and non-acceptable in the relations between the sexes, as Sedgwick has noted.[47] Historically speaking, homosociality has been recognized in the sexological and psychiatric press as 'dangerous' for the development of same-sex attachments and possible sexual activity. One only has to think of the attention devoted to averting the perils inherent in same-sex environments such as ships, prisons, barracks and schools. In the eighteenth and nineteenth century, for example, it was deemed acceptable for young women to engage in highly demonstrative attachments with members of the same sex, and even indulge in sexual acts, as long as this was seen as an 'apprenticeship' for marriage.[48] Amongst men, displays of affection, including kissing, were common in several European countries and had no 'taint', at least until the middle of the nineteenth century, of homosexuality.[49]

If homosociality contained these hidden dangers, it was homosexuality itself that was viewed by the sexual sciences as the greatest danger of all. Homosexuality would play a similar regulatory role to its not so distant cousin homosociality: '[T]he importance – an importance – of the category "homosexual" . . . comes not from its regulatory relation to a nascent or already-constituted minority of homosexual people or desires, but from its potential for giving whoever wields it a structuring definitional leverage over the whole range of male bonds that shape the social constitution.'[50]

Homosexuality is, of course, the most recent category of the five variants listed above in Halperin's scheme, referring uniquely to the object of sexual desire. In this way, it may differ from sexual inversion in the sense that, as many a commentator observed, it was impossible to tell a homosexual and a 'normal' man apart. Observable gender deviance does not necessarily characterize homosexuality.

Of course, it would be laborious for the writer and tedious for the reader if this schema were to be followed category by category throughout this book. What this framework allows us to do, however, is to avoid the projecting back of the 'homosexual' through time (even as a 'queer cultural essentialism') as though there were a constant subject to be discovered throughout the latter part of the nineteenth and the beginning of the twentieth century. What we have tried to do instead is to illustrate how questions such as the 'dangers' of effeminacy and sexual inversion have been evoked in different contexts in order to create a kind of porous condition that was thought by doctors, legal experts and literary writers to be in need of intervention in order to save the child, the individual or the nation. Tracing connectivity (or following the 'pure little lines of mutation', as Deleuze has called them)[51] between the discourses and individuals produced around these issues does not have the advantage of making its claim to one subject and one subject alone. In the absence of this simplicity, as with all constructionist or genealogical approaches, it is possible that the subject we intend to study disappears as he (in this case) dissolves in a sea of discontinuities. Conscious of this danger, our task would consist of what one historian has called the tracing of 'sexually deviant subject formations' over time.[52]

By ranging over such permeable categories as effeminacy, and by being conscious of how emerging subjectivities that established some kind of relationship with same-sex sexuality came about, we can trace an illusive subject or cluster of signifiers around what became 'homosexuality'. Such a strategy shifts the lens off homosexuality alone and allows us to scrutinize the 'normal', to focus on how it is constructed and how it in turn constructs insiders and outsiders.[53] Perhaps the most illustrative points in our history are those overlaps, or alliances, so to speak, between self-aware subjects and those disciplines which intersected with their lives.

A kind of sensibility was created in Spain in a number of areas such as legal medicine, the hygiene movement, the literary world, and in discourses on the nation around issues that became important for the demarcation of different kinds of sexuality and their significance for wider questions. In many of the writings we have traced, the task of finding homosexuality in the most recondite places of the body or psyche obtains a medical and cultural significance, which somehow overflows its own actual importance. For example, in some circles doctors paid little attention to homosexuality as anatomical disease, preferring to focus on tuberculosis or syphilis, but the cultural menace presented by homosexuality was inflated far beyond its immediate medical or legal interest.

For this reason, despite the fact that we have relied heavily on discourse on the subject in specialist legal and medical areas, such as pedagogy and psychiatry, it cannot be said that homosexuality was merely a creation of expert discourses; the notion 'homosexuality' drew on a much broader base. We therefore emphasize a multiplicity of discourses and practices that contributed to the construction of an area, 'homosexuality', which raised fears, concerns and calls for intervention. But this was not a one-way process. The calls for intervention from doctors, for example, often backed up by very real police and legal persecution, in itself was not devoid of a reverse or counter-discourse. If all discourses, as Foucault has remarked, produce a counter-discourse, 'homosexuality' in Spain produced its spaces for self-affirmation or resistance. These important spaces, seen increasingly as the 1920s wore on, suggest how resistances are 'forged in conflict with medico-scientific discourses which pathologize homosexuality' and show how subjects become 'excessive' to the discourses from which they (at least partially) emerge.[54]

In this way, we have not given primacy to either self-aware identities (while not, on the other hand, ignoring them) or to expert discourses as the creator of these identities *ex nihilo*, as if discourse brought them into being, and could equally in a flourish extinguish them. We have not tried to resolve what we think is the sterile dilemma of whether the homosexual was created by medical science or whether medical science responded to the existence of homosexuals in order to embark on its taxonomical project.

George Chauncey, after producing one of the first accounts of the historical creation of sexual inversion and its transformation into homosexuality in New York at the turn of the twentieth century, admitted that he had overemphasized the role of medicine in producing those categories. In a postscript to his original article he wrote:

> I would now argue even more strongly... that the medical discourse did not 'invent' the homosexual; doctors did not create new categories on which people based their identities as homosexual or lesbian. Subsequent research has shown that doctors reproduced the categories and prejudices of their culture. The men doctors called 'inverts' in their medical journals were already called 'fairies' and 'queers' on the streets and in the popular press, and many of them, as several doctors noted in astonishment, resisted doctors' efforts to condemn them as 'perverts'.[55]

This dialectical relationship between the named and those doing the naming has been revisited by Harry Oosterhuis in his study of the writings and cultural milieu of the psychiatrist Richard von Krafft-Ebing. Oosterhuis argues that the disciplining effects of medical attention have been overemphasized, resulting in a neglect of individual voices and the socio-psychological formation of sexual subjectivity. Oosterhuis in his study focuses, therefore, on the 'patients' in order to assess the impact of medical theories on them and how they received such theories. He argues that in general medicine, diagnosis and 'objective' accounts substituted patients' accounts, but this was not so in psychiatry.[56] In contrast however, we, like Hacking, prefer to see how categories were mutually formed, with particular kinds of persons coming into being at the same time as the kind itself was being invented. This does not mean that we cannot trace the discourses involved in such a process, or the interests to which they may have responded, or their relationship to wider processes of nation-building, professional aspirations or political motivations, or to the emergence of modern subjectivities.

Despite these comments relativizing the importance of medicine in the construction of homosexuality, it must be acknowledged that a large proportion of the material we have located is related in some manner to medical or psychiatric discourse on the subject. Medical discourse becomes, in this sense, the starting point of the study in Chapters Two and Three and the impact of these medical theories is explored in a number of scenarios in subsequent chapters. In these two chapters we trace how medical attention on the subject of homosexuality was not static and how conceptualizations evolved primarily in the light of foreign theories that entered the Spanish medical and legal professions in the latter half of the nineteenth century.

Chapter Two concentrates on the 'formative' period of 1850 up to 1915 which saw the arrival of a number of theories from abroad in constant renovation. Older ideas which explained delinquent acts, such as murder, mental illness or sodomy as states induced by an aberrant mental condition, 'monomania', slowly gave way to newer psychiatric and nervous disease models of sexual pathology. These models recognized that there was something constitutionally 'wrong' with an emerging group of individuals who liked to engage in same-sex sexual acts. Gone was the old idea of 'vice', to be replaced by a number of causes which provoked a specific set of individuals with congenital characteristics to commit such acts. Or did the idea of vice die out? In reality, what we see was a kind of curtailed medicalization of homosexuality during this period, which laid new concepts over old ideas that continued well into the twentieth century and to some degree coexisting in specific expert fields. Vice, contagion and predisposition formed a complex set of explanations for sexual 'deviance'.

Rather than theorize this coexistence as incoherent or as an inadequacy in the Spanish medical field, we would rather see this as a product that has three principal roots. First, it can be seen as the result of the uneven development of Spanish science in general. There were remarkable differences between Spanish legal medicine and the field of pathology in terms of their acceptance of new ideas. Second, throughout the whole period studied, there is a tendency for multiple and even contradictory ideas to coexist in accordance with either the desire to minimize differences for the sake of the advances of science (an attitude that can be seen in Gregorio Marañón's work, for example), or the strong tendency or claim to eclecticism that all scientific fields, including those in the arts and humanities, aspired to. Third, the very dynamism of the period is witnessed by the multiplicity of terms and explanations that were voiced with respect to homosexuality. Some of these terms, such as those found in José de Letamendi's work of the late nineteenth century,[57] were short-lived and soon lost to history. This combination of factors meant that many terms and aetiological categories coexisted for reasons that cannot be explained by recourse to Spanish science's 'lack of consistency'.

Chapter Three continues this inquiry into the medicalization of homosexuality by concentrating on the period 1915–39. We argue that, after the initial flourish of interest on homosexuality principally in medico-legal contexts, this period signified the end of isolation for medical and psychiatric theories on the question. Whereas in the preceding years, it must be admitted, there was in fact relatively little interest devoted to the question in academic reviews, manuals and texts, partly because of the lack of legal framework that condemned most expressions of homosexuality, in the period from the mid-1910s and certainly from the 1920s, medicine (and psychiatry in particular) became steadily integrated into the state and into political, social and medical prerogatives, such as 'modernization', nation-building and eugenics, and the homosexual question received renewed interest.

This interest in homosexuality was, in fact, a reflection of a much broader social and medical interest in all matters sexual, from questions of birth control and gynaecology to sexual morality and sexual science. This heightened sexological interest was most pronounced in the 1920s and 1930s. It represents a significant change in qualitative and quantitative terms with respect to the interest that was only germinating in the nineteenth century. The increasingly vocal discussions on sexuality in general and 'sexual perversions' in particular allowed, as more modest discussion had done in the second half of the nineteenth century, for a number of paradigm shifts in the conceptualization of homosexuality, and permitted the eventual preference for the term 'sexual inversion'; a term which in Spain (unlike the United States) denoted both gender and sexual deviance from its inception. This medical and psychiatric model thus connected with and reinterpreted existing scientific as well as lay ideas on the subject of gender and sexual deviance: the *marica* became the sexual invert. But, as we have already suggested, the arrival of the invert did not necessarily replace previously existing categories; it coexisted with them.

Another group of specialists who argued for their place in this new world of discipline and knowledge were educationalists. Chapter Four outlines how from the eighteenth century onwards a different notion of childhood began to take hold, particularly in bourgeois circles, later extending to the working classes. This science of pedagogy, sometimes Catholic and at other times secular, notably from the beginning of the twentieth century onwards, formulated the notion of 'childhood in danger', recalling thus one of Foucault's 'great strategic unities' forming 'specific mechanisms of knowledge and power centred on sex'.[58] This particular concept would end up in the figure of the masturbating child, the personification of the 'fall' into 'counter-natural practices' as a result of the failure of 'Parents, families, educators, doctors, and eventually psychologists [who] would have to take charge . . . of this precious and perilous, dangerous and endangered sexual potential' of the child.[59]

These perils emerged clearly in the writings of these experts in the form of a whole series of recommendations on the subject of the proximity of the child to his or her educator, to the priest, to other members of the school and family, with emphasis on the possible contagion of 'unnatural' acts: primarily onanism (either solo or mutual) and actual homosexuality. As in other areas of specialist knowledge, however, there is much slippage between concepts of contagion and congenitality. Commentators constantly moved back and forth between the malleability of children and their propensity to imitate others and the relationship between contagion and eventual homosexuality as a lifestyle once the child was grown up. If a child 'infected' another with the desire to masturbate did this desire spring from the environment, the same-sex school, for example, or from some deeper deviation in the child's background?

Much of the emphasis in this kind of pedagogical writing was placed on the creation of healthy children who would in turn become useful adults in their mission to establish a deviance-free nation state. This aim must be understood not merely as emanating purely from the medical and pedagogical sciences but also from a cluster of political and social concerns that arose in the late nineteenth century and which could be grouped broadly under the banner of *regeneracionismo* ('regenerationism'). Chapter Five examines how the notion of effeminacy as a lack of virility was deemed by many political, philosophical and social commentators as one of the reasons – in tandem with structural deficiencies in the Spanish economy, political institutions and psyche – why Spain had fallen behind other nations and had become 'decadent'.

This late nineteenth-century interpretation of Spain's historic decline from the 'Golden Age' of the sixteenth century was buttressed by the fallout from the loss of the last major colonies of the once extensive Spanish empire in 1898. The collective recipe for the 'regeneration' of Spain included a number of ingredients. One was the recuperation of virility in the form of strong men and institutions to extirpate the cancerous growths which marred Spanish attempts at improvement and which sank the nation in abulia or extreme apathy.

Chapter Six attempts, in broad brushstrokes, to paint a picture of what homosexual life may have been like in the years 1850 to 1939. This is necessarily an impressionist picture and one whose canvas, if the metaphor can be continued, is still not dry. Once more, material is taken from published expert accounts of male homosexuality, and thus must be treated with caution, but the chapter weaves into those sources the much more sparse memoirs, literary publications, and other contemporary materials from participants themselves in what was a varied same-sex subculture. The relationship between these different representations – between the expert eye and the often lone voice of the variably 'self-aware' invert or homosexual – is deeply problematic. Some key instances, nevertheless, allow us to reconstruct a history that goes beyond discourses on both sides to capture the mentality of the period and the tactical alliances which were forged between, for example, medicine, law and the literary form, notably in the book *El Ángel de Sodoma* authored by A. Hernández-Catá. In this novel, the protagonist is inexorably led to his doom as he slowly realizes that he is attracted to other men. Full of pathos, the work is nevertheless a cry for a more dignified treatment of the homosexual individual. It is accompanied, in its second edition of 1929, by commentaries from Gregorio Marañón, the endocrinologist and theoretician of the 'intersexual states', and from Luis Jiménez de Asúa, the legal expert and architect of the republican constitution of 1931.

It is perhaps alliances such as these which allow us to evince the specific characteristics of debates around homosexuality in a particular period, to appreciate the ballast that still underpinned the subject and the value of essentialist and 'social constructionist' arguments for greater tolerance. A question, however, is how far did this kind of textual production affect the lives of homosexual subjects? Beyond the more educated classes the likely answer is, very little. Despite this, a sensibility towards class differentials has allowed us to begin to plot the various subcultures within the subcultures that existed during the period and the different modus operandi of aristocratic homosexuals and working-class 'trade'.

Our conclusions focus on how different Spain is in terms of the already written history of male homosexuality in the West and other parts of the world and how useful the Foucauldian model is in our attempts to better understand homosexual history in Spain. We provide an assessment of the significance of the assimilation into Spanish medicine of the various new categories – inversion, homosexuality – which served to describe same-sex sexual activities, and how these related to changing social and legal circumstances. We also acknowledge some of the tentative aspects of our work and suggest some future possible areas for exploration.

There is no doubt that what we publish here leaves many
questions unanswered and many topics untouched. We have, as
we have said, limited our study to the years 1850–1939, thus
leaving the whole of the Franco period, and the Transition and
the advent of 'democracy', apart from some allusions, out of our
account. The number of studies on post-1975 gay and lesbian
subcultures has mushroomed in recent years,[60] and during the
writing of this book gay life under Franco was receiving increased
treatment.[61] As some of the published materials on this later
period suggest, because of the legal constraints on particularly
male homosexuality, court proceedings may well hold many clues
for the construction of official and public attitudes towards
homosexuality. Other questions requiring research would be the
punishment of same-sex acts in the armed forces, governed by
their own codes. The urban/rural divide is a matter that deserves
more research. Cities historically have attracted more homosexuals but a history of rural attitudes towards homosexuality would
no doubt be illuminating. Transvestism and its association with
homosexuality received attention in the post-Franco years with
the rise of the drag queen but little had been written about the
matter in previous years.[62]

We should say some words about the history of lesbianism. As
we have indicated at the start of this chapter, there are few
references to historical aspects of lesbianism in Spain.[63] Given
that, historically, the contours of lesbian history have been in
many ways very different from those of male homosexuality, we
decided not to try to construct a 'lesbian and gay history' for
Spain. Too often, the lesbian side of such studies for other
countries is under-represented and it is assumed that the medical,
social and gender aspects of lesbianism are more or less similar to
those governing male homosexuality.[64] Because we do not wish to
commit this kind of misrepresentation, we generally leave the
history of lesbianism in Spain aside, although we have drawn on
some illustrative comparative examples between lesbianism and
male homosexuality in order to reinforce our arguments.

Finally, some comment on the title of this book is required. We
have chosen to place 'Los Invisibles' in the title, not just in
response to the kind of concerns that some other volumes have
voiced – the 'recovery' of history from a forgotten, lost or
deliberately hidden past, even though this is a process that we
believe is necessary – but more from a perspective that plays on

the schism of visibility/invisibility and its operations as a historical process.[65] Spanish homosexual life has not suddenly been 'discovered' by us, two historians working in different countries. It was there and it informed life as part of that fundamental heterosexual/homosexual division that Sedgwick has discussed in relation to Western social relations in general. Our 'recovery' of discourses on homosexuality and our account of homosexual life brings to the fore not something forgotten as such, but something often silently evoked, something peripheral but equally central to contemporary Spanish life. Our evocation of invisibility also, we hope, implies visibility and presence in the period studied.

NOTES

[1] A. Nin Frías, *Alexis o el significado del temperamento urano* (Madrid: Morata, 1932), p. 14. Nin Frías' words were: 'Nunca se ha buscado tanto como ahora el explicar al ser humano a través del objeto de su líbido.'

[2] A. Nin Frías, *Homosexualismo creador* (Madrid: Morata, 1933).

[3] See H. Graham and J. Labanyi, 'Culture and Modernity: The Case of Spain', in H. Graham and J. Labanyi (eds), *Spanish Cultural Studies* (Oxford: Oxford University Press, 1995), pp. 1–19.

[4] On the Inquisition period see R. Carrasco, *Inquisición y represión sexual en Valencia. Historia de los sodomitas (1565–1785)* (Barcelona: Laertes, 1985) and F. Garza, *Quemando mariposas. Sodomía e imperio en Andalucía y México, siglos XVI–XVII* (Barcelona: Laertes, 2002, trans. Lluís Salvador).

[5] Our first review of the sources available to the historian, which has informed and guided the present volume, was R. Cleminson and F. Vázquez García, '"Los Invisibles": Hacia una historia de la homosexualidad masculina en España, 1840–2000', *International Journal of Iberian Studies*, 13, 3 (2000), 167–81. A recent exception to the general lack of work on the subject is the cultural-literary history by A. Mira, *De Sodoma a Chueca: Una historia cultural de la homosexualidad en España en el siglo XX* (Barcelona/Madrid: Egales, 2004). A useful introduction to the current state of historical discussions of homosexuality in Spain is A. Martínez Expósito, *Escrituras torcidas: Ensayos de crítica «queer»* (Barcelona: Laertes, 2004), pp. 11–27.

[6] There are, of course, too many works to name here. As examples, the following may be considered. For reasons related to constraints of the time in which it was written and given the book's rights-oriented thrust, the historical element in J. R. Enríquez (ed.), *El homosexual ante la sociedad enferma* (Barcelona: Tusquets, 1978) is principally constrained to Armand de Fluvià's brief comments on the 1930s in his essay 'El movimiento homosexual en el estado español' (pp. 149–

67). More could reasonably be expected from studies such as B. Enguix Grau, *Poder y deseo: La homosexualidad masculina en Valencia* (Valencia: Edicions Alfons del Magnànim/Generalitat Valenciana, 1996) or from Ó. Guasch, *La sociedad rosa* (Barcelona: Anagrama, 1991), where historical sources are almost entirely Anglo-American. L. Sanfeliú's historical account of lesbianism, *Juego de damas. Aproximación histórica al homoerotismo femenino* (Málaga: Universidad, 1996) is practically devoid of references to Spain.

[7] One has only to recall the furore around the publication of A. Mira (ed.), *Para entendernos* (Barcelona: Libres de l'Index, 1999). Amongst other reasons, however, the debate and subsequent passing of legislation on same-sex marriage in Spain in 2005 has placed homosexuality on centre stage.

[8] E. Hobsbawm, *Age of Extremes: The Short Twentieth Century, 1914–1991* (London: Michael Joseph, 1994), p. 3.

[9] An excellent example is the recent monographic issue of the *Journal of the History of Sexuality* on 'Sexuality and German Fascism'. The richness of articles and perspectives on that period of history in Germany show, amongst other things, how much further advanced sexuality studies are in that country in comparison to Spain. See, in particular, the editor's essay, D. Herzog, 'Hubris and Hypocrisy, Incitement and Disavowal: Sexuality and German Fascism', *Journal of the History of Sexuality*, 11, 1/2 (2002), 3–21.

[10] A. McLaren, 'National responses to sexual perversions: the case of transvestism', in F. X. Eder, L. Hall and G. Hekma (eds), *Sexual Cultures in Europe. Themes in Sexuality* (Manchester: Manchester University Press, 1999), pp. 121–38.

[11] We take our lead from the work of Michel Foucault, especially from volume one (*La volonté de savoir*) of his *History of Sexuality* (Harmondsworth: Penguin, 1990, trans. Robert Hurley).

[12] That the 'nineteenth-century thesis' is now accepted is often illustrated by comments by sociologists and those working in other disciplines that historians would be wary of uttering. O. Viñuales in her *Lesbofobia* (Barcelona: Bellaterra, 2002) opens with the confident 'La homosexualidad, al igual que la heterosexualidad, entendida como identidad, es un fenómeno reciente. Ambas se inventaron en el siglo XIX . . . ' [Homosexuality, like heterosexuality, understood as an identity, is a recent phenomenon. Both were invented in the nineteenth century . . . (p. 19).

[13] The connection with Michel Foucault's work here is clear. Slightly before Foucault published his ground-breaking accounts, however, a still largely neglected essay that analysed the significance of sexual acts and identities in different social contexts was M. McIntosh, 'The Homosexual Role', *Social Problems*, 16 (1968), 182–92.

[14] See E. Stein (ed.), *Forms of desire: sexual orientation and the social constructionist controversy* (New York/London: Routledge, 1992).

[15] R. Llamas, *Teoría torcida. Prejuicios y discursos en torno a «la homosexualidad»* (Madrid: Siglo XXI, 1998), pp. 21–30, has concluded that the debate in Spain has already been exhausted.

16 E. K. Sedgwick has discussed the natural/unnatural divide as one of many Western binaries in *Epistemology of the Closet* (New York/London: Harvester Wheatsheaf, 1991), pp. 94–7. See also the useful ideas advocated by A. Fausto-Sterling as a way of moving beyond this dichotomy for epistemological purposes, but not ignoring its effect on 'reality' in *Sexing the Body: Gender politics and the construction of sexuality* (New York: Basic Books, 2000), pp. 20–9.

17 D. Eribon, *Réflexions sur la question gay* (Paris: Fayard, 1999), pp. 290–1.

18 H. Oosterhuis, 'Male Bonding and Homosexuality in German Nationalism', in H. Oosterhuis and H. Kennedy (eds), *Homosexuality and Male Bonding in Pre-Nazi Germany* (New York: Harrington Park Press, 1991), esp. pp. 247 ff. Oosterhuis notes that the Nazi lawyer Rudolf Klare sustained in 1935 that potentially all male Germans were exposed to possible seduction by homosexuals and that the homosexuality, if not curtailed, would spread like an epidemic (p. 249). This does not seem to have been a stable Nazi position, however. See S. Micheler, 'Homophobic Propaganda and the Denunciation of Same-Sex-Desiring Men under National Socialism', *Journal of the History of Sexuality*, 11, 1/2 (2002), 95–130 (96).

19 R. Norton, *The Myth of the Modern Homosexual: Queer history and the search for cultural unity* (London: Routledge, 1997), p. 12.

20 J. R. Searle, *The Construction of Social Reality* (Harmondsworth: Penguin, 1996).

21 I. Hacking, 'Making Up People', in Stein, *Forms of desire*, pp. 69–88 (p. 78).

22 Two clear examples, despite their differences, are J. Weeks, *Coming Out: Homosexual Politics in Britain, from the Nineteenth Century to the Present* (London: Quartet, 1977) and G. Chauncey, *Gay New York: The Making of the Gay Male World, 1890–1940* (London: Flamingo, 1995).

23 Foucault, *The History of Sexuality*, vol. I, p. 43.

24 The actual complexity of Foucault's model is discussed in Eribon, *Réflexions sur la question gay*, pp. 345–486.

25 F. Tomás y Valiente, 'El Crimen y Pecado contra natura', in F. Tomás y Valiente, *et al.*, (eds), *Sexo Barroco y Otras Transgresiones Premodernas* (Madrid: Alianza Universidad, 1990), pp. 37–8.

26 R. Trumbach, 'The Birth of the Queen: Sodomy and the Emergence of Gender Equality in Modern Culture, 1660–1750', in M. B. Duberman, M. Vicinus and G. Chauncey (eds), *Hidden From History: Reclaiming the Lesbian and Gay Past* (Harmondsworth: Penguin, 1991), pp. 129–40; R. Trumbach, *Sex and the Gender Revolution*, vol. I, *Heterosexuality and the Third Gender in Enlightenment London* (Chicago/London: University of Chicago Press, 1998).

27 Weeks, *Coming Out*, shows some signs of this movement as does the early work of G. Chauncey, 'From Sexual Inversion to Homosexuality: The Changing Medical Conceptualization of Female "Deviance"', in K. Peiss, C. Simmons and R. Padgug (eds.), *Passion and Power: Sexuality in History* (Philadelphia: Temple University Press, 1989),

pp. 87–117. Chauncey's article, originally published in 1982–3, contains a useful postscript that revises the definitiveness with which the author had originally traced the shift from inversion to homosexuality. D. M. Halperin, *One Hundred Years of Homosexuality and Other Essays on Greek Love* (New York: Routledge, 1990) also followed this schema. Important revisions of his framework were suggested in D. Halperin, 'How to do the History of Homosexuality', *GLQ: A Journal of Lesbian and Gay Studies*, 6, 1 (2000), 87–124.

[28] Chauncey, 'From Sexual Inversion to Homosexuality', pp. 108–9.

[29] The Braudelian notion of 'multiple temporality' is useful here, where historical time is divided into geographical, social and individual time, intersecting in productive ways. See Braudel's *The Mediterranean and the Mediterranean world in the age of Philip II*, 2 vols, (London: Collins, 1972–3).

[30] An eloquent example of this is J. R. Ackerley's autobiographical *My Father & Myself* (1968) in which he recalls how mystified he was when a Swiss friend asked him around 1918 whether he was 'homo' or 'hetero'. His response was that he 'had never heard either term before'. The incident is mentioned in Halperin, *One Hundred Years*, p. 17. A fictional example would be Stephen's realization that she was a lesbian in R. Hall, *The Well of Loneliness* (Paris: Pegasus Press, 1928).

[31] The notion of 'resignification' reflects the conflict between Derrida's perspective on discourse, with his insistence on the 'iterability' ad infinitum of the signifier, and Foucault's emphasis on the 'speech act' as unique and unrepeatable. This multiplicity is a modification of Foucault's 'unity in discourse' to incorporate Derrida's perspective of a polysemic discourse articulated in the work of Sedgwick and Butler. A useful analysis of these differences can be found in A. Campillo, 'Foucault y Derrida: historia de un debate sobre la historia', in *La Invención del Sujeto* (Madrid: Biblioteca Nueva, 2001), pp. 109–48.

[32] H. [*sic*, for Alfonso] Hernández-Catá, *El Ángel de Sodoma* (Valparaíso: 'El Callao', 1929).

[33] A. Mira, 'Modernistas, dandis y pederastas: articulaciones de la homosexualidad en la "edad de plata"', *Journal of Iberian and Latin American Studies*, 7, 1 (2001), 63–75.

[34] See Halperin, 'How to Do the History of Homosexuality'.

[35] See, for example, L. McNay, *Foucault and Feminism: Power, Gender and the Self* (Cambridge: Polity, 1992); R. M. Strozier, *Foucault, Subjectivity, and Identity: Historical Constructions of Subject and Self* (Detroit: Wayne State University Press, 2002), esp. pp. 79–110.

[36] Chauncey, 'From Sexual Inversion to Homosexuality', 'Postscript', p. 108.

[37] Guasch, *La Sociedad Rosa*, pp. 47–73. This too absolute process of subjectification has been critiqued in the work of R. Norton, *Mother Clap's Molly House: The Gay Subculture in England 1700–1830* (London: Gay Men's Press, 1992), who argued for the existence of a 'self-aware' 'gay' subculture well before the rise of the homosexual. Others, like Trumbach, *Sex and the Gender Revolution* and G. Dall'Orto, '"Socratic Love" as a Disguise for Same-Sex Love in the Italian Renaissance', in

K. Gerard and G. Hekma (eds), *The Pursuit of Sodomy: Male Homosexuality in Renaissance and Enlightenment Europe* (New York/London: Harrington Park Press, 1989), pp. 33–65, have argued that same-sex sensibilities are to be traced before the advent of the 'homosexual'. For a broad discussion of these issues see G. Hekma, 'Same-sex relations among men in Europe, 1700–1990', in Eder *et al.*, *Sexual Cultures in Europe. Themes in sexuality*, pp. 79–103 (pp. 79–82).

[38] Despite what we say here, the 'marica' was also a Portuguese phenomenon at least from the seventeenth century. See the mention of the homosexual fruit picker from Coimbra, 'Manoel Maricas', in L. Mott and A. Assunção, 'Love's Labors Lost: Five Letters from a Seventeenth-Century Portuguese Sodomite', in Gerard and Hekma (eds), *The Pursuit of Sodomy*, pp. 91–101 (p. 92).

[39] See A. Mira, 'Laws of silence: homosexual identity and visibility in contemporary Spanish culture', in B. Jordan and R. Morgan-Tamosunas (eds), *Contemporary Spanish Cultural Studies* (London: Arnold, 2000), pp. 241–50 (pp. 244–5).

[40] M. Rocke, *Forbidden Friendships: Homosexuality and Male Culture in Renaissance Florence* (New York/Oxford: Oxford University Press, 1996), has noted that comparative research on homosexuality in southern Europe after 1700 is needed to chart the decline of the 'old' sodomite model and its possible persistence into the twentieth century (p. 282, n. 5).

[41] The terms 'marica', 'maricón' and the female 'bollo' are still used today verbally and in print. Admittedly, in the mouths of some users their significance has changed – in similar fashion in the Anglo-American world 'queer' has been re-appropriated. For a militant usage of terms like 'marica' see B. Preciado, *Manifiesto contra-sexual: Prácticas subversivas de identidad sexual* (Madrid: Opera Prima, 2002), p. 17.

[42] R. Cleminson, 'The Review *Sexualidad* (1925–28), Social Hygiene and the Pathologisation of Male Homosexuality in Spain', *Journal of Iberian and Latin American Studies*, 6, 2 (2000), 119–29; R. M. Cleminson, 'The Significance of the "Fairy" for the Cultural Archaeology of Same-Sex Male Desire in Spain, 1850–1930', *Sexualities*, 7, 4 (2004), 412–29.

[43] A similar situation is reflected in other related case scenarios where doctors attempt to fit their culturally-bound assumptions surrounding gender and sex with medical notions of the 'hermaphrodite'. See A. D. Dreger, 'Hermaphrodites in Love: The Truth of the Gonads', in V. A. Rosario (ed.), *Science and Homosexualities* (New York/London: Routledge, 1997), pp. 46–66.

[44] R. Norton, *The Myth of the Modern Homosexual*; R. Trumbach, 'Sodomitical subcultures, sodomitical roles and the Gender Revolution of the Eighteenth Century', in R. P. Maccubin (ed.), *'Tis Nature's Fault: Unauthorized Sexuality during the Enlightenment* (Cambridge: Cambridge University Press, 1985), pp. 117–18. See also Rocke, *Forbidden Friendships*, p. 88, who notes that there were changes in perceptions around sodomy in Florence from 1700 onwards. Adult males were

frequently found having sex with other adult males, as opposed to with youths. There was a more fluid active/passive divide, homosexuality became associated with effeminacy and distinctive subcultures emerged.

45 A. Sinfield, *The Wilde Century: Effeminacy, Oscar Wilde and the Queer Moment* (London: Cassell, 1994). In the United States the medical linking of homosexuality with effeminacy in the late nineteenth century was a new departure. See D. F. Greenberg, *The Construction of Homosexuality* (Chicago/London: University of Chicago Press, 1988), p. 384.

46 Cleminson, 'The Review *Sexualidad*', 119–29; S. Wright, 'Gregorio Marañón and "The Cult of Sex": Effeminacy and Intersexuality in "The Psychopathology of Don Juan" (1924)', *Bulletin of Spanish Studies*, 81, 6 (2004), 717–38.

47 E. K. Sedgwick, *Between Men: English Literature and Male Homosocial Desire* (New York: Columbia University Press, 1985), p. 1.

48 L. Faderman, *Surpassing the Love of Men* (London: The Women's Press, 1991).

49 H. Oosterhuis, *Stepchildren of Nature: Krafft-Ebing, Psychiatry, and the Making of Sexual Identity* (Chicago/London: University of Chicago Press, 2000), pp. 245–8, has discussed the homosocial aspects of men's friendships in literary and academic circles in Britain and Germany.

50 Sedgwick, *Between Men*, p. 86.

51 G. Deleuze, 'The Rise of the Social', foreword to J. Donzelot, *The Policing of Families* (London: Hutchinson, 1979), pp. ix–xvii (p. xi).

52 D. Penn, 'Queer: Theorizing Politics and History', *Radical History Review*, 62 (1995), 24–42 (25).

53 This point was made in R. Cleminson, 'Male Homosexuality in Contemporary Spain: Signposts for a Sociological Analysis', *Paragraph: A Journal of Modern Critical Theory*, 22, 1 (1999), 35–54 (41), drawing on M. Warner, 'Introduction', in *Fear of a Queer Planet: Queer Politics and Social Theory* (Minneapolis/London: University of Minnesota Press, 1993), pp. vii–xxxi (p. xxvi).

54 J. Terry, 'Theorizing Deviant Historiography', *differences: A Journal of Feminist Cultural Studies*, 3, 2 (1991), 55–74 (55).

55 Chauncey, 'From Sexual Inversion to Homosexuality', p. 109.

56 Oosterhuis, *Stepchildren of Nature*, pp. 11–12. The author focuses on northern and central Europe.

57 J. de Letamendi, *Curso de Clínica General*, 2 vols, (Madrid: Imp. de los Sucesores de Cuesta, 1894).

58 Foucault, *The History of Sexuality*, vol. I, p. 103

59 Foucault, *The History of Sexuality*, vol. I, p. 104.

60 Of the many studies one could cite: X. M. Buxán (ed.), *ConCiencia de un singular deseo* (Barcelona: Laertes, 1997), and J. V. Aliaga and J. M. G. Cortés (eds), *Identidad y diferencia: sobre la cultura gay en España* (Barcelona/Madrid: Egales, 1997).

61 Perhaps a key to this history under Franco lies in regional studies as a first port of call. A short but rich section on homosexuality in

Asturias is contained in R. García Piñeiro, 'Actitudes sociales en la Asturias de postguerra', in J. López Álvarez and C. Lombardía Fernández (eds), *Valentín Vega: Fotógrafo de calle (1941–1951)* (Gijón: Ayuntamiento, 2001), pp. 73–165 (pp. 138–40). See also P. Fuentes, 'Modos de vida y relaciones sociales', in P. Fuentes, *En clave gay* (Madrid: Egales, 2001), pp. 55–87; A. Arnalte, *Redada de Violetas: La represión de los homosexuales durante el franquismo* (Madrid: La Esfera de los Libros, 2003); F. Olmeda, *El látigo y la pluma: homosexuales en la España de Franco* (Madrid: Oberon, 2004); and the recent monograph of *Orientaciones; revista de homosexualidades*, 7 (2004) on 'Represión franquista'.

[62] An exception is L. Litvak, *Antología de la novela corta erótica española de entreguerras. 1918–1936* (Madrid: Taurus, 1993).

[63] See F. Vázquez García and A. Moreno Mengíbar, 'La Sexualidad Vergonzante', in I. Morant (ed), *Historia de las Mujeres en España y América Latina. Del siglo XIX a los umbrales del XX*, vol. III (Madrid: Cátedra, 2006), pp. 207–33.

[64] There are many works that have addressed the difficulties and specificities of lesbian historical research. One piece which tackles these very successfully is C. Dean, 'The Making of Lesbian Sexuality', in *The Frail Social Body: Pornography, Homosexuality, and Other Fantasies in Interwar France* (Berkeley/Los Angeles/London: University of California Press, 2000), pp. 173–215.

[65] See, for example, the 'Introduction' by G. Chauncey, M. Duberman and M. Vicinus, in Duberman, Vicinus and Chauncey (eds), *Hidden from History*, pp. 1–13.

Chapter Two

The Birth of the 'Invert': a Truncated Process of Medicalization

Office of the Mayor's Lieutenant, Second Brigade, to the Mayor:

> On the afternoon of the fourth of this month, on being called by José Ruiz, resident at 10 Maizal Street, the bailiff José Coldión proceeded to help in the arrest of a man who had by force taken one of Ruiz' younger boys to a house of prostitution, known as the house of La Valenciana, in order to perform obscenities with the said boy. The bailiff proceeded immediately to the house and detained the man, by the name of Manuel Montemayor, resident at 83 Soledad Street. It was necessary to take him to the office of the Civil Guard given the cries and shameless acts he proffered . . . Public opinion designated Montemayor as demented. In faith, Cadiz, 6 July 1846. Juan Rafael Durán.

Letter from Montemayor's father to the Mayor:

> With all due respect, Montemayor, resident of this town, directs himself to the esteemed Mayor: that as appears in the request made to this office on 28 April last . . . I pleaded for the release of my son from the Capuchinos refuge on condition that if his dementia increased he would be transferred to the Casa Hospicio in order to be attended there as a demented person, as his disorders and manias which border on crimes permit no other measure. His flight from two other asylums, the scandal of the night of the 21st of last month in which he attempted . . . to murder this writer, the disorders and robberies that he is committing in the neighbourhood, the events of last Saturday . . . all show the imperious need of the Mayor to concede the request made above in all its effects . . . Cadiz, 6 July 1846. Antonio Montemayor.

> [in the margins:] the medical doctors should examine Montemayor to determine if he is demented or not. Signed: José López.

Medical report:

> In order to fulfil the order made by the Mayor we have examined
> the detainee D. Manuel Montemayor with the object of
> determining his dementia and we declare: by the answers he has
> given to our questions and inquiries it does not seem that
> Montemayor suffers from said illness. The official in charge of the
> house where Montemayor was detained declares that over the days
> when he was in [unreadable] he has not observed any act that
> would confirm his madness. However, it cannot be sustained that
> Manuel does not suffer from this illness, given the fact that his
> father has declared that it is intermittent. In the light of this, the
> Mayor can dispose as to whether Montemayor should be placed in
> observation or whether he is indeed mad, in which case he can be
> transferred to the department in charge of those thus
> designated . . . Cadiz, 9 July 1846.[1]

These texts from 1846 can be compared with the following, from
1904:

> Given that no analogous case can be found in the recent
> contemporary and now classic works of Westphal, Laségue [*sic*],
> Charcot, Magnan and von Krafft-Ebing, just to cite the great
> masters, I dare to expose before this Section, abusing the attention
> of those assembled here, the following case. It may be that the
> range of expertise of legal medicine will be enhanced by its
> analysis, if I examine the notions and the symptoms which have an
> undeniable scientific character in this sexual pervert, from all of
> which, in general, medicine until recently shied away in horror,
> retreating from the noble duty of discovering and analysing them,
> however abominable, immoral and unworldly these acts may seem
> if viewed by the eye of ignorance . . .

> It is the case of a subject (U. L.), of forty-one years of age, from the
> Low Pyrenees (France) who, on being caught during one of his
> frequent sexual encounters he had with children, was denounced
> to the Justice Administration. The following case was heard by the
> Criminal Court, which pronounced itself as follows: 'This is a case
> of a degenerate who suffers from a limited state of partial madness,
> in accordance with his sexual inclinations, which propels him
> against his will to realize acts of the kind he is accused of and he is
> thus deprived of the freedom whereby to commit those acts'.
> However, the Jury, believing that in order that the accused be
> deemed irresponsible of his acts there should exist a complete and
> total state of madness in all aspects of his existence, merely

understood this as an attenuating circumstance, and condemned the accused in consequence . . .

By way of summary of all that we have said, we can state that the physiological-pathological antecedents of the family and the inheritance of the accused can be described as follows: the father, the mother, the oldest brother and the degenerate himself are short-sighted (myopic); the father, a paternal aunt, the mother and a maternal grandmother suffer from nervous disease; his brothers and sisters suffer from psychic stigmas, Pablo from illusions of grandeur, Adriano is taciturn and avaricious, José, known as 'La Mariposa' and his two sisters [also suffer from nervous disease]. We also found constitutional illnesses, infections and intoxications in his family . . . together with some stigma, including the asymmetry of the brain, which is platicephalic . . . and whose constitution is eminently scrophulous . . . to sum up, this subject possesses disorders in his sentiments and in his will, with obsessions, impulses and clear physical stigmas, and should be considered a mental degenerate, who is congenital, suffers abulia, displays psychopathic homosexual manifestations, characterized by his dedication to masturbation, in preference by the mouth, suffering erection and voluptuous ejaculation when he realises such immoral manoeuvres and unworldly suctions.[2]

Between Two Worlds

These two accounts relate the medico-legal consequences of two instances of sexual contact between adult males and boys. They come from different periods and in each case the diagnosis performed responds to very different criteria and explanatory repertoires. This difference is not merely one of precision when describing the acts or the degree of specialization in the language employed. Nor does it refer solely to a different relationship between the non-specialist field (the neighbours, the father, the guardian of the place of internment of the criminal in the first account and the 'mundo ignorante' [ignorant world] mentioned in the second account) and that of the experts. What is remark-ably different is the status of what is deemed important in order to reach a decision on the culpability of the miscreant concerned and the ways in which reality is constructed through a series of representations (in terms of classificatory systems, definitions and concepts) which change radically from one scenario to the next.

In the case of Montemayor, madness is associated with an explosion of rage, a brief and intermittent burst of disequilibrium. The sexual misdemeanour committed is performed amongst 'gritos y desvergüenzas' [cries and shameless acts], 'escándalo' [scandal], the 'fuga' [flight] of the person concerned and the attempted murder of the father. In addition, any madness is thought to derive from a process of defective rationalization in the individual given the 'contestaciones que se nos ha dado a las preguntas y cuestiones' [answers he has given us to our questions and inquiries]. This implies that the subject was the victim of a form of delirium. But it is precisely the absence of delirium that makes the diagnosis more difficult for the experts.

In the second scenario, the case of the priest U. L., the diagnosis relies upon a completely different set of criteria. The madness of the subject is not now seen to derive from an absence of reason, but from the malfunctioning of the instinct or will. The actual sexual conduct of the subject is what concerns the experts most and this is described in detail. This rooting of the problem in the instincts permits two connected explanations to emerge. On the one hand, the problem is located in visible signs on the organism ('estigmas físicos' [physical stigmas]); on the other, it is seen to derive from an evolutionary process (the 'antecedentes fisio-patológicos de la familia' [physiological-pathological antecedents of the family]). Pinpointing this inheritance becomes the principal objective of the diagnosis. The family itself, and not the space of the asylum, becomes the locus of medico-legal attention. There is, therefore, a complete shift in the conceptualization of the problem. From the 'demencias' [dementia], 'manías' [mania] and intermittent nature of reason in the first case, we arrive at the 'degeneración' [degeneration], the 'herencia de los instintos' [inheritance of instincts], the perversion and 'manifestaciones psicopáticas homo-sexuales' [psychopathic homosexual manifestations] of the second.

The two accounts present other interesting differences worthy of note. From one case to the other, there is a change in the relationship between the spheres of penal justice and mental hygiene. In the first case, that of Montemayor, it is suggested that his 'dementia' means that he is not responsible for his actions.

The father suggests that he is a madman and not a criminal and it is for this reason that he requests for his son to be locked up in an asylum rather than sent to prison. In the second scenario, however, the diagnosis changes completely. There is a difference of opinion between members of the court. The jury, apparently more acquainted with the psychiatric theories of the time, saw no degree of incompatibility between madness, which affected the will and the instinct of the priest rather than his ability to reason, and criminality.

What must have taken place in the space of fifty years to alter dominant conceptualizations of sexual activity between adults and minors? What allowed the category of 'homosexual perversion' or simply 'homosexuality' to become incorporated into psychiatric knowledge by the early 1900s?

Forensic Medicine and Sodomy

In Spain, between the years 1830 and 1928 there was almost no divergence between medical and legal attitudes towards homosexuality. This was not the case in countries such as Germany and, later on, England where the law condemned homosexual activity and medicine advocated its decriminalization often on the basis of the argument that homosexuality was a congenital, and therefore unavoidable, condition.

From the end of the eighteenth century, as Huertas and Martínez have pointed out,[3] legal medicine in Spain institutionalized cooperation between doctors and judges. Medical professionals not only aided the latter in cases where their expertise was drawn upon but they also participated in the drawing up of new legal codes and laws. Law and medicine, therefore, effectively became two main technologies of 'governmentality' in the liberal period in the nineteenth century. What Foucault has termed 'bio-power', the regulation of the life of the population in accordance with the demands of a market economy and state power, made its appearance in Spain in the form of this cooperation between the two professions as well as in other senses such as the adoption of a single currency, the construction of national identity and the selling off of church properties.

The Legal Code of 1822, which was barely implemented, was inspired by the Napoleonic Code of 1810 and successive alterations (in 1848, 1850, 1860 and 1870) did not criminalize sexual acts between individuals of the same sex. As a result, there was no penalization of these acts and no medical discourse that proposed their decriminalization.

The liberal conception, in contrast with that of the Old Regime, was concerned with the separation of public crimes and private 'vice'. Sodomitical acts did not merit the attention of the law unless they passed the boundaries of the private realm. It was only in the proposed Penal Code of 1928, in the dying days of the dictatorship of Primo de Rivera, that any separation of medicine and law in this sense occurred.

Despite this general trend, there was a period of criminalization of homosexuality in the years between the end of the 'Liberal Triennium' and the 1848 Code, resulting from a modification in the statutes of the 1822 Code. During this period, medical professionals were asked to draw up reports on the phenomenon of sodomy, to be punished by hanging.[4] The category 'sodomy' dates from the Old Regime and is specifically named as a crime in the *Novísima Recopilación*. One jurist, De Tapia, in the section on 'sodomy' in his *Tratado del Juicio Criminal* (1829), after noting laconically that these acts constituted a 'delito execrable' [execrable crime] of which 'el pudor impide mayor explicación' [modesty prohibits further discussion] referred the reader to the section on 'bestiality' in the same volume.[5] In this way, 'el acceso carnal de un hombre o una mujer con una bestia' [carnal acts between a man or a woman and a beast][6] and carnal acts between members of the same sex or 'inappropriate' acts between members of different sex were considered in much the same light. These acts were conceived as being 'against nature' and contrary to the natural order as created by Providence.

The principal medico-legal texts of the time displayed the same kinds of concept as de Tapia. Examples include the work of P. M. Peiró and J. Rodrigo (*Elementos de Medicina y Cirugía Legal*, 1839), Pedro Mata (*Vademécum de Medicina y Cirugía Legal*, 1844) and that of Mateo Orfila (*Tratado de Medicina Legal*, 1847). In all these cases the author expressed his moral repugnance at having to deal with the issue of sodomy or pederasty and both terms were used interchangeably. These crimes were considered alongside those committed against public morality and rape, forced sexual relations and adultery.[7]

While sodomy was generally understood to include acts of 'inappropriate' sexual intercourse, Mata, one of the most influential medical figures of the time, defined it more closely as the 'concúbito de hombre con hombre o de mujer con mujer' [joining of man and man or woman and woman][8] and he understood same-sex institutions and the homosociality permitted by them as one major cause of same-sex practices: 'en los cuarteles, en las cárceles, en los presidios y en los buques es muy frecuente la pederastia' [in barracks, in prisons and on ships pederasty is very common].[9]

Orfila, professor of legal medicine in Paris, for his part, established a direct connection between sodomy and sexual relations with minors. Sodomy, Orfila wrote, 'se comete por lo general con niños a quienes se emponzoña la vida' [is generally committed with minors whose lives are poisoned] as a result.[10] We must recall that in France the crime of 'paedophilia' had been established in 1832, an initiative that entailed a veritable witch-hunt of suspects, particularly school masters.[11] Despite all these concepts and measures, the sodomite was not seen to possess a particular character or personality. At most, he displayed a kind of moral inclination but nothing more. From the eighteenth century the sodomite had been associated with a 'libertine'; his acts were the 'producto de una imaginación desarreglada y del libertinaje más escandaloso' [product of a disturbed imagination and the most scandalous expression of libertinage].[12]

The task of the medico-legal practitioner was to identify physical signs that betrayed the practice of sodomitical acts. In Orfila's words, it was a matter of identifying the signs of an 'introducción preternatural' [preternatural introduction] of an inappropriate nature. Those individuals dedicated to this kind of vice displayed 'el recto ensanchado en forma de embudo' [a rectum distended in the form of a funnel], their sphincter was 'dilatado y sin resistencia' [dilated and offered no resistance], the surrounding flesh was 'gruesa, floja y abotargada' [thickened, slack and inflamed] and if 'el atentado acaba de cometerse habría rubicundez e hinchazón, las márgenes del ano podrían estar rasgadas y doloridas si el miembro era muy voluminoso' [the crime has just been committed, we will see irritation and swelling and the anus may be torn and painful if the member was large].[13]

In all cases, it is always the receptor or 'passive' partner that is examined. The doctors in question suggest that the 'victim' of active sodomy, once corrupted, becomes a habitual passive sodomite. However, a number of difficulties made for problematic diagnoses. How can the habitual passive sodomite be distinguished from the victim of sodomy against the person's will?

The precariousness of this medico-legal diagnosis was plain to see in the famous Boulton and Park case in England in 1870;[14] in Spain a similar case arose in Alfaro (Alicante province). The victim was a girl aged nine called Gregoria who worked as a servant in a house near her parents' home. She declared in 1846, two years after the events, that she had been penetrated anally by the owner of the house: 'la levantaba las sayas, ejecutaba con las manos tocamientos en los órganos sexuales de ella, y le introducía la guía por el *ojal* del cuerpo' [he lifted up her skirts, touched her sexual organs, and introduced his member into the girl's orifice]. After a detailed examination of the girl, it was acknowledged that it was difficult to prove the crime, especially as two years had passed since the crime was allegedly committed.[15]

What is interesting in this case is not just the difficulty that experts admitted in determining with any degree of accuracy the facts of the case. What is also evident is the degree of unequal treatment of the two people concerned. The young servant girl is examined fully but the accused, a male and property owner, is invisible throughout the whole process. The girl, the object of the sexual satisfaction of another, now becomes the object of science and she is examined 'en distintas ocasiones y en presencia siempre de su madre' [on several occasions always in the presence of her mother]. The active partner is not examined. Only the passive sodomite can betray the indelible marks of his or her condition.

The Penal Code of 1848, returning to the articles contained in the Code of 1822, eliminated sodomy as a crime against public morality. The 1870 Code, drawn up in light of the 1869 Constitution, followed suit. However, legal and medical figures tended to interpret this change not as proof of a softening of attitudes towards sodomy as a private sexual act, but rather as a linguistic measure. The expression 'abusos deshonestos' [crimes against decency], introduced in Article 364 and in the last paragraph of Article 366 of the 1848 Code (corresponding to Articles 454 and the last paragraph of 458 in the 1870 Code) after the elimination of sodomy as a crime against public morality was in reality a veiled reference to the same thing. Romero Gil-Sanz, a lawyer and member of parliament commented in his version of the forensic manual written by Briand, Bouis and Casper that the words 'el que abusare deshonestamente de persona de uno u otro sexo' ['he who commits dishonest abuse with a person of the same or the other sex'], or a 'crime of decency', as we shall refer to it from now on, were too general. The notion of 'abuse', he argued, did not refer specifically to any act out of respect for custom or, indeed, decency itself. In reality, it was the crime of sodomy or pederasty that was alluded to.[16]

Mata, less directly, alluded to the same phenomenon in his often republished *Tratado de Medicina y Cirugía Legal*, understanding that the category 'crimes against decency' included adultery, rape, sex with minors, forced sexual relations and sodomy and masturbation, that is, 'todo otro acto, ora sea un concúbito efectuado por vías no naturales, ora suplementos de la cópula llevados a efecto con las diferentes formas que la lujuria sugiere a los lascivos' [that is to say, all acts effected by non-natural means and all those substitutes of the copula undertaken by the lascivious in response to whatever means luxuriousness disposes them towards].[17]

The more or less literal interpretation of 'abusos deshonestos' as sodomitical acts allowed legal medicine to continue its incursion into the field of homosexuality and to formulate a more complete set of understandings on the subject of sexual relations between members of the same sex. Spanish commentators from now on began to experience renewed interest in the subject and the major legal figures of other European countries were drawn upon in a number of texts. Johannes Casper, of the University of Berlin, and Ambroise Tardieu of the Medical Faculty of Paris, were cited as authors of fundamental works on the question of 'pederasty', a term which slowly replaced others such as 'sodomy' or acts 'contranaturaleza' [against nature] in Spanish accounts from the 1850s onwards.[18]

Perhaps the most significant of these works was that written by Tardieu, the *Étude Médico-Légale sur les Attentats aux Mœurs* (1857).[19] The volume described the pederastic world in different countries of Europe and in an extensive chapter 'De la Pederastia a la Sodomía' [From Pederasty to Sodomy] for the first time in any detail, medicine began to think of pederasts as individuals who displayed specific anatomical peculiarities and particular sociological qualities (such as lifestyle, and social and sexual habits).

Although, as we have seen, some medico-legal experts such as Pedro Mata had offered certain details on the lifestyle of pederasts, indicating where they were to be found most easily (in barracks, prisons, ships) and the ways in which this vice was to be cultivated (young boys were seduced or forced to prostitute themselves to escape poverty), there is little reference to pederasts' physiognomy or habits until after the arrival of Tardieu in Spain. Mata's 'pre-Tardieu' exposition concentrates almost entirely on anatomical characteristics and on the signs any examining officer should look for in order to detect sodomites.

Tardieu's *Étude*, however, represented a fundamental change in the ways in which legal medicine considered such phenomena. The French author did not just portray the acts themselves or describe any evidence left by them on the body of the sodomite. From an extremely detailed ethnographical study (based on 212 cases, a very high number when compared to the inexperience of his Spanish counterparts) Tardieu described the anatomical and social peculiarities of individual pederasts. Drawing on the categories supplied by Heinrich Kaan, he described this class of subjects as 'morally perverse'. He emphasized the frequent association between pederasty and serious crime, as if the practice was itself a school of delinquency: 'la pederastia ha servido de pretexto, y en algún modo de cebo para el asesinato' [pederasty has served as the pretext and in some way as an inducement for murder].[20] Despite this, his use of statistics allows him to destroy certain prejudices such as the idea that marriage and pederasty are two mutually exclusive categories and also some ideas with respect to 'active' and 'passive' practices. Not only are the physical attributes of the pederast made clear in his text but he also records different aspects of homosexual lifestyles, language and codes. In this way, even the most innocent and trivial of mannerisms are understood as symptoms of a particular sexual type or proclivity towards a sexual act.

The most obvious indication in the recognition of the pederast would be, perhaps not surprisingly, his physical appearance, as if his sexual habits were seen to take on physical form. We progress from the identification of specific physical indices (the dilation of the anus, for example) to the characterization of a type of subject:

the pederast. Tardieu discusses the dimensions and form of the penis *in extenso*. Pederasts would possess 'un miembro muy delgado, agudo y afilado por la punta' [very thin, tapered, pointy member] which 'recuerda enteramente el *canum more*' [reminds one entirely of the *canum more*].[21] From this moment on, the expert eye must roam beyond the anus of the individual examined to take in other aspects: 'del mismo modo que en el ano es donde se buscan las huellas de los hábitos pasivos, así en el miembro viril es donde debe esperarse hallar el rastro de los hábitos activos' [in the same way that the anus is the place where the evidence of passive habits must be looked for, it is in the virile member that evidence of active habits will be found].[22] Another important element in Tardieu's account is the association he establishes between pederasty, physiognomy and effeminacy. This relationship is found more often amongst those who engage in 'hábitos pasivos' [passive habits], the vast majority of the sample (177 cases).[23]

The passive pederast is a simulacrum of woman and he is thus an example of gender deviance even though such qualities are only surface manifestations displayed on the individual's visible body. A further conceptual development would have to take place before these physical elements would be overtaken by the psychiatric model and for physical androgyny to be internalized in order to make way for the 'hermaphroditism of the soul' described by Foucault.[24] As the concepts marshalled by Tardieu and Casper declined in influence they were replaced by a whole new series of terms such as 'Uranism' (Ulrichs, 1864), 'homosexuality' (Benkert, 1869), 'contrary sexual feeling' (Westphal 1870) and 'inversion of the sexual instinct' (Charcot & Magnan 1882).

In Spain, however, these developments would come slightly later than in other European countries such as France and Germany. It is possible that, as was the case in England,[25] amongst medical experts pederasty was seen as a foreign practice and therefore unworthy of scientific attention. There are other examples of this kind of patriotism when considering the sexual 'vices'. Pedro Mata attributed the existence of dildos in Spain to foreign imports[26] and the translators of Tardieu's book were keen to impress on the reader that pederasty was fortunately not common in Spain: 'En España no se ha propagado afortunadamente tan asqueroso vicio del modo que lo ha hecho en el vecino Imperio . . . En ocho años sólo hemos reconocido tres individuos en quienes se notaban hábitos pasivos de pederastia: dos niños de 8 a 9 años y una prostituta'. [It is fortunate that in Spain such a revolting vice has not spread to the same degree as it has in the neighbouring country [France] . . . In eight years we have examined only three individuals with signs of passive pederasty; two boys of 8 or 9 years and a prostitute].[27]

The work of Casper and Tardieu was to be the dominant schema adopted by Spanish legal experts. Pedro Mata and Teodoro Yáñez follow almost to the letter the criteria and observations of these two authorities. Both engaged in the examination of the rectum in the case of passive pederasty and of the penis in the case of suspected active pederasty.[28] They also conceded that there was a relationship between pederasty and violent crime. Mata mentions, for example, 'un hecho acaecido en Madrid en 1862' [an event which occurred in Madrid in 1862], whereby a young parcel carrier fell victim to some individuals who introduced a nutcracker up his anus. The incident resulted in the death of the boy.[29]

But the most delicate and difficult problem consisted in determining 'si el pederasta activo adolece de ese vicio, o si, por uno de esos momentos desgraciados que tiene el hombre, se ha dado por excepción a este acto; y si el *pático* o el *andrógino* es tal, es un ser degradado con esa prostitución, o bien una pobre víctima que por primera vez se ve atacada de esa suerte' [whether the active pederast engages in this vice, or if, as a result of one of those unfortunate moments that men pass through, his involvement in such acts was exceptional. And [the problem also consisted in determining] if he is *pathic* or *androgynous*; that is, whether he is a person degraded by prostitution or rather a poor victim who has fallen foul for the first time].[30]

Another device employed by doctors in their identification of the ever increasing number of pederasts in Spanish cities was the association they made between passive pederasty and effeminacy. Mata was to note on this subject: 'Creo que deberíamos aceptar esas denominaciones distintivas, llamando pederastía al uso de un hombre o de una mujer *a tergo*; pederasta a la parte active, y *andrógino, kinodo* o *pático*' [I think we should accept these distinctive categories and call pederasty the use of man or woman *a tergo*. The pederast is the active partner and the passive partner is called *androgynous, cynaedus* or *pathic*].[31] Yáñez was to formulate this question in similar ways:

Los pederastas son de dos especies, activos y pasivos, según que dan o que reciben; esto es, según que buscan los placeres en los muchachos y hombres o en las mujeres por el ano, o según que, de uno u otro sexo, se prestan a ser víctimas de tales ataques. Algunos autores quieren reservar el nombre de 'pederasta' o *anófilo*, solo al activo, y el *andrógino*, *kinodo* o *pático* al pasivo, pero entendiendo que sólo cuando este vicio es habitual en ellos.[32]

[Pederasts are of two species: active and passive, according to whether they give or take. That is to say, according to whether they seek pleasure with boys and men or with women by the anus, or whether, with one sex or the other, they dispose themselves to be victims of such attacks. Some authors wish to reserve the name 'pederast' or *anophile* for the active partner only and the descriptions *androgynous*, *cynaedus* or *pathic* for the passive element, but only on the understanding that this vice is habitual in them.]

In other words, the millenarian Mediterranean distinction between active and passive does not just refer to differences in sexual practices but actually creates differences between types of person.[33] One of these types, the passive pederast, is recognizable by his effeminate aspect. This new device also allows for distinction between the 'innocent', those upon whom such practices were forced and those who anally penetrated another person in a moment of weakness, and the 'guilty', those who possessed a particular physiognomy and a certain defined inclination. Those in the latter category were seen as more effeminate and were more clearly identified in the public eye: 'porque dependiendo estos gustos particulares e inclinaciones sexuales de la constitución física de los sujetos' [because these particular likes and sexual inclinations would depend on the physical constitution of the subjects], Yáñez would explain. Further, 'decimos que esas inclinaciones pasivas dependen algo de la organización afeminada de los sujetos' [we would also say that these passive inclinations depend to some degree on the effeminate organization of these subjects]; they communicate amongst themselves and 'understand' one another.[34]

Around the same time, Spanish medicine began to associate the anatomical ambiguity of supposed physical hermaphrodites with ambiguous sexual tastes. Some suggested that the latter were merely an expression of the former. Pedro Felipe Monlau, Professor of Hygiene at the University of Madrid, followed this line of reasoning:

¿Existen en la especie humana verdaderos hermafroditas o individuos que reúnan los dos sexos? No. Lo que hay es uno que otro varón imperfecto que presenta muchos de los caracteres exteriores de las hembras, así como una que otra hembra con varios de los atributos masculinos. Lo que hay son algunos maricas, u hombres de textura floja, de facciones mujeriles, voz afeminada, carácter tímido y aparato genital poco desarrollado; y también algunas marimachos o mujeres hombrunas (*viragines*), de costumbres masculinas, voz ronca, barba poblada, clítoris muy abultado.[35]

[Do true hermaphrodites or individuals that combine both sexes really exist amongst humankind? No. What exist are some imperfect men who present many of the external characters of females, just as there are females who display some male characteristics. There are *maricas*, men of weak textures, of womanly aspect, with an effeminate voice, with a timid character and poorly developed genitalia. There are also *viragines*, *marimachos* or manly women who act like men, have deep voices, developed facial hair and large clitorises.]

What we see, then, is that at the same time that pederasts were understood to possess a particular physiognomy, especially passive or 'androgynous' pederasts, supposed hermaphrodites were also understood to possess a peculiar psychic structure. From these figures, there would emerge an individual who places not only sexuality, but also gender, in question. What begins to haunt medical doctors, pedagogues, moralists, politicians and novelists during the last third of the nineteenth century is not so much sexual deviance but more the trope of gender deviance, something which is held to occasion the ruin of the family and the nation. In order to arrive at this new figure – the 'invert' as a 'sexual pervert' – and the eclipse although not the disappearance of the active/passive and the natural/unnatural divide, it will be necessary to depart from anatomical criteria, prevalent in legal medicine, to arrive at psychiatric explanations, characteristic of the school of mental hygiene.

A 'Truncated' Process of Medicalization: From Monomania to the Perversion of the Genital Instinct

The discussions around 'sodomy' from the mid century and pederasty from the 1870s did not take place within the field of mental illness. Instead, these activities were usually located in the province of criminality. During the same period, psychiatric examinations were one of the principal tasks performed by legal doctors in court cases.[36] The psychiatrist's task was to decide whether or not the individual who had committed a crime was mentally sound or not and hence deserving of punishment.

In the case of sexual acts which were proscribed by law, how was it possible to determine whether the individuals that performed them were responsible for their acts or not? At the time of the cases of the young girl Gregoria and that of Montemayor the prevailing school of legal medicine was that of 'alienism',[37] a theory elaborated in France and whose standard reference text came to be *Des Maladies Mentales* (1838) written by Esquirol. The text was translated into Spanish and published in 1847 even though some aspects of the theory had already percolated Spanish medicine. By 1846, the treatise written by José Pérez Vilargoitia, *De los Remedios para mejorar en España la suerte de los enajenados* and Pedro Mata's *Tratado de Medicina y Cirugía Legal* had appeared.

Mata followed the conceptual framework provided by French alienism and analysed the sexual 'deviations' as an expression of phenomena contained in the broader field of 'monomania'. This concept denoted a 'partial delirium' as opposed to the general delirium suffered in cases of complete mania. This partial delirium altered the instincts and passions of the individual momentarily but left his mental faculties intact, even though such a state could, according to the theory, produce hallucinations. However, not all manifestations of unusual sexual activity implied the presence of monomania. For this reason, the expert had to determine whether the sexual transgression was simply a crime (such as rape, adultery or crimes against decency) or whether it was indeed a symptom of partial madness for which the individual in question was not responsible.

Monomania in the sexual behaviour of individuals was termed 'erotic monomania' and, according to Mata, could be of two classes. First, there were those in whom the 'reproductive impulse' was unleashed through conscious excitation ('erotomania') and, secondly, those in whom the impulse resulted directly from an anomaly in the genital organs, such as 'satyriasis', 'nymphomania' and 'necromania'.[38]

In direct contrast to erotomania, nymphomania and satyriasis were not directed at a particular individual object. Instead of idealized and conscious representations of a desired person, these pathologies were directed towards others in general. The first affected women and the second men. At the base of these illnesses was the exaltation of the 'reproductive apparatus'. Nymphomania was considered to be the more dangerous of the two because it prevented women from fulfilling their 'social function'.[39] Satyriasis, on the other hand, was rare even though it could lead to the most extravagant of sexual transgressions.

Pederastic acts and sexual relations between individuals of the same sex remained outside the framework provided by monomania and therefore strictly outside the parameters of mental hygiene. Mata, who around the 1870s was becoming acquainted with the new degenerationist psychiatry,[40] was reluctant to call sodomy and lesbian acts pathological: 'Tal vez deberían figurar aquí como tipos de esas horribles aberraciones ciertos hechos de amor socrático y lésbico, y de sodomía tan fuera del orden común que no parecen posibles en un estado de razón' [perhaps certain forms of Socratic love, lesbianism and sodomy should figure here as types of those horrible aberrations which are so far removed from normality that they do not seem to be possible within a state of reason], he mused.[41]

Mata cites as an example the historic case of 'monstrous infanticide' committed by Gilles de Rais. His analysis of this case never goes beyond the conceptual frameworks of alienism and its categories of monomania. In order for a particular sexual behaviour to attain the designation of illness it has to be so exceptional ('tan fuera del orden común' [so far removed from normality]) that it is impossible within a state of reason. With Mata, we are still in the realm of acts associated with kinds of delirium; the articulation of particular perverse psychic states will have to wait some years.

The new psychiatric theories which would break with the old alienism and theories of monomania and which developed the idea of the 'sexual perversions' would be consolidated in Europe in the years 1850–70, particularly in France and Germany. In

alienist thought, as we have noted, any mental illness was understood as a manifestation of delirium, which could be 'partial' as in
monomania. The madman was a victim of this state or error and,
as such, was not responsible for his acts. In the new psychiatry,
from the times of Griesinger, Baillarger, Morel and later Magnan
and Lombroso, the key explanatory device became the instinct. In
this new formulation, it was a question of the involuntary drive of
the instinct which pushed the individual towards certain acts. All
these factors were understood as regressions or atavisms in the
march towards progress.[42] The main concern of this kind of
psychiatry was not the curing of madmen but the detection of
abnormality, that is, the identification of those individuals who
transgressed social codes while still lucid and in possession of
their mental faculties and who allowed instinct to triumph over
their will. The question of responsibility is thus replaced by a
concern about how dangerous the individual may be.[43]

One of the major areas of interest of this new psychiatry was
the domain of sexual psycho-pathology. Sexual behaviour was
understood as a manifestation of the instinct and was thus classified and explained in its many varieties. This entailed a number of
innovations. Firstly, it was held that the sexual instinct was separate from what had been termed the 'reproductive instinct'.
Children were understood to possess a sexual instinct which
'pre-dated' the reproductive imperative.[44] Secondly, the sexual
instinct needed to be satisfied and from this the individual
derived pleasure. The intermediary between the instinct and
pleasure was the imagination. Thirdly, the sexual instinct was
inscribed in a developmental or evolutionary process. This in turn
obeyed certain laws and a particular teleology. Normal evolution
consisted of the subordination of the sexual instinct to that of
reproduction, which demanded the channelling of previous
undifferentiated desire towards that one end. On the other hand,
'abnormal' sexuality consisted of a kind of imbalance whereby the
superior brain functions, associated with the will, would become
subordinated to the inferior brain functions, associated with the
involuntary sphere. This had much in common with the model of
epilepsy constructed by the French degenerationist school.[45]

These theoretical elaborations permitted several shifts. Medical
discourse on sexual questions could be unified under its auspices
and the differences in explanations coming from mental hygiene
and legal medicine could be resolved. All sexual 'deviations', from

masturbation through to rape, could be included under the banner of 'abnormalities' of the sexual instinct. The dualisms of voluntary and involuntary expression of deviant acts and that of ontogenetic and phylogenetic development allowed for neurological explanations within a developmental or evolutionary framework.[46] The organicism and the evolutionary connotations of the new psychiatry had their roots in this kind of dualism and it is this which informed the diagnosis of cases such as that of U. L., discussed at the beginning of this chapter.

Before 1900 this kind of discourse was only encountered in Spanish psychiatry in a fragmentary form. The categories that alienist thought had supplied for the understanding of the sexual 'deviations', particularly 'erotic monomania' were to persist right up to the end of the nineteenth century.[47] It is not unusual to find them alongside the new categories of 'sexual perversion' in medico-legal treatises published in Spain in the latter decades of the nineteenth century.

A good example of this kind of mixture is the work of Ignacio Valentí y Vivó (1841–1924), who was Professor of Legal Medicine and Toxicology at the University of Barcelona and one of the pioneers of the eugenic movement in Catalonia.[48] His two-volume *Tratado de Antropología Médica y Jurídica* was published in 1889–94. If one compares his treatment of the 'sexual deviations' with that of other volumes at a similar time, such as Yáñez's *Elementos de Medicina Legal y Toxicología* (1884), substantial differences come to light. Yáñez continues to subscribe to the old frame of 'erotic monomania',[49] and, with respect to pederasty, as noted above, he relied entirely on Tardieu and Casper.[50] In contrast, Valentí y Vivó introduced a whole new range of concepts into his work and relied on Lassègue, Charcot and Westphal to diagnose states such as exhibitionism, inversion of the sexual instinct, feminism, tribadism, and other aberrations of this ilk.[51]

Valentí Vivó drew upon several notions contained in the new psychiatry such as degeneration, morbid inheritance, organodynamic anomaly, dysgenics and syndrome. He also associated the existence of the 'sexual aberrations' with the decline of civilization, casting them as threats of a return to the 'carnal brutality' of times past.[52] Sexual anomalies in his account would derive from hereditary or acquired pathological deviations. In this way, the author distanced himself from Lombrosian determinism and innatism and admitted the effects of adaptation and morbid environment as factors in the generation of stigmas. He distinguished 'sexual abnormality' from 'sexual monstrosity', the latter constituting the 'negación de aptitud – absoluta, relativa – generadora por aberración de órganos e imposibilidad completa y heredada de funciones, tanto por la cópula como para la fecundación' [negation of reproductive ability, either absolute or relative, due to aberration of the organs and the complete and inherited impossibility of the function, both in terms of the copula and in the ability to fertilise].[53] At the same time, old concepts such as erotomania persisted relatively unchanged. While this concept was viewed as having been incorrectly associated with hysteria and nymphomania, there was no further elaboration on the matter as there was in the work of Binet in 1887, for example.[54]

Finally, it is worth noting that the usual neutral and 'objective' style seen in other commentators on the 'sexual perversions' is absent in Valentí Vivó. The age-old ideas and vocabulary of 'abomination' and crimes 'against nature' are maintained. Sexual practices between members of the same sex ('relaciones libidinosas con sexualidad homóloga' [libidinous relations with homologous sexuality])[55] are described as 'anti-natural' acts, together with other expressions of sexual 'deviation', such as 'cópula con brutos' [copulation with beasts]. Valentí uses the term 'Teraselgia' (from the Greek *aselgeia*, 'libertinage' or 'sexual excess') in order to refer to the 'estudio de la lascivia contranatural' [study of anti-natural lasciviousness].[56]

The concepts of degeneration, the conceptualization of the invert as an androgyne (following Tardieu) and the old rhetoric on anti-natural vice coincided in another alienist and medico-legal doctor, José María Escuder.[57] Escuder had participated as an expert witness in the trial of the priest Galeote, the murderer of the bishop of Madrid-Alcalá in 1886.[58] In his work *Locos y Anómalos* some cases of sexual inversion are mentioned where degenerative stigma, genital abnormalities, and the preference for members of the same sex all coincide. The case of a 'loco que pasa por cuerdo' [madman who passes as sane], a 39-year-old doctor possessed by a 'homicidal-suicidal delirium' is described in the following terms after Escuder's observations:

> I noted the following: the penis coincided in terms of size and
> shape with that of a boy of nine years, in marked contrast with the

hairiness of developed virility. The scrotum, which was very small
and shrivelled, contained but one testicle. This right testicle was as
large as a duck egg and was lodged in the upper section of the sac.
The left testicle was absent and had not yet descended from the
abdominal cavity, a cryptorchidia uncommon even in those
suffering degeneration of the sexual organs. This deficiency of the
genitalia suggested the presence of sexual inversion. It was with
deep regret that, in this human companion of mine, who was mad
and poor, I moved on to perform an anal examination. I noted that
the hairs that surrounded the orifice were turned inwards towards
the centre and above a clear infundibulum, formed by the dilation
of the sphincter and the elevation of the dilated opening, whose
folds had been erased completely. To my inquiries he replied that
he had never known woman as he felt repugnance towards this
act.[59]

Later on, in the section dedicated to the 'genesic aberrations',
Escuder discussed the few inverts that according to him existed in
Spain, amongst the 'vida refinada y muelle de las ciudades, entre
la molicie de los agotados y decadentes' [pleasure-seeking and
loose life of the cities, amongst the *mollitie* of the exhausted and
decadent].[60] He depicts them as 'errata de la naturaleza que
incluyó un cerebro masculino en un cuerpo femenino' [errata of
nature, which united a male brain to a female body]. In the
description of the life of these unfortunates, Escuder combined
anatomical and physiological stigma with those of a psychological
and moral nature. In this way, inverts' pelvis, thighs and busts
would be woman-like, their feet would be small, and 'su voz es
atiplada, de falsete' [their voice is high-pitched and falsetto]. On
the other hand, 'aman la contemplación de las formas masculinas' [they love to contemplate the male form]; 'imitan a las
mujeres, o mejor aún, proyectan al exterior sus gustos femeninos:
los perfumes, los colores vistosos, la poesía lírica' [they imitate
women, or rather, they project outwards their feminine tastes,
such as perfumes, bright colours, and lyrical poetry].

For Escuder, inverts thus constituted a 'tercer sexo, un género
neutro, adverso a todos' [third sex, a neutral gender, adverse to
all] and a difficult legal situation which 'conspira contra la
naturaleza y las gentes' [conspired against people and nature] as
their behaviour drew them to the limits of criminality, including
thievery, deceit and murder as a result of extreme jealousy.[61] On
the other hand, Escuder utilizes the language of degenerationism

and Lombrosian descriptions of atavism.[62] The doctor suspected of inversion discussed above is diagnosed as a 'degenerado típico, tal como Morel y Morselli lo estudiaron' [typical degenerate, just like Morel and Morselli noted].[63] This veritable *bricolage* of concepts taken from the model of the hermaphrodite, the degenerate and the sodomite, is combined with a highly moral tone which condemns the invert:

> Siendo hombres según la ley, claro está que donde un maricón de éstos se introduce, colegio, cuartel, cofradía, convento o sociedad masculina, ha de ser un foco de depravación, de corrupción y deshonra. Oprobio de la especie humana, malean a los que con ellos se relacionan.[64]

> [As they are men, at least according to the law, it is clear that wherever a *maricón* appears – in a barracks, school, brotherhood, convent or any male society – he will be a site of depravation, corruption and dishonour. The opprobrium of human kind, he will contaminate all he touches.]

As a study of Valentí Vivó and Escuder shows, the new repertoire of psychiatric terms coming from degenerationist perspectives incorporated from 1880 onwards did not entail the complete disappearance of the old theoretical positions. Even the old ideas on sodomy and anti-natural acts and the active/passive divide did not altogether disappear.[65] Instead, all these old terms of reference are incorporated and 'resignified' as part of the new theoretical framework which affords the sodomite a particular character or exotic psychic nature. The process of the medicalization of the sodomite did not actually impede the return of this age-old figure; it reincorporated it. Rather than seeing this medicalization process, therefore, as anything 'complete' or progressive, we see an irregular and hybrid approximation to new theoretical paradigms. This does not mean, however, that these new medical categories did not have any effects on collective experience or on the creation of new types of 'person'. But the medicalization of sexuality was neither a linear process nor was it 'vertical' affecting all branches of medical knowledge equally.[66] The process of medicalization, as several authors have pointed out, depended on a number of institutional factors, relatively external to medical discourse, to which the latter adapted. Some of these factors were unique to the Spanish case, as we will show towards the end of this chapter.

This process of 'resignification' as a reiteration of difference and rupture of unity obliges us to reconsider a version of the history of homosexuality which has relied on a narrow reading of Foucault in order to construct linear and unitary explanations of the rise of the 'homosexual'.[67] According to this version, sodomy would have been slowly but progressively replaced by the new category of homosexuality. Chauncey has rectified this linear account by finding a 'missing link', that of the sexual invert who is more of a figure pertaining to gender inversion than to the overt sexual 'deviance' of the homosexual.[68] Chauncey's modification goes someway to correcting this model, but still suffers from a certain degree of lineality. In addition to Valentí Vivó and Escuder, there were many others in Spain who would confound this version of history. We concentrate on two important medical texts in the next section.

The Old in the New: The Limits of Medicalization

Our first example is taken from the work of José de Letamendi, Professor of General Pathology and Dean of the Faculty of Medicine at the University of Madrid. Author of *Curso de Clínica General o Canon perpetuo de la práctica médica* (1894), Letamendi is a curious figure in late nineteenth-century medical circles. At the time of the rise of positivist perceptions of life and nature, Letamendi defended a holistic and romantic conception akin to German *Naturphilosophie*. Letamendi occupied an in-between space in Spanish medicine, projecting what was essentially fast becoming an out-dated perception but from a prestigious chair in medicine. His ideas produced supporters and critics in the medical reviews of the period.

The second volume of his *Curso de Clínica General* contained some 850 aphorisms, typical of the Hippocratic tradition but already outmoded by the 1890s, covering all aspects of medical practice. The fourth section of this volume is dedicated to the 'Genetic Processes' (where 'genetic' refers to the act of 'generation' of new beings), and he covers both 'physiological and aberrant' sexual conduct. Letamendi believed that his work played an important part in literature of this type given 'el lamentable vacío que los patologistas y los clínicos dejan en la enseñanza' [the lamentable lacunae left by pathologists and clinicians in their teaching], who had maintained a complete silence on these matters.[69]

The sources employed by Letamendi are not easily determined. His aphoristic style does not allow for the mentioning of other works and his rhetoric, full of Latin phrases, Greek lexical items and neologisms of his own making, hardly aids the identification of his sources. For example, Letamendi speaks of the 'sexual impulse' as 'aphrodism'. This is divided into 'natural aphrodism' and 'para-aphrodism', the category which includes 'preternatural or aberrant' sexuality. 'Natural aphrodism' follows the logics of attraction and repulsion, or sympathy and antipathy, and is itself composed of three categories: friendship (attraction for moral reasons); luxuriousness (attraction for sensual motives); and love ('psycho-physical, integral attraction').[70]

Most of the text is devoted to the discussion of the 'para-aphrodisias'. These expressions of sexuality are explained as returns to atavism, to an original hermaphroditic state, to a lack of sexual differentiation characteristic of the lower species and the first stages of individual development. This atavistic origin would explain the universal presence of 'erotic aberrations' in the human species and amongst irrational beings.[71]

These innate 'hermaphroditic remains' inherent to human nature, the influence of which was expressed in practically invincible sexual aberrations, would, nevertheless, be broken down into several different categorizations.[72] In accordance with the degree of atavism present in these 'erotic aberrations' there would be: (1) innate conditions as a result of anatomical structure; (2) innate conditions due to neurotic inheritance; (3) those due to spontaneous vice; (4) those resulting from bad example; (5) those due to pure necessity; and (6) those produced by auto-suggestion and caprice. Medicine, according to Letamendi, could only operate with any degree of success in the cases outlined in (3), (4) and (5).

In addition, five different types of aberrations are identified.[73] These are: 'pseudo-pornia' (coition in an inappropriate vessel); 'autoerastia' (the 'solitary vice');[74] 'homoerastia o sodomía o singenesia' [homoerastia, sodomy or syngenesia] 'amor al de igual sexo' [love of those of the same sex]; 'pederasty' ('love of children'); and 'thesierastia', the 'sin of bestiality'.

With respect to the classification of 'pseudo-pornia', Letamendi believed that it was practised by many women as 'sodomitical pseudo-pornia' in order to avoid pregnancy and as a
concession to their libidinous tendencies. Those who practised
'autoerastia' did so because of the lack of an appropriate object of
the other sex, a 'recurso supletorio' [alternative resort] or
because of hermaphroditic atavism. The latter would include
those who engaged in 'rectal autoerastia'.[75]

Amongst homoerastic subjects there are those who 'are naturally so' and those who are 'so through passion and those
occasional'. Those who can effectively choose respond to 'secondary atavism or incomplete hermaphroditism (crossed para-
aphrodism)'.[76] In this way, Letamendi coincided with the modern
notion of 'inversion' as 'psychic hermaphroditism', divorced from
any anatomical abnormality. He argued that homoerastia in males
could be accompanied by an external virile countenance and that
'viraginity' (homoerastia among women) could be found among
females whose appearance was entirely feminine. 'Viraginity',
Letamendi pointed out, 'es condición encefálica y general, no
cutánea' [is a cephalic and general condition, not a cutaneous
one].[77]

However, amongst homoerasts and viraginists, whether innate,
temporary or occasional, certain 'feminine sodomites' can be
identified who like to reveal their desires and 'se gozan en
revelarse tomando a honor su propia infamia' [enjoy displaying
themselves, projecting their infamy as something honourable].
These individuals would combine the worst of both sexes, even
though they were capable of, in contrast to 'virile sodomites', 'una
asombrosa resistencia orgánica al libertinaje' [an astonishing
degree of organic resistance to libertinage], that is, they
restrained themselves sexually. Breaking with tradition, Letamendi distinguished 'homoerastia' from 'pederasty', the attraction to children. In the latter, in any case, 'los niños no siempre
son víctimas por concepto de violencia' [children are not always
the victims of violence].[78]

Theoretically, the work of Letamendi is both innovative and
incoherent. As already noted, he combined conceptual frameworks of extremely diverse origins. For example, together with the
Lombrosian reference to atavism and the interruption of normal
developmental patterns as a cause of anomalies (a notion that
goes back to the Teratology of Geoffroy de Saint-Hilaire)[79] there

is mention of Ernst Haeckel's analogy of the relationship between ontogenetic and phylogenetic development, current at the time,[80] and discussion of the theory of hermaphroditism and lack of sexual differentiation, taken from Darwin and the nascent school of sexology.[81]

The reliance of Letamendi on some of the principles of German *Naturphilosophie* in order to explain sexual attraction (in terms of sympathy and antipathy) constitutes a refusal to take positivism on board. To complete this eclectic picture, Letamendi discussed the notion of the invert as a male body with a female soul, as first expounded by Karl H. Ulrichs and disseminated by psychiatrists and sexologists such as Westphal, Magnan, Krafft-Ebing and Moll. The Spanish pathologist understands this gender deviance (as hermaphroditic atavism) and sexual deviance (as 'homoerastia') as a kind of personality, an innate special form of psyche. In the last analysis, all the 'erotic aberrations' would reside, according to Letamendi, in the transgression of gendered spheres; in all of them there is a return to the undifferentiated organism or original hermaphrodite.

Letamendi tried to harmonize these new medical and anthropological insights with archaic conceptual frameworks. He maintained the great divide between the natural and the unnatural by defining the erotic 'aberrations' as 'preternatural'. Furthermore, even though he distinguished between 'homoerastia' and 'pederastia', he maintained the distinction between 'active' and 'passive' roles. He also, despite first not defining those acts included in 'para-aphrodisia' as abominable or monstrous, evoked the moral condemnation of previous periods, referring as he did to vice, libertinage and luxury.[82]

Our second example of the truncated nature of the medicalization of same-sex sexuality in Spain at the turn of the century is taken from the field of criminal anthropology, a buoyant discipline in the country at the time. Criminal anthropology was given added impetus by the arrival and criticism of Lombrosian theories and by the perceived need to govern deviance in the city.[83] Like the naturalist and realist novel, criminal anthropology illuminated a demimonde created by urban overcrowding and poverty and it was keen to show how dangerous such elements were for the health of the nation. The three great names of this period, the three 'little Lombrosos' as Trinidad Fernández described them,[84] drawing in turn on Baroja's expression, were Rafael Salillas,

Dorado Montero and Constancio Bernaldo de Quirós. Bernaldo de Quirós, together with J. M. Llanas Aguilaniedo, published the remarkable *La Mala Vida en Madrid. Estudio psicosociológico con dibujos y fotografías del natural* in 1901.[85]

This text was written between 1899 and 1901. It was the fruit of a long process of research based on a variety of literatures, statistics and oral interviews, photographs and anthropometric studies carried out in a Madrid prison. At the same time, Salillas pioneered his Laboratory of Criminality, assiduously attended by the authors of *La Mala Vida en Madrid*.[86] The book was published as part of a broader late nineteenth-century genre about the 'low life' of several cities in Europe and Latin America. The subjects of the criminologists' inquiries were the city's criminals, prostitutes and beggars.

The section of the book devoted to sexual inversion appeared in the chapter on prostitution. Amongst the many interesting aspects of this text are the taxonomical resources employed by the authors (such as Uranism and tribadism) and their theorization of same-sex practices. Like Letamendi, the authors displayed a marked degree of eclecticism, relying on the degenerationist models espoused by Garnier, Raffalovitch, Benjamin Ball, Dalle-magne and Roux. But they also drew upon emerging sexological works such as those of Krafft-Ebing (e.g. *Psychopathia Sexualis*) and on the volume on sexual inverts co-written by Havelock Ellis and John A. Symonds. There are also, as is to be expected, references to Spanish authors such as Letamendi himself and to Italian criminal anthropologists such as Ferri.

This extremely diverse theoretical arsenal gave rise to a tax-onomy which, despite its sophistication, nevertheless reflects older conceptual frameworks. Inverts are classed in four main groups: 'pure inverts'; 'pseudo-inverts'; 'unisexuales dimorfos' [dimorphic unisexuals]; and 'polysexuals'. In each variety the characteristics of males and females are identified. 'Pure inverts' tended in an irresistible manner 'comportarse como individuos del sexo contrario' [to behave like individuals of the opposite sex]. They were divided into those 'platonic', in whom passion manifested itself as a form of erotomania, seen in poets, artists and admirers of strength, superiority and toughness;[87] the second group of 'pure inverts' were the sexual variety. Here were placed all those who in addition to adopting the role of the opposite gender ('maricas' and 'marimachos') also tended to adopt the corresponding role in the sexual act – subordinate in males and dominant in females. In the case of men, this submission converted them, the authors continued, into 'masturbators', 'succubi' or the 'effeminates of Krafft-Ebing' and even combinations of these.[88] A third class of 'pure inverts' comprised those capable of alternating the 'pure' role and the 'sexual' role according to circumstance.

'Pseudo-inverts', who popularly went by the name of *bujarrones*, conserved the gender role of their sex for outside appearances but could vary this gender role according to the sexual practice engaged in. Thus, according to Bernaldo de Quirós and Llanas Aguilaniedo, pseudo-invert males were capable of adopting passive or active roles but pseudo-invert women could adopt the passive role only. This whole class of inverts could be divided in turn into platonic, sexual and alternate inverts.

The class of 'dimorphic unisexuals' or *dígamos* are 'homosexuales de bodas dobles' [homosexuals of two marriages]. By this the authors meant that they could act as pseudo-inverts or inverts according to circumstances. Finally, the 'polysexuals' were those that combined the traits of the three classes mentioned above with the practice of heterosexual relations.

According to the two authors, this schema exhausted all possibilities in the terrain of sexual inversion and it was applied systematically to all the subjects observed in the study. These consisted of nineteen case studies some of which we will examine below. Despite this extensive schema, which is bound by traditional concepts of gender and sex, there may be, the authors admit, some types which have escaped their attention.[89]

As was the case of the typology constructed by Letamendi, the one employed by the two authors of *La Mala Vida* was equally ambivalent. On the one hand, they coincided with contemporary sexological criteria with respect to the supposed link between physical inversion (eunuchoid genital anatomy, effeminacy in men, a large clitoris in women and masculine appearance) and inversion of the sexual instinct. The authors admitted that 'no siempre, en efecto, coincide la inversión de los caracteres sexuales físicos con la inversión del instinto sexual' [not always, in fact, does inversion of the physical characters coincide with inversion of the sexual instinct].[90] Inversion of the sexual instinct was to be found in Uranians and tribades that possessed peculiar personalities rather than anatomical types. On the other hand, the two

authors insisted that 'sodomy' was not the only sexual practice
that inverts engaged in: 'la masturbación recíproca, el coito bucal,
etc, son manifestaciones uranistas corrientes' [mutual masturbation, oral coition, etc., are common Uranian practices].[91]

From schemas such as this, we can deduce that the long-
standing separation between active and passive sexuality characteristic of Mediterranean sexual codes drove the modern category
of the invert in Spain. For this reason, those males that practised
the insertive role, including 'pederasts' and those 'impassioned by
children' were not real inverts but pseudo-inverts and their
practices were more the result of vice than of their specific
nature.[92] A similar understanding is afforded of the *dígamos* and
the polysexuals. Their desires stem from 'curiosidad malsana,
vicio, voluptuosidad, deseo de lucro, etc' [unhealthy curiosity,
vice, voluptuousness, desire for monetary gain, etc].[93] This divide
between natural and apparent or artificial inverts draws on an old
but increasingly outdated distinction between the natural and the
anti-natural.

To speak of 'incubi through vice', 'unhealthy curiosity' and
'unfortunate aberrations' is obviously to adopt a moral tone. This
tone coexists uncomfortably with the attempt to craft an 'objective' typology or labelling technique. Bernaldo de Quirós and
Llanas Aguilaniedo also refer to the smells of some Uranians, in
whom 'a la perversión del instinto sexual se asocia la perversión
del instinto olfativo' [the perversion of the sexual instinct is
associated to the perversion of the olfactory instinct] and many
'perfúmanse con olores repugnantes' [perfume themselves with
repugnant odours].[94] This association between perverted sexual
and olfactory instincts had already made its appearance in the
work of Tardieu, Mata and Yáñez and it appears to have something in common with the sulphurous smells supposedly accompanying Satan and devils.[95] Indeed, the identification of sodomy
with a plague, vice or pestilence, all referred to in *La Mala Vida*,
goes back at least to the beginnings of modernity in Spain.[96] The
ambivalent discourse of this unequal process of medicalization
would possess as a constant feature the homophobia of yester-
year.[97]

In addition, it is worth mentioning briefly the work of the
Catalan pedagogue Max Bembo, whose *La Mala Vida en Barcelona*
followed shortly after the work authored by Bernaldo de Quirós
and Llanas Aguilaniedo in 1912.[98] This work, discussed more

extensively in Chapter Six, devoted a large amount of space to inversion and eliminated the condemnatory tones seen in many other studies. The theoretical framework offered by Bembo coincides broadly with that of the authors of *La Mala Vida en Madrid* and degenerationist proponents such as Magnan, Lacassagne and Binet are hailed over and above the more deterministic somatic theories of Lombroso. Combined with this is a large swathe of sexological theories taken from Moll, Raffalovitch, Westphal and Krafft-Ebing.

Although Bembo admits that sexual inversion could be a natural phenomenon, he coincides with Moll and Raffalovitch in arguing that it is a phenomenon which arises from a 'predisposition' rooted in morbid inheritance.[99] Inversion is not an instinct, he argues, but the degeneration of an instinct. His discussion of the 'naturalness' or otherwise of sexual inversion draws, once more, on the old antithesis between natural and anti-natural, seen above. Inversion becomes a disease that is at the heart of all other deviations of the sexual instinct. The presence of sexual inversion in an individual should be seen, Bembo argues, as the result of both a biological trait and of environmental factors which may include certain types of food, literature, and various kinds of psychic disturbance.[100] An innovative feature of Max Bembo's account of Barcelona is his admission that there may not be such a rigid divide between hetero and homo sexuality. Bisexuality might be a middle course or a transition stage. Anomalous and degenerate admittedly, the invert is no longer a strange monster, an 'unexplainable' freak of nature.

The Dissemination of Sexological Literature

If the limits of medicalization can be seen in texts such as those of eminent pathologists (Letamendi), medico-legal doctors (Valentí Vivó, Escuder, Piga Pascual), criminologists (Bernaldo de Quirós and Llanas Aguilaniedo) and educationalists (Bembo), a similar process can be traced in hygienic and sexological material. Sexological literature in Spain emerged in the last quarter of the nineteenth century as a variant of the conjugal hygiene literature of the mid-century, the most emblematic work of which was that of Pedro Felipe Monlau, *Higiene del Matrimonio* (1853).

The new literature was characterized by its general recommendations on health matters and was written by medical doctors and essayists of less renown than psychiatrists. Married life was a prime concern of these texts but they also dealt with the sexual 'aberrations' and more piquant subjects. They often cited or even reproduced entire paragraphs extracted from foreign literature on the subject.

One of the first authors of this genre was the Catalan Amancio Peratoner. Although his status as medical practitioner is somewhat dubious,[101] he was the author of some twenty books on sexual matters. One of the most significant for our purposes is his *Los Peligros del Amor, de la Lujuria y del Libertinaje*, published in 1874. The text includes in an annex a section reproduced from Tardieu on pederasty which first appeared in the French author's *Atentados contra la Honestidad*.

Peratoner himself referred to the question of pederasty, but unlike some of the authors we have discussed above, he was overtly condemnatory of the practice, describing it as the 'último grado de la humana depravación' [last point on the scale of human depravation]. Nevertheless, he did recognize, in accordance with the first psychiatric theories on 'moral madness' that in some cases pederasty had something to do with an 'unhealthy perversion of sensibility' and an 'aberration of the moral faculties'. In most cases, notwithstanding, pederasty would be due to 'desenfrenada lujuria y a una sensibilidad depravada' [untamed luxuriousness and depraved sensibility]. This 'brutal passion' was most common in the cities and gave rise to a particular form of prostitution offered by 'un enjambre de barbilampiños corrompidos y ociosos' [a swarm of beardless corrupt and lazy] individuals. The pederast became a 'libertine' converted into a client in this equation.[102]

The question is treated more extensively in the series of twenty volumes written between 1891 and 1893 by the Catalan Dr Suárez Casañ. The little volumes of his encyclopaedic 'Conocimientos para la Vida Privada' [Knowledge for Private Life] were addressed to a more popular audience.[103] There were at least twenty editions of these works, a fact that underscores their popularity amongst the Restoration public.[104]

Volumes Six and Nine are entitled, respectively, *La Pederastia* and *El Amor Lesbio*. They offer the reader an often incoherent amalgam of stories and reflections, of moral condemnations and concepts drawn from other medical and historical sources. In *La Pederastia* Suárez Casañ justifies his use of the term pederasty by declaring that it was a catch-all term, describing both active and passive variants. The biblical term 'sodomy' is considered to be ambiguous and the colloquial expressions *bujarrón* and *maricón* do not, for the author, capture the full significance of pederasty.

Pederasty finds a home in the section on 'anti-natural unions'.[105] It is described as a 'repugnante y odiosa aberración que apenas el médico y el filósofo se explican' [repugnant and odious aberration hardly to be explained by the doctor or the philosopher].[106] Given such language, the work of Suárez Casañ can be seen to be leagues away from the attempts of figures like Letamendi to achieve a certain degree of clinical distance. In accordance with his desire for more lurid accounts, Suárez Casañ draws extensively on experts such as Tardieu and Casper but only in order to paint a picture of the infamy and murderous traits purportedly present in the pederast. For this purpose, the child-murderer Gilles de Rais is discussed at length and thus 'el pederasta es, en nuestro concepto, el ente más degradado de la naturaleza y lo consideramos capaz de las mayores monstruosi-dades' [the pederast is, in our understanding, the most degraded being in nature and we believe him capable of the greatest monstrosities].[107]

After a grand tour of pederastic prostitution in the European cities of Paris, Rome, Naples and Barcelona, Suárez Casañ, draw-ing on Mata, Casper and Tardieu once more, denotes the most relevant signs that any medico-legal doctor must focus upon in order to identify the pederast. Following this, the 'causes' of pederasty are examined. It is argued on the one hand that pederasty constitutes a kind of madness, 'an aberration of the senses', but on the other hand it arises from 'el desenfreno de las pasiones, la lujuria y el libertinaje' [the unleashing of passions, luxury and libertinage].[108] An intricate coalition between mad-ness and luxuriousness is thus established: 'El hombre que vive sólo para las sensualidades parece que va perdiendo poco a poco su racionalidad convirtiéndose en una especie de bestia feroz y repugnante' [Any man that lives for sensuality alone seems to lose, little by little, his reason and becomes a kind of ferocious and repugnant beast].[109]

Such a situation would arise, the author argued, when a variety of circumstances coincided including the lack of contact with

women, a 'carácter tímido, apocado y afeminado' [timid, diminished and effeminate character], fear of venereal disease, having
been a victim of abuse in childhood, impotence, castration and
hermaphroditism. In any case, it was necessary, Suárez Casañ
argued, to determine the culpability of the pederast. Citing the
influential article on inversion published by Charcot and Magnan
in 1882, Suárez Casañ wondered '¿pero no cabría establecer la
diferencia entre los pederastas que lo son a causa de la locura y
los pederastas que lo son por lujuria?' [would it not be best to
establish the difference between those pederasts who are so
because of madness and those whose cause is luxuriousness?][110]

Suárez Casañ went on to argue that the most common examples of the pederast were situated between these two limits;
pederasts would be neither exclusively irresponsible nor were they
completely consumed by vice. Vice, nevertheless, once repeated
often enough could result in the corruption of the nervous
system which in turn and in time would affect the sexual instinct.
'Inversion of the reproductive sense', therefore, could be interpreted as a result of actual sexual behaviour.[111] This continuous
play between cause and effect is characteristic of Suárez Casañ
and many other commentators. It is for this reason that he, like
Letamendi (not referred to by Suárez Casañ) believed that
residual hermaphroditism could function as a predisposition
towards inversion.[112] In this way, without forgetting the effects of
luxuriousness and vice, Suárez Casañ accepts some form of
hereditability of the sexual perversions. This constant movement
between a moral tone, which foregrounds vice and virtue, free
will, luxuriousness and passion, and a technical language which
refers to atavism and hereditary stigma, is found elsewhere, as we
have seen, in the domain of psychiatry.

While Suárez Casañ used the term 'pederasty', another author,
Fernando Mateos Koch, continued to employ the category 'sodomy' at the beginning of the century. This doctor advertised his
clinic and remedies in his many books published around 1900.[113]
Practising in Madrid, Koch's books fit into the genre of marriage
hygiene guides but, like Monlau's volume, also discussed the
sexual aberrations. 'Sodomy', Koch held, 'es el coito rectal y lo
mismo la practica el hombre con la mujer que con el mismo
hombre o con el niño' [is rectal coition whether between man
and woman or between man and boy].[114] Such practices were
widespread, we are told, in the cities and in all those places where

men were housed together or came into contact: 'los marinos, los soldados, los presos y muchos de los que están en contacto con los niños, en los hospicios y escuelas' [sailors, soldiers, prisoners and many of those who are in contact with children in hospices and schools].[115]

Other texts insisted on hermaphroditism as an interpretive device for same-sex sexuality. *Higiene Sexual del Soltero* (1902) written by Ciro Bayo, was republished in 1919. In the eighth chapter of this work dedicated to the question of the 'sexual aberrations', Bayo distinguished between Sapphism (also termed 'tribadism' and 'lesbian love') and pederasty. According to Bayo, Sapphism was the 'faz de la inversión sexual del placer hetero-sexual en la mujer, correspondiente al uranismo o pederastia en el hombre' [expression of the sexual inversion of heterosexual pleasure in women, comparable to Uranism or pederasty in men].[116] Here, the term 'heterosexual' was employed in its original meaning, denoting 'bisexuality', in accordance with the observations made by the historian J. Katz.[117] Bayo also remarked that the popular term for pederasty and Sapphism was 'hermaph-rodism'.[118] The relationship established between residual her-maphroditism and homosexuality was common in sexological literature (as it had been in other discourses discussed above) and lasted up to the 1920s,[119] when it was reformulated in endocrino-logical terms, particularly by Marañón in his notion of the 'intersexual states'.

Bayo engaged in an extensive survey of inversion and admitted that such a practice was a constant in human experience. This notion of constancy allowed him to argue that it was not a phenomenon provoked by the 'nervousness of our generation' or by 'sexual fatigue'.[120] Here we see a reference to the broad notion of neurasthenia, a disease thought to arise from over-civilization, a sedentary state and the exaltation of the intellectual faculties over and above the dynamics of the will, resulting in impotence and loss of virility.

If it was a constant in human civilization, what were the conditions that induced sexual inversion according to Bayo? A heterogeneous and rather disordered set of conditions were tabled by the author running the gamut of organic and mental pathologies ('congenital psychoses', 'epilepsy', 'senile dementia') and the often referred to 'bad habits'.[121]

Finally, Bayo noted that pederasts were particularly interested in youths, taking a leaf out of Krafft-Ebing's book: 'pierden el cuerpo y el alma de los jóvenes' [they destroy the body and soul of youth], he sentenced.[122] The theory of contagion, noted by Suárez Casañ,[123] was also invoked and the practices of pederasts including 'marriages' and 'baptisms' in certain Madrid clubs sealed the association between homosexuality and secret societies.[124]

Sexual Inversion and Gender Anxiety in Restoration Spain

As we have seen, sexological literature published between the Restoration era and the First World War is even more diverse in its conceptual base than the texts on criminology and legal medicine that we first reviewed. In this literature the old 'pre-medical' divisions between active/passive and natural/anti-natural/ preternatural, coexisted with the modern concepts of the psychopathology of the perversions. Also present were old concepts deriving from a framework based purely on anatomical characteristics such as the 'vices of conformation', women with oversized clitorises, hermaphroditism, together with notions that came from alienism (such as nymphomania) blended together with a marked moral tone.

Despite this eclectic conceptual mix one common point of crossover between popular sexological texts, works of general pathology, legal medicine and criminology, was the connection made between gender deviance and the sexual aberrations rather than an emphasis on actual sexual acts. In this framework, the 'invert' is conceived above all in this period up to the mid 1910s as someone who transgresses the limits drawn between masculinity and femininity; hence the recourse to the concept of hermaphroditism (whether biological or psychical). The male invert or aesthete and the female variety, the mannish woman, display a physiognomy, form of dress and set of gestures of their own. The extent to which these characteristics were viewed as definable and real can be seen by looking beyond the medical sciences into the arts. For example, in *La Luz y La Pintura* (1894), written by the ophthalmologist and President of the Academy of Fine Art, President of the Provincial Government (Diputación) and Mayor of Cadiz, Cayetano del Toro,[125] a number of guidelines are included on how to represent figures with particular trades, temperaments and characteristics. It is worth citing at length the section devoted to the description of the aesthete, accompanied by a sketch (figure 560 in Del Toro's book):

> Aesthetes. There are certain men who are effeminate and certain women who are mannish and who have extremely marked characteristics; a true disgrace for both sexes. The effeminate man exaggerates as much as he can the movements and attitudes of women. But he becomes nothing more than a copy or imitation, a true caricature. Thus they make the tone of their voices more shrill and carry their arms closely to their torso, one folded over the other and their hands crossed in the region of the stomach. As they walk, the tips of their feet are turned inwards so imitating the sweet sway that women are obliged to undertake given the nature of their pelvic cavities and their thighs. Their faces are well cared for and shaven and it is not rare that they employ make-up and rouge or at least use powders to whiten their visage. Their lips are painted bright red or they might paint their eyelids dark, drawing an almost black horizontal line. It is not rare for them to paint beauty spots on their cheeks, or for them to wear their hair long, shiny and combed into partings. They often use a necktie or brightly coloured cravat, a very clean shirt, tight clothing, generally trousers, waistcoat and short jacket, sometimes of velvet. Some dress in a blouse instead of a jacket and wear a little felt hat or cap with or without a peak and with a tie or multicoloured adornment behind. Others, carrying much further the imitation, pierce their ears and wear earrings, and others still mortify their bodies with corsets. They clean their hands carefully and wear rings, if they can, and carry a fan or handkerchief.[126]

The actual sexual contact between individuals of the same sex is considered as just one more aspect of the make-up of the invert. For this reason, to return to Bernaldo de Quirós and Llanas Aguilaniedo, these authors continued to consider 'pseudo-inverts' as part of the broader class of inverts who were active and dominant in their relations. Letamendi had described his 'homo-erasts' as an effect of atavistic hermaphroditism. In reality, the homosexual, as a different personage, had not yet been distin-guished from the invert. The same phenomenon will be encoun-tered later when we discuss some aspects of the conceptual basis of psychiatry. It would seem that this lack of specificity and the predominance of gender deviance as a trait of the invert would mark Spain as different from the United States and some European countries around 1900.[127] It would appear that Spain had more in common in this sense with, for example, Argentina.[128]

Another clear example of the connotations around gender deviance that inversion primarily invoked can be drawn from the medical profession. A clinical case study was published in 1892 in the prestigious review *El Siglo Médico* by Vicente Ots Esquerdo. Ots Esquerdo was the medical doctor of Carabanchel mental asylum and one of the first degenerationist psychiatrists. The case related by the doctor was termed 'Inversión Sexual Intelectiva Sistemática' [Systematic Intellective Sexual Inversion]. According to the author of the report, who considered himself to be well informed with respect to the 'phrenopathic literature' of the period, no 'case of similar delirium' had been found in the annals of psychiatry.[129]

The case history is one of a 36-year-old woman identified only by the initials 'R. N.' who was married and had five children. The sudden death of one of her children produced in her 'una serie de ataques de naturaleza francamente histérica, seguidos más tarde de trastornos psíquicos e impulsos suicidas' [a series of attacks of a frankly hysterical nature, followed later by psychic upsets and suicidal impulses]. The woman stated that she did not know her own father and that the latter had handed her over when still a child to a guardian. A revelation follows: 'Hasta los cinco años fue un chicho rollizo y bien conformado aparentemente, que se llamaba Timoteo' [Up to the age of five, she was a healthy lad who was apparently well formed, and went by the name of Timoteo]. But when his tutor discovered a genital anomaly he was operated upon and was designated a woman. At the age of fifteen, as a result of a secret sexual relationship, she became pregnant and gave birth to a 'monster', the doctor noted, which died shortly afterwards. A year later, she was secuestered, taken to North Africa and was sold to a Moroccan who incorporated her into his harem. She became pregnant once again and once more gave birth to a monstrous child. She then escaped her captor and roamed through different lands finally arriving in Tangiers. From here, she made her way to Madrid 'y como llamase la atención por las formas y aspecto afeminado de su cuerpo, pidió ropas de mujer, y vestida con este traje entró de criada en una casa' [and as her effeminate form and general aspect drew attention, she asked for female clothing and thus dressed became a servant]. When she was nineteen a beard began to grow; she was considered to be male and was expelled from the house in which she served. Some time later, once more in the hands of her tutor, 'volvió a tomar todas las apariencias de mujer, permitiéndole esta retrocesión a su falso sexo trabajar como triple bailarina en el Real' [she once again took female clothes and this return to her false sex allowed her to become a dancer in the Royal Ballet]. Soon afterwards, she fell into a state of dementia and was married off to the man who was at the time of writing, 1892, still her husband. She became pregnant eight times, none of which entailed a monstrous birth. For this reason, she believed that her children were not really hers but that she had been tricked into thinking so.[130]

The woman stated that six years previously she had had a hallucinatory experience while listening to the National Anthem and this allowed her to shake herself out of the daze in which she had hitherto lived. She then began to recall all the events of her past life. From that moment on, she tried to recover her 'posición, traje, costumbres, etc., adecuados a su verdadero sexo; pero su marido y tutor' [position, dress, customs, etc., appropriate to her true sex, but her tutor and husband] stopped her and they were 'empeñados en que siguiese siendo mujer' [determined that she continued to be a woman]. Ots Esquerdo recorded that she begged them for 'un traje de hombre y la dejemos en libertad, que ella se buscará una casa, café o fonda, donde sea admitida como criado' [men's clothing and that we leave her in peace. She would find a house, café or inn where she could be admitted as a servant].

The psychiatrist, on describing R. N.'s desire to be recognised as a man, remarked that the subject presented 'una lucidez perfecta en todas sus manifestaciones intelectuales, y en ninguna ocasión hemos observado la menor incoherencia mental' [perfect lucidity in all her intellectual manifestations, and on no occasion have we observed the least mental incoherence]. In order to diagnose the case, Ots Esquerdo summed up all the facts and considered the various classifications available to him. He decided that hers was not a case of 'instinctive sexual inversion' as described by Westphal, because this state indicated an exclusively genital basis, that is, sexual attraction towards members of the same sex. Here, 'el cambio de sexo no es un pretexto para buscar las caricias y atenciones de la mujer, sino que, al contrario, procura apartarse de todas sus compañeras siempre que dejan al descubierto alguna de las regiones ocultas de su cuerpo' [the sex change is not a pretext in order to seek the attention and caresses of women but, on the contrary, she always tries to distance herself from her female companions when they uncover any parts of their body].[131]

Ots Esquerdo did not believe that he was before a case of erotomania, either. There were no indices of 'erotic madness' in this case, or of any 'persecution delirium'. It was not a case of 'dual consciousness' or one of 'dual personality' since the two consciousnesses, those of man and woman, did not coexist in the woman. Instead of all these diagnoses, Ots Esquerdo came up with a completely novel one: 'systematic intellective sexual inversion'. In one sense this was sexual inversion like other cases. But this form of sexual inversion demanded that the person integrated this state 'en su verdadero derecho a participar de los vestidos, trabajos, derechos y deberes del sexo contrario, del masculino' [into their real right to share the clothes, labours, rights and duties of the opposite sex, the male sex].[132] We are not faced with a perversion of the sexual instinct, however; what we have here is an alteration of the representation of the sex of the person. As such, it relied upon an intellectual basis not an instinctual one.

In terms of aetiology, Ots Esquerdo revealed the degenerationist basis of his diagnosis and he tried to explain the disease as the consequence of morbid inheritance, even though he admitted that he was unable to detect any illustrative antecedents.[133]

The case of R. N. is illuminating because it described the subversion of gender roles but did not allude to any sexual transgression. Why was sexual inversion mainly ascribed to acts of gender deviance rather than to those of sexuality? One reason may be, as we have already noted, that as the medicalization of homosexuality in Spain did not respond to a campaign for the decriminalization of same-sex acts, there was less emphasis on the sexual aspects of the question. There was no specific legislation at the time on homosexuality, even though the elastic interpretation of 'crimes against decency' and 'sodomy' could result in prosecution. This is one hypothesis, but in any event, the Spanish situation appears to be similar to that of France,[134] where there was also concern about broad gender aspects such as the 'de-virilization' of the race, as expressed in the words of many politicians, doctors and legal experts in the last years of the nineteenth century as well as certain laws against cross-dressing.

In Spain at the same time, medicine, pedagogy, religion, philanthropy, the novel and the arts were all engaged in drawing clear demarcations between the sexes and, therefore, between the public and private, between production and reproduction, as a way of guaranteeing the family and national identity. Doctors were interested in sexuality because it was one way of regulating family life as the repository of privacy and affection. Jo Labanyi has described how the writers of Restoration novels (Galdós, Pardo Bazán, Valera, Clarín, amongst others) effectively functioned as a technology of government and a way of producing 'Spaniards', in the same way as Cánovas through his centralizing policies and state construction hoped to create a feeling of nationhood.[135] This is a project which has been described as 'the nationalization of the masses'.[136] One place where these subjects are manufactured is the domestic scenario, characterized by a clear dividing line between maleness and femaleness. The rogue figures in this domestic scene are the adulterous women[137] and weak or effeminate men who are not strong enough to rule the roost. The passive husband faced his counterpart in the dominant wife, who was often termed a *marimacho*.[138] Seducers and perverts of various descriptions also found a home amongst those who constituted a threat to family life and they inundate the pages of the realist and naturalist novel.[139] To figures such as these, the presence of the invert in the large cities is to be added. This presence was increasingly remarked upon for example in the work of Tardieu (1863), in the autochthonous work *La Mala Vida en Madrid* and in Max Bembo's 1912 work. This preoccupation was no doubt in part a result of the rapid urban expansion experienced between 1877 and 1900 in Spain and the high levels of internal male migration to the industrialized Basque Country and Catalonia or to cities based on services, such as Madrid.[140]

In France, the concern over lost virility was intricately connected to fears of a low birth rate. The absence of a numerically strong and physically vigorous race, doctors and national pundits warned, resulted from the use of contraception (the 'birth strike'), the proliferation of 'conjugal fraud' (non-reproductive sex), the sexual aberrations and the exhaustion of the nervous system as a result of over-refinement and a life of increased luxury amongst the upper classes. Rivalry with Germany, which was perceived as vibrant and disciplined, merely served to exacerbate this feeling.

But in Spain, preoccupation with the genders did not arise from a concern over a low birth rate. The birth rate remained high, except for Catalonia, in all regions around 1900.[141] Loss of virility was instead associated with the decline of political and military clout; a fear that was clearly expressed in elocutions such as that of Lord Salisbury's 'dying nations' speech.[142] Political instability, economic dependence on other countries, the lack of individual initiative, corruption, favouritism and class struggle accounted for the rest. These factors, discussed extensively in Chapter Five, were in turn attributed to a lack of will power and organic coherence of the nation and the exhaustion of collective energy, all of which were seen to have resulted in the decline of the 'race'.

A further factor causing concern with respect to gendered relations was the rise of an incipient culture of consumption amongst the richer urban classes in the latter years of the nineteenth century.[143] The tastes and excesses once reserved for the aristocracy seemed to have reached the 'middle classes': 'El amor excesivo al lujo y a los placeres entre las clases más instruidas de la sociedad, [es] una de las causas que más influyen en el desarrollo de la prostitución clandestina' [The excessive taste for luxuries and pleasure amongst the educated classes of society [is] one of the causes of greatest influence in the development of covert prostitution], noted one social analyst. Certain customs had spread from the aristocracy to the other social classes 'de modo que ciertas costumbres, no bien anotadas en el código de la moral, que antes constituyeron un privilegio de la aristocracia, hoy día se han democratizado y han penetrado en las clases sociales que se hallan ligadas con ella' [Because of this certain customs not mentioned in the moral code and which were formerly the privilege of the aristocracy have nowadays become democratized and have been adopted by those social classes that are connected to it [the aristocracy].][144]

The seeking of luxury which drives women to forget their obligations as wives and mothers, the attraction of young men and women to the sensuous life of Bohemia, aestheticism and to passing pleasures,[145] are the targets of this disciplinary discourse. In addition, fashion, the desire for luxurious goods,[146] and sexual inversion itself were seen as foreign imports, particularly French ones. According to commentators of the time, this resulted in the denaturalization of gender relations and neglect of the task of each sex; maternity was under attack as the number of effeminate men continued to rise. Adultery and the 'sexual aberrations' were seen to be related to the consumption of superfluous goods, which extended the gap between the natural and the non-natural, between the masculine and feminine. As we will now see, the new psychiatry of the beginning of the twentieth century also responded to these concerns as it continued to place sexual deviation within the broad remit of gender transgression.

Psychiatry and Degenerationist Thought

In comparison with the texts from the areas of legal medicine, criminal anthropology and sexology that we have examined up to now, the discourse of clinical psychiatry was much more rounded theoretically and maintained a much more neutral and less condemnatory stance on sexual questions. Despite this innovation, we cannot assume that the new psychiatry was a complete break with the past. In fact, as we will see, like any 'new' discipline, many of its conceptual referents drew on those of the past, particularly those of a moral nature. Psychiatry also possessed another element which distinguished it from earlier alienism: a hygienic dimension which allowed intervention in a variety of scenarios including the school, the workplace and the domestic sphere. Interest in the 'abnormalities' effectively converted psychiatry into a technology of government which reached far beyond the old boundaries of the asylum and placed it firmly in the social sphere.[147] This was most obviously felt by the family, a unit transformed by the new sciences of evolution and heredity into an endless fount of pathological disorders.

It can generally be argued that between the years 1900 and 1920 the model of French degenerationist thought held sway in Spanish psychiatry.[148] While somewhat slow to be accepted and unequal in its influence, this theory held that degeneration was a condition that resulted from adaptation to a morbid environment, a condition which was then immediately converted into something fixed in the heredity of the person and thus transmitted from one generation to the next.[149] The use of this concept permitted a kind of negotiation between heredity and environment, avoiding both classical voluntarism (common amongst jurists) and Lombrosian determinism (first defended by Spanish criminologists). The reception of degenerationism was, as has been recently shown, highly eclectic and varied in the Spanish sciences. It gave rise, for example, to the acceptance of some of the ideas of British sex psychology (Symonds and Ellis),[150] German psychopathology (Westphal, Moll,[151] Krafft-Ebing,[152] Hirschfeld), and psychoanalysis (Freud).[153]

With respect to sexual inversion, Spanish commentators began to ask the same questions as their European counterparts: was sexual inversion a hereditary, congenital or acquired condition? Were there any psychical or physical stigmas that allowed for its diagnosis? How dangerous was the invert for society? One way of answering these questions was to establish a system whereby different types of sexual inversion were distinguished.

Before discussing Spanish degenerationists' views on sexual inversion, some introductory remarks on the reception of these ideas are called for. There were two principal readings of degenerationism, conforming more or less to what has now been articulated as the 'nature' versus 'nurture' division. In some cases, the biologistic and deterministic view of Magnan, the foreign author most translated in the Spanish medical press of the period, was adopted.[154] Degeneration was equated with an inherited imbalance which manifested itself in terms of a physical lesion affecting the functions of the brain. In other cases, the older variant of the theory was preferred, as articulated by Morel, which accepted a certain degree of acquired degeneration or which authors tried to render compatible with certain religious tenets.[155] Those most critical of the first theory insisted upon the distinction to be made between that which was inherited and that which was congenital; during the formation of the embryo alterations could occur that would affect all subsequent development. In both cases, however, Prosper Lucas's notion of 'dissimilar heredity' was accepted: 'the hereditary transmission of a morbid process would also predispose towards the suffering of other illnesses'.[156] Thus, in all the classifications of degenerates made, the perversions of the sexual instinct (including sexual inversion) featured prominently.

A final common element was the importance attributed to psychic stigmas and mental and behavioural qualities which may indicate a morbid predisposition. Physical stigmas were also discussed and certain constitutional and anatomical elements were understood to be definitive signs of degeneration. Lombrosian degenerationists tended to emphasize physical stigma over and above others, primacy being given to craniometry and to photographic techniques. In Bembo's *Mala Vida de Barcelona*, for example, there is discussion of these techniques and their use on a number of inverts, although this empiricist methodology did not give rise in the text to deterministic readings. Other techniques employed included genealogical trees, graphs and drawings which allowed for the description of the heredity of an individual and any pathological transmission.[157]

As examples of Spanish degenerationist thought, in what follows we focus on four paradigmatic contributions which all discuss sexual inversion in the light of this theory. Differences abound, however. The first two examples are closer to the reductionist and biologistic account; the last two are more flexible, less deterministic and more open to environmental influences on mental states.

In 1899 Martínez Valverde published the first treatise of Spanish psychiatry in a degenerationist vein.[158] In this volume, sexual inversion is described by referring to the contributions made by Westphal and Ulrichs. Considered in this light, sexual inversion was understood by the author to constitute a defect in the 'genital instinct' observed in both men and women, in such a way that 'siendo una mujer físicamente mujer, psíquicamente es hombre, y viceversa, un hombre físicamente hombre, es mujer psíquicamente' [a woman who is physically a woman, is psychically a man and vice versa, a man who is physically a man, is psychically a woman].[159] With such a description we have moved some distance away from the model of physical hermaphroditism, eunuchoid men and women with oversized clitorises evoked by the sexological literature of the last years of the nineteenth century.

In order to determine the 'causes' of this anomaly, Martínez Valverde relied on the thought of Ball and Magnan, and placed sexual inversion in the camp of 'obsessions of a sexual nature' and 'neurotic madness':

> Estas depravaciones genésicas revisten la forma de sodomía, bestialidad, safismo, necrofilia o violación de cadáveres, mutilaciones mortuorias, ninfomanía, onanismo (este último en

especial en los idiotas e imbéciles), y otras muy diversas obsesiones eróticas, de las cuales una de las más notables por su importancia social y que, por tanto, merece alguna más detenida atención, es la inversión del sentido sexual.[160]

[These reproductive depravations cover sodomy, bestiality, Sapphism, necrophilia or the violation of corpses, the mutilation of corpses, nymphomania, onanism (seen especially in idiots and imbeciles), and other various erotic obsessions. One of the most notable of these given its social importance and thus the attention that it merits is the inversion of the sexual sense.]

The origins of this process (for degeneration was held to be a process rather than a finished state) 'can be congenital or acquired' but generally, Martínez Valverde conceded, this particular 'aberration' occurred in individuals with an inherited predisposition.[161]

As was frequent in literature of this type, Martínez Valverde related the clinical observation of an individual in which all the usual degenerationist concepts are laid bare. There is some comment on family antecedents, the physical and psychic stigmas currently present in the individual and in his family, the concept of dissimilar heredity appears and the individual's artistic talents are discussed. Artistic precocity was a characteristic, according to Dolsa y Ramón, another Spanish degenerationist, of young degenerates who cultivated the arts and poetry, 'hábitos que le hacen erótico para, al final, caer en el más funesto de los vicios, la masturbación' [habits which eroticise him and make him, in the end, fall into the worst of the vices; masturbation].[162] The nexus between onanism, excessive intellectual or artistic talent, mental exhaustion and sexual inversion form a constellation of degenerative stigmas which undermined gender differences and led to the destruction of the family and the nation. Martínez Valverde, for example, discussed the case of a young woman whose father died in a mental asylum, whose paternal grandmother was senile, and in whose family there had been one suicide. On the mother's side:

se encuentran estigmas hereditarios, si no tan precisos, bien evidentes. Hacia los veinte años dicha muchacha contrajo una violenta pasión por otra muy bellísima joven, que como caso curioso de locura de dos, o por sugestión, correspondió a dicho amor, fugándose de sus respectivas casas paternas para mejor entregarse a los lúbricos placeres de su delirio; despreciando la opinión del mundo y olvidándose de sus familias, y sólo viviendo para ellas.[163]

[one also found degenerative stigmas, although less precise, but very evident. At around the age of twenty, this young woman experienced a violent passionate feeling for another extremely beautiful girl who, as an interesting case of madness of the two, or through suggestion, reciprocated that love. They both fled from their respective homes in order to engage more successfully in the lubricious pleasures of their delirium, turning against public opinion and spurning their families, living but for themselves.]

After his clinical observations, Martínez Valverde considered the medico-legal consequences of the young woman's acts. Here, the vocabulary of degenerationism ('hereditary predisposition', 'stigmas', etc.) surprisingly gave way to moral interdictions ('acts contrary to nature', for example). The forensic doctor asked himself whether sexual inversion was a vice or an irresistible pathological impulse: 'Nos hemos detenido algo en el estudio de este último trastorno mental por la importancia médico-legal que tiene, pues entre el vicio y la impulsión morbosa a ciertos actos contrarios a la naturaleza y a la moral frecuentemente es difícil pronunciarse' [We have spent some time on the study of this last mental illness given the medico-legal importance it holds. It is difficult to pronounce whether such acts against nature and morality respond to vice or to a morbid impulse.][164]

For some, the solution to this problem was to go beyond the limits of the tenets of classical liberal law. With respect to inverts, the question should not be whether they were responsible for their acts or not, but rather whether they were dangerous for society and hence required 'security measures', as Dorado Montero would argue.[165] This intervention against subjects that were considered dangerous opened up a whole new terrain encapsulated by the theory of 'the defence of society' in the late nineteenth and early twentieth century.[166] Both criminologists and jurists espoused such a theory but any actual legal measures were late in coming; at least in the case of sexual inversion, legislation was finally drawn up in 1928.

Our second example of degenerationist thought is taken from another clinical case with medico-legal effects from the early twentieth century. The case once more shows the difficulties in which the courts found themselves when discussing cases of sexual crime, instances when psychiatrists were increasingly called in to offer their expert views. The case was related to the XIV International Congress of Legal Medicine and Toxicology held at Madrid in 1903 (the clinical examination took place in 1901) by Dr. Fernando Bravo y Moreno who practised in Santander.

The study referred to by Bravo y Moreno and partly reproduced at the beginning of this chapter is of a priest identified only as the forty-one-year-old U. L., of French nationality, and who was tried in Santander accused of the 'frecuentes tratos sexuales que tenía con los niños' [frequent sexual practices that he maintained with boys].[167]

First of all, Bravo y Moreno alluded to the judicial conflict that the case gave rise to. Even though he admitted that this was not his central concern he noted that the jury had emphasized the lack of free will exercised in the individual who was understood to have suffered from 'partial limited madness'. The Defence insisted that the individual was not responsible for his acts since the state of madness was not total. Finally, after an appeal, the Supreme Court held that U. L. 'era un ser degenerado y no un criminal' [was a degenerate being and not a criminal].[168] Such complexity shows the difficulties for a legal system caught between the old classical concepts of free will, responsibility and proof and the new medical categories of the degenerate, a figure not necessarily responsible or answerable for his acts.

Bravo y Moreno began his exposition in this prestigious international forum by referring to the extraordinary nature of the case. Nothing similar, he averred, could be found in the textbooks of the grand masters of psychiatry of whom he cites Westphal, Lassègue, Charcot and Krafft-Ebing. The doctor was also keen to underline the distances that separated, in his view, the neutral scientific vocabulary ('las nociones, los síntomas que tengan un carácter científico innegable en el examen de este pervertido sexual' [the notions, the symptoms that possess an undeniable scientific character in the examination of this sexual pervert]) and the terms of the 'ignorant world' that surrounded science, however abominable or immoral the acts committed may have seemed.[169]

After describing the events which led to his expert intervention in the case, in the usual degenerationist style Bravo y Moreno went on to examine the family history of the individual to be judged. Here, numerous physical and psychical stigmas are located, from the kleptomania of a paternal aunt to the neuralgia and diarrhoea of the mother; from the megalomania of the maternal grandfather to the strangeness of his siblings (the hysterical convulsions of Ana, the alcoholism of Pablo, the anaemia and nervousness of María, the cruelty of José towards animals).

The personal history of U. L. was also entered into in order to focus on his physical and mental inheritance. Much is said of his masturbatory habits with others (his brother, fellow seminarists, disciples, domestic animals) and alone: 'se entrega con furor al onanismo en su época de estudiante' [he engages furiously in onanism in his student days]. His sexual precocity ('en él se despierta el instinto genésico a los seis u ocho años' [the sexual instinct is awakened in him at the age of six or eight]) and his inclination towards other boys and lack of desire for the other sex were also seen as evidence of his condition. The analysis of his 'present state' is full of references to physical and psychic stigmas. His lack of application towards his studies, his liking of history, various forms of delirium ('creyéndose obispo y papa, otra vez, trasladado al Paraíso, en medio de los ángeles' [he believed he was bishop and Pope, once more in Paradise, amongst the angels]), abulia and his desire to collect things are interpreted as other expressions of his state. Bravo y Moreno, leaning towards the more somaticist side of the degenerationist repertoire,[170] concedes greater importance, however, to the physical stigma:

De cráneo asimétrico, platicéfalo, el pabellón auricular derecho y, sobre todo, el lóbulo libre desprendido y más desarrollado que el del lado izquierdo; muy corto de vista, con adenitis cervicales muy pronunciadas; nada de anómalo en los órganos genitales, si no es un poco de engrosamiento de la piel escrotal; el muslo, la pierna y pie del lado izquierdo, nótanse disminuidos en su volumen, comparándolos con los del lado derecho.[171]

[He is of an asymmetric cranium; platicephalic; the right ear cavity and, above all, the earlobe which is large and hanging down are more developed than those of the left side. He is very short-sighted, with pronounced inflammation of the neck glands; has nothing anomalous in the genital region, even though there is a slight thickening of the scrotal tissue; the left thigh, leg and foot are of lesser volume in comparison to those of the right-hand side.]

The most important element in this case of perversion seems to be the extent of sexual deviation. In the final diagnosis it is noted that U. L. 'debe ser considerado como un degenerado mental, congénito, abúlico, con manifestaciones psicopáticas homo-sexuales' [should be considered as a congenital mental degenerate, with abulia and with homosexual psychopathic manifestations].[172] Homosexuality would be the most palpable sign of this degenerative disorder. But a closer analysis reveals the presence of other important conceptual elements.

It is noted on two occasions that among the psychical stigma of the subject there was a certain frequency of hallucinations. In one of these, U. L. believed that he had changed sex and had become a woman. Sexual inversion as gender deviation, then, is also made apparent in the subject's obsessions even though there is no anatomical ambiguity and nothing amiss with the genitalia. In addition, his lack of strong character ('se deja dominar con facilidad' [he allows himself to be dominated easily]), his timidity and his habit of taking the subordinate position in sexual relations, practising oral sex with youths or masturbating animals and other people, are all seen as signs of inversion. There may be an allusion towards some interest in Socratic pederasty in the doctor's observation that U. L. was in the process of taking notes 'para la publicación de algunos estudios sobre las costumbres de los pueblos en la antigüedad' [for the publication of some studies on the customs of ancient peoples].[173] All such allusions draw on the age-old divide between passive and active in the sexual relation and their corresponding divisions between female and male.

In this case, rather than an emphasis on the deviation of the sexual instinct, directed towards members of the same sex, our attention is drawn towards the effeminate and passive nature of U. L. and it is these aspects that are understood as characteristic stigmas of this particular 'degenerate' individual. This case of 'homosexual psychopathy' is, therefore, not simply the case of an individual attracted to members of the same sex. Despite this, there follows a series of recommendations to parents on the sharing of beds (single beds would be best, it is argued), the separation of the sexes during childhood and the dangers that surround children in boarding schools as means of preventing any temptations towards homosexuality.

If Martínez Valverde and Bravo y Moreno represented the more somaticist and deterministic interpretation of French degenerationist thought, the psychiatrists César Juarros and Gonzalo Rodríguez Lafora began to break that mould before 1920. Both tended to dissolve the strict association between degeneration and hereditary illness that the first two authors had relied upon.

In the case of César Juarros, the reception of degenerationist thought responded much more closely to the Morelian variant with its acceptance of the existence of acquired degeneracy. Before graduating from the Medical Faculty, Juarros had become interested in questions of both psychopathology and legal medicine.[174] After obtaining his certificate to practise, he took up post as military medical officer. He later became established as a neuro-psychiatrist in Madrid. He was also professor of forensic psychiatry in the Spanish Criminological Institute (Madrid).

Juarros was instrumental in the introduction of French psychiatric texts to a Spanish audience. In 1906 he translated and annotated *El Contagio Mental*, by the two French doctors Vigouroux and Juquelier, and in 1914 edited the *Tratado de Psiquiatría* by Régis. In both cases, references to the sexual perversions and sexual inversion in particular are common. The thesis offered by the authors of these two books is adopted by Juarros himself as witnessed by his two publications *Psiquiatría Forense* (1914) and *Psiquiatría del Médico General* (1919), commented upon more extensively in the next chapter.

Régis, Vigouroux and Juquelier all coincided in understanding that sexual inversion, or Uranism as they sometimes called it, was the expression of a psychic anomaly of a degenerative nature. Coinciding with the ideas of Ulrichs, these authors believed that individuals who displayed such anomalies combined the body of one sex and the soul of the other. Régis (on whom Martínez Valverde had also drawn) relied on the work of Krafft-Ebing, Ulrichs and Raffalovitch to buttress his theories. Sexual inversion was conceptualized by Régis as a 'morbid predisposition'; Vigouroux and Juquelier would consider sexual inversion in similar terms in their *El Contagio Mental*.[175]

Juarros, nevertheless, believed that the predispositions that characterized the psychically abnormal individual were not *necessarily* inherited.[176] He admitted, like Morel, the existence of predispositions that could well be congenital or acquired in the womb.[177] Sexual inversion could therefore have been generated by environmental factors. Vigouroux and Juquelier placed greatest importance on the concept of 'mental contagion' in the array of environmental factors that supposedly gave rise to sexual inversion. These authors, basing their arguments on those of Tarnowsky, believed that 'un muchacho atacado de inversión sexual internado en un colegio, puede propagar esta afección alrededor de él' [a boy attacked by sexual inversion who is in a boarding school could propagate the affection to those around him].[178] The 'attack' (one has to recall the vocabulary of epilepsy used here) could be contagious in those individuals who possessed some kind of predisposition and who had practised mutual masturbation in school. In most subjects 'las primeras relaciones sexuales normales hacen desaparecer el gusto de la masturbación mutua; pero en un pequeño número de degenerados los hábitos de pederastia persisten y pueden ser el punto de partida de una inversión total' [the first normal sexual relations make the desire for mutual masturbation disappear. But in a small number of degenerates the habit of pederasty persists and can become the basis of complete inversion].[179]

The importance accorded to masturbation as the origin of many mental illnesses was a common recourse of the period.[180] Juarros himself had emphasized its dangerous role in a conference on the subject in 1911.[181] But in reality, the supposed connection between onanism and homosexuality was not new; Tissot and others had made that link in their dissertations on the weakening of masculinity and general diseases brought about by the solitary vice in the eighteenth century. Juarros, amongst the psychiatrists, was particularly keen to revive that link and would repeat it well into the 1930s even though its conceptual frame altered in accordance with successive innovations in the sexological and psychiatric sciences (for example, endocrinology, the impact of Kraepelin's thought and psychoanalysis).

The combination of the presence of homosexuality, the development of childhood and the insights of Morelian degenerationist thought were also present in the last of the figures we analyse. The leading psychiatrist of the Madrid School, Gonzalo Rodríguez Lafora, was a disciple of one of the followers of Ramón y Cajal, Nicolás Achúcarro.[182] Lafora also enjoyed an excellent international reputation and had worked in France, Germany and the United States; a product of the new generation of scientists spawned by the Junta para Ampliación de Estudios (founded in 1907) whose generosity in grants to study abroad is well known.

Lafora's book, *Los Niños Mentalmente Anormales* (1917) was the result of his researches into 'mentally weak' children, a new domain of medico-pedagogical intervention in European societies in the early twentieth century.[183] Lafora, together with Achúcarro, had established a psychological clinic based at the Institute of the Deaf and Dumb in 1912.[184] In 1914 he was named vice secretary of the Wayward Youth Institute (Patronato de Anormales) and he often published in the general press as part of his attempt to raise the issue of 'abnormal' youth.

The book itself, a pioneering text in the subject area in Spain, embraced largely the precepts of degenerationist thought. However, the volume is not without its theoretical innovations given the variations and criticisms that Lafora made of established paradigms, resulting in yet another eclectic text.[185] Following the line of argument proposed by Juarros, Lafora insisted that degeneration must be understood as separate from heredity. Familiar with Mendelian genetics, Lafora further distinguished between 'congenital transmission' – alterations acquired during the foetal period – and 'hereditary transmission' – modification of the 'germs' transmitted according to Mendel's Law.[186] In this light, diseases such as alcoholism, syphilis, neuropathies and endocrinal disorders were transmitted congenitally but not via the genes. This meant that degeneration was not present in all the inherited disorders but just 'aquéllos que presentan varios signos degenerativos verdaderos' [those which present various true degenerative signs].[187]

What was the status and origin of homosexuality in Lafora's thought? The Madrid psychiatrist was one of relatively few at the time (1917) to employ the new term 'homosexuality' to describe this practice in a section devoted to the 'sexual perversions'. He considered homosexuality to be relatively common among 'imbecile' children, prone to exaltation or overexcitement of the sexual instinct.[188]

Lafora began by referring to Freud's theory of the stages of the sexual life. From primitive narcissism and infantile auto-eroticism the child passed through a 'fase de vacilación' [phase of doubt] in the sexual instinct, until 'la decisiva diferenciación sexual en el sentido de que los sexos opuestos se atraen' [the decisive sexual differentiation in the sense that the opposite sexes attract] took place.[189] In the intermediate phase, homosexual inclinations were common in children, Lafora argued, and could include 'simpatías, prácticas pederásticas, masturbaciones recíprocas, etcétera' [affections, pederastic practices, mutual masturbation, etc.], through imitation or spontaneously.

Why would these inclinations persist in some individuals? Lafora outlined three main theories to explain this phenomenon. First, there were theories of 'extrinsic circumstances' as elaborated by Freud, Binet and Garnier. From this perspective, there would exist a 'congenital predisposition', acquired during the embryonic stage towards homosexuality. This only became a 'permanent perturbation' if certain external factors accompanied it such as perverse influences, giving rise to 'homosexuality or Uranism'.[190]

The second theory is mentioned without reference to its makers. Lafora could have cited here Weininger's influential book translated into Spanish as *Sexo y Carácter* (1902) given the 'bisexuality thesis' that was discussed. According to this model, all individuals were in their making 'bisexual' (i.e. the two sexes were present in any one person). The actual proportion of each sex in each individual varied from one person to the next. Amongst heterosexuals the traits of one sex predominated over the traits of the other, even though vestiges of the other sex still remained. In homosexuals, the process of differentiation had not evolved fully and they were 'stalled' in their development. Although Lafora did not mention them, this argument implied the presence of endocrinological disorders, discussed in other parts of the book in relation to other pathologies resulting from a lack of differentiation.[191] The connection with Marañón's thought on 'intersexuality' is evident. This subject is discussed in the following chapter.

The third group of theories that Lafora mentioned covered the idea of the 'third sex'. Lafora cited Hirschfeld, Römer and Näcke as advocates of this explanation. The true homosexual would be so *ab initio*, from birth, congenitally, as would be the true heterosexual. Environmental influences could not change this basic conformation. This third theory was the one that would admit most freely that 'la homosexualidad no es una enfermedad ni un síntoma de degeneración, sino sólo una variación biológica' [homosexuality is neither an illness nor a symptom of degeneration, but simply a biological variation].[192]

Lafora, without actually inclining towards one theory or the other (the first allowed for a distinction between inversion and homosexuality; the last two were closer to the 'psychic hermaphroditism' theory) did, however, reject the supposed normalcy of homosexual individuals. The psychiatrist arrived at this conclusion by two principal means: firstly, the identification of normality through the statistical norm, something that was part of the positivist project offered by Comte, Quêtelet and Claude Bernard.[193] Secondly, Lafora relied on the old notion of 'anti-natural' and of the 'designs' of nature to disqualify homosexuality: 'es lo cierto que es una desviación de la tendencia común en la mayoría de los normales y de los designios de la naturaleza' [it is clear that it [homosexuality] is a deviation from the common tendency in the majority of normal people and from the designs of nature].[194] What is striking here, in the heart of the most sophisticated version of degenerationist thought that was produced in Spain, is the return of an age-old idea. This return to the most archaic expression of thought on the question – the 'natural' and the 'unnatural' – surrounded by theoretical and conceptual innovation, seems to be the leitmotif of the first stage of the medicalization of homosexuality in Spain between 1850 and 1920.

NOTES

1   Municipal Archive of Cadiz, C/1.131 (R), containing a sheaf of documents (no. 71, 1846) in which this report (no. 5) appears with the title 'Personas escandalosas que no caben en el mundo' [Scandalous persons who have no place in this world]. For questions of space, several long passages in this chapter have been given in English translation only.

2   F. Bravo y Moreno, 'Exposición de un caso clínico médico-legal de psicopatía homo-sexual', in *Actes du XIC Congrès International de Médecine*, publiés sous la direction de Ms. le Dr. Fernández-Caro. Section d'Hygiène, Épidémiologie et Science Sanitaire Technique (Madrid: Imp. de J. Sastre, 1904), pp. 96–102.

3   R. Huertas García-Alejo, *Orfila. Saber y Poder Médico* (Madrid: CSIC, 1988), p. 31; J. Martínez Pérez, 'Sexualidad y Orden Social: la visión médica en la España del primer tercio del siglo XIX', *Asclepio*, 42 (1990), 119–35.

4   P. Mata, *Vademécum de Medicina y Cirugía Legal* (Madrid: Imp. Calle de Padilla, 1844), vol. II, p. 48.

5   E. de Tapia, *Tratado del Juicio Criminal* (Valencia: Imp. de Ildefonso Mompié, 1829), p. 167.

6   De Tapia, *Tratado*, p. 82.

7   Even Mariano Cubí i Soler, responsible for the introduction of phrenology into Spain and one of the pioneers of criminal anthropology (see A. Galera, *Ciencia y Delincuencia. El determinismo antropológico en la España del siglo XIX* (Seville: CSIC, 1991), pp. 10–11), considered sodomy as a 'pecado nefando' [nefarious sin]. He believed that the 'perversión de la amatividad' [perversion of amativity], of the sexual instinct, was located in the brain and 'produce exceso de población, estupro, mil especies de demencia a causa de vicios nefandos a que conduce, y todos los males que se enumeran bajo el encabezamiento de "pervertida"' [produces an excess in population, sex with minors, a thousand species of dementia because of the disgraceful vices which it entails, and all the ills that can be lodged under the heading of 'perversion'] (M. Cubí i Soler, *Sistema Completo de Frenología* (Barcelona: Don Juan Oliveres Impresor, 1846), p. 151.)

8   Mata, *Vademécum*, p. 47.

9   Mata, *Vademécum*, p. 70. Mata did distinguish between active sodomites (who forced 'niños o muchachos' [children or boys] to have sex) and passive sodomites. The latter were corrupted, according to Mata, by their active partners 'o por la seducción o por la miseria se prostituyen, sustituyendo asquerosamente a la mujer' [either through seduction or prostitution, a product of poverty, substituting women in the most revolting way] (Mata, *Vademécum*, p. 70). The reference to 'Sodomy' in the *Vocabulario Médico-Quirúrgico* by Hurtado de Mendoza refers the reader to 'Pederasty'. This is identified as love between men: 'es el amor ilícito entre hombres: vicio infame reprobado por moral, la naturaleza y la razón' [it is illicit love between men; an infamous vice rejected by morality, nature and reason]. (M. Hurtado de Mendoza, *Vocabulario Médico-Quirúrgico* (Madrid: Boix, 1840), p. 618.)

10   M. Orfila, *Tratado de Medicina Legal* (Madrid: Imp. de D. José Mª Alonso, 1847), vol. I, p. 459.

11   J. P. Aron and R. Kempf, *La Bourgeoisie, le Sexe et l'Honneur* (Brussels, Ed. Complexe: 1984), pp. 42–4; J. Danet, *Discours Juridique et Perversions Sexuelles (XIXᵉ et XXᵉ siècles)* (Nantes, Université de Nantes: 1977), p. 25; M. Foucault, *Los Anormales. Curso del Collège de France (1974–1975)* (Madrid: Akal, 2001), p. 154.

12   Orfila, *Tratado*, p. 459. Peiró and Rodrigo refer to 'individuos culpables de este vicio' [individuals culpable of this kind of vice]. (P. M. Peiró and J. Rodrigo, *Elementos de Medicina y Cirugía Legal arreglados a la Legislación Española* (Madrid: Imp. de la Compañía General de Impresores y Libreros, 1841), p. 77. Mata alludes to 'criaturas depravadas' [depraved creatures], an 'abominable aberración de la voluptuosidad' [abominable aberration of voluptousness], and 'placeres hediondos' [disgusting pleasures]. (Mata, *Vademécum*, pp. 69–70).

13   Orfila, *Tratado*, p. 459.

14   I. D. Crozier, 'The Medical Construction of Homosexuality and its

Relation to the Law in Nineteenth-Century England', *Medical History*, 45 (2001), 61–82 (67–9).

[15] This quotation and the previous ones relevant to this case were taken from M. González de Samano and A. Francés, 'Dictamen acerca de un presunto atentado de sodomía presentado al juzgado de 1ª instancia de la ciudad de Alfaro', *Boletín de Medicina, Cirugía y Farmacia*, 1 (1846), 231–2 (232).

[16] J. Briand, J. Bouis and J. L. Casper, *Manual Completo de Medicina Legal y Toxicología*, 2 vols, (Madrid: Moya y Plaza, 1872), vol. I, p. 112.

[17] P. Mata, *Tratado de Medicina y Cirugía Legal Teórica y Práctica*, 4 vols, (Madrid: Bailly-Baillière, 1874), vol. I, p. 378. T. Yáñez, Professor of Legal Medicine at the University of Madrid, in his *Lecciones de Medicina Legal y Toxicología* (Madrid: Librería de Saturnino Calleja, 1878), p. 305, stated explicity that what was in reality being discussed was 'la pederastia y sus congéneres', that is, 'anti-natural relations'.

[18] Yáñez, *Lecciones*, p. 336.

[19] Aron and Kempf, *La Bourgeoisie*, pp. 47–78; P. Haan, *Nos Ancêtres les Pervers* (Paris: Olivier Orban, 1979), pp. 193–214; R. Huertas García-Alejo, 'El concepto de "perversión sexual" en la medicina positivista', *Asclepio*, 42, 2 (1990), 89–99 (91–4); R. Nye, 'Sex Difference and Male Homosexuality in French Medical Discourse, 1830–1930', *Bulletin of the History of Medicine*, 63, 1 (1989), 32–51 (49).

[20] A. Tardieu, *Estudio Médico-Forense de los Atentados contra la Honestidad*, (Madrid: Imp. Médica de Manuel Álvarez, 1863 trans. Nemesio López Bustamente and Juan de Querejazu y Hartzensbuch), p. 114.

[21] Tardieu, *Estudio*, p. 140.

[22] Tardieu, *Estudio*, p. 139.

[23] Mata, *Tratado*, vol. I, p. 486.

[24] A. I. Davidson, 'Sex and the emergence of sexuality', *Critical Inquiry*, 14 (1987), 16–48 (19–23); Foucault, *History of sexuality*, vol. I, p. 43; H. Oosterhuis, *Stepchildren of Nature: Krafft-Ebing, Psychiatry, and the Making of Sexual Identity* (Chicago/London: University of Chicago Press, 2000), pp. 241–58 (p. 248).

[25] Crozier, 'The Medical Construction', 70–1.

[26] Mata noted that 'En París esta prostitución ha llegado a un estado espantoso y hasta lleno de peligros para la sociedad' [In Paris this form of prostitution has gained shocking proportions, being dangerous for society], (Mata, *Tratado*, vol. I, p. 486).

[27] Tardieu, *Estudio*, p. 125. There are several other accounts of the relatively scant presence of pederasty in Spain. Sereñana y Partagás noted: 'Existe otra clase de prostitución, que pudiéramos llamar masculina, o sea, el *cenydismo* o pederastia. Afortunadamente escasa entre nosotros, esta forma especial es asquerosa e indigna de la especie humana' [There exists another form of prostitution, which we could call masculine, or cenydism, or pederasty. This special form is disgusting and unworthy of humankind and is fortunately scarce amongst us], (P. Sereñana y Partagás, *La prostitución en la ciudad de*

Barcelona (Barcelona: Imprenta de los sucesores de Ramírez y Compañía, 1882), p. 125). On the use of the term *kinaidos* or *cinaedus*, see J. J. Winkler, *The Constraints of Desire: The Anthropology of Sex and Gender in Ancient Greece* (New York/London: Routledge, 1990), *passim*, and, C. A. Williams, *Roman Homosexuality: Ideologies of Masculinity in Classical Antiquity* (New York/Oxford: Oxford University Press, 1999), *passim*. The forensic psychiatrist José María Escuder wrote: 'No es España un país donde abunden las anomalías o aberraciones genésicas, y por eso resulta difícil reunir casos concretos de psicopatías sexuales . . . No negaré que existen algunos casos singulares de esta anomalía psíquica del amor; pero quizá por la virilidad de este pueblo, por su rudeza, ocupaciones agrícolas, sobriedad, apartamiento de las grandes ciudades y escaso consumo de alcohol . . . las aberraciones genésicas orgánicas son hechos raros y excepcionales' [Spain is not a country where sexual anomalies or aberrations are common and for this reason it is difficult to present concrete cases of sexual psychopathies . . . I do not deny that some unusual cases of this psychic anomaly of love exist. But perhaps because of the virility of this people, because of its roughness, agricultural occupations, sobriety, distance from the great cities and low consumption of alcohol . . . organic sexual aberrations are rare or exceptional]. (J. Mª Escuder, *Locos y Anómalos* (Madrid: Establecimiento Tip. de Sucesores de Rivadeneyra, 1895), p. 175).

28   Mata, *Tratado*, vol. I, pp. 488–90; Yáñez, *Lecciones*, p. 334.

29   Mata, *Tratado*, vol. I, p. 492.

30   Mata, *Tratado*, vol. I, p. 487.

31   Mata, *Tratado*, vol. I, p. 487.

32   Yáñez, *Lecciones*, p. 333.

33   I. Hacking, 'Five parables', in R. Rorty, J. B. Schneewind and Q. Skinner (eds), *Philosophy in history: essays on the historiography of philosophy* (Cambridge: Cambridge University Press, 1984), pp. 103–24; B. Hansen, 'American Physicians' "Discovery" of Homosexuals, 1880–1900: A New Diagnosis in a Changing Society', in C. E. Rosenberg and J. Golden (eds), *Framing Disease: studies in cultural history* (New Brunswick: Rutgers University Press, 1992), pp. 104–33 (p. 107).

34   Yáñez, *Lecciones*, p. 335.

35   P. F. Monlau, *Higiene del Matrimonio o El Libro de los Casados* (Madrid: Imp. M. Rivadeneyra, 1865 [1853]), p. 156.

36   A. M. Rey González, *Estudios médico-sociales sobre marginados en la España del siglo XIX* (Madrid: Ministerio de Sanidad y Consumo, 1990), p. 55.

37   R. Castel, *El Orden Psiquiátrico. La Edad de Oro del Alienismo* (Madrid: La Piqueta, 1980).

38   This classification did not appear suddenly in Mata's thought. In the first edition of his *Tratado de Medicina y Cirugía Legal* (1846), he refers to 'monomania' but there is no detailed elaboration of its types. In the fourth edition of the work (1866), however, a typology appears. Mata differed in opinion from Esquirol, however. The latter did not

class nymphomania and satyriasis as mental disorders but instead as purely physical illnesses (E. Esquirol, *Des Maladies Mentales* (Paris: J. B. Baillière Ed., 1838), vol. II, pp. 32–3).

39   F. Vázquez García, 'Ninfomanía y construcción simbólica de la femineidad (España siglos XVIII–XIX)', in C. Canterla (ed.), *VII Encuentro de la Ilustración al Romanticismo. La Mujer en los siglos XVIII y XIX* (Cadiz: Universidad de Cádiz, 1994), pp. 125–35.

40   F. Álvarez-Uría, *Miserables y locos: medicina mental y orden social en la España del siglo XIX* (Barcelona: Tusquets, 1983), p. 185. The first degenerationist analyses of sexual 'perversion' arrived around this time; see G. Lanteri-Laura, *Lecture des Perversions. Histoire de leur appropriation médicale* (Paris: Masson, 1979), pp. 47–52 and Huertas García-Alejo, 'El concepto de "perversión sexual", 89–99. The work by Lassègue on 'exhibitionism' was reviewed in 1877 by Anon., 'Los exhibicionistas', *El Siglo Médico* (1877), 429–30. R. Campos Marín, 'La Teoría de la Degeneración y la Profesionalización de la Psiquiatría en España (1876–1920)', *Asclepio*, 51, 1 (1999), 185–203 has shown that degenerationist psychiatry was received in Spain in the 1870s and applied in medico-legal examinations at that time. Foucault, however, has indicated that it was around 1845–50 that sexuality came to occupy a central place in studies of mental illness, in contrast with the relatively minor role it was accorded in classical alienism.

41   Mata, *Tratado*, vol. II, p. 377.

42   Between the concept of 'monomania' and that of the 'perversion of the instinct' we can place the notion of 'moral madness'. According to Simarro, 'con ella [la locura moral] se asocian de ordinario las perversiones e inversiones sexuales que constituyen a veces una variedad de la misma' [with it [moral madness] are usually associated the sexual perversions and inversions which often constitute a variety of the same]. See L. Simarro, 'Sobre el concepto de locura moral', *Revista Iberoamericana de Ciencias Médicas*, 2 (1900), 396–8 (398).

43   R. Álvarez Peláez and R. Huertas García-Alejo, *¿Criminales o locos? Dos peritajes psiquiátricos del Dr. Gonzalo Rodríguez Lafora* (Madrid: CSIC, 1987), pp. 43–8; M. Foucault, 'L'évolution de la notion d'individu dangereux dans la psychiatrie légale', *Déviance et Société*, 5 (1981), 403–22; Foucault, *Les Anormaux*, pp. 281–2; Lanteri-Laura, *Lecture des Perversions*, p. 58.

44   The doctor Victoriano Garrido y Escuín, who practised in the asylum of Carabanchel Bajo, commented on the case of a boy of ten who could not be left alone with his younger sisters in his *La Cárcel o el Manicomio. Estudio Médico-Legal sobre la Locura* (Madrid: Casa Editorial de D. José Mª Faquineto, 1888), p. 160. Garrido was a disciple of Esquerdo and one of the pioneers of degenerationist thought in Spain.

45   Garrido classified those forms of impulsive madness associated with the sexual instinct as 'accesses' of 'sexual epilepsy' (Garrido y Escuín, *La Cárcel*, pp. 199–200). Amongst Spanish doctors at the turn of the century, sexual inversion is often referred to as an 'attack' along the lines of an epileptic fit.

46   Foucault, *Los Anormales*, p. 279.

47   Álvarez-Uría, *Medicina y locos*, pp. 184–8; Campos Marín, 'La Teoría de la Degeneración', 187; J. J. Plumed Domingo and A. Rey González, 'La introducción de las ideas degeneracionistas en la España del siglo XIX. Aspectos conceptuales', *Frenia. Revista de Historia de la Psiquiatría*, 2, 1 (2002), 31–48 (32).

48   R. Álvarez Peláez, 'Origen y desarrollo de la eugenesia en España', in J. M. Sánchez Ron (ed.), *Ciencia y Sociedad en España. De la Ilustración a la Guerra Civil* (Madrid: El Arquero/CSIC, 1988), pp. 178–204 (p. 184).

49   In this period, Spanish degenerationist psychiatrists had already begun to believe that 'monomania' was an out-dated notion used to identify a whole range of expressions of 'impulsive madness' associated with malfunctions of the brain, thus implying the cancellation of will-power. See, for example, Arturo Galcerán, 'Ensayo de clasificación anatomo-patológica de las vesanias', *El Siglo Médico*, 36 (1889), 407–9, 470–2, 486–9.

50   T. Yáñez, *Elementos de Medicina Legal* (Madrid: Imprenta de Enrique Rubiños, 1884), pp. 173–9.

51   I. Valentí Vivó, *Tratado de Antropología Médica y Jurídica* (Barcelona: Imp. de Jaime Jepús Roviralta, 1889), vol. II, p. 414.

52   Valentí Vivó, *Tratado*, vol. II, p. 408. Antonio Piga Pascual, physician to the Royal Family and lecturer at the Institute of Legal Medicine, followed this line of thought some years afterwards. He wrote in his *Higiene de la Pubertad* (Toledo: Imp. de la Vda. e Hijos de J. Peláez, 1910), p. 8, that 'la salud social está perturbada profundamente por la lujuria colectiva que disputa al alcoholismo el papel de elemento preponderante entre las causas de la criminalidad' [social health is gravely disturbed by the collective luxuriousness which vies for first place with alcohol as the most important cause of criminal behaviour].

53   Valentí Vivó, *Tratado*, vol. II, p. 393.

54   Valentí Vivó, *Tratado*, vol. II, p. 409. See also Nye, 'Sex Difference and Male Homosexuality', p. 41. This same mixture of different concepts from alienism and from the new psychiatry can be seen clearly in the naturalist novels published in Spain during the period. See P. Fernández, '*Scientia sexualis* y el saber psiquiátrico en la novela naturalista decimonónica', *Asclepio*, 49, 1 (1997), 227–44 (240–1).

55   Valentí Vivó, *Tratado*, vol. II, p. 403.

56   Valentí Vivó, *Tratado*, vol. II, p. 406.

57   E. Monzón in his *Antropología y Antropologías. Ideas para una historia crítica de la antropología española. El siglo XIX* (Oviedo: Pentalfa, 1991), pp. 462–3, considers Escuder to be one of the first disseminators of Lombrosian thought in Spain.

58   See J. Varela and F. Álvarez-Uría, *El Cura Galeote Asesino del Obispo de Madrd-Alcalá* (Madrid: La Piqueta, 1979). For the involvement of Escuder, see pp. 103–7.

59   The inset quotation and the references in the preceding paragraph are taken from Escuder, *Locos y Anómalos*, pp. 171–2.

60 Escuder, *Locos y Anómalos*, p. 176.
61 Escuder, *Locos y Anómalos*, p. 177.
62 See Galera, *Ciencia y Delincuencia*, pp. 23–4.
63 Escuder, *Locos y Anómalos*, p. 170.
64 Escuder, *Locos y Anómalos*, p. 177.
65 Piga Pascual, *Higiene de la Pubertad*, p. 28, divides 'inversion' into four categories: 'active and passive pederasty, tribadism and Sapphism.'
66 G. Chauncey, 'From Sexual Inversion to Homosexuality'; H. Ooster-huis, 'Medical Science and the Modernisation of Sexuality', in F. X. Eder, L. Hall and G. Hekma (eds), *Sexual Cultures in Europe. National Histories* (Manchester: Manchester University Press, 1999), pp. 221–41 (pp. 221–2); Hansen, 'American Physicians' "Discovery"', 106–7.
67 On the question of resignification and reiteration see J. Butler, *Excitable Speech. A Politics of the Performative* (New York: Routledge, 1997), p. 163, and, J. Derrida, 'Firma, acontecimiento, contexto', in *Márgenes de la Filosofía* (Madrid: Cátedra, 1998), pp. 347–72 (pp. 367–72). For a critique of an overly schematic reading of Foucault with respect to the creation of the homosexual, see D. M. Halperin, 'How to do the History of Homosexuality', *GLQ: Gay and Lesbian Quarterly*, 6, 1 (2000), 87–121 (89–92).
68 G. Chauncey, *Gay New York* (London: Flamingo, 1994) and the postscript to his 'From Sexual Inversion', pp. 108–9.
69 J. de Letamendi, *Curso de Clínica General* (Madrid: Imp. de los Sucesores de Cuesta, 1894), 2 vols, vol. II, p. 105.
70 De Letamendi, *Curso*, vol. II, p. 110.
71 De Letamendi, *Curso*, vol. II, p. 119.
72 De Letamendi, *Curso*, vol. II, p. 120.
73 De Letamendi, *Curso*, vol. II, p. 120.
74 Within the category of 'autoerastia' Letamendi identifies 'rectal autoerastia'. Individuals in this group enjoy introducing instruments into their anus, something which the author differentiated from 'homoerastia'. A case of this variety was described in *El Siglo Médico* in 1902, whereby S. D., a Spanish subject of 29 years, sought medical attention to extract from his rectum the handle of a knife holder of some 8 cm. He supposedly introduced this item into his anus to stop the diarrhoea from which he was suffering. He was operated upon and the item was removed. His case was classified as one of 'morbid eroticism'. See J. F. Arteaca, 'Cuerpo extraño en el recto', *El Siglo Médico*, 49 (1902), p. 59.
75 De Letamendi, *Curso*, vol. II, pp. 122–3.
76 De Letamendi, *Curso*, vol. II, p. 126.
77 De Letamendi, *Curso*, vol. II, p. 127.
78 The references in this last paragraph can be found in De Letamendi, *Curso*, vol. II, pp. 127–8.
79 For comments on Lombroso and Saint-Hilaire, respectively, see P. Tort, *La Raison Classificatoire* (Paris: Aubier Montaigne, 1989), pp. 469–74 and pp. 193–203.

80 G. Canguilhem *et al.*, *Du Développement à l'évolution au XIX siècle* (Paris: PUF, 1985), pp. 39–43.

81 L. Birken, *Consuming Desire. Sexual Science and the Emergence of a Culture of Abundance, 1871–1914* (Ithaca/London: Cornell University Press, 1987), pp. 10–11.

82 De Letamendi, *Curso*, vol. II, p. 106.

83 See L. Maristany, *El Gabinete del Doctor Lombroso (Delincuencia y fin de siglo en España)* (Barcelona: Anagrama, 1973) and P. Trinidad Fernández, *La Defensa Social. Cárcel y Delincuencia en España (siglos XVIII–XX)* (Madrid: Alianza Universidad, 1991), pp. 248–82.

84 Trinidad Fernández, *La Defensa Social*, p. 267.

85 C. Bernaldo de Quirós and J. Mª Llanas Aguilaniedo, *La Mala Vida en Madrid. Estudio psicosociológica con dibujos y fotografías del natural* (Madrid: B. Rodríguez Sierra, 1901).

86 L. Maristany, 'Introducción', in the republished C. Bernaldo de Quirós & J. Mª Llanas Aguilaniedo, *La Mala Vida en Madrid. Estudio psicosociológico con dibujos y fotografías del natural* (Huesca: Instituto de Estudios Altoaragoneses/Egido Editorial, 1998 [1901]), XXXIII–LVIII (XXXIX–XL).

87 For the categories referred to in the next paragraphs, see Bernaldo de Quirós and Llanas Aguilaniedo, *La Mala Vida en Madrid*, 1901 edition, pp. 259–62.

88 The distinction between Incubus and Succubus was one originally made in demonology with respect to the actions of the devil. The devil took the form of incubus to penetrate women and of succubus with men. See J. Delumeau, *El Miedo en Occidente (siglos XIV–XVIII)* (Madrid: Taurus, 1989), p. 382.

89 Bernaldo de Quirós and Llanas Aguilaniedo, *La Mala Vida*, 1901 edition, p. 262.

90 Bernaldo de Quirós and Llanas Aguilaniedo, *La Mala Vida*, 1901 edition, p. 278.

91 Bernaldo de Quirós and Llanas Aguilaniedo, *La Mala Vida*, 1901 edition, p. 284.

92 Bernaldo de Quirós and Llanas Aguilaniedo, *La Mala Vida*, 1901 edition, pp. 260–1.

93 Bernaldo de Quirós and Llanas Aguilaniedo, *La Mala Vida*, 1901 edition, p. 261.

94 Bernaldo de Quirós and Llanas Aguilaniedo, *La Mala Vida*, 1901 edition, p. 285.

95 On Satan and smells, see R. Muchembled, *L'invention de l'Homme Moderne. Culture et sensibilités en France du XVᵉ au XVIIIᵉ siècle* (Paris: Fayard, 1987), p. 47, and, A. Corbin, *Le Miasme et la Jonquille. L'odorat et l'imaginaire social, XVIIIᵉ au XIXᵉ siècles* (Paris: Flammarion, 1986), p. 23.

96 See F. Garza, *Quemando mariposas. Sodomía e imperio en Andalucía y México, siglos XVI–XVII* (Barcelona: Laertes, 2002, trans. L. Salvador), pp. 17–18. On the relationship formed in the Low Middle Ages between the hyena, plague, polysexuality and sodomy, see J. Boswell, *Christianity, Social Tolerance, and Homosexuality: Gay People in Western*

Europe from the Beginning of the Christian Era to the Fourteenth Century (Chicago/London: Chicago University Press, 1980), pp. 138–43. On the relationship between sodomy and the devil, see R. Carrasco, *Inquisición y represión sexual en Valencia. Historia de los sodomitas (1565–1785)* (Barcelona: Laertes, 1985), pp. 42–3 and Garza, *Quemando mariposas*, pp. 25–6. On the other hand, C. del Toro, *La Luz y la Pintura* (Cadiz: Real Academia de las Bellas Artes, 1901), 2 vols, vol. I, p. 628 establishes a contrast between the cleanliness and general correct external appearance of the 'aesthete' and the lack of care characteristic of the 'mannish woman'.

[97] F. Eribon, *Réflexions sur la Question Gay* (Paris: Fayard, 1999), p. 107.

[98] M. Bembo, *La mala vida en Barcelona. Anormalidad, miseria y vicio* (Barcelona: Maucci, 1912).

[99] Bembo, *La mala vida*, pp. 28–9.

[100] Bembo, *La mala vida*, p. 32.

[101] E. Amezúa, 'Cien años de temática sexual en España: 1850–1950. Repertorio y análisis. Contribución al estudio de materiales para una historia de la sexología', *Revista de Sexología*, 48 (1991), 1–197 (138).

[102] A. Peratoner, *Los Peligros del Amor, de la lujuria y del libertinaje en el hombre y en la mujer* (Barcelona: Establecimiento Editorial de José Miret, 1874). References in this paragraph are from pp. 62–3.

[103] Amezúa, 'Cien años', p. 139.

[104] We have used the twentieth edition, published in 1910 and corrected and expanded by Dr Pío Arias Carvajal, former head of the Sección de Higiene in Barcelona.

[105] V. Suárez Casañ, *Conocimientos para la Vida Privada*, vol. VI, *La Pederastia* (Barcelona: Casa Editorial Maucci, twentieth edition, 1910), p. 13.

[106] Suárez Casañ, *La Pederastia*, p. 7.

[107] Suárez Casañ, *La Pederastia*, p. 54.

[108] Suárez Casañ, *La Pederastia*, p. 52.

[109] Suárez Casañ, *La Pederastia*, pp. 52–3.

[110] Suárez Casañ, *La Pederastia*, pp. 88–9.

[111] Suárez Casañ, *La Pederastia*, p. 89. The autor referred to 'inversión del sentido genésico'. The more psychiatry-oriented authors would often write of the 'instinct' rather than the 'sense'.

[112] Suárez Casañ, *La Pederastia*, p. 90.

[113] Amezúa, 'Cien años', p. 139.

[114] F. M. Koch, *Venus Sexual: tratado de las enfermedades que resultan de los excesos sexuales, hábitos solitarios . . .* (Madrid: Imp. El Resumen, 1903), p. 61.

[115] Koch, *Venus Sexual*, p. 62.

[116] C. Bayo, *Higiene Sexual del Soltero* (Madrid: Librería de Antonio Rubiños, 1919 [1902]), p. 101.

[117] J. N. Katz, *The Invention of Heterosexuality* (New York: Penguin, 1995), p. 4.

[118] Bayo, *Higiene Sexual*, pp. 109–10.

[119] See, for example, L. Comenge, *Generación y Crianza ó higiene de la familia* (Barcelona: José Espasa Editor, s.f.), pp. 146–7; J. Gómez

Ocaña, *El sexo, el hominismo y la natalidad* (Madrid: Editorial Saturnino Calleja, 1919).

[120] Bayo, *Higiene Sexual*, p. 110.

[121] See his discussion of tribadism in Bayo, *Higiene Sexual*, pp. 111–12.

[122] Bayo, *Higiene Sexual*, p. 112.

[123] Suárez Casañ, *La Pederastia*, p. 55.

[124] An aspect noted by Yáñez, *Elementos*, p. 323 and, later, by Bernaldo de Quirós and Llanas Aguilaniedo, *La Mala Vida en Madrid*, 1901 edition, p. 283.

[125] See A. Orozco Acuaviva, 'El doctor Don Cayetano Del Toro Quartiellers', *Archivo Iberoamericano de Historia de la Medicina y Antropología Médica*, 14 (1972), 261–84.

[126] Del Toro, *La Luz y La Pintura*, 1901, vol. I, p. 628. The 'mannish woman' was described on the same page and was depicted in Figure 561.

[127] See Chauncey, 'From Sexual Inversion to Homosexuality', p. 93, and, Oosterhuis, 'Medical Science', p. 230.

[128] See J. Salessi, 'The Argentine Dissemination of Homosexuality, 1890–1914', *Journal of the History of Homosexuality*, 4, 3 (1994), 337–68 (338). Despite this similarity, the importance given to the active/passive divide amongst Argentinian doctors and criminologists is not so central in Spanish commentators. Garza, *Quemando mariposas*, pp. 45–9, has discussed the need to break with the ethnocentric assumptions made in the history of homosexuality, which still employs north-western European and North American realities as the principal paradigm from which to consider the question.

[129] V. Ots Esquerdo, 'Inversión sexual intelectiva sistemática', *El Siglo Médico*, 39 (1892), 664–98 (665).

[130] References in this paragraph are taken from Ots Esquerdo, 'Inversión sexual', 665–6.

[131] References in this paragraph are taken from Ots Esquerdo, 'Inversión sexual', 686.

[132] Ots Esquerdo, 'Inversión sexual', 665.

[133] Ots Esquerdo, 'Inversión sexual', 665.

[134] Nye, 'Sex Difference and Male Homosexuality', 36–7; R. Nye, *Masculinity and Male Codes of Honor in Modern France* (Oxford/New York: Oxford University Press, 1993), pp. 108–26.

[135] J. Labanyi, *Gender and Modernization in the Spanish Realist Novel* (Oxford: Oxford University Press, 2000), p. 65.

[136] J. Álvarez Junco, *Mater Dolorosa. La idea de España en el siglo XIX* (Madrid: Taurus, 2001), p. 546.

[137] Labanyi, *Gender and Modernization*, p. 47; P. Muñoz López, *Sangre, Amor e Interés. La Familia en la España de la Restauración* (Madrid: Marcial Pons/UAM Ediciones, 2001), pp. 223–7.

[138] Muñoz López, *Sangre, Amor e Interés*, p. 220.

[139] Labanyi, *Gender and Modernization*, pp. 80–2; P. Fernández, *Eduardo López Bago y el Naturalismo Radical* (Amsterdam: Rodopi, 1995); P. Fernández, 'Moral y *scientia sexualis* en el siglo XIX. El eros negro de

la novela naturalista', *Analecta Malacitana*, 11 (1997), 192–4; P. Fernández, '*Scientia sexuales* y el saber psiquiátrico en la novela naturalista decimonónica', *Asclepio*, 49, 1 (1997), 227–44.

140 B. Magnien, 'Cultura urbana', in S. Salaün and S. Serrano (eds), *1900 en España* (Madrid: Espasa Calpe, 1991), pp. 107–30 (108–9); D. S. Reher, *La Familia en España. Pasado y presente* (Madrid: Alianza Universidad, 1996), pp. 302–3.

141 Reher, *La Familia*, pp. 238–51.

142 R. de la Torre, 'La prensa madrileña y el discurso de Lord Salisbury sobre las "naciones moribundas" (Londres, Albert Hall, 4 mayo 1898)', *Cuadernos de Historia Moderna y Contemporánea*, 6 (1985), 163–80.

143 The connections between the rise of sexology and the emergence of a capitalist society of consumption have been discussed by Birken, *Consuming Desire*, pp. 29–32, and, Oosterhuis, 'Medical Science', p. 238.

144 P. Hauser, *Madrid desde el punto de vista Médico-Social* (Madrid: Editora Nacional, 1979), 2 vols, vol. II, p. 146.

145 Suárez Casañ in *La Pederastia*, p. 43, was to write on the supposed relation between pederasty and literary figures by discussing Wilde and Poe, who were reflected, he noted, in certain unnamed Spanish figures: 'en España no tendríamos que esforzarnos mucho para recordar nombres de literatos, alguno de ellos eminente que han sido o son víctimas de esta aberración incomprensible' [in Spain it would not be too hard to recall the names of literary figures, some of whom are eminent ones, who have been or are victims of this incomprehensible aberration]. See also A. Mira, 'Modernistas, Dandis y Pederastas: articulaciones de la homosexualidad en la "edad de plata"', *Journal of Iberian and Latin American Studies*, 7, 1 (2001), 63–75. On Wilde in Spain, see L. E. Davis, 'Oscar Wilde in Spain', *Comparative Literature*, 35 (1973), 136–52; R.A. Cardwell, 'Oscar Wilde and Spain: Medicine, Morals, Religion and Aesthetics in the *Fin de Siglo*', in F. Bonaddio and X. de Ros, *Crossing Fields in Modern Spanish Culture* (Oxford: University of Oxford, 2003), pp. 35–53.

146 Labanyi, *Gender and Modernization*, pp. 109–14.

147 J. Mª Comelles, *La Razón y la Sinrazón. Asistencia psiquiátrica y desarrollo del Estado en la España Contemporánea* (Barcelona: PPU, 1988), p. 106.

148 R. Campos Marín, 'La teoría de la degeneración y la clínica psiquiátrica en la España de la Restauración', *Dynamis*, 19 (1999), 429–56 (431); Campos Marín, 'La Teoría de la Degeneración y la Profesionalización', p. 187; Plumed Domingo and Rey González, 'La introducción', p. 32.

149 Plumed Domingo and Rey González, 'La introducción', p. 32.

150 Ellis' *Studies in the Psychology of Sex* were partially translated into Spanish between 1906 and 1913, in seven volumes published by Hijos de Reus Editores, Madrid. Volume Two, with the title *Inversión Sexual*, was published in 1913 with no mention of the translator.

151 Albert Moll's *Las Perversiones del Instinto Sexual* was published in Spanish in 1896, according to L. S. Granjel, 'El Sexo como Problema

en la España Contemporánea (pesquisa bibliográfica)', *Cuadernos de Historia de la Medicina*, 13 (1974), 111–31. In 1909, a text by Moll on sex education appeared as 'La Educación Sexual', in the *Boletín de la Institución Libre de Enseñanza*, 33, 294–6. Bembo in *La mala vida en Barcelona*, p. 23, mentions Moll's work.

152 Although Krafft-Ebing was often cited by criminologists (see Bernaldo de Quirós and Llanas Aguilaniedo, *La Mala Vida en Madrid*, 1901 edition, pp. 260, 261, 273, 279) legal medical figures (e.g. Piga, *Higiene*, p. 30) psychiatrists (e.g. Garrido y Escuín, *La Cárcel*, p. 175; Bravo y Moreno, 'Exposición', p. 96; A. Sánchez Herrero, 'Un caso de imbecilidad avanzada', *El Siglo Médico*, 57 (1910), 774–5), popular sexologists (T. de R. Climent, *Higiene Sexual del Soltero y la Soltera* [Barcelona: La Vida Literaria, *c*.1910], pp. 18, 24; Suárez Casañ, *El Amor Lesbio*, p. 63) and pedagogical experts (F. Giner de los Ríos, 'La nerviosidad y la educación según el Dr. Pelman', in *Obras Completas de Francisco Giner de los Ríos*, vol. XVI, *Ensayos sobre Educación y Enseñanza* [Madrid: Imprenta Julio Lozano, 1927], original article from 1889, pp. 221–2, 228; Bembo, *La mala vida en Barcelona*, pp. 23–6) his *Psychopathia Sexualis* had to wait until 1955 to be fully translated into Spanish in a version published in Argentina and taken from a French version edited by Albert Moll. Most Spanish commentators used the Italian version of Krafft-Ebing's work published in 1889.

153 The complete works of Freud were published in Spain by Biblioteca Nueva in 1922. Before then, Fernández Sanz's *Histerismo, Teoría y Clínica* (1914) was crucial for the reception of Freud in Spain. See T. Glick, 'El impacto del psicoanálisis en la psiquiatría española de Entreguerras', in J. M. Sánchez Ron (ed.), *Ciencia y Sociedad en España*, pp. 204–21 (pp. 209–13). One of the first public discussions of Freud's work took place in the Academia Médico-quirúrgica Matritense on 23 April 1917. Amongst those who participated were the doctors Sánchez Ramos, Lafora and Salazar. See Anon., 'Teoría Psicoanalítica de Freud. Sesión del día 23 de abril. Academia Médico-Quirúrgica de Madrid', *El Siglo Médico*, 64 (1917), 320–1.

154 A résumé of Magnan's celebrated conference 'Des anomalies, des aberrations et des perversions sexuelles', given on 13 January 1885 in the Paris Medical Academy, appeared in *El Siglo Médico* the same year, Anon., 'Noticias', *El Siglo Médico*, 32 (1885), 92. Those affected by 'inversion of the genital sense' were classed more specifically as 'enfermos espinales cerebrales anteriores'. According to the author, this was 'una influencia psíquica . . . la que obra sobre el centro genitor-espinal; pero la idea, el sentimiento, la inclinación están pervertidos' [a psychic influence that . . . operates on the genito-spinal centre; but the idea, the sentiment, the inclination are perverted]. These are men and women who 'dirigen sus deseos hacia individuos del mismo sexo y nada más que a ellos, desde la edad más tierna, antes de que hayan podido adquirir malos hábitos' [direct their desires towards individuals of the same sex and to no others, from the earliest age, before any bad habits may have been acquired]. One of the first texts by Magnan to be translated into

Spanish was his 'Consideraciones generales sobre la locura', published in *El Siglo Médico*, 34 (1887), 104–6, 118–20. Here, the 'sexual perversions' were classed as degenerative psychic stigma, a product of inheritance. Garrido y Escuín comments on Magnan's description of an inverted university teacher in his *La Cárcel o el Manicomio* (1888). This individual is described as displaying 'una voluptuosa curiosidad por las desnudeces masculinas y una inclinación lujuriosa y tenaz por los jóvenes' [a voluptuous curiosity towards male nudity and a luxurious and tenacious inclination towards youths] (pp. 239–40).

155 Plumed Domingo and Rey González, 'La introducción', p. 32; Campos Marín, 'La teoría de la degeneración', 442.

156 Campos Marín, 'La teoría de la degeneración', 436; On Lucas' theory of 'dissimilar heredity', see D. Pick, *Faces of Degeneration: A European disorder, c.1848–c.1914* (Cambridge: Cambridge University Press, 1989), pp. 48–50.

157 L. Agote, 'Neuropatología. Nuevo método gráfico para fijar la herencia', *Revista Iberoamericana de Ciencias Médicas*, 7 (1902), 402–7.

158 Plumed Domingo and Rey González, 'La introducción', p. 37.

159 J. Martínez Valverde, *Guía del Diagnóstico de las Enfermedades Mentales* (Barcelona: Hijos de Espasa Editores, 1899), p. 34.

160 Martínez Valverde, *Guía del Diagnóstico*, p. 33.

161 Martínez Valverde, *Guía del Diagnóstico*, p. 34.

162 L. Dolsa y Ramón, 'Contribución al estudio de la hebefrenia', *Revista de Ciencias Médicas de Barcelona*, 15, 11 (1899), 401–3 (403).

163 Martínez Valverde, *Guía del Diagnóstico*, pp. 34–5.

164 Martínez Valverde, *Guía del Diagnóstico*, p. 35.

165 Trinidad Fernández, *La Defensa Social*, p. 325.

166 J. L. Aranguren, *Moral y Sociedad. La Moral Española en el siglo XIX* (Madrid: Taurus, 1982), p. 145; Trinidad Fernández, *La Defensa Social*, pp. 322–7.

167 Bravo y Moreno, 'Exposición', p. 96.

168 Bravo y Moreno, 'Exposición', p. 97.

169 Bravo y Moreno, 'Exposición', p. 96.

170 Campos Marín, 'La teoría de la degeneración', 447.

171 Bravo y Moreno, 'Exposición', p. 101.

172 Bravo y Moreno, 'Exposición', p. 102.

173 Bravo y Moreno, 'Exposición', p. 100.

174 P. Samblás Tilve, 'César Juarros y el *Tratamiento de la Morfinomanía:* ¿cura u ortopedia?', *Frenia. Revista de Historia de la Psiquiatría*, 2, 1 (2002), 123–37 (128).

175 E. Régis, *Tratado de Psiquiatría* (Madrid: Imp. Saturnino Calleja Fernández, 1911), p. 109; A. Vigouroux and P. Juquelier, *El Contagio Mental* (Madrid: Daniel Jorro Ed., 1914), p. 258.

176 C. Juarros, *Psiquiatría Forense* (Madrid: Imp. de Antonio Marzo, 1914), p. 24; C. Juarros, *La Psiquiatría del médico general* (Madrid: Imp. Ruiz Hermanos, 1919), p. 10.

177 Campos Marín, 'La teoría de la degeneración', 444, 453.

178 Vigouroux and Juquelier, *El Contagio Mental*, p. 259.

[179] Vigouroux & Juquelier, *El Contagio Mental*, p. 258.

[180] F. Vázquez García, 'Gobierno de la infancia y educación sexual (España 1900–1936)', *Cahiers Alfred Binet*, 661, 4 (1999), 33–48 (42).

[181] C. Juarros, 'Diagnóstico de las neurastenias', *Revista Médica de Sevilla*, 30 November 1911, 289–96.

[182] E. González Duro, *Historia de la Locura en España*, vol. III, *Del Reformismo del XIX al Franquismo* (Madrid: Ediciones Temas de Hoy, 1996), pp. 131–5.

[183] G. Rodríguez Lafora, *Los Niños Mentalmente Anormales* (Madrid: Ed. de la Lectura, 1917).

[184] G. Moya, *Gonzalo R. Lafora. Medicina y Cultura en una España en Crisis* (Madrid: Universidad Autónoma de Madrid, 1986), p. 72.

[185] R. Huertas García-Alejo, 'Niños degenerados. Medicina Mental y regeneracionismo en la España del cambio de siglo', *Dynamis*, 18 (1998), 157–79 (172).

[186] Campos Marín, 'La teoría de la degeneración', 443–4; Rodríguez Lafora, *Los Niños Mentalmente Anormales*, p. 72.

[187] Rodríguez Lafora, *Los Niños Mentalmente Anormales*, p. 72.

[188] Rodríguez Lafora, *Los Niños Mentalmente Anormales*, pp. 114, 368.

[189] Rodríguez Lafora, *Los Niños Mentalmente Anormales*, p. 430.

[190] Rodríguez Lafora, *Los Niños Mentalmente Anormales*, pp. 430–1. In a later article on the subject of a case of psychic impotence with paranoid derivations (G. Rodríguez Lafora, 'Consideraciones sobre el mecanismo genético de las psicosis paranoides', *El Siglo Médico*, 68 [1921], 1201–5), Lafora shows his closeness to degenerationist thought and his ambivalence with respect to psychoanalysis. On the one hand he accepts the Freudian stages of sexual development and subjects the patient to psychoanalytic techniques. On the other hand, he rejects the Freudian interpretation of this kind of impotence and paranoid delusion as a result of repressed homosexual desire. He believes that the patient shows a fixation of the libido not in the homoerotic phase but in the incest phase. This fixation, furthermore, is not the cause of 'heterosexual failures' but rather their effect. Lafora believed that hardly anyone did not suffer some kind of sexual failure at least once in their life. In these circumstances 'los individuos con constitución mental normal se adaptan a estos conflictos y los que tienen una constitución paranoide desarrollan una psicosis' [those individuals with a normal mental constitution adapt to those conflicts and those who possess a paranoid constitution develop a psychosis] (p. 1204). Fixation of the libido in stages previous to the normal heterosexual development only takes place in those individuals with the requisite 'individual and family predisposition'.

[191] Huertas García-Alejo, 'Niños degenerados', 173–4.

[192] Rodríguez Lafora, *Los Niños Mentalmente Anormales*, p. 431.

[193] G. Canguilhem, *Le Normal et le Pathologique* (Paris: PUF, 1966), pp. 18–51.

[194] Rodríguez Lafora, *Los Niños Mentalmente Anormales*, p. 431.

Chapter Three

The Sexological Context, 1915–1939: Sexual Inversion, Marañón's 'Intersexuality' and the 'Social Dangerousness' of the Homosexual

The last chapter focused on the important changes in the conceptualization of mental disorders, nervous disease and medico-legal questions related to sexuality in Spain in the period 1840–1915. In the last quarter of the nineteenth century, the epistemological and terminological framework in which homosexuality was discussed was transformed, particularly by means of the arrival in Spain of foreign authors' work such as that of Tardieu as a new psychiatric model of sexuality was developed.[1] Throughout the nineteenth century discussions of the hermaphrodite became one of several means of introducing a discussion of all those bodies and practices that did not conform precisely to accepted male and female morphologies and, later, behaviours. These 'vices de conformation', as Tardieu called them, allowed for doctors to introduce a discussion of questions more closely related to sexual practices. This interest in the hermaphrodite was renewed as new medical technologies allowed for the determination of sexual identity in the field of the anatomical sciences in the twentieth century. These changes also had an effect on the conceptualization of gender and sex deviance in the early part of the twentieth century. In tandem with the new psychiatric and sexological sciences, the old category of sodomy was revised and the idea of sexual inversion became more current.

Sexual inversion, however, in the period up to 1915 was primarily a category that denoted gender deviance and only later acquired an explicit sexual dimension. In the period 1915 to 1939 we see how sexual inversion came to denote both gender and sexual deviance. In this way, it is possible to argue, sexual inversion as this dual category delayed the reception of 'homosexuality' as a primarily sexual state in Spain. Furthermore, the elaboration of theories such as Gregorio Marañón's 'intersexuality' added another dimension to aetiologies and taxonomies of same-sex sexuality, blending biological with psychical explanations. In this chapter, we trace the development of both sexual inversion and homosexuality as theories, their interface with intersexuality and the competition between different frameworks for their understanding which drew not only on the new psychiatry but also on renovated biological accounts, especially endocrinology.

It is important to note, however, that those streams of medical theories on sexuality that came from other countries (particularly France and Germany) did not necessarily imply that Spanish doctors accepted and reproduced them faithfully, without modification, or took all of their consequences to heart. While Mata reiterated the categories that Tardieu established on the subject of same-sex sexuality,[2] others, such as José de Letamendi, created their own taxonomic framework that testified to the attractiveness of this new field for medical experts.[3] Related to doctors' desire to create their own specialisms and to mark out their own terrain in the *fin de siècle* years, the creation of whole new, but often short-lived, taxonomies for homosexuality and other 'perversions' was a characteristic of the profession.

Despite this renovation of concepts, what cannot be ignored is the fact that mid-nineteenth-century terms of reference that explained homosexuality as some form of monomania, madness or mental illness (deriving from the work of alienists such as Esquirol) ran concurrently, for some time, with ideas which depicted same-sex activity basically as a moral question (sodomy). The resource of monomania and sodomy coincided with newer psychiatric and nervous disease models of sexual 'pathology' well into the twentieth century. It is difficult, therefore, to affirm that in Spain there was a clear and progressive shift from 'sodomy' to 'sexual inversion' through to 'homosexuality' in this period, as could be argued more easily for some other European countries

and the United States. Instead of a linear and progressive movement towards 'homosexuality', what predominates during the
period 1850–1939 in Spain is a proliferation of terms designating
same-sex sexuality and the concepts that they struggled to contain. Such a non-linear and polysemic development is strikingly
confirmed by the return of the use of 'sodomy' by medico-legal
and Catholic figures (albeit with a measurably different meaning)
during the Franco period to describe male same-sex sexual activity.

Despite the fragmentation of ideas on homosexuality, the
period discussed in this chapter denotes the end of isolation for
medical and psychiatric theories that concentrated on sexuality
and it entails their incorporation into the imaginary of the elite
professions and, to some degree, into the apparatus of the state.[4]
This, at least, was the aspiration of many psychiatrists who became
steadily more involved in diverse projects from the description of
sexual delinquency with a view to demanding more severe punish-
ments, to involvement in discussions in the Cortes on the female
vote.[5]

The period from the mid 1910s, and especially from the early
1920s onwards, was characterized by what can be described as a
sexological ferment, the 'take-off' of the sexual question in ways
that were only germinating in the nineteenth century.[6] This rise
of medical explanations for all kinds of sexual expression must be
understood, furthermore, within the more general context of the
institutionalization of medical knowledge, the important questions raised by the *fin de siècle* and the debates on the direction of
national politics and the health of the race. These elements, when
combined with a reliance on medical theories to explain disease,
degeneracy and crime, made for potent 'bio-political' discourses
on sexuality.

As noted elsewhere, in Spain in the nineteenth century and to
a large degree in the twentieth, psychiatry was the principal
vehicle by which theories on sexuality began to permeate the
national consciousness, from the professional to the popular
level, although in concert with the sexual sciences and new
educational theories.[7] Psychiatry, with its increased involvement
in the apparatus of the state, its plea for doctors to become more
familiarized with psychiatric concepts, and the continuous renova-
tions of the discipline particularly at the beginning of the twentieth century, was, as we have suggested, a potent force when

coupled to the social and literary examinations of sexuality which emerged at the end of the nineteenth century. The connections between psychiatry and its approximation to the newer, more strictly sexological sciences, and to eugenics and genetics, fields that encapsulated the aspirations of the elites to purify society and to regenerate its base elements, made up a set of extremely strong – and for some, extremely attractive – apparatuses allowing for the government of sexual and other causes of deviance in the first decades of the twentieth century.

Expert areas such as psychiatry and sexology did not just emerge on their own, as some prosthesis growing out of the ruling elite's desire to control, in response to an impersonal 'power' that sought the secret of sex, or even simply as a strategy followed by medical doctors or psychiatrists. Specialisms such as these were part of a set of responses to the urgent questions that were posed notably by the middle and reforming classes. The growth of these disciplines may also have reflected the concerns of homosexuals themselves who sought an explanation of desires that were posited as 'deviant' by medical doctors and psychiatrists.[8] Before considering psychiatric discourse on homosexuality, the first section of this chapter focuses on biological or somatic theories of (homo)sexuality. Despite their more somatic approach, however, as we will see, considerable concessions were made to psychological and psychoanalytic explanatory frameworks.

Psychic Hermaphroditism or Gonadal Intersexuality?

While in the United States, for example, somatically oriented theories of sexuality began to decline and the idea of the psychic hermaphrodite superseded that of the physical hermaphrodite as the power of mental explanations was consolidated,[9] in Spain a number of doctors revived a physical theory of hermaphroditism by evoking the power of the internal secretions as the determinants of sexual expression. The most renowned figure in this field was Gregorio Marañón, whose first analyses of the subject took place around 1918.[10] As we will see, however, Marañón was not just interested in the science of hermaphroditism; his theories of 'intersexuality' covered a variety of sexual states, from virilized women through to homosexuality per se. Indeed, in contrast to some of his medical colleagues who were more interested in anatomical differences between the sexes, endocrinology for Marañón came to be a resource for the explanation of gender deviance and homosexuality itself.

Marañón's doctrine of internal secretions was not, therefore, merely a vulgar biological theory. In a response to a critique of his theories of intersexuality for their alleged over-reliance on biology made by the Hungarian psychiatrist Oliver Brachfeld in 1932, Marañón rejected the assertion that he ignored psychiatric theories on sexual pathology in favour of biological ones. On the contrary, he argued, without being a psychiatrist, he read as much old and new psychiatry as he had time to and he cited many such texts in the bibliography of his work. In fact, he wrote, it was psychiatrists who were often ignorant of the work of biologists and pathologists and not the other way around: 'También he dicho en varias ocasiones que una parte de las concepciones de los psiquiatras modernos peca de escaso conocimiento de la fisiología y de la patología humanas' [I have also said on many occasions that some aspects of modern psychiatric concepts are guilty of a lack of knowledge of human physiology and pathology].[11]

Marañón's theory of intersexuality developed from nineteenth-century theories on physical and, to a lesser degree, psychic hermaphroditism. In order to understand this 'return' to older theories, it is worth briefly recalling the interest in hermaphroditism in medical circles from the 1850s. While in the medieval period the magical or monstrous figure of the hermaphrodite was an accepted part of lore and medicine, in the mid nineteenth century it was acknowledged that real hermaphroditism in humans was rare, if not impossible.[12] What medical doctors such as Pedro Mata argued in the 1870s was that, in reality, some subjects shared some of the primary, secondary or even tertiary characteristics of the other sex, making them rather than hermaphrodites, 'pseudo-hermaphrodites'. This was a period in which the old 'one sex' model had declined; it was now thought that there were two different sexes, female and male, who had essentially different characteristics.[13]

The same period saw the growth in psychiatric circles of the idea of the 'psychic hermaphrodite', an individual who may not, and probably did not, combine the physical aspects of both sexes but rather combined what were deemed to be the psychic characteristics of the other sex. This was materialized in preferences, demeanour, voice and sexual interests of the subject studied. If a man was sexually aroused by another male he was 'in reality' a woman because his psychic or instinctual urges were directed towards the male sex. This sexual economy admitted of just one sex drive: towards the other sex. Any deviations from this could only be explained in the very terms of this same model.

While from the early 1870s hermaphroditism in Spanish medico-legal texts often formed a kind of preface to the introduction of accounts of pederasty and non-procreative sexual acts in general, anatomical accounts of hermaphroditism remained closely tied to somatic explanations and consequences of sex/body disharmony. For many medical doctors of the early twentieth century some kind of somatic or hormonal explanation for gender and sexual 'anomalies' was common. That doctors more closely associated with the non-psychiatric branches of medicine used this framework is exemplified in the work of, for example, Luis Comenge, José Gómez Ocaña and Ricardo Nóvoa Santos. Comenge held, amongst other positions, the directorship of the Barcelona Instituto de Higiene Urbana; Gómez Ocaña held a chair in physiology in Madrid and Nóvoa Santos a chair in medical pathology. In 1910 Comenge argued that real hermaphrodites did not occur in the human species; what had been observed in the past were apparent hermaphrodites, whose external organs of generation were incorrectly formed, to use the terminology employed by Tardieu.[14] This medical category should, the author argued, be investigated above all because of the suffering it caused in the marital sphere. What Comenge refused to discuss were those individuals who suffered genital defects in combination with gender deviance, such as *maricas*, viragos and *marimachos*: 'No incumbe á la hygiene el estudio de estos seres desgraciados y monstruosos' [It is not the province of medical hygiene to discuss these unfortunate and monstrous beings].[15] This lack of discussion of gender and sexual 'deviants' was not uncommon. In a section on hermaphroditism in his *Manual de Patología General* the pathologist Nóvoa Santos did not mention sexual instincts or desires and his was a purely biological account of the differences between the sexes.[16]

The scientific fields that allowed some doctors, including Marañón, to go beyond mere morphological accounts of hermaphroditism included histology and endocrinology and we see growing tensions in the old somatic models used by medical doctors to study hermaphroditism as the 1920s wore on. As Nelly Oudshoorn has argued, the gonads became the designator of the true sex of the individual; an explanation that was in competition with truths related in some way to the psyche.[17] The insights of endocrinology were incorporated into medical accounts on hermaphroditism in the mid 1920s and appear in influential medical journals of the time such as *La Medicina Ibera* and the *Gaceta Médica Española*. Usually, they appeared in the gazette section of these reviews, where institutions and individual doctors supplied details of case histories for other doctors' attention.[18]

What is clear from these case studies is that like Westphal's 'contrary sexual feeling', discourse around hermaphroditism became a device that allowed for a tentative, although not as yet theoretical discussion of same-sex sexuality in the specialized field of pathological anatomy. It would not be long before a renovated version of the hermaphrodite, as the origin and one form of 'intersexual', would become one of the major paradigms for understanding homosexuality in Spain in the twentieth century in the form of Marañón's endocrinological theories. What was to change around 1918, from the time of Marañón's first exposition of his understanding of the working of the 'internal secretions',[19] was the articulation of a specific theory that combined both the somatic and gonadal aspects of hermaphroditism and a discussion of sexual instincts. Marañón's use of the concept of the hermaphrodite permitted a whole set of explanations for phenomena, including homosexuality, which were grouped under the copious umbrella of 'intersexuality', a theory which was elaborated in detail in a number of essays and most famously in his 1930 publication *Evolución de la sexualidad y los estados intersexuales*. This stance also allowed a medico-legal defence of homosexuality to be articulated from the 1920s onwards.[20]

Marañón's *opus* is large and our attention here will be confined to two principal publications which express the endocrinologist's ideas on intersexuality and homosexuality from 1928 and 1930.[21] In the first of these works, 'Nuevas ideas sobre el problema de la intersexualidad y sobre la cronología de los sexos' [New ideas on the problem of intersexuality and the chronology of the sexes],

Marañón is quick to dispel the commonly held prejudice that the two sexes are discrete phenomena; rather, human beings, to a greater or lesser degree, harbour characteristics of the two sexes within the same body. Marañón argues that the gonad or sexual gland is an undifferentiated organ, is 'bisexual' (meaning it is capable of developing into one sex or the other since both sexes are contained within), and potentially hermaphroditic up to a certain stage of embryonic development. The action of the sex glands determines whether the organism will be male or female. It is important to note, however, that 'esta diferenciación de la gónada en uno u otro sentido sexual y esta diferenciación paralela de la morfología y de la fisiología hacia la feminidad o la masculinidad, no se verifican de una manera absoluta. No es que un sexo se desarrolle y el otro desaparezca. Lo que ocurre es que uno se hipertrofia y el otro se atrofia' [the differentiation of the gonad towards one or other of the sexes and the accompanying differentiation of the morphology and physiology towards femininity or masculinity, does not take place in any absolute sense. It is not the case of one sex developing and the other disappearing. What happens is that one hypertrophies and the other atrophies.][22]

Despite a male or female morphology and physiology, then, a number of signs or primary or secondary characteristics of the 'other' sex remain according to a scale of masculinity and femininity.[23] Thus, both sexes persist in the human individual throughout his or her life, 'mezclados según dosis distintas; y no en proporción inmutable, sino variable en el curso de la vida ulterior; es decir, con la posibilidad de que el sexo principal se debilite y de que, en cambio, el secundario se acreciente bajo la acción de determinadas influencias fisiológicas o patológicas' [mixed up in accordance with different dosages and not in unchangeable proportions but in variable ones as life progresses. That is, with the possibility that the principal sex is weakened and, by contrast, the secondary sex is strengthened through the action of particular physiological or pathological influences].[24] Such a notion allowed Marañón to argue in a later article, that in order to resolve this 'bisexuality' satisfactorily, it was the task of every individual to destroy the 'fantasma del otro sexo que cada cual lleváis dentro; sed hombres, sed mujeres, y entonces, las mujeres y los hombres que andan por el mundo no serán para vosotros más que fuentes de castidad' [ghost of the other sex that you all carry within; be men, be women, and then the women and men that walk the earth will be nothing more than founts of chastity].[25]

The two sexes (Marañón refers to them as the two 'sexualities'), however, do not follow the same stages or rhythms of development. Marañón points out that it is not a case of *synchronic* development but of *successive* development according to the sex of the individual. Employing a Darwinian framework, the female in Marañón's thought is a stage of development less advanced than that of the male. The 'correct' development of the individual moves towards maleness and away from femaleness, as far as is possible: 'Lo femenino es una fase que sigue a la adolescencia y procede a lo masculino, etapa terminal de la evolución' [The feminine is a phase that follows adolescence and proceeds to the masculine, the final stage of evolution].[26] Every male, therefore, passes through a period of femininity and, likewise, the female through a period of maleness. This period, however, or 'crisis' in Marañón's terminology, arrives at a different time for each sex. In the case of the male, it appears in puberty and in the case of the female in the climacteric period. The degree to which each person surpasses this crisis determines his or her 'success' as a person who is *predominantly* male or female and heterosexual.

When this evolutionary process is not successful, when the 'killing off' of one sex by the other is not decisive, an 'intersexual' state is the result. These anatomical and characterological states (Marañón employs the terminology 'organic forms of undifferentiated sexual characters', where 'organic' comprises somatic and psychic elements) can be grouped into permanent and transitory intersexual states. Amongst the former, Marañón, basing his account on the theories of Goldschmidt, includes hermaphroditism, pseudo-hermaphroditism, virilization, feminization, 'homosexualities' and inversions of psychology, affection and social behaviour. Amongst the transitory manifestations is included circumstantial homosexuality as a result of inebriation, cocaine intoxication or deprivation of the other sex.

In his 1928 article Marañón focuses on those intersexualities which are 'critical', that is, those which appear only at the beginning and the end of sexual evolution. It is these critical intersexual states that allow us, Marañón argues, to understand how psychosexual behaviour works. It is during these moments of crisis that the full expression of male or female sexuality becomes blurred or diminished. In the male crisis, puberty, the subject displays an 'auténtica intersexualidad feminoide' [authentic femi-noidal intersexuality].[27] Women acquire 'viriloid' intersexuality in the climacteric phase.

But this period of crisis is not merely a crisis of maleness or femaleness. It may also become a crisis of sexual object choice. The male period of intersexual femininity is an underestimated danger zone; it is these pubertal adolescents that produce the 'contingente más copioso de las futuras anormalidades sexuales' [most extensive contingent of future sexual abnormalities].[28] These adolescents are usually placid, intellectual, show a particu-lar aptitude for mathematics and music, are inept in sports, and their sexual interest is late in developing. Their libido, Marañón continues, is polymorphous, a quality that 'coloca al adolescente en un estado de indefensión específica contra las sugestiones perversas, que, precisamente, encuentran en la morfología muelle, androginoide ... un particular punto de atracción' [places the adolescent in a state of vulnerability with respect to perverse influences, which, precisely in the androgynous, soft morphology ... find a definite pole of attraction].[29] The shyness of such individuals paves the way for the homosexualization of the boy; a process which, Marañón notes, Adler had argued was a reaction to timidity.

The crucial element in all this process, however, is not the morphology of the individual in itself, his shyness or any kind of perverse suggestions. The key to an individual's development is contained in the action of the glands both in the embryonic stage of development and in the period of crisis. While youthful female homosexuality is explained with difficulty in this paradigm (women acquired viriloid intersexuality in the climacteric phase), male homosexuality is seen to arise from a combination of endocrinological, morphological and psychosexual factors of varying intensity. In this way, in the male the permanent acquisi-tion of female characteristics (including the desire towards other men, seen as a 'female' desire in Marañón's framework) is a concession to an atavistic past, to a regressive process of evolution, the 'bisexual' or hermaphroditic state. Marañón once more: '*Los dos sexos no se oponen, por lo tanto, sino que sencillamente, se suceden*' [*The two sexes are not opposed to each other, therefore, but rather, simply, they follow on from one another*].[30]

This diachronic rather than synchronic process contains the explanation of 'sexual inversion' and all human intersexual states:

'En la mujer, la inversión, la virilización, *es un fenómeno superativo* en cierto modo progresivo. En el hombre la inversión *es un fenómeno regresivo*' [In woman, inversion and virilization *are positive phenomena*, to a certain extent progressive. In man inversion *is a regressive phenomenon*].[31] The male invert or homosexual, as an intersexual, is, according to Marañón, closer to the female as he has lost his virility and has lost the battle against the 'other sex within': 'Al hombre le basta *que su virilidad se debilite* para acercarse a la mujer. Para que la mujer se acerque al hombre es precisa una influencia compleja *de superación de la feminidad*' [For a man to become more like a woman, all that is needed is that his *virility become weakened*. For a woman to become like a man, what is required is a complex process of *overcoming femininity*].[32] Here, Marañón meets Freud in his assertion that homosexuality is a fully 'natural' expression rooted in the freedom to range over female and male object choice found in early childhood, in primitive states of society and early periods of history.[33]

Marañón's thought, revolutionary for the Spain of the 1920s and 1930s, rooted sexual behaviour primarily in the endocrine glands while conceding some influence to other factors such as psychology and environment and was thus faithful to his admission of psychiatric and psychoanalytic explanations for homosexuality as part of an eclectic aetiology, an aspect we will discuss later in the light of a number of criticisms of his theories. The workings of the sexual glands as a biological origin of sexuality became enmeshed in a social context which also had its part to play in guiding its ultimate heterosexual or homosexual expression. While Marañón believed that homosexuality should not be punished since its criminalization was not only 'una insensatez en el terreno científico, sino, socialmente, de una táctica a más de inhumana, notoriamente contraproducente' [a mark of insensitivity in the scientific field but in social terms a tactic that, more than inhuman is notoriously counterproductive],[34] he was to argue in a different forum that everything possible should be done to educate youth on the subject of sexuality and to promote sexual differentiation as a means of avoiding the 'fall' into sexual 'indifferentiation', or a form of intersexuality that could harbour the spectre of homosexuality.[35]

While Marañón was a major voice in the field of medical theories of homosexuality in the 1920s, he was not a lone voice; the decade spawned a number of contrasting positions, which, although eclectic once again, favoured the predominance not of biological explanations but psychological ones. The pathologist Roberto Nóvoa Santos, for example, writing at the same time as Marañón, viewed puberty as the critical age for the development of healthy adult sexuality but, in contrast to Marañón, he believed that homosexuality, in part at least, developed from a faulty process of *psychosexual* differentiation.[36] Nóvoa Santos naturalized homosexuality as a trait that might appear in perfectly formed youths in body and spirit; sooner or later, however, sexual differentiation would continue to develop such that heterosexuality would be attained in the majority of cases. Any perversion of instincts, or 'sexual inversion' in Nóvoa Santos's terms, was usually the result of a congenital abnormality in degenerate individuals, producing the perversion of the sexual instinct explained by recourse to 'una anomalía en la esfera psicosexual, a una diferenciación psicosexual imperfecta o aberrante' [an anomaly in the psychosexual sphere, to imperfect or aberrant psychosexual differentiation].[37] He conceded, nevertheless, that sexual inversion could also occur as a result of 'viciousness' or vice, without the person having shown any degenerative signs, an economy with which we are, by now, familiar.

While Nóvoa Santos differed from Marañón in the aetiology of inversion, he coincided in other aspects. For example, he noted that 'en la inmensa mayoría de casos de inversión sexual los órganos genitales están perfectamente conformados desde el punto de vista anatómico y fisiológico' [in the vast majority of cases of sexual inversion the genital organs are perfectly formed from the anatomical and physiological point of view];[38] Marañón had also been keen to stress the lack of necessary relationship between alterations in body type or in the genitalia and homosexuality. Despite the lack of physical bodily traits, Marañón noted from his clinical experience that something like two thirds of homosexual men presented some clear secondary or tertiary signs of sexual inversion, including gestures, gait or habits.[39] This open debate on any possible relationship between physiological type and sexual orientation shows how medical commentators in the 1920s and 1930s were able to admit that homosexuality was not necessarily a visible gender deviation but one which manifested itself primarily in sexual terms, an aspect that inverted the framework employed in the case of 'sexual inversion' in the years

1850–1915, which viewed the latter primarily as a gender disorder, only later to incorporate actual sexual deviance. While 'sexual inversion' steadily became more sexualized, the newer category of 'homosexuality' was primarily a sexual category, with a number of gradations between the two extremes evident in a variety of works.[40]

Marañón's desire to trace intersexuality, to a greater or lesser degree as a reality or a potentiality in all human beings, led him to argue that it was possible, despite the normality of the morphology of the genital organs, that the damaged sexual instinct of some male adolescents could well persist beyond puberty. One result of this potentiality would be homosexuality but another would be the 'hypervirile' or effeminate (but heterosexually inclined) man. The persistence of a damaged psychosexuality could result, in turn, in numerous exemplars of the type of 'Don Juan'.[41]

Marañón's sexual analysis of a figure of national importance such as Don Juan created a storm in the mid 1920s onwards,[42] to the degree that Barco Teruel was to claim: 'De la noche a la mañana, Marañón se convierte en un tema nacional de polémica. Por todas partes, se hablaba de Marañón y de su versión del donjuanismo . . .; se comentaba, ora con curiosidad, ora con auténtica cólera, la flamante feminidad de Don Juan' [Overnight, Marañón became a national polemical subject. Everywhere, people were talking about Marañón and his interpretation of donjuanism . . .; the arresting femininity of Don Juan was discussed with curiosity by some and with real anger by others].[43]

While the figure of Don Juan had attained literary and scientific attention in previous years, Marañón was the first to analyse Don Juan as a figure that was emblematic of the 'hypererotic' spirit of the age, part of the 'cult of sex' and an example of 'false' or quantitative virility. It was this 'pseudovirility' that was, in Marañón's mind, lamentably common in the Spain of the early twentieth century. While men should be involved in worthy activities such as science or work, the archetypal Don Juan was devoted to wooing women, cultivating his image and to frittering away valuable male resources. This lack of real content was thus typical of the female spirit and encouraged a 'feminization' of society.

To a large degree the figure of Don Juan came to signify a site of danger for the stability of gendered and sexual traits. While, of course, Marañón acknowledged that all human beings were but a mixture of the sexes, Don Juan became symbolic of the feminine in men; he was prone to lying, was somewhat foppish or effeminate in dress and was passive in that he waited for women to approach him.[44] This femininity became iconic in some cultural quarters. Elias Salaverría's portrait of Don Juan from 1927 was described by Bernadino de Pantorba as disturbing in its depiction of an effeminate Don Juan adorned with 'todas sus galas y joyas, *donjuaneando*' [all his best apparel and jewels, *donjuaneando*].[45] Was this 'donjuaneando' practically a form of 'mariconeando'? It would seem so, or at least the danger was present, for in 1940 Marañón affirmed that his own portrait of Don Juan was of 'un hombre afeminado, casi un homosexual' [an effeminate man, almost a homosexual].[46] The slip into active homosexuality was one that other commentators preferred not to accept.[47]

The consideration of the hypervirile yet ineffective sexuality of Don Juan, however, was just part of Marañón's repertoire of 'failed' sexual types. The development of his theory of intersexuality was to undergo various revisions and it is now that we come to discuss in detail his 1930 *Evolución de la sexualidad y los estados intersexuales* with respect to homosexuality. It cannot be denied that Marañón proposed a more humanitarian treatment of homosexuals and, in his own words the inclusion of homosexuality amongst the intersexual states 'supone un enorme progreso en la comprensión de esta anomalía del instinto' [supposes enormous progress in the understanding of this anomaly of the instinct].[48] The homosexual was as faithful to his own peculiar sexual instinct as those who sought the 'opposite' sex. The difference, he argued however, was that the homosexual's instinct was 'torcido' [twisted]: 'El invertido es, pues, tan responsable de su anormalidad como pudiera serlo el diabético de su glucosuria' [The invert is, therefore, as responsible of his abnormality as the diabetic is of his glycosuria].[49]

Despite this lack of responsibility of the individual invert, it was society's duty to try to prevent the multiplication of homosexuals: 'El papel de la sociedad, por lo tanto, frente al problema de la homosexualidad, es estudiar los orígenes profundos de la inversión del instinto para tratar de rectificarlos' [The role of society, therefore, with respect to the problem of homosexuality, is to study the origins of sexual inversion in order to try to correct them].[50] What were these origins? For Marañón, as we have already seen, a major factor was the original 'bisexuality' of the body – its mixture of male and female bodily and psychic elements. Agreeing with Ulrichs's notion of a female soul in a male body to explain male homosexuality, Marañón wrote that 'En la actualidad no puede dudarse de que la homosexualidad es un fenómeno condicionado por un estado de bisexualidad del organismo' [Today, one cannot doubt that homosexuality is a phenomenon conditioned by the bisexual state of the organism].[51] This organism would betray a 'functional disorder' far more profound than any anatomical disorder found in other forms of intersexuality. So, homosexuality in this equation was not equivalent to physical hermaphroditism and could not necessarily be identified immediately merely by looking at the subject. On this question as with many others, as we shall see, however, Marañón was not decisive. He admitted that '*en un gran número de homosexuales se puede descubrir, junto con la inversión del instinto, una significativa inversión paralela de los caracteres somáticos*' [*in a large number of homosexuals one can find, together with the inversion of the instinct, a significant parallel inversion of the somatic characteristics*].[52] In contrast to Freud, whom he cites as not finding any anatomical differences, and others, Marañón lists alterations in the skeleton, height, hair, voice, skin and gestures of homosexuals.[53]

The causes of homosexuality were also somewhat unclear. We have seen, for example in the work of degenerationist psychiatrists, a wavering relative importance of the physical and the psychic, of the influence of heredity and environment and Marañón's work appears to be equally inconclusive, if not more so. Marañón admitted the interaction between 'psychological factors' and the hormones: 'Esta afirmación nos pone, de una vez para siempre, al margen de las censuras, que muchos psicólogos, pedagogos y sociólogos dirigen a los médicos por su intento de explicar estos complejos estados del espíritu por el mero juego químico de las hormonas. Las hormonas no lo son todo. Pero sí mucho; y lo inadmisible es prescindir de su intervención' [This statement places us, once and for all, outside the censure that many psychologists, educationalists and sociologists cast on doctors for their attempt to explain these complex states of the spirit by reference to the chemical mix of hormones alone. Hormones are not everything. But they are a lot and it is inadmissible to rule out their intervention].[54] With this in mind, Marañón set out the principal 'facts' behind the intersexual state of homosexuality.

The first of these was related to the notion that the libido in its original manifestation was triggered by a hormonal origin. Working within the paradigm of heterosexual desire alluded to above, for Marañón it was evident that if a man was attracted to another man, it was clear that 'está sometido a una influencia erótica de sentido femenino' [he is subject to an erotic influence in the feminine sense].[55] Secondly, amongst others, Steinach had claimed to have found in the testicle of homosexuals the decisive proof of the bisexuality of the gonad – this would explain how certain individuals would result in a mix of female and male. The evidence provided by current histology however, Marañón noted, was not decisive even though this did not mean that such a conclusion would be reached in the future.[56]

Thirdly, scientists such as Voronoff had tried testicular implants in homosexuals in order to alter their erotic desires 'with favourable results', but not without a degree of criticism.[57] Fourth, as we noted above, 'a large number' of homosexuals did show a degree of inversion in their somatic characteristics. It was necessary to look for the 'little signs' of intersexuality, which could include those physical elements listed before such as skeleton size, hair consistency and tenor of voice.[58]

But if these 'facts' formed the basis of the homosexual variant of intersexuality, what ultimately would the causes be? It was not, Marañón believed, just a case of the existence of a female hormone in a male body. Given that there were so many categories of intersexuality present in humans, other causal factors had to be adduced: 'Todo esto nos indica que *si la bisexualidad hormónica es una condición necesaria para el desarrollo de la homosexualidad, no basta, sin embargo, para que la homosexualidad se produzca*' [All of this shows that *if hormonal bisexuality is a necessary condition for the development of homosexuality, it is not enough in itself, however, for homosexuality to be produced*].[59] This led Marañón to make a daring admission that few authors would subscribe to: given that organic intersexuality was so frequent it was possible that all human beings would have the potential to become homosexual, whether this potential developed or not. Such an appreciation coincided to some degree with Freud, Stekel and in Spain Letamendi, who explained homosexuality on the basis of the original bisexuality of the organism and Martí Ibáñez, who followed Marañón's thought on this subject to the letter.[60]

Within this paradigm of the dangers inherent in the original bisexuality or intersexuality of the organism, Marañón regarded the need to differentiate the sexes from an early age as a key measure to prevent sexual confusion. Childhood, with its polymorphous and indeterminate sexual object stage so clearly described by Freud, was a danger zone signalled by educationalists of all types (see Chapter Four). The male homosexual's sexuality was not strictly close to feminine or passive sexuality as some commentators believed; instead it was more akin to infantile, undeveloped sexuality, which had not undergone the process of differentiation between the sexes. This was a major cause of future homosexuality when added to by psychic factors of sexual development: 'a *este retraso de la diferenciación de la libido, que consideramos esencial en la génesis del homosexualismo* ... se unen después los mismos factores psicológicos condicionadores del reflejo erótico' [to *this delay in the differentiation of the libido, which we consider to be essential in the genesis of homosexuality* ... afterwards are added the psychological factors that condition the erotic reflex].[61] Puberty, then, on this basis is a '*moment of maximum delicacy*'; it is the '*momento equívoco en que se engendran o se deciden la mayoría de las perversiones sexuales*' [equivocal moment in which the majority of sexual perversions are created or consolidated].[62]

While original bisexuality and the lack of sexual differentiation in puberty were two key factors in the generation of the sexual perversions for Marañón, there were additional factors complicating an individual's homosexuality. Once again, childhood was deemed a dangerous period, not only because of the possible seduction of the child into homosexual acts but also because of an excessively long and intense maternal influence over the child. Many a homosexual was, Marañón warned, the only child or the last child of a long line of siblings.[63] Other factors favouring the development of homosexuality included narcissism, which was reinforced by masturbation, previous sexual failure, fear and revulsion towards women.[64] These 'external factors' were for Marañón important and given that the 'intersexual predisposition' was so common amongst people homosexuality was a distinct possibility in many.

But what was the relationship for Marañón between the acquisition of homosexuality and its innate quality? Eschewing a strong hereditarian paradigm that many of his psychiatrist colleagues such as Juarros (as we will see below) would entertain, Marañón declared 'no admitimos la clásica división de los homosexuales en *congénitos* y *adquiridos*. *Para nosotros, todos son congénitos; y a la vez, todos son adquiridos*' [we do not accept the classical division of homosexuals into *congenital* and *acquired*. *For us, all are congenital and at the same time all are acquired*].[65] This was not merely an easy way out for Marañón; it responded to a real attempt to fuse environmental factors with the 'morbid predisposition' towards homosexuality. Some psychiatrists would try to privilege one factor over the other but not Marañón: 'un sujeto, dotado de un fuerte lastre constitucional de intersexualidad, denunciará la alteración de su instinto desde la niñez; y otro, con la intersexualidad orgánica latente, no se nos mostrará como tal invertido, hasta que actúen con vigor las causas determinantes del medio. El primero podrá, sin embargo, no llegar nunca, a pesar de la congénita tendencia, a ser un homosexual, si los influjos externos son contrarios a la perversión' [a subject, endowed with a strong constitutional element of intersexuality, will show the alteration of his instinct from childhood, and another subject, with latent organic intersexuality, will not become this invert until the determining factors of the environment act on him with force. The first type may not ever become a homosexual, however, in spite of the congenital tendency, if the external influences counter inversion].[66]

As we can see, Marañón's theory of intersexuality and its extension to the aetiology of homosexuality was a complex one. It was also en eclectic theory in that it did not formally privilege hormonal explanations, psychological elements or environmental factors, even though the thesis of the original bisexuality of the organism or the gonads was an indispensable part of his theory of intersexuality. In later years, however, Marañón was to concede that he had perhaps over-privileged hormonal explanations for intersexuality.[67]

Perhaps because of the eclectic nature of his theories as expressed in *La evolución de la sexualidad* and because of the humanitarian (although intensely medicalized) position he adopted with respect to homosexuality, he was to experience strong criticism in the form of a refutation in the prestigious *El Siglo Médico* by Medical Academy member Francisco Criado y Aguilar.[68] The articles by Criado referred to the theoretical aspects of Marañón's work but were also sprinkled with references to 'immorality', 'sensualism' and 'abominable aberrations'. The second part of his article finished with the exhortation that Marañón's theory of intersexuality be erased from the annals of medical thought: 'Bórrese, pues, de los anales de la Medicina todo lo referente a la intersexualidad humana, porque no existe' [Let us delete from the annals of medicine everything that refers to human intersexuality because it does not exist].[69]

On the other hand, for progressive doctors and those in the legal profession who advocated the decriminalization of homosexuality or its consideration under 'scientific' auspices, endocrinological and hormonal theories of sexual development offered a bridge for the suffering homosexual and his scientific 'rehabilitation'. Such was the interpretation that some gave to the hormonal and testicular grafting experiments of surgeons such as Voronoff and Steinach in the 1920s. In this sense, Dr Ángel Pulido Martín, of the San Juan de Dios Hospital, Madrid, embraced the modernity of glandular theories of sexual functioning.

The insertion of sex hormones into laboratory animals was held to modify male and female behaviour, often 'renovating' the 'appropriate' sex instinct of either male or female. The therapeutic possibilities of this surgery were made explicit by Pulido. If, he argued, in animals the substitution of one sex gland for another, before the original gland had begun to function, could effectively modify their sexual behaviour the possible application of such treatments for homosexuals was not inconceivable. If sexual behaviour could thus be modified, and animals could take on the sexual instinct 'appropriate to their sex', human homosexual behaviour could effectively be modified. Biological modification of the homosexual would also entail social consequences: 'Si gracias a estos trabajos, son considerados los homo-sexuales congénitos, desde un punto de vista científico, y se llevan a la teratología sacándolos del ridículo y del crimen donde la ignorancia les ha tenido hasta hoy, se habría hecho una obra buena, que siéndo [sic] de comprensión resultará de caridad' [If, thanks to this work, homosexuals are considered to be congenital, from a scientific view, and they are placed in the field of teratology and removed from ridicule and crime where ignorance has placed them to date, then a positive act will have been performed and from this comprehension charity will result].[70]

While positions on the question of homosexuality were to remain staunchly divided, in the case of Marañón his ideas grew out of a liberal, humanitarian scientific milieu that viewed science as generally objective and progressive, a tool that could be employed to raise humanity out of its state of misery to gain a more dignified existence. Marañón viewed the sexual question – like many of his profession – as one of the most pressing concerns for Spanish doctors and for Spanish society at the time. His critique of the backwardness of Spain in its lack of openness in broaching the sexual question is often repeated in his work.[71] Marañón's medical project cannot, therefore, be isolated from the overlapping social and scientific concerns of those engaged in the sex reform movement, which emerged as a powerful force by the late 1920s and which saw its heyday in the 1930s.

Despite this, Marañón's thought betrays not only a hierarchical justification of the sexual order but also essentially the view that homosexuality was a disorder. That he was a man of his time is shown by the degree to which he drew on a mixture of nineteenth-and twentieth-century scientific paradigms. Glick has argued that Marañón fused Darwinian evolutionary concepts and Freudian explanations of sexual development.[72] In accordance with this fusion, Marañón's theory of sexuality relied on an evolutionary model of development of the sexes whereby female-ness was viewed as a developmental stage through which creatures must pass towards completion, something synonymous with male-ness. This 'logic of recapitulation' suggested that 'the fully evolved human male himself passed through a female stage of development'.[73] In this way, ontogeny was to recapitulate phylogeny; the embryo of any animal recapitulates in its development the entire history of the animal kingdom. Marañón (and Freud) believed that children recapitulated the phylogeny of the species, resembling their own human ancestors and, at the same time, contemporaneous 'primitive' peoples who were supposed to be at the same phylogenetic level. Women's bodies and minds were, by extension, phylogenetically older and had more primitive stages to be passed through in the obtaining of a higher, male, level. Homosexuality, as Letamendi had said, was always a derivation of an atavistic past.

Renovated Psychiatric Explanations: The Period from 1910 Onwards and New Theories from Abroad

While Marañón refined his theories of intersexuality throughout the 1920s, and incorporated into them some concessions to the psychiatric and psychological sciences, the latter constituted an important reservoir of ideas on homosexuality far beyond the audience they received in endocrinological frameworks. Psychiatry had undergone, according to Michel Foucault, a revolution in the second half of the nineteenth century that obliged it to construct a number of what he called 'large theoretical edifices'. These slowly replaced the idea that a certain crime was a symptom of an underlying pathology that burst forth at a particular moment (i.e. monomania) with the idea that a crime was committed by an individual with permanent physical or mental stigmas.[74] According to this thesis, the three principal changes that psychiatry underwent in this period were, firstly, the description not now of symptoms of an illness but syndromes of an illness. These constituted a whole set of deviant or aberrant behaviours. Syndromes were significant in their own right: 'those people . . . do not carry the symptoms of illness but rather abnormal symptoms in themselves, of oddities consolidated into anomalies'.[75] Such conditions, which responded to something internal in the person that characterized his or her whole character and behaviour, included kleptomania, agoraphobia, exhibitionism and eventually, the sexual perversions including sexual 'inversion'.

A second characteristic of this new psychiatry was the return or the re-evaluation of the idea of 'delirium' that allowed for the concept of the instinct to permeate psychiatry, coupled with the notion of pleasure. The instinct thus became fundamental to the designation of abnormalities. Third was the appearance of the idea of the 'state', introduced by Falret in the 1860s, and which became coupled to the expression 'psychic foundation'. Once one had a 'state', one could be 'predisposed' towards an abnormality and, as such, the state was the ultimate explanatory resource: 'its aetiological extent is total and absolute. The state can produce absolutely anything, at any time and to any degree'.[76] What kind of body and mind could produce such a state? The answer lay in the affected person's ancestry. It was necessary, therefore, to investigate the delinquent's hereditary character and, eventually, to institute a series of measures to defend society against the rise of the 'degenerate'.

Foucault's analysis of the changing face of psychiatry was, to a large degree, based on his interpretation of the French discipline. Nevertheless, it can be argued that Spain underwent a similar process, despite differences in timescales. It is important to note, however, that despite the entry of, for example, Tardieu's ideas and those of other foreign psychiatrists from the 1860s onwards, it was only in the second decade of the twentieth century that psychiatrists in Spain in their majority moved on from biological interpretations of the mind to embrace a more instinctual model.[77]

César Juarros, attached to the Madrid Instituto Criminológico, is illustrative of Foucault's third period of psychiatry whereby the psychic state of the individual, influenced by a combination of ancestral and environmental factors, could 'predispose' him or her towards a certain abnormality. Juarros is significant not only for his own work on the causes of mental illness, in which the sexual perversions were included, but also for his role in translating and disseminating the ideas of foreign authors. Before turning to Juarros's considerable publications throughout the decade of 1910–20 we focus on the significance of his role in the dissemination of new psychiatric ideas coming from abroad, notably in the context of his translation of the work by the French psychiatrist Emmanuel Régis, *Tratado de Psiquiatría* (1911).[78]

The work by Régis exemplified the areas that the theories of psychopathology were attempting to occupy at the beginning of the twentieth century. Régis noted that the causes of psychopathological states could result from a huge variety of determinants: 'En realidad no hay una condición patógena, hereditaria ó adquirida, individual ó colectiva, moral ó física, externa ó interna, que no pueda convertirse en determinadas circunstancias, en una causa de psicopatía' [In reality, there is no pathogenic, hereditary or acquired, individual or collective, moral or physical, external or internal condition that cannot become, under certain conditions, a cause of psychopathy].[79] This left little terrain free from a degree of pathology. A number of 'predispositional' causes, which might result in mental illness included race, political circumstances, religious ideas, inheritance, age, sex, climate and civil state. There were also 'occasional' causes which were divided into the psychic (including fatigue, the passions, contagion, puberty), physiological (menstruation, pregnancy and birth, lactation) and pathological (infections, illnesses of the nervous system, endocrine disorders) and these, once more, included a huge range of possible sources.[80]

Régis followed the theories of the most renowned psychiatrists of the time to classify and explain the 'sexual perversions'. In a section on the 'sexual impulses', he took his principal framework from Krafft-Ebing and noted that the sexual perversions resulted, above all, from a morbid predisposition, a degenerate terrain upon which exhibitionism, fetishism, sadism, masochism and homosexuality grew.[81] Régis also argued in favour of changes in the taxonomy and typology of those who engaged in same-sex activity. His principal term of reference was 'Uranism', but he also referred to sexual inversion and to 'homosexuality'. On this subject he noted 'Nos limitaremos á señalar aquí el uranismo, inversión genital ó sexual, homo-sexualidad, perversión caracterizada por la dirección exclusiva de la inclinación amorosa hacia personas del mismo sexo' [We will confine ourselves to Uranism, sexual or genital inversion, homosexuality, a perversion characterized by the exclusive interest in the amorous inclination towards persons of the same sex].[82] The newness of such thought is shown by Régis's comment that authors who had studied the subject, above all in Germany, had insisted that Uranism was very different from common pederasty. Uranism, he continued, was above all a psychic disturbance, in which the soul and body of the individual did not conform to the same sex. What would spark off this morbid predisposition? The psyche of such individuals was so fragile and so damaged that any incident susceptible of harming the imagination of the subject by creating a 'psycho-genital' association in their childhood or youth 'orienta su vida sexual exclusiva, impulsivamente, hacia una perversión en relación con el incidente primitivo' [would orient, exclusively and impulsively, his life towards a perversion in accordance with the original incident].[83] Once more, the importance of the inheritance of certain traits was coupled to particular environmental conditions that could spark off the slide into perversion is evident in this psychiatric account.

It is striking that Juarros, on writing his *Psiquiatría forense* imitated not only much of the structure of the French psychiatrist's book but also its contents to the extent of using in some places practically the same wording as Régis. This was basically a degenerationist analysis, and Juarros covered the concepts of hereditary and non-hereditary predisposition extensively in the volume which was arranged in twenty lessons or chapters.[84] When it came to the 'sexual perversions', Juarros followed Régis's account, understanding these as symptoms of mental illness, and added to Régis's list by including some others of a much more archaic variety such as nymphomania and satyriasis.[85] The sexual perversions were listed from (a) to (i), beginning with masturbation, passing through exhibitionism, fetishism, sadism, masochism, and finally Uranism.[86] 'Uranism', Juarros declared, was love towards another of the same sex: 'Antes se tenía de los uranistas un concepto totalmente distinto del actual' [Before, one had a totally different idea about Uranians].[87] Furthermore, it was necessary to distinguish the Uranian from the pederast 'que llega á esta perversión arrastrado por una vida de crápula' [who arrives at this perversion through a life of debauchery]. The Uranian, Juarros wrote on the other hand 'es físicamente hombre y psíquicamente mujer ó viceversa' [is physically a man and psychically a woman or vice versa].[88] In contrast, Juarros was then to note, 'El *pederasta* es un hombre que prefiere el amor de otro hombre' [The *pederast* is a man who prefers the love of another man]. In this schema, the Uranian would have been predisposed to engage in the sexual acts hinted at or would have a hereditary condition making him do so, if the degenerationist framework were to be made explicit. On the other hand, the pederast would have lent himself to acquired tastes. Both, nevertheless, were either dangerous for the individual concerned or for society at large.[89] How the Uranian could be distinguished from the pederast was not explained.

Such a framework was equally explicit in his 1919 work, *La Psiquiatría del médico general.*[90] Among the causes of mental illness ('enfermedades mentales' or 'psiconeuroses') Juarros listed degeneration, inheritance and predisposition. He was careful to separate the latter two concepts, which, he noted, had become confused in the writings of many psychiatrists of the time. An inherited trait would eventually become manifest, while a predisposition had to be triggered by some event or state of affairs.[91] The 'deformations' that degeneration could entail were manifested in physical and psychic symptoms or stigmas which could be detected clinically.[92] The causes of mental illness, thus broken down, coincided with those he detailed in his *Psiquiatría forense*

(1914) and included degeneration, hereditary factors, predisposition, infection, fatigue, race, age and sex, contagion and profession. From these causes of mental illness, a number of 'symptoms' could arise such as a dysfunctional memory, delirium, phobias, questions of conscience, physical symptoms such as blood disorders and insomnia and a number of instincts. In the latter case, there were two kinds of symptoms, individual and 'los instintos de la especie'.[93] These 'instincts of the species', the sexual instincts, were understood to be 'El instinto eje de la vida de la especie' [The key instinct in the life of the species].[94] Interestingly, they could be both the cause and the symptom of mental illness: 'por ser tan hondo, tan recio, tan indomable, el instinto sexual desempeña un papel importantísimo en la Psiquiatría como síntoma unas veces, como causa otras' [because it is so profound, so strong, so indomitable, the sexual instinct plays an all important role in psychiatry as a symptom some times and at other times as a cause].[95] Homosexuality was understood in this section to be a symptom of psychic inhibition or of the influence of civilization, which 'ha introducido en las manifestaciones sexuales un elemento psíquico que explica esta última reciprocidad entre el instinto y lo puramente intelectual' [has introduced in sexual life a psychic element that explains this reciprocity between instinct and that which is purely intellectual].[96]

Was homosexuality purely a volitional or intellectual symptom or something larger then? Juarros did not wish to imply this. Homosexuality and sapphism, he wrote, 'tienen su punto de partida en la infancia, que como hemos dicho, es bisexual. En ciertos individuos se conservan ambas tendencias; son varios los homosexuales que además tienen relaciones sexuales con mujeres, como abundan las safistas que desdeñan buscar también el placer entre brazos masculinos' [have their starting point in childhood, which, as we have said, is bisexual. In certain individuals both tendencies are conserved; there are many homosexuals who also have sexual relations with women, just as there is an abundance of sapphists who do not eschew pleasure in the arms of men].[97] Apart from childhood influences, these individuals also betray stigmas of degeneration 'pero la alteración sexual no tiene carácter constitucional' [but the sexual deviancy has no constitutional character].[98]

The actual causes of homosexuality (in the forms of Uranism and pederasty), in Juarros's schemes as detailed in his *Psiquiatría*

forense and his *Psiquiatría del médico general*, begin to become less
and less clear. As we have seen in the work of Marañón, and will
see from discussions held in later years with respect to homosexuality, the acquired/congenital conundrum that many psychiatrists
and others entered into was never really resolved satisfactorily.
Juarros had declared that degeneration was something constitutional which was rooted in the subject's ancestors. Despite having
declared that sexual deviancy was not constitutional in one part of
his book, he went on to write that the 'sexual perversions' were
'always a degenerative stigma',[99] resulting from the union, in most
cases, of physical and psychic sexuality. Thus, most 'sexual perversions' would be constitutional, either because of physical or
psychic causes, or a combination of both: 'Podrá ocurrir que la
influencia del medio, o el contagio mental determinan en algunos sujetos la aparición de perversiones y aberraciones sexuales;
pero esto es lo excepcional, lo común es que tales aberraciones y
perversiones sean traducción de un estado degenerativo' [It may
come to pass that the influence of the environment or mental
contagion determines on some occasions the appearance of
sexual aberrations and perversions. But this is exceptional and
what is more common is that these aberrations and perversions
are the product of a degenerate state].[100] The definition of the
pervert as a constitutional degenerate in many respects still
retained elements of the volitional, an aspect that was characteristic of the days in which Mata spoke of those who 'had the *habit* of
committing a [pederastic] act' and those who did not.[101]

Another foreign work of psychiatry, written by E. Bleuler, was
published in Spain in 1924. In his prologue to this work the nerve
specialist and histologist Santiago Ramón y Cajal lamented the
fact that few Spanish psychiatrists were acquainted with the
German language and the 'conceptos elaborados allende el Rin'
[concepts elaborated on the other side of the Rhine].[102] Part of
the objective of translating foreign works such as those of Régis,
Bleuler and Bumke[103] in the first two decades of the twentieth
century was, naturally, the dissemination of psychiatric ideas on
mental illness and, concomitantly, on the 'sexual perversions'. If
the percolation of such ideas in the Spanish medical sciences was
slow, or if such ideas were resisted in some quarters as was the case
of the more somatic sciences discussed earlier, two areas where
they were to find a home was in the disciplines of pedagogy (see

Chapters Two and Four) and, as we will see below, the more popularly oriented sexology of the 1930s.

Psychological and Psychoanalytical Frameworks from the 1920s Onwards

The reception of psychoanalytic ideas in Spain was not predominantly Freudian, at least until the mid 1920s; nor was it overwhelmingly, as a consequence, in favour of Freud's theory of pansexualism.[104] In addition, there were huge theoretical differences between psychiatric frameworks heavily influenced by new psychoanalysis and the more biological and positivist psychology of the end of the nineteenth and early twentieth century.[105]

Opposition to Freud's theory of pansexualism, to the sexual significance of everyday objects and as a key to understanding the genesis of neuroses was acute from approximately 1914 onwards. Enrique Fernández Sanz, despite being one of the first to introduce Freud into Spain,[106] was highly critical of Freud in his 1914 work on hysteria.[107] The final words of his work left no room for doubt: 'En suma, la escuela psicoanalítica pasará a la historia estigmatizada por la reprobación de los pensadores imparciales. No es probable que desaparezca todo el material de estudio por ella acumulado, pues quedarán algunas de sus minuciosas investigaciones sobre los mecanismos de la actividad sexual. *En cuanto al psicoanálisis, como metodo* [sic] *terapéutico, debe radicalmente desecharse por ser, no sólo inútil, sino además perjudicial*' [In sum, the psychoanalytic school will pass into history stigmatized by the rejection of impartial thinkers. It is not probable that all the research material accumulated by it will disappear as some of its minute studies on the mechanisms of sexual activity will remain relevant. *Psychoanalysis as a therapeutical method should be rejected without question as it is not only useless but also harmful*].[108]

These kinds of thought found echoes in prestigious medical journals such as the *Archivos de Medicina, Cirugía y Especialidades*. In the pages of this review, there were several attacks on what authors viewed as an overemphasis on the importance of sexuality in childhood and on sexuality as a means of explaining neuroses. As part of a repudiation of the desire of psychoanalysis to conquer all fields and to award primacy to Freud's pansexualism, a number of national and foreign authors made strident contributions. Henri

Roger, of the Marseilles Medical School, was to comment that 'El psico-análisis sexual no se acantona en los dominios psicológicos y neuro-psquiátricos. Equivocadamente quiere invadirlo todo' [Sexual psychoanalysis does not limit itself to the psychological and neuro-psychiatric domain. It wants to invade everything].[109]

This kind of critique of psychoanalysis, followed by another from Fernández Sanz a few weeks later,[110] was contested by José Sanchis-Banús who argued that the importance of the libido in neuroses was confirmed in that it was not the sexual instinct itself that was a cause of later problems but rather the repression of the morbid inclinations of sex.[111] In order to achieve ontogenetic mental health it was necessary that the individual passed through all the phases that had been suffered by the whole species: autoeroticism, incest, homosexuality, to finally, emerge into heterosexuality, displaying a standard, if vulgarized psychoanalytic understanding of human sexual development.

The refusal to confine psychoanalysis to the Freudian school was followed through by major figures in the discipline such as Emilio Mira y López, who was to become professor of psychiatry at the Autonomous University of Barcelona from 1931 to 1939. His 1926 work, *El psicoanàlisi*, did not follow one school of thought and was typically eclectic (Mira cited, amongst others, Stekel, Rank, Jung and Adler). His analysis offered an interpretation of the libido that was not sexual, but vitalist, following a Bergsonian model of energy. Mira also argued, like Jung, that neuroses may have their origin in the present rather than exclusively in the past. Sexual conflicts in the present made people return to child-like beings.[112] Others followed suit: in 1936 J. J. López Ibor critiqued the pansexualism of Freud and proposed a fusion between the three systems envisaged by Freud, Adler and Jung.[113]

An indicator of the reception of psychoanalytic ideas and the eclectic frameworks that were followed is offered by the *Archivos de Neurobiología*, founded in 1920. The initial organizing committee of the review was as eclectic as its subject matter comprising amongst others, Ramón y Cajal, Augusto Pi Suñer, Ricardo Nóvoa Santos, Juan Negrín, Gregorio Marañón, Pío del Río Hortega, Luis Simarro, José Sacristán and Gonzalo Rodríguez Lafora.[114] The title of the review – in its full form, *Los Archivos de Neurobiología, Psicología, Fisiología, Histología, Neurología y Psiquiatría* – illustrates not only how Spanish psychiatry at the time was still strongly rooted in nineteenth-century concepts, awarding primacy, or at least a great deal of emphasis to biological and somatic elements, but it also illustrates how the review in its very title was an attempt to integrate the rather disparate moods of the science at the time.[115] This 'fusion' was carried forward into the 1930s and beyond and is once more indicative of the desire for collaboration and the marking out of a professional space, which held primacy over coherence or compatibility of theoretical positions. This was yet another tactical alliance. While differences existed, for example, in the sphere of legal medicine, or in treatises on criminology, what united experts was an *esprit de corps* not seen to the same extent in England or France, where divergences and disputes more readily reached the pages of specialist reviews.

It is quite possible that this equivocal relationship between psychiatrists, psychoanalysts and the conflictive reception of ideas by European theorists such as Freud, Adler and Jung had a detrimental effect on the articulation of theories of sexuality from a psychoanalytic viewpoint. Certainly, the most vociferous accounts of sexual and gender deviance came not from psychoanalysis but from applied psychiatry and, as we have seen, from renovated somatic accounts of hermaphroditism and endocrinology. In the late 1920s and early 1930s these ideas increasingly surpassed the limits of specialist journals and became integrated into the public imaginary. This, at least, was the explicit aim articulated by one major forum where such ideas were expressed. The extraordinary psychiatric review *Sexualidad*, published in Madrid from 1925 to 1928, was replete with the latest theories on sexuality articulated within a psychiatric and eugenic framework combined with a strong moral stance.[116] Such dissemination in more popular forums also allowed for a political dimension to emerge around the category of homosexuality, particularly in the light of new attempts to criminalize the practice, and further during the period opened up by the Republic in 1931. We now consider these new dimensions emergent in the late 1920s.

Tactical Alliances?

It is possible that given the social and political situation in which Spain found itself towards the end of the 1920s, the dominant uniting cause amongst liberal or progressive scientists was the modernization project that had enabled the suspension of the ideological battles of the pre-1898 period. The 'civil discourse' thus formed by establishment politicians and scientists alike would make the playing down or disappearance of theoretical differences the order of the day.[117] Rather, tactical alliances were forged. Even though the uses made of Freud amongst sex reformers in the Cortes of the Second Republic were substantially different – Marañón and Nóvoa Santos appropriated Freudian concepts to underline characterological types more in tune with traditional sex roles, while Sanchis Banús and Juarros used Freud to attack the old morality[118] – the lack of defined fields, the degree of eclecticism or the generosity of the players, meant that the most unlikely disciplines could be assembled together to do battle.

Emblematic of this kind of alliance was the linkage established by Marañón between criminology and the science of endocrinology. Conceding that the ability of the glands to determine behaviour had perhaps been overemphasized, Marañón was to acknowledge in his prologue to Saldaña's 1936 book on criminology that the effects of the internal secretions were in fact rarely decisive.[119] The approach offered by Saldaña in his *Nueva criminología*, however, was less flexible. Heredity, he wrote, was the prime factor guiding human actions, even though in the majority of cases human beings could modify its influence. Nevertheless, in tune with Marañón's words of praise for those penologists who had taken the biological aspects of criminality seriously, Saldaña was willing to accept a strong link between sexual life and criminality: 'Si el Psicoanálisis nos enseña cómo toda la vida del hombre . . . es vida sexual, directa o transformada, todo delito, en su etiología psicológica profunda, sería *delito sexual*' [If psychoanalysis teaches us that the whole of human life . . . is essentially a sexual life, whether directly so or in modified form, all crimes in their deep psychological aetiology are *sexual crimes*]. Within this context homosexuality was viewed as one source of crime.[120]

As was the case of the review *Sexualidad* mentioned above, Saldaña had made this link between criminality and homosexuality towards the end of the 1920s and more extensively in a book published in 1930.[121] In this latter account, which was strongly pedagogical in tone, Saldaña viewed masturbatory narcissism, an idea he took from Hesnard's *Psicología homosexual*, as a point of departure for the development of full homosexuality. Acknowledging the specialism that had grown up in Germany on the relationship between sexual inversion and crime, Saldaña warned that the spectre of homosexuality which had haunted society from the days when sodomy was punished in early Christian times was still alive and well. While on the one hand he noted that the Penal Code of 1928 punished male homosexual acts with a fine, something which he believed unjust because the grown-up homosexual had once been seduced himself by other 'unfortunates', on the other hand Saldaña invited much more draconian measures to combat these 'half men' who exhibited a 'state of homosexual dangerousness'. Firm security measures were required; Forel, he noted, advocated deporting homosexuals to a desert island. For Saldaña 'Mejor sería el forzoso tratamiento psiquiátrico, en sanatorios adecuados. Para eso fuera preciso admitir como prueba el reconocimiento facultativo, por buenos médicos, del órgano perisexual de los invertidos (eso, por otra parte, les placería a ellos sobremanera)' [It would be better to provide obligatory psychiatric treatment in special sanatoria. In order to do this, it would be necessary to carry out a medical examination as proof [of their sexual inversion] of the perisexual organ [the region of the anus] of inverts by good doctors. (This, by the way, would please them to no little degree)].[122]

The uniting of late nineteenth-century medico-legal examinations together with a belligerent campaign of repression, within the framework of 'social dangerousness', with the added abuses that psychiatry was prepared to afford, would not have to wait long: Franco's regime placed homosexuals in prisons and concentration camps, set up a department of the state on the 'homosexual question', and used electro-shock treatment and other means to combat the state of dangerousness that homosexuals were considered to engender.[123]

NOTES

[1]   See R. Huertas García-Alejo, 'El concepto de "perversión sexual" en la medicina positivista', *Asclepio*, 42, 2 (1990), 89–100 (91–4), and F. Vázquez García and A. Moreno Mengíbar, *Sexo y Razón. Una Genealogía de la Moral Sexual en España (siglos XVI–XX)* (Madrid: Akal, 1997), p. 31. On the impact of Tardieu and his thought generally see V. A.

Rosario, *The Erotic Imagination: French Histories of Perversity* (New York/Oxford: Oxford University Press, 1997), pp. 72–7. Tardieu's book was translated into Spanish in 1863 by the Madrid forensic doctors Nemesio López Bustamente and Juan de Querejazu y Hartzensbuch from the third French edition and appeared as *Estudio médico-forense de los atentados contra la honestidad* (Madrid: Manuel Álvarez, 1863).

2   There are significant differences between one edition and another of Pedro Mata's *Tratado de Medicina y Cirugía Legal.* The first edition came out in 1846, the third in 1857 and the expanded fifth in 1874, published by Bailly-Baillière of Paris. The arrival of Tardieu's thought significantly altered the contents of Mata's *Tratado,* the insights of which are incorporated into the four-volume edition of 1874. On these changes see R. Cleminson and R. M. Medina Doménech, '¿Mujer u hombre? Hermafroditismo, tecnologías médicas e identificación de sexo en España, 1860–1925', *Dynamis,* 24 (2004), 53–91 (72–80) and R. M. Cleminson, 'The Significance of the "Fairy" for the Cultural Archaeology of Same-Sex Male Desire in Spain, 1850–1930', *Sexualities,* 7, 4 (2004), 412–29 (417–20).

3   J. de Letamendi, *Curso de Clínica General,* 2 vols, (Madrid: Imp. de los Sucesores de Cuesta, 1894).

4   The ways in which psychiatrists were slowly incorporated into the legal mechanism of the state, often tailoring their thought in accordance with the exigencies of the period, are discussed in R. Campos Marín, 'La teoría de la degeneración y la profesionalización de la psiquiatría en España (1876–1920)', *Asclepio,* 51(1), 1999, 185–203. The author argues that psychiatrists would use degenerationist theories in court extensively but would be more reticent to do so in the clinic. Part of the reason for this was psychiatrists' desire to become integrated into the apparatus of the state thus confirming their professional status.

5   For a discussion of some of these matters see T. Ortiz, 'El discurso médico sobre las mujeres en la España del primer tercio del siglo veinte', in M. T. López Beltrán (ed.), *Las mujeres en Andalucía. Actas del 2º encuentro interdisciplinar de estudios de la mujer en Andalucía,* vol. I (Málaga: Diputación Provincial de Málaga, 1993), pp. 107–38 and M. Nash, 'Género y ciudadanía', *Ayer,* 20, (1995), 241–58. On the 'dangers' of the female vote see J. Gómez Ocaña, *El sexo, el hominismo y la natalidad* (Madrid: Editorial Saturnino Calleja, 1919), esp. p. 51.

6   R. Álvarez Peláez, 'Introducción al estudio de la eugenesia española (1900–1936)', *Quipu,* 2, 1 (1985), 95–122; R. Álvarez Peláez, 'El Instituto de Medicina Social: primeros intentos de institucionalizar la eugenesia', *Asclepio,* 40 (1988), 343–58; E. Amezúa, 'Cien años de temática sexual en España: 1850–1950. Repertorio y análisis. Contribución al estudio de materiales para una historia de la sexología', *Revista de Sexología,* 48 (1991), 1–197; E. Amezúa, 'Los hijos de Don Santiago: paseo por el casco antiguo de nuestra sexología', *Revista de Sexología,* 59–60 (1993), 1–281; R. Cleminson and E. Amezúa, 'Spain: the political and social context of sex reform in the late nineteenth

and early twentieth centuries', in F. X. Eder, L. Hall and G. Hekma (eds), *Sexual Cultures in Europe. National Histories* (Manchester, Manchester University Press, 1999), pp. 173–96.

7   Vázquez García and Moreno Mengíbar, *Sexo y Razón*, pp. 32–43.

8   The notion that the medical sciences in their consideration of homosexuality were a response to other concerns outside medicine or even from homosexuals themselves, as a 'reverse discourse', is contained in G. Chauncey, 'Christian Brotherhood or Sexual Perversion? Homosexual Identities and the Construction of Sexual Boundaries in the World War One Era', *Journal of Social History*, 19 (1985), 189–211. For an extensive discussion of related ideas see H. Oosterhuis, *Stepchildren of Nature: Krafft-Ebing, Psychiatry, and the Making of Sexual Identity* (Chicago/London: University of Chicago Press, 2000).

9   G. Chauncey, 'From Sexual Inversion to Homosexuality: The Changing Medical Conceptualization of Female "Deviance"', in K. Peiss and C. Simmons (eds), *Passion and Power: Sexuality in History*, (Philadelphia: Temple University Press, 1989), pp. 87–117 (p. 99), originally published in 1982–3, republished here with a postscript.

10   See G. Marañón, *La doctrina de las secreciones internas* (Madrid: Corona, 1918), originally given as a conference at the Madrid Ateneo in 1915.

11   G. Marañón, 'Acerca del problema de la intersexualidad', *El Siglo Médico*, 4082 (1932), 243–7 (245). Brachfeld's article was 'Crítica de las teorías sexuales del Dr. Marañón', *El Siglo Médico*, 4081 (1932), 214–21.

12   On the process of extinction of the 'marvellous' hermaphrodite by the mid nineteenth century see M. Foucault, *Los Anormales. Curso del Collège de France (1974–1975)* (Madrid: Akal Universitaria, 2001), pp. 57–78, and, F. Vázquez García, 'La imposible fusión. Claves para una genealogía del cuerpo andrógino', in D. Romero de Solís, J. B. Díaz-Urmeneta Muñoz and J. López-Lloret (eds), *Variaciones sobre el cuerpo* (Seville: Universidad de Sevilla, 1999), pp. 217–35.

13   On the change from the 'one-sex' model to the 'two-sex' model see T. Laqueur, *Making sex: body and gender from the Greeks to Freud* (Cambridge, Mass./London: Harvard University Press, 1990), pp. 25–62, 149–92. On the history of hermaphroditism in Spain, see Vázquez García, 'La imposible fusión'; Cleminson and Medina Doménech, '¿Mujer u hombre?'; M. J. de la Pascua Sánchez, '¿Hombres vueltos del revés? Una historia sobre la construcción de la identidad sexual en el siglo XVIII', in M. J. de la Pascua, M. del Rosario García-Doncel and G. Espigado (eds), *Mujer y deseo* (Cadiz: Universidad de Cádiz, 2004), pp. 431–44.

14   Comenge wrote in his *Generación y Crianza ó higiene de la familia* (Barcelona: José Espasa, Editor, n.d.) 'Lo que sé se ha observado es el hermafrodita *aparente* en quien los órganos exteriores de la generación mal conformados' [What I know to have been observed is the *apparent* hermaphrodite in whom the poor conformation of the external organs of generation], which engendered doubt as to the 'true' sex of the individual (p. 147).

15 Comenge, *Generación y Crianza*, p. 147.
16 R. Nóvoa Santos, *Manual de patología general*, 3 vols, (Santiago de Compostela: Tipografía El Eco de Santiago, 1916–19), vol. I (1916), pp. 414–17. In his later third volume of 1919, there is mention of the role of psychosexual disorders in the production of sexual inversion. This matter is discussed below. This kind of somatic approach continued more or less untouched by the insights of both psychiatry and psychoanalysis in works well into the third decade of the twentieth century. See, for example, the Spanish translation of the collective work, mainly of foreign authors, by J. Rof Carballo, *Tratado de fisiología patológica especial* (Barcelona: Editorial Labor, 1936). Here, masculinization and feminization of rats after hormonal addition are discussed, as is 'pseudo-hermaphroditism', which is still seen in terms of a 'vicio de conformación'.
17 N. Oudshoorn, 'Endocrinologists and the conceptualization of sex, 1920–1940', *Journal of the History of Biology*, 23, 2 (1990), 163–86.
18 It is difficult to assess the impact of these usually short accounts in the wider medical field. The fact that they appeared in reputable and influential journals indicate that hermaphroditism in particular and sexuality in general were areas that were of interest to the profession. No such accounts appeared, however, in other, equally reputable journals. For example, the *Revista Ibero-americana de ciencias médicas* from 1915–20 and from 1923–34 contained no major article on hermaphroditism, intersexuality or homosexuality, according to its index. The same was the case of *Los Progresos de la Clínica* from 1927–30 and from 1932–5. The *Revista Médica de Barcelona* contained few reports on the subject area in the years 1924 through to 1935. A fuller discussion of these materials takes place in Cleminson and Medina Doménech, '¿Mujer u hombre?'.
19 Marañón, *La doctrina de las secreciones internas.*
20 That Marañón entered the medical and popular imaginary as a figure who fought for a more progressive treatment of homosexuals as well as a more fluid conceptualization of what we now term gender is shown by the praise and criticism afforded to him by figures as diverse as Hildegart, San de Velilla and Martí Ibáñez. See, respectively, Hildegart, *El problema sexual tratado por una mujer española* (Madrid: Morata, 1931); A. San de Velilla, *Sodoma y Lesbos Modernos: Pederastas y Safistas, estudiados en la clínica, en los libros y en la historia* (Barcelona: Carlos Ameller, 1932); F. Martí Ibáñez, 'Consideraciones sobre el homosexualismo', *Estudios*, 145 (1935), 3–6. The fact that Marañón became associated with matters sexual in general to the level of the Spanish Cortes is shown by his presence in the parliament in the first period of the Republic and the references made to his ideas therein. See, for example, the mention of hysteria invoked around the debate on the female vote recorded in C. Campoamor, *Mi pecado mortal: el voto femenino y yo* (Seville: Instituto Andaluz de la Mujer, 2001 [1936]), p. 58. That this was a lasting phenomenon is shown by the scurrilous treatment that Marañón's work received in the paranoid work of M. Carlavilla del Barrio, *Sodomitas* (Madrid:

Editorial Nos, 1956), esp. pp. 77–124, where his work is denigrated as part of 'La escuela científica sodomizante' [The sodomizing scientific school].

21 What follows is a discussion drawn firstly from G. Marañón, 'Nuevas ideas sobre el problema de la intersexualidad y sobre la cronología de los sexos', in *Obras Completas*, vol. IV (Madrid: Espasa-Calpe, 1976), pp. 165–83 (original 1928). Marañón later elaborated on his theory of intersexuality and homosexuality in *Los estados intersexuales de la especie humana* published in 1929. This was one of many revisions and discussions on hermaphroditism, intersexuality and homosexuality which developed into our second source, *La evolución de la sexualidad y los estados intersexuales*, in *Obras Completas*, vol. VIII (Madrid: Espasa-Calpe, 1972), pp. 499–710. This book was published as a second edition by Morata, Madrid, in 1930. Throughout the 1940s and beyond Marañón returned to the subject area. We concentrate here on his 1928 essay, usually neglected by historians who focus preferentially on his 1930 work. Because Marañón continually revised his ideas and since our aim is not to write a full history of these ideas here, the 1928 essay, with some comments drawn from the 1930 book, form the bulk of our subject matter.

22 Marañón, 'Nuevas ideas', 165.

23 In this sense, Marañón's ideas were a precursor to Kinsey's own scale of masculinity and femininity developed in the 1940s and 1950s. Kinsey did come to Madrid and he met Marañón. For a brief note on the encounter, see Amezúa, 'Los hijos de Don Santiago', 15–19.

24 Marañón, 'Nuevas ideas', 165.

25 G. Marañón, 'Educación sexual y diferenciación sexual', in *Ensayos sobre la vida sexual*, in *Obras Completas*, vol. VIII, pp. 247–364 (p. 345).

26 Marañón, 'Nuevas ideas', 178.

27 Marañón, 'Nuevas ideas', 169.

28 Marañón, 'Nuevas ideas', 169.

29 Marañón, 'Nuevas ideas', 170.

30 Marañón, 'Nuevas ideas', 182. Emphasis in original.

31 Marañón, 'Nuevas ideas', 182. Emphasis in original.

32 Marañón, 'Nuevas ideas', 182. Emphasis in original.

33 Glick, 'Marañón, Intersexuality', where a note written in the 1915 edition of Freud's *Three Essays on the Theory of Sexuality* is cited.

34 Marañón, *La evolución de la sexualidad*, p. 608.

35 G. Marañón, 'La educación sexual y la diferenciación sexual', *Generación Consciente*, 31 (1926), 15–18 and *Generación Consciente*, 32 (1926), 42–5. Marañón notes, for example, 'Puede asegurarse que el homosexualismo, producto aún de la insuficiente diferenciación sexual. . . ' [We can be sure that homosexualism, another product of the lack of sexual differentiation . . .] (45). Perversion, however, was not on the increase, despite what some commentators argued. Human evolution, coupled with sound education, would eliminate the perversions: 'Pensemos que un Dios justiciero y preocupado de la moral de sus criaturas no tendría hoy, al cabo de tantos siglos, que

recurrir al fuego para destruír ninguna nueva Sodoma: le bastaría con unos cuantos hombres inteligentes, repartidos por las escuelas y los confesonarios' [Let us believe that a just God who looks alter the morality of his creatures today would not, after so many centuries, have to have recourse to fire in order to destroy any new Sodom. What he would need are a few intelligent men shared out amongst the schools and confessionals] (45).

[36] Nóvoa Santos, *Manual de Patología General*, vol. III, p. 119.

[37] Nóvoa Santos, *Manual de Patología General*, vol. III, p. 120.

[38] Nóvoa Santos, *Manual de Patología General*, vol. III, p. 120.

[39] Marañón, *La evolución de la sexualidad*, p. 614.

[40] This partial separation of homosexuality from gender deviance was evident, as we have seen, in the nineteenth century but increasingly in the twentieth, especially from the 1920s onwards. An early example of this partial separation is Max-Bembo, *La mala vida en Barcelona. Anormalidad, miseria y vicio* (Barcelona: Maucci, 1912). A later example, A. Martín de Lucenay, *Homosexualidad* (Madrid: Editorial Fénix, 1933), will be discussed below in Chapters Four and Six.

[41] Marañón, 'Nuevas ideas', 171.

[42] See G. Marañón, 'Notas para la biología de Don Juan', in *Obras Completas*, vol. IV, *Artículos y otros trabajos* (Madrid: Espasa-Calpe, 1968), pp. 75–93 (original published in the *Revista de Occidente* in 1924). Marañón's conference in the Royal National Academy of Medicine in Madrid of the same year was entitled 'Psicopatología del donjuanismo', reproduced in *Obras Completas*, vol. III, *Conferencias* (Madrid: Espasa-Calpe, 1967), pp. 75–93. An excellent recent study of Marañón's medicalization of Don Juan is contained in S. Wright, 'The "Cult of Sex", Effeminacy and Intersexuality in Early Twentieth-Century Spain: Gregorio Marañón's "The Psychopathology of Don Juan" (1924)', *Bulletin of Spanish Studies*, 81, 6 (2004), 717–38.

[43] Barco Teruel, *Elogio y nostalgia de Gregorio Marañón* (Barcelona: Barca, 1961), p. 41, cited in Wright, 'The "Cult of Sex"', 731–2. Marañón was not to remain a merely a national polemical figure, as we have seen with respect to Oliver Brachfeld's criticism of his work. In addition to Brachfeld, Alfred Adler refuted Marañón's explanations of homosexuality and denied its congenital basis. For him, as expressed in his *El problema del homosexualismo* (Barcelona: Apolo, 1936), homosexuality resulted from environmental causes, particularly timidity with respect to the other sex.

[44] Wright, 'The "Cult of Sex"', 739.

[45] Cited in Wright, 'The "Cult of Sex"', 732.

[46] Gregorio Marañón, *Don Juan. Ensayos sobre el origen de su leyenda*, in *Obras Completas*, VII, *Biografías* (Madrid: Espasa-Calpe, 1971), pp. 179–250 (p. 213). Cited in Wright, 'The "Cult of Sex"', 733.

[47] G. Rodríguez Lafora, for example, rejected Marañón's notion of 'frontier homosexuality' in Don Juan. While he accepted that Don Juan was hypereroticised and of hysterical character, he extended, as had many others, the idea of hysteria to cover men without any

notion of femininity. Lafora postulates two possible theories to explain Don Juan's behaviour. First, that a first love in his youth was so strong that he cannot commit to another, hence his scepticism in finding a love that would surpass it. Second, his butterfly-like approach to women can be explained by his voluble, melodramatic, erotic and polygamous spirit. His devotion to eroticism means that he cannot settle on one object. See G. Rodríguez Lafora, 'La psicología de Don Juan', in *Don Juan, Los milagros y otros ensayos*, Alianza, Madrid, 1975 [1927], pp. 7–44 (pp. 31–3).

[48] Marañón, *La evolución de la sexualidad*, p. 607.

[49] Marañón, *La evolución de la sexualidad*, p. 608.

[50] Marañón, *La evolución de la sexualidad*, p. 608. Elsewhere in this book Marañón discussed the experiments with testicular transplants by Steinach and Lipschütz but suspended judgement on them. For Marañón the emphasis was placed on prevention rather than cure. See Marañón, *La evolución de la sexualidad*, p. 608.

[51] Marañón, *La evolución de la sexualidad*, p. 609.

[52] Marañón, *La evolución de la sexualidad*, p. 610. Emphasis in original

[53] Marañón, *La evolución de la sexualidad*, pp. 611–13.

[54] Marañón, *La evolución de la sexualidad*, p. 609.

[55] Marañón, *La evolución de la sexualidad*, p. 609.

[56] Marañón, *La evolución de la sexualidad*, pp. 609–10.

[57] Marañón, *La evolución de la sexualidad*, p. 610.

[58] Marañón, *La evolución de la sexualidad*, pp. 611–13.

[59] Marañón, *La evolución de la sexualidad*, p. 615. Emphasis in original.

[60] Marañón, *La evolución de la sexualidad*, p. 616. Marañón noted that Stekel, whose theory of homosexuality relied on the original bisexuality of the organism, believed that the heterosexual impulse dominated the homosexual in normal persons and the inverse in homosexuals. In either case, the other tendency could occasionally overtake and the primarily heterosexual individual could engage in homosexual acts. The reverse could take place especially if the homosexual was under the effects of alcohol or dreams (Marañón, *La evolución de la sexualidad*, p. 609, n. 2). The work by Stekel referred to by Marañón was *Onania und Homosexualität* (Berlin, 1923). For Letamendi's ideas see J. de Letamendi, *Curso de Clínica General* (Madrid: Imp. de los Sucesores de Cuesta, 1894), 2 vols, vol. II, pp. 119–21. Letamendi wrote that 'Toda aberración sexual humana es acto de atavismo, que radica en la condición hermafrodita' [All human sexual aberrations are the result of atavism, which is rooted in the hermaphroditic condition] (p. 119). For F. Martí Ibáñez see his 'Consideraciones sobre el homosexualismo'.

[61] Marañón, *La evolución de la sexualidad*, p. 620.

[62] Marañón, *La evolución de la sexualidad*, p. 621.

[63] Marañón, *La evolución de la sexualidad*, p. 622.

[64] Marañón, *La evolución de la sexualidad*, pp. 623–5.

[65] Marañón, *La evolución de la sexualidad*, p. 625.

[66] Marañón, *La evolución de la sexualidad*, p. 625.

[67] In 1936 Marañón acknowledged that he had perhaps overestimated

the determining action of the endocrine glands in human behaviour. The action of internal secretions was now viewed by him as one factor in human personality amongst many others of diverse sources. See Marañón's prologue, 'La endocrinología y la ciencia penal', in Q. Saldaña, *Nueva criminología* (Madrid: M. Aguilar, 1936), pp. 7–18.

68 See the two-part 'Refutación de las teorías de la intersexualidad', *El Siglo Médico*, 4085 (1932), 321–5, and in *El Siglo Médico*, 4090 (1932), 457–63 by Criado y Aguilar.

69 Criado y Aguilar, 'Refutación de las teorías de la intersexualidad', 463.

70 Á. Pulido Martín, 'Algunos conceptos modernos sobre la potencia sexual', *El Siglo Médico*, 3498 (1920), 977–9 (978).

71 See his 'Prólogo' to I. Bloch, *La vida sexual contemporánea*, 2 vols, (Madrid: Editora Internacional, 1924), vol. I, pp. v–xvi.

72 T. F. Glick, 'Marañón, Intersexuality and the Biological Construction of Gender in 1920s Spain, *Cronos*, 8 (1), (2005), 121–37. This paragraph is largely drawn from Glick's argument.

73 C. E. Russett, *Sexual Science: The Victorian Construction of Womanhood* (Cambridge, Mass.: Harvard University Press, 1989), p. 55.

74 M. Foucault, *Los Anormales. Curso del Collège de France (1974–1975)* (Madrid: Akal, 2001), pp. 265–91, esp. pp. 282–91.

75 Foucault, *Los Anormales*, p. 283.

76 Foucault, *Los Anormales*, p. 285.

77 See F. Álvarez-Uría, *Miserables y locos: medicina mental y orden social en la España del siglo XIX* (Barcelona: Tusquets, 1983); Huertas García-Alejo, 'El concepto de "perversión sexual"'; M. Richards, 'Spanish Psychiatry *c.*1900–1945: Constitutional Theory, Eugenics, and the Nation', *Bulletin of Spanish Studies*, 81, 6 (2004), 823–48.

78 E. Régis, *Tratado de Psiquiatría* (Madrid: Saturnino Calleja Fernández, 1911). The translation was from the fourth French edition. The fact that Juarros translated the work by Régis, which spoke of the 'impulsos sexuales' as instincts and bearing in mind that Juarros himself wrote his *Psiquiatría forense* (Madrid: Imprenta de Antonio Marzo, 1914), following the same ideas and even, at times, the same wording of Régis, would allow us to reaffirm the periodization of psychological accounts offered by H. Carpintero, 'Influencias germánicas en la psicología española', in J. de Salas and D. Briesemeister (eds), *Las influencias de las culturas académicas alemana y española desde 1898 hasta 1936* (Madrid/Frankfurt: Ibero-americana/ Vervuert, 2000), pp. 223–37. Carpintero argued that psychology in Spain underwent three main periods from 1876 to 1936. These were: 1876–1907, a period characterized by psycho-physical thought which drew on the work of Krause and Spencer; a second period, from 1907–19, including the European push favoured by the creation of the Junta para Ampliación de Estudios (1907), which drew mainly on a biological notion of the mind; and a third period from 1919–36, marked by the translation of foreign works and the application of psychological knowledge to juridical, educational and criminological

fields. Psychiatry, in its intellectual and profession development, seems to have been further advanced than its co-discipline psychology.

79 Régis, *Tratado*, p. 17.
80 Régis, *Tratado*, pp. 17–18.
81 Régis, 'Impulsos sexuales', in *Tratado*, pp. 104–9.
82 Régis, *Tratado*, pp. 108–9.
83 Régis, *Tratado*, p. 109.
84 Juarros, *Psiquiatría forense*, pp. 20–5.
85 The sexual perversions were covered in 'Lección Cuarta. Síntomas de las enfermedades mentales', which included general ailments in a person such as depression, 'trastornos' or disorders in the activity of a person, disorders in dress and cleanliness.
86 Juarros, *Psiquiatría forense*, pp. 54–7.
87 Juarros, *Psiquiatría forense*, p. 55.
88 Juarros, *Psiquiatría forense*, p. 55. It is interesting to note that Juarros viewed 'psychic hermaphrodism' (commonly employed in Germany and England, at least, as a marker for 'homosexuality') as the propensity of an individual to enjoy intimacy with both sexes (p. 56).
89 Juarros, *Psiquiatría forense*, p. 56.
90 C. Juarros, *La Psiquiatría del médico general* (Madrid: Ruiz, Hermanos, 1919).
91 Juarros, *La Psiquiatría del médico general*, pp. 9–12.
92 Juarros, *La Psiquiatría del médico general*, p. 9.
93 Juarros, *La Psiquiatría del médico general*, p. 85.
94 Juarros, *La Psiquiatría del médico general*, p. 90.
95 Juarros, *La Psiquiatría del médico general*, p. 90.
96 Juarros, *La Psiquiatría del médico general*, p. 90.
97 Juarros, *La Psiquiatría del médico general*, p. 91.
98 Juarros, *La Psiquiatría del médico general*, p. 92.
99 Juarros, *La Psiquiatría del médico general*, p. 321.
100 Juarros, *La Psiquiatría del médico general*, p. 321.
101 P. Mata, *Tratado de Medicina y Cirugía legal* (5th edn, 1874), p. 487. Emphasis added.
102 S. Ramón y Cajal, 'Prólogo de la edición española', in E. Bleuler, *Tratado de psiquiatría* (Madrid: Calpe, 1924), no page number [ix]. Bleuler was professor of psychiatry at the University of Zurich.
103 O. Bumke, *Tratado de las enfermedades mentales* (Barcelona: Francisco Seix, 1920). Bumke, we note in passing, was much less liberal with respect to homosexuality than either Régis or Bleuler. While homosexuality and other 'sexual perversions', for Bumke, should be punished by law (Bumke, *Tratado*, p. 286), Bleuler was of the opinion that all 'normal' men contained an element of homosexuality and that the latter was not susceptible to cures, except possibly in those cases where the incidence was not deep-rooted. Otherwise, 'los enfermos deben acostumbrarse a conformarse con su destino' [the sick should become accustomed to accepting their destiny] (Bleuler, *Tratado*, p. 426). Other differences include some recourse to psychoanalytic explanations for the acquisition of the sexual perversions.

Nevertheless, Bleuler was adamant that homosexuality not be viewed a vice, that is, something consciously attained: 'Antes se había discutido si la homosexualidad era un vicio; hoy no necesitamos hablar de eso. Si ello es una enfermedad es cosa que pertenece a las cuestiones tontas, sobre todo mientras no se pueda limitar el concepto de la enfermedad y no se sepan las consecuencias que pueden sacarse de ello' [Yesterday, we asked if homosexuality was a vice. Today we do not need to speak of this. If it is an illness, it is relegated to a trivial question, above all if we cannot define the concept of illness and we are ignorant of the consequences that result from it] (Bleuler, *Tratado*, p. 424). The kind of scientific reflexivity and care for the consequences of scientific and legal thought for the lives of subjects will reappear in the work of Marañón and other liberal doctors. Most importantly, in this kind of work, what was seen as necessary was to find out whether homosexuality was a congenital disorder or an acquired one, in which case it would be avoidable (Bleuler, *Tratado*, p. 425).

[104] Alfred Adler's work was particularly popular amongst political progressives and the left. See, as an example of his influence amongst the legal profession, L. Jiménez de Asúa, *Valor de la psicología profunda (Psicoanálisis y psicología individual) en ciencias penales* (Madrid: Editorial Reus, 1935), and the critique of Freudian psychoanalysis therein. De Asúa believed that Adler's 'Individual Psychology' offered greater hope in the victory of law and society over crime (p. 9). On Jung in Spain see V. Mestre and H. Carpintero, 'Unas notas sobre la entrada de Jung en España', *Historia de la Psicología*, 10, 1–4 (1989), 139–48.

[105] On the history of psychology from the impact of Wundt in Spain to the 1930s see M. Yela, 'La psicología española', in E. Quiñones, F. Tortosa and H. Carpintero (eds), *Historia de la psicología; textos y comentarios* (Madrid: Tecnos, 1993), pp. 593–603. An example of more biological and positivist psychology would be T. Mestre, *Introducción al estudio de la psicología positiva* (Madrid: Bailly-Baillière é Hijos, 1905). Mestre's volume (and the prologue to it written by S. Ramón y Cajal) was certainly 'old school', with chapters on the brain as the organ of the psyche, the histological constitution of the nervous system and a chapter on biological inheritance. The latter chapter made reference to the work of Pinel, Krafft-Ebing, Maudsley, Lamarck, Wallace, Darwin, Spencer and Weismann, but contains little of interest with reference to sexuality.

[106] M. V. Mestre and H. Carpintero, 'Enrique Fernández Sanz y la introducción de las ideas de Freud en España', *Historia de la Psicología*, 4, 1 (1983), 69–84.

[107] E. Fernández Sanz, *Histerismo. Teoría y clínica* (Madrid: Librería de Francisco Beltrán, 1914).

[108] Fernández Sanz, *Histerismo*, p. 239. Emphasis in original.

[109] H. Roger, 'Psicoanálisis y concepto sexual freudiano de las psiconeurosis', *Archivos de Medicina, Cirugía y Especialidades*, 141 (1924), 277–300.

[110] E. Fernández Sanz, 'Observaciones polémicas sobre psico-análisis', *Archivos de Medicina, Cirugía y Especialidades*, 154, 17 May 1924, 311–18.

[111] J. Sanchis-Banús, 'La cuestión del psicoanálisis', *Archivos de Medicina, Cirugía y Especialidades*, 150 (1924), 136–42. Despite the differences between the Madrid and Barcelona schools of psychiatry, collaboration, naturally, did occur. An example is the translation of foreign works such as that of Oswald Bumke discussed above, which was translated by E. Mira from the Barcelona school, and the prologue of which was written by José Sanchis-Banús from Madrid.

[112] Mestre and Carpintero, 'Unas notas sobre la entrada de Jung en España', 140–1.

[113] J. J. López Ibor, *Lo vivo y lo muerte del Psicoanálisis* (Barcelona: Luis Miracle, 1936).

[114] J. M. Peiró and H. Carpintero, 'Historia de la psicología en España a través de sus revistas especializadas', *Historia de la Psicología*, 2, 2 (1981), 143–81 (147).

[115] Carlos Castilla del Pino has argued that psychiatry at the time was still rooted in nineteenth-century concerns and was of 'claro sabor arcaico' [evident archaic qualities] in *La cultura bajo el franquismo* (Barcelona: Ediciones del Bolsillo, 1977), p. 80.

[116] The review was edited by Antonio Navarro Fernández, who had published *La prostitución en la villa de Madrid* (Madrid: Ricardo Rojas, 1909). For a more extensive account of the review, its contents and place in the sexual sciences consult R. Cleminson, 'The Review *Sexualidad* (1925–28), Social Hygiene and the Pathologisation of Male Homosexuality in Spain', *Journal of Iberian and Latin American Studies*, 6, 2 (2000), 119–29.

[117] This is an extension of the argument used by T. F. Glick in 'La "idea nueva": ciencia, política y republicanismo', in B. Ciplijauskaité and C. Maurer (eds), *La voluntad de humanismo: Homenaje a Juan Marichal* (Barcelona: Anthropos, 1990), pp. 57–90 (p. 61).

[118] Glick, 'La "idea nueva"', pp. 67–8.

[119] G. Marañón, 'La endocrinología y la ciencia penal', prologue in Q. Saldaña, *Nueva criminología* (Madrid: M. Aguilar, 1936), pp. 7–18 (p. 10).

[120] Saldaña, *Nueva criminología*, pp. 293–6. Quotation from p. 293.

[121] Saldaña mentions his 1928 essay 'Nueva Criminología' in Saldaña, *Nueva criminología*, p. 293. His 1930 text was *La Sexología (Ensayos)* (Madrid: Mundo Latino).

[122] Saldaña, *La Sexología*, p. 262.

[123] There was a large number of homosexuals in the Miranda de Ebro concentration camp according to the testimony of Fernando Barros Santos recorded in R. Torres, *Víctimas de la Victoria* (Madrid: Oberon, 2002), pp. 104–5. On the situation of homosexuals under Franco, see the monograph 'Represión franquista', *Orientaciones. Revista de homo-sexualidades*, 7 (2004).

Chapter Four

'Quien Con Niños se Junta': Childhood and the Spectre of Homoerastia

Introduction

As several historians have pointed out, the history of male friend-ship in the West is a story of a long decline, from overt sexual relationships through to a highly codified set of permissible interactions where sexuality was to be the element least sought. Associated in Greek culture with a whole stylistics of existence, although carefully articulated through permissions and prohibi-tions according to the status of the persons involved, *philia*, with its expression in *eros paidikós*, would gradually lose ground and be eliminated as acceptable social practice. It was first to be substi-tuted by the *amicitia* of the time of Cicero. Later, with the advance of Christianity and the rise of the evangelist *agape*, friendship is displaced by a love whose metaphor is the family: *fraternitas*.[1] Friendship is slowly uncoupled from any sensual connotation. Homosociality, men living together in close contact, was no longer seen as the expression of an exemplary kind of love or eroticism or as a means of resisting effeminacy or emasculation. Homosociality would be regarded with suspicion, surrounded by prohibition and distance in order to avoid any carnal contact.

Of course, these developments would not prevent the concur-rent expression of love relationships between men and, in certain periods, of a buoyant homoerotic subculture. But, in reality, the fate of homoerotic relationships was, at least for the time being, sealed and at the same time that Western modernity has centred love in the family and in the conjugal sphere it has tried to separate eroticism from men and their friendships with one another. The triumph of sexual dimorphism, as irreconcilable difference between males and females, from the eighteenth century, which in turn associated masculinity with the public sphere and femininity with the values of intimacy and private existence, reinforced the incompatibility between male friendship and sexuality.

In Spain, fears surrounding the 'excessive' expression of friendship between boys or between adults and youths, particularly in the boarding school environment, are literally written into institutions' rulebooks and into the treatises of the Counter-Reformation.[2] In order to govern the space of the boarding schools, a kind of 'total institution' in Goffman's terms, a whole set of precautionary disciplinary measures was put in place.[3] In this sense the nineteenth century did not introduce any revolutionary change but rather continued the separation of the sexes in educational institutions, considering that their proximity encouraged sexual precociousness or led to a loss of masculinity in men and a masculinization of women.[4] What was new in the nineteenth century was that the fears around homosociality were no longer expressed simply in moral terms or by cataloguing the inappropriate feelings or expressions of vice that may arise between individuals of the same sex. Hygienists, pedagogical experts, architects, law makers, psychiatrists and novelists would increasingly tend to pathologize this homosocial space and relate its dangers to the national picture, predicating the need to secure a robust and healthy population.

The second place which concerned pedagogues and hygienists was the public street and its homosocial potential. The main concern in this respect responded to fears around the recruitment of young boys into the arms of male prostitution. In Spain this question would only reach noticeable levels from circa 1890 onwards and became integrated into fears around the 'white slave trade', female prostitution, and child sex. These fears were given a collective basis in the form of the notion of 'childhood in danger' and even 'dangerous children' in need of surveillance in the big cities.[5]

There were, then, two principal spaces around which the problematization of children, and particularly their possible homoerotic relations, occurred: the school and the street. The first of these spaces concerned mainly middle-class children and disciplinary measures functioned in two ways, one 'horizontal' and the other 'vertical'. 'Bad company' was to be avoided among the children themselves in the boarding school, particularly with those pupils experienced in masturbation. But also teachers and tutors were the focus of attention for their potential to enrol their charges in the ranks of pederasty. The second of these spaces involved primarily children of working-class origin who were poor and often cast out on to the street by their parents. There was also a horizontal and vertical dimension to this second group. Itinerant children, and waifs and strays could operate as contacts for the world of prostitution. Brothel owners, men of high society, *señoritos* with strange tastes and professed inverts represented the 'vertical' threat.

In addition to these two spaces, but of lesser importance, we might add the domestic sphere. Social reformers also saw this scenario as a locus for the corruption of minors. Two great periods can be identified when this panic was at its height. The first covers the years 1850 up to the first two decades of the twentieth century, a period characterized by the explosion of the concept of 'childhood in danger' and the application of policies of child protection. The second period dates from the 1920s and takes us up to the Civil War. These years see the incorporation of the notion of the corruption of children as part of the burgeoning 'sexual question' with its manuals on sex education for the school and family.[6]

The Pupil as Seduced and as Seducer

The triple relationship between the school, the street and the family as foci of concern over the pederastic initiation of children in Spain appears well before the end of the nineteenth century in the work of Suárez Casañ who described how pederasty sought out its victims:

> La pederastia recoge a sus víctimas, generalmente en el arroyo, abusando de la miseria y apoderándose de los niños vagabundos sin familia y sin hogar . . . .. Pero volviendo a los niños, no solamente los hijos del arroyo son las víctimas de esta clase de atentados, sí

[*sic*] que también, y con harta frecuencia desgraciadamente, los que pertenecen a las familias más acomodadas, en los colegios, por parte de profesores indignos, que abusan de su debilidad y de su inocencia.[7]

[Pederasty picks up its victims generally in the street [the *arroyo*, or torrent, as many hygienists would term it; a fluid, fast-moving, hence dangerous place], taking advantage of their poverty and taking up vagabond children with no home or family . . .. But, to return to children, it is not only the sons of the *arroyo* that are the victims, but unfortunately it is frequently those who belong to comfortable families in the school setting, where they are victims of shameless teachers who abuse their weakness and innocence].

What kinds of measures would be taken in the school environment against such an eventuality? In this case we are talking about children from comfortably-off families;[8] in Spain at the beginning of the twentieth century secondary education was reserved for the middle and upper classes. These children's 'inocencia y debilidad' [weakness and innocence], in Suárez Casañ's words,[9] were taken advantage of by experienced seducers in charge of their education. Those who had been seduced, hygienists argued, would then in turn spread seduction like contagion throughout the school. This process of seduction would take place surreptitiously and invisibly, both from the adult to the child and from child to child.

Who were precisely the 'shameless' instructors that Suárez Casañ referred to and what legal means allowed for their capture and prosecution? Through a series of discursive means, doctors, hygienists and pedagogues narrowed their attention down onto suspicious persons and situations that gave rise to sexual seduction. Those who might seduce children were a varied set of individuals, making the task even more difficult. They could be schoolmasters, spiritual tutors, or the private educators of middle-class or bourgeois houses of the late nineteenth century. These private educators, halfway house figures between school and home, were seen by one eminent medical figure, José de Letamendi, indeed as a potential danger: 'no des nunca asentimiento á la institución de pedagogo interno ó parásito, en el seno de las familias, ni varón, ni hembra, sin distinción de clases ni de traza personal; de donde le hallares ya instalado, tenle siempre en estudio' [never agree to the institution of a private educator or extraneous individual into the heart of the home, whether male or female, without regard to class of personal traits. Where one such educator is already installed, keep a watch over him].[10]

But it would be priests who were seen as the most likely culprits in the perversion of children. They were omnipresent in the boarding houses and schools of the religious orders; the rich were under the wing of the Jesuits and the popular classes under the Escolapians.[11] In the wake of the Concordat of 1851, a whole new series of congregations emerged and were revitalized during the Restoration. As will be detailed in the next chapter, the long-standing battles between liberalism, republicanism, the revolutionary left and the Catholic Church left a rather pejorative legacy, to say the least, in terms of the representation of clerics. The vow of chastity and continence was understood as a source of sexual psychopathologies and aberrations. Amongst these, of course, lay pederastic tendencies.

Priests often figured as the protagonists of pederastic episodes, especially those religious figures who were young, enthusiastic and who had children in their care. Letamendi believed that a 'tendencia mística exagerada' [excessive mystical tendency], particularly amongst the young, 'suele ocultar semilla de aberración sensual' [usually masked the seed of some sensual aberration].[12] Essays on sex education, a genre that was established around 1910 in Spain, explained this tendency as an inexorable effect of forced chastity. For example, González Carreño, professor of philosophy and one of the first in Spain to write about the pedagogy of sex, believed that 'con frecuencia las inclinaciones amorosas invertidas tienen por origen la violencia que han debido sufrir' [often inverted amorous inclinations are the fruit of the violence that they [clerics] must have suffered] given the difficulties priests experienced in expressing their sexuality in the 'natural' way.[13] Despite this, however, the author goes on to state that the best kind of instructor with respect to sexuality is indeed the monk, given his exercise of chastity.[14]

Other writers, from the fields of hygiene or psychiatry, declared themselves in open opposition to Catholic celibacy, and considered it to be in conflict with the demographic interests of the state,[15] or to be the origin of sexual perversions.[16] The value or otherwise of continence and its possible relation with perverse sexuality became a focus for several authors.[17] It was discussed alongside the question of coeducation and will be analysed more fully later on in this chapter.

In Chapter Two the priest, U.L., who abused children was discussed at length. The case was first highlighted by Bravo y Moreno and this medical figure made several recommendations in the course of his presentation to the XIC International Medical Congress in order to prevent similar situations from arising and to prevent the incidence of 'homo-sexual' psychopathy in internees.[18] He is clear on the dangers supposedly personified in priests: 'Son peligrosas las relaciones particulares – educación e instrucción – de todo adolescente con personas que por su estado, profesión, etc, tienen una continencia forzada' [personal relationships, that is, those of learning and instruction, of adolescents with people who maintain forced chastity because of their status, profession, etc., are dangerous].[19]

But the huge cohort of dangerous adults does not just stem from the cloisters and chastity vows.[20] There are also long-standing masters who are well versed in the practice of pederasty and who try to inculcate the same in their pupils. Once more, Suárez Casañ in the sixth volume of his sexological library focuses on the warning signs. Quoting Tardieu and Casper directly, he relates a number of cases in which abusive relationships invariably ended up in violent orgies or blood-letting violations of minors. On occasion, the guilty partner is a cook or other functionary in the school environment. In France, which is mentioned as the veritable centre of this kind of crime, the alarm bells had already sounded in the early nineteenth century in the light of the number of incidences from the 1820s onwards, resulting in more than one public lynching of those assumed guilty. A law of 1832 institutionalized the crime of 'paedophilia' and condemned all sexual acts with a minor below the age of 11, including caresses and attempts at seduction.[21] At the centre of the most famous of these cases were often schoolmasters. The 'instititeur' Ferré was at the heart of such a case in 1844, discussed in turn by Tardieu,[22] and Lessablé was the subject of another in 1845.[23] In 1863 the age of the minor was raised to thirteen.

In Spain, in contrast, documentary sources such as medico-legal treatises, criminal anthropology, and legal essays and documents suggest that the issue enjoyed public attention later on, at the turn of the nineteenth century and beginning of the twentieth. One of the most famous cases of the period was that of Padre Meliá who was murdered in 1898, uncovering the existence of a pederastic circle. Another was the crime perpetrated by 'Chato del Escorial' against the young boy 'Pedrín'.[24] But again in contrast to the French case, these were mainly crimes against street urchins rather than those of the middle classes in boarding schools.

It was only in 1928 that any kind of legislation was placed on the books as part of an extensive apparatus to detect the corruption of minors, particularly with respect to cases of homosexuality and when the accused were schoolmasters or had children in their care.[25] The Penal Codes of 1848 and 1870 did not explicitly mention cases of 'crimes against decency' between individuals of the same sex; young ladies and women were always referred to. However, in both codes, the section pertaining to rape and 'dishonest abuse', on the one hand, and to corruption of minors on the other, added an article[26] and a paragraph,[27] respectively, which allowed for readings on pederastic abuse. This interpretation consisted in identifying 'crimes against decency' with sodomy, pederasty and masturbatory practices and seems to have become accepted around 1870 amongst jurists and medico-legal experts. The new article on 'rape and crimes against decency' allowed for the prosecution of adults who had maintained sexual relations with youths below the age of twelve. The legislation also allowed for prosecution of those who had had sexual relations with youths aged between twelve and twenty-three but only if there was evidence of some kind of deception having taken place or abuse of authority by an adult in whose care the child or young person was placed. In the latter case, the priest and the schoolmaster, amongst other figures, were mentioned explicitly.

The Penal Code of 1928 was written in the dying days of the dictatorship of General Miguel Primo de Rivera. It came after a long period of child-protection legislation and moral panics created by the sexual abuse of children or a perceived danger arising from sexual 'promiscuity' in various forms (the sexual promiscuity and incest of working-class families; child prostitution; hereditary syphilis and pornography). This code also contemplated the punishment of homosexual acts between consenting adults. Within the section of the law on public scandal, Article 616 sanctioned homosexuality with a fine or prison.[28] In addition, dishonest abuse of persons of the same sex was also punished more severely than that of persons of the other sex (from two to twelve years in prison for the first and from six months to three years in the latter case). Finally, the code paid special attention to cases of abuse by those responsible for the education of children. Educators would be punished not only if any activity had taken place but also if they were proven to be accessories or facilitators in such acts. The punishment could include a fine, prison, or the suspension from such duties for up to twenty years.[29]

Literary representations of the schoolmaster as seducer of boys were also current at the time in certain genres. For example, the novelette published by Álvaro Retana in 1919, *Los Extravíos de Tony (confesiones amorales de un colegial ingenuo)*, presents a kind of diary or memoir of the erotic activities of Antonio Fontanar ('Tony') from the age of fifteen when he enrolled in the *Colegio Aristocrático* in Madrid. An orphan brought up by his aunt and uncle, Tony discovers a whole erotic world in the latter's library. The uncle by day is a bank manager but by night pens erotic stories. He is the archetype, nevertheless, of moral rectitude and he rules the roost impeccably in tune with Christian virtues. For this reason, he worries about the possible bad influence that his nephew might pick up in the school environment and delays his enrolment by contracting a private tutor.[30]

When Tony finally goes to school he does not delay practising what he has read about in his uncle's study. Amongst the various characters in the school there is Don Fernando, a young sketching teacher who has a taste for young boys. Fernando invites Tony to visit his painter's studio and he invites him to pose nude. This strategy was always employed by the teacher as a prelude for his amorous encounters with pupils. But Tony resists the suggestions of Don Fernando and disregards the academic blackmail of his teacher.[31] Don Fernando uses the excuse of getting to the root of the practice of pederasty amongst the schoolboys in order to lure boys into his grasp.[32]

Of interest are the ways in which the seducer is represented together with the wiles used in order to achieve his aim. In some cases, such as the description offered by Suárez Casañ, the 'shameless' instructor is a person who abuses his authority in order to deceive and then terrify the pupils in his power who are innocent and weak. In other representations, however, a different image is drawn.

Commentators acknowledged that there was a kind of friendship between master and pupil that denoted a form of homoeroticism *in potentia*, even though it never transgressed a purely sentimental expression. José de Letamendi, once again, can be taken as an example of one expert who discussed this kind of relationship. After differentiating friendship from love and from luxuriousness, Letamendi warns his readers that 'la amistad no deja de ofrecer sus peligros, ya entre sexos diferentes, ya dentro del mismo' [friendship is not devoid of danger, whether between members of different sex or members of the same sex].[33] For his part, Juarros, aware of the theories on inversion and acquainted with psychoanalytic concepts of the development of homosexuality, discusses the admiration between males that goes beyond the 'canón habitual de la amistad' [usual canon of friendship] and which may hint at a sexualized inclination.[34] It is this kind of chaste but intense homosexual love that we see in the relationship between Pedro Miguel, the Gypsy choirboy, and the Basque priest of *Pasión y Muerte del Cura Deusto* (1924) written by Augusto D'Halmar. Kisses and gentle embraces and intense glances are the only form of carnal contact between man and boy in the story.[35]

But the tables could also be reversed and the child, instead of appearing as the innocent victim of the wiles of a perverted adult, was also represented as a veritable monster of sexual precocity, constantly seeking erotic favours from the adults in their midst:

> En las relaciones pederásticas los niños no siempre son víctimas para el concepto de violencia; la segunda infancia en los varones oculta un gran fondo de precocidad sexil [*sic*] que fácilmente toma un carácter provisional femíneo: de donde resultan no pocos niños cuya petulancia para con los maestros, compañeros, mayores, etc., constituye la provocación de las relaciones pederásticas. Ya Petronio nos dejó escrita una viva muestra de ese tipo infantil.[36]

> [In pederastic relationships children are not always the victims of [sexual] violence. The second childhood in boys contains huge amounts of sexile [*sic*] *precociousness which easily takes on a provisional feminine character. It is from here that the petulance with which these children treat their masters, companions and adults springs together with the provocation of pederastic relations. Petronius has supplied us with a written testimony of that kind of infantile type.*]

Precocious and provocative children allowed for a number of interpretations from the closing years of the nineteenth century onwards. During this period, theories were generally somaticist and commentators spoke of congenital traits, predispositions and degenerative atavism. Later on, these children would become the seed houses of epidemic sexual inversion which would run rampage in educational establishments. Before discussing these developments, some further comment is required on the figure of the child as seducer. Those in charge of children's education were particularly at risk. Martín de Lucenay, the most well known of the sexological popularizers of the period, related the case of a child of twelve years who befriended a dock worker in North Africa:

> De cuando en cuando le llevaba tabaco y otros regalos hasta que una vez le ofreció darle cincuenta pesetas si le enseñaba a nadar. El cargador, que ya había simpatizado con el pequeño, le prometió unas lecciones de natación desinteresadamente, y al segundo día, en ocasión en que se bañaban, el muchacho fingió un calambre con el fin de que su profesor le trasladase en brazos hasta la playa.[37]

> [From time to time he took him tobacco and other presents and one day offered him fifty pesetas if he taught him to swim. The dock worker, who was by now friends with the youngster, promised him swimming lessons at no charge and on the second day while bathing the boy faked cramp in order that his teacher would take him to the shore in his arms.]

Afterwards, the boy was interned in a school in Algeria but after a short while was returned to his father on account of having fallen in love with a teacher.

When Martín de Lucenay related this case the power of degenerationist theories was already on the wane. Other theories took their place. For some, the homosexuality of children and adolescents was viewed as a stage of lack of sexual differentiation or sexual passivity of the libido,[38] which made them 'extraordinariamente propicia a la seducción' [extraordinarily prone to seduction].[39] Infantile homosexuality is, therefore, seen as a perfectly normal stage in the development of adult sexuality, in accordance with the stages of sexual development established by Freud.[40] The theses of Marañón were, of course, extremely influential in this field. Marañón, however, spoke in the language of hormones and internal secretions. Infantile homosexuality in this schema would be the product of a lack of sexual differentiation characteristic of that period of life when the hormones had not reached their 'mature' expression. This 'bisexuality' would be a

normal phase in the 'battle' waged during puberty in the definition of the sexes. In the transitional phase, 'es muy frecuente que
el muchacho adquiera, primero, ciertos acentos físicos o psíquicos, de feminidad, porque el sello vivil es más tardío que el
femenino' [it is very common that the male child acquires, first,
some of the physical or psychical traits of femininity, because the
stamp of masculinity comes later than that of femininity].[41] In
Marañón's terms, bisexuality becomes pathological only when it
does not develop beyond an intersexual state – as is the case of
homosexuality – which is when there is a fault in the glandular
mechanism resulting in stunted development. The task of pedagogy is to assist 'natural' development and to favour the tendency
towards marked sexual differentiation.[42]

In the case of those who adopted a Freudian argument,
homosexuality appeared as a libido stagnated in a pre-oedipal
phase of sexual development. The problem here was not seen in
terms of regressive biological development but as an association
of images.[43] These images came from the subject's immediate
environment and would fix the libido on a particular object. In
both the endocrinological and the psychoanalytical model, the
behaviour of the teacher or instructor[44] could be decisive in terms
of the production of the sexual differentiation sought (in
Marañón's scheme); or it could produce a trauma or a communicative disorder (cf. Freud) which would favour a homosexual
object choice.[45]

But how was this homosexual desire in adults transferred onto
children or youths? A number of arguments were made to explain
this phenomenon. Letamendi believed that all forms of sexual
aberrations were expressions of 'atavismo hermafrodítico' [her-
maphroditic atavism], that is, congenital regressions to a primitive
state of sexual indifferentiation. Homoerastia ('amor al de igual
sexo' [the love of the same sex]) is clearly differentiated from
pederasty ('amor a niños' [love of children]) in Letamendi's
scheme.[46] Piga Pascual, whose ideas were modelled closely on
degenerationist thought, considered that pederasty could be
either congenital or acquired. The first was the case in effeminate
men who pursued children. These would possess underdeveloped
masculine characteristics and would be 'púberes, por regla general mal desarrollados física y psíquicamente, de tipo mujeril, con
fisonomía imberbe, formas redondeadas, órganos genitales
pequeños, y voz atiplada, de niño' [pubertal, as a general rule

poorly developed physically and psychically, womanly, beardless, with rounded [bodily] forms, small genitalia, and a high-pitched voice, like children], according to the forensic doctor.[47] This type of person sought children of either sex.

Other authors, however, found the roots of this behaviour in racial characteristics or in the degree of civilization of the individual concerned. At the height of the controversy over the inherence of 'donjuanism' as part of the Spanish character, Marañón discussed with Pérez de Ayala its possible origins: 'Pérez de Ayala, en un admirable ensayo sobre el donjuanismo, insiste certeramente en que el núcleo biológico de esta modalidad sexual, esto es, la transmutación del centro de gravedad de la atracción amorosa desde la mujer al hombre, es de origen mahometano' [Pérez de Ayala, in an admirable essay on donjuanism, is correct to insist that the biological core of this sexual practice, that is, the shifting of the centre of gravity of amorous attraction from woman to man, is of Mohammedan origin].[48] But Marañón was to add a further element. In addition to the supposed Moorish origins of donjuanism there was an inescapable Catholic component: the notion of sin, without which the character of Don Juan was impossible. Don Juan 'no podía nacer entre harenes, en una ciudad mora, sino precisamente en Sevilla, la ciudad de toda la tierra en la que ese injerto moro cristiano toma un apariencia de realidad más vigorosa' [was not born in the harem, in a Moorish city, but precisely in Seville, the one place on the whole earth where this grafting of Moorish and Christian elements made its most vigorous appearance].[49]

César Juarros also believed that desire for both young men and women (this kind of invert was termed an *anfígeno* by him) was of Moorish origin, something shared with the ancient Greeks: 'la homosexualidad mora escoge efebos, casi niños, de apariencia femenina' [Moorish homosexuality tends towards ephebes, almost children, of feminine looks].[50]

The School and Dangerous Friendships

Most commentators coincided in believing that the adult pederast resulted from a process of childhood or adolescent initiation by another, consolidated by a more or less congenital tendency. According to this model, the most precocious children would initiate neophytes into perverse sexual activity. A vicious circle is thus established in schools which would soon assume, according to the literature of the time, apocalyptic proportions.

The discovery of the rituals of pederasty in schools was not made overnight. As mentioned already, the persecution of sodomy in educational establishments was undertaken by moralists in the Counter-Reformation, and even before. What is new in the nineteenth century is the way in which medical hygiene, psychiatry, legal medicine, and later sexology and psychoanalysis, take this question to the heart of their concerns and codify it in their own language. Some experts in Spain had already found the presence of sodomy in all-male enclaves such as schools, prisons, on ships and in barracks by the 1870s.[51] But it would be hygienists who later on, by alluding to the pathologies entailed in mutual masturbation in schools, would contribute significantly to the moral panic around sexual inversion in these establishments. In this way, a connection was established between two processes seen by Foucault as differentiated in the *Volonté de Savoir*: the 'psychiatrization of perverse pleasure' (the creation of the homosexual) and the 'pedagogization of children's sex' (the medical persecution of masturbation).[52]

Around the mid-nineteenth century, pedagogical experts and medical hygienists baptized onanism with the name of the 'vicio escolar' [school vice]. If the practice of masturbation in a bedroom in the domestic setting was conceived as a *solitary* vice,[53] then masturbation in a more public setting, such as schools, was given a collective dimension, to which converts were continually added.[54] The medical campaign against the 'school vice' was in essence one drawn up against homosexuality in the school environment.

Giné y Partagás, one of the eminent figures of Catalan medical hygiene, had already discussed in passing the ease with which masturbation was learned in schools. The disadvantages of the state school included precisely an environment 'tan favorable al contagio del mal ejemplo' [favourable to the contagion of bad examples]. The state school was devoid of religious instruction and those children already in the grip of the solitary vice 'para cohonestar su vergonzoso extravío, ponen todo su conato en perder los que todavía se conservan en la inocencia' [in order to mitigate their own shameful course, try their hardest to inveigle those who still conserve their innocence].[55]

Some years later, in the treatise on hygiene written by the Cadiz professor Benito Alcina, mutual masturbation was alluded to directly and the presence of pederasty was hinted at. If children slept over in schools this brought untold dangers: there was 'poca vigilancia en los lugares excusados, y el tolerar ciertos cabildeos entre los escolares, se favorece la masturbación, ya individual, ya mutual, bien la pederastia, que desgraciadamente abunda en el templo de la ciencia' [little surveillance in the private quarters, and the tolerance of certain indecorous familiarities amongst the children, favours masturbation whether individual or mutual, and even pederasty, which unfortunately abounds in the temple of science], wrote Alcina.[56]

Solitary masturbation, then, was held to lead to mutual masturbation and almost inexorably to the practice of pederasty.[57] The propensity of children to spread this contagion was seen as something practically criminal and those well versed in these practices would become inverts for life. This process was described in detail by the reputed hygienist from Valencia, José María Escuder. The culprits were those children who were:

> Más precoces que los niños de su edad, más casquivanos, románticos e idealistas, enamóranse al principio platónicamente del macho más fuerte, del que les protege, aunque abuse; aman la contemplación de las formas masculinas; en los colegios inician a los demás en la masturbación prematura, en los deslices solitarios o a dúo . . .

> [More precocious than the other children of their age, more frank in their treatment with others, romantic and idealist, they fall in platonic love first of all with the strongest male who protects but abuses them at the same time. They delight in the contemplation of the male form. In schools they initiate others in the early practice of masturbation, whether solo or with others . . .]

Later on these same individuals would become the invert 'grown-up':

> más tarde, cuando la pubertad aparece, diseña en ellos una forma especial, ciertos rasgos exclusivos que les diferencian del hombre; predomina en ellos la pelvis, las nalgas y las mamas; balancean las caderas al mover con paso menudo sus pies pequeños; su voz es atiplada, de falsete; imitan a las mujeres, o mejor aún, proyectan al exterior sus gustos femeninos.

[when puberty appears, it does so in a special way and certain traits differentiate them from men. Their pelvis, thighs and busts predominate; they swing their hips as they walk in quick steps with their little feet. Their voice is high-pitched and falsetto. They imitate women or rather they project externally their feminine desires.][58]

It would be these 'inverts-in-the-making' that would return to the school to continue their perverse acts and their conversion of other children.[59] This circular process was described extensively in many treatises on hygiene[60] and pedagogy[61] of the time and, as we have already seen, the literary tradition was not blind to the same kind of concern. We have already seen how in Álvaro Retana's *Los Extravíos de Tony* (1919) the perverse adult would try to convince the youths in his care to engage in pederastic practices. But the process was also tied up in the activities of the children themselves, as Tony, the protagonist, was to relate.

Tony's immediate friends were an unusual trio, two of whom had an effeminate air (Pepito Ribes and Rodrigo Díaz de Vivar) and a third doubtful pupil, Mansilla. The three were always together, shared everything from tricks, laughs and 'dirty' jokes and they made up a trio composed of 'dos duquesitas' [two duchesses] and an obese 'abate de los tiempos de Mozart' [abbot of the times of Mozart].[62] Intrigued by these somewhat strange friendships and driven by a desire to share erotic experiences, Tony is led to the bedroom occupied by Pepito Ribes. Once inside, the two 'duchesses' turn off the light, dress up as damsels and invited the protagonist to share 'algo que suelo hacer a veces sin intervención ajena' [something that I usually do without others' intervention].[63]

A few months later, the trio has become a true 'cofradía' [brotherhood] formed by a half-dozen children.[64] Amongst them figures a Neapolitan youth who has brought with him certain customs of the schools of Italy. The group continues to grow and practices veritable orgies where transvestism and masturbation competitions take place.[65] The group even participates in Carnival with their own float as the *Capricious Romans*.[66] A crescendo is reached and some of the members of the group are expelled: 'Todo el colegio está en antecedentes de las excentricidades – llamémoslas así – del napolitano y medio Colegio Aristocrático sabe cómo las gastan 'las duquesas', Mansilla y Rafaelito Carvajal' [The whole school is on the look out for the 'eccentricities' – let us call them that – of the Neapolitan and half the Aristocratic School knows what such practices are in the case of 'the duchesses' Mansilla and Rafaelito Carvajal]. These vices spread and 'concluirán probablemente adueñándose de los doscientos alumnos que integramos el Colegio Aristocrático si Dios no manda dos arcángeles para anunciarnos un fin semejante al que tuvieron los habitantes de Sodoma' [they will probably take over the two hundred pupils that are in the Aristocratic School if God doesn't send down two archangels to announce the same kind of fate that befell the inhabitants of Sodom].[67]

In the 1920s the panic over pederasty in Spanish schools reached its height.[68] At the same time, the campaign in the press against the presence of sexual inverts in the large cities was especially virulent, as can be seen, for example, by a study of the pages of the review *Sexualidad* (discussed in Chapter Three). It could be argued that the passing of new legislation on homosexuality in 1928, referred to above, was in direct response to these concerns.[69]

We have seen how children could begin as masturbators and 'progress' to pederasty with their classmates. We have seen how adults could pervert children with their wiles (and vice versa). But how did the perverse child become the perverse adult? What is the 'missing link' between the two? The answers to this question, were, predictably, extremely varied. Some emphasized hereditary factors and others the environment as a causal factor. As is well known, by the 1920s the corpus of foreign sexological works translated into Spanish was extensive. The question of the connection between masturbation practised in the 'critical age' of pre-adolescence and sexual inversion per se was an important issue in these works.[70] It was this matter that had received sustained attention in the Symposium on Masturbation organised by the Viennese Psychoanalytical Association in 1910.

In some cases, a direct link was established between masturbation and homosexuality. Krafft-Ebing in his famous *Psychopathia Sexualis* (1886) maintained that those individuals who, through a hereditary taint, were unable to differentiate the orientation of their sexual instinct could adopt homosexuality as a practice if they engaged in mutual masturbation with individuals of their own sex.[71] Others, such as Forel, argued that onanism in schools, engaged in before the sexual orientation of the individual was 'set', did not have the same significance as it did in adults.[72]

Onanism could signify merely a passing tendency or it could, he admitted, on the contrary be the sign of a congenital predisposition towards sexual inversion. But in either case, it was considered more of a symptom than a cause.

The French commentators Régis, drawing once more on Krafft-Ebing,[73] and Vigouroux and Juquelier, who relied on Tarnowski,[74] believed that masturbation in schools did not just reveal a morbid predisposition towards inversion but that it actually brought it to life and reinvigorated it. Any feelings of latent sexual inversion were activated when the pre-adolescent became used to associating pederastic imagery with the acts undertaken and the pleasures experienced in the school environment. The imitation of these practices produced the 'mental contagion' of inversion in schools, even though it was only the predisposed who developed full-blown sexual inversion.

The British sexologist Havelock Ellis, following Moll, believed that 'excessive' and early masturbation if not a direct cause of sexual inversion could help to develop it. The onanistic habit was reinforced at an early age and the child began to disassociate physical and psychic pleasure from one another and this led to impotence, sexual precocity and possibly homosexuality.[75] Finally, Freud in the Symposium mentioned above, pointed to the difficulties of pinpointing any 'qualitative condition for the ill effects of masturbation'.[76] A different question, however, was the effect of masturbation in the genesis of neuroses and the differences between the ill effects of the practice and its repression.[77]

Two examples in the Spanish sexological literature of the time show how the general arguments of international authors were to a large extent heeded. We refer once more to the work of Rodríguez Lafora and César Juarros. Lafora, for his part, broaches the question in both his *Los Niños Mentalmente Anormales* published in 1919 and in his *La Educación Sexual y la Reforma de la Moral Sexual* (1933). Lafora adopts Freud's stages of sexual development. In this light, homoerotic attachments and experiences in schoolchildren should be seen as indicators of a normal expression of congenital homosexuality, he asserted. In turn, this was viewed as a characteristic of the 'doubts' experienced during post-puberty.[78] However, negative or perverse influences, such as those possibly provided by precocious schoolmates, could make what was a passing phase into something much more permanent.[79]

Lafora recognized the transcendental importance of 'los acontecimientos de orden sexual en la edad infantil' [events of a sexual nature in the infantile stage], thus coinciding with Freud, and their possible consequences 'en la vida ulterior del sujeto, en sus reacciones caracteriológicas y en el desarrollo de neurosis' [in the subject's later life, in their characterological make-up and in the development of neuroses].[80] But at the same time, in a mix with which we are now familiar, purely somatic factors, both those hereditary and those deriving from endocrinological development, were deemed to be important.[81] In this way, mutual masturbation amongst schoolchildren could be a cause of future homosexuality or a sign of latent congenital or innate homosexuality.[82]

The eclecticism of Juarros is even more extreme than that of Lafora.[83] As we have seen in previous sections, Juarros had adopted a degenerationist perspective which conceptualized the invert as a congenital degenerate although not necessarily with an innate basis.[84] Like his two French counterparts, Vigouroux and Juquelier, he accepted the effects of 'mental contagion' whereby masturbation could rekindle a predisposition to sexual inversion. Juarros also incorporated Marañón, Moll and, more problematically, Freud, into his extensive publications of the 1920s and 1930s, such as *Normas de Educación Sexual y Física* (1925), *El Amor en España. Características Masculinas* (1927), *Los Horizontes de la Psicoanálisis* (1928) and *Sexualidad Encadenada* (1930).

The relationship between onanism and sexual inversion was underwritten in *Normas de Educación Sexual y Física* where Juarros discussed Moll's thesis on the erogenous zones.[85] In agreement with Marañón, but dissenting from Freud, Juarros believed that homosexuality, even though it did consist of a lack of differentiation between the sexes stemming from the phase of the oedipal complex, never actually produced exclusive homosexual practice.[86] Instead, individuals who engaged in homosexuality were seized by a kind of psychic hermaphroditism since they aped 'las maneras, ademanes, adornos y afeites del sexo opuesto' [the mannerisms, gestures, adornment and hairstyles of the opposite sex].[87] Juarros, as can be seen, still theorized same-sex activity as part of sexual inversion rather than 'homosexuality'.

On the other hand, following Marañón, he established an affinity between precocious sexual expression and passivity, both characteristics of the masturbator and the effeminacy of the invert. This, in turn, was connected to a peculiar national ethnology of the mores of love, which went as follows: the average Spaniard's sexual initiation began at school. Confidences accompanied by mutual or group masturbation could give rise to 'pederastic manoeuvres'.[88] Once adolescence was over, the average male Spaniard began to frequent the brothel. However, the most timid,[89] cowardly or passive youths, those least virile, preferred to devote themselves to auto-eroticism.[90] But those who did go to the brothel, Juarros continued, did not become satisfactory male types. Instead, and with some common ground with Marañón's 'Don Juan' thesis, Juarros argued that the preference for this kind of sexual relationship betrayed the man's derision towards women and a lack of definition in sexual object choice. This 'unconscious homosexuality' impregnated all forms of Spanish male sociability,[91] whether in the bordello, café, boxing ring, football supporters' groups, or bullfighting circles.[92] Once more coinciding with Marañón, Juarros argued for a kind of sex education that would reinforce sexual difference and 'strengthen man and effeminize woman'.[93]

From the Healthy School Environment to Sex Education

Around the middle of the nineteenth century hygienists' criticism of the education system in Spain had become fairly marked.[94] The unhealthy nature of the school was seen by them to be manifested in the fact that children spent long periods shut indoors, with little physical movement and whose education was mainly based on intellectual exercises rather than the development of physical or affective capacities.[95] With respect to the sexual question, hygienists believed that the hothouse school environment led to the degradation of the 'reproductive instinct' through children's contact with early masturbation and the loss of childhood innocence. One of the greatest fears was the 'contagion' of pederastic habits between pupils or between master and pupil.

Pedagogical experts, however, believed that any sexual corruption came not from the school itself but from the promiscuity and general lack of morality and care in the working-class family. The vice of masturbation, and indeed pederasty, was born of domestic origins, even though both spread their tentacles to the educational environment.[96]

Between the middle of the nineteenth century and the first years of the twentieth, educational experts took on board the concerns of medical doctors and launched a noisy campaign in favour of the 'healthy school'.[97] One immediate result of this alliance was the introduction of the subject of school hygiene into the curriculum of aspiring teachers and in primary education.[98] Perhaps the most resounding of all the measures taken with respect to health and sexuality were those introduced under the auspices of the Institución Libre de Enseñanza (ILE).[99]

The members of the ILE, in addition to promoting liberal values in education, defended the superiority of education in the home over that of the school. Despite this, and given the lack of awareness of educational matters amongst most families, the school should step in, they argued, to assume those responsibilities.[100] Their arguments in favour of coeducation, physical education, outdoor activities and school visits, can all be understood within the framework of regenerationist concerns.[101]

As will be pointed out in Chapter Five, regenerationists contrasted instruction with education. The former would be a purely intellectual form of training while the latter was a much broader formation of character and will. The body, the affections, the emotions, the will; all these elements should be the prime target of any educational endeavour. In accordance with these priorities, the ILE, in the words of one of its main supporters, Cossío, encapsulated the aim of 'crear sujetos vigorosos de cuerpo y alma, cultos y varoniles' [creating subjects vigorous in body and soul, cultured and manly].[102]

Here, once more, we see the connections forged between emerging educational strategies and the prevention of effeminacy. This quality was seen to be the result of an excess in intellectualism and a sedentary life which, according to critics, characterized Spanish schooling. The latter produced individuals who lacked character and who suffered from an excess in what was termed 'celebration',[103] and an absolute lack of character.[104] In turn, this lack of equilibrium could result in an overexcited state which could produce 'neurasthenia'.

The dangers of a 'nervous childhood' were taken seriously by eminent members of the ILE such as Francisco Giner de los Ríos, who drew on Pelman and Krafft-Ebing to support his analysis.[105] One of the traits of these children was sexual precocity and this was linked, as we have seen, to masturbation and the creation of

'vices which remain secret'.[106] To counter weakness and effeminacy in the child the worth of gymnastics,[107] physical exercise and
outdoor games were championed,[108] to take place as part of
countryside walks and in school 'colonies' outside the city.[109] It
was also understood that coeducation from the earliest years of
schooling,[110] far from 'de-virilizing' youth,[111] countered sexual
precociousness and the 'mysteries' of the other sex.

Some hygienists believed that the overexcitation of the intellectual faculties had similar effects on the sexual instinct, leading to
'la lujuria, y con ella a las aberraciones sexuales y a la homoerastia' [luxuriousness, and with this, the sexual aberrations and
homoerastia].[112] The frequency of homosexuality among geniuses
and in civilizations characterized by a strong intellectual or artistic
life would further underpin this kind of understanding.

While the links between these new educational strategies and
the prevention of the aberrations of the sexual instinct were not
necessarily explicit, we can see that the formation of a healthy,
'natural' and well developed child was seen as the basis from
which to combat the many degradations of the physique and the
psyche. The lack of explicitness of this project is confirmed by the
Institutionalists' resistance to formal sex education. From their
liberal and non-interventionist perspective, collective sex education coming from the state was viewed with some caution; the
domestic environment was still, for them, the forum from which
to approach these questions.[113]

Those who defended the introduction of sex education into
the daily curriculum of schools were in effect proposing a whole
new system of governance of the body and sexuality. Instead of
the old measures advocated by hygienists and pedagogues in the
nineteenth century with respect to masturbation in school and at
home, a new kind of strategy was adopted. Rather than a permanent and individualized examination of behaviour and the surveillance of spaces and the detection of any traces left by
masturbation, from the early twentieth century experts relied on
a communicative method, a conversational strategy that alluded
to the consequences of the practice. This shift from the private or
personal to the collective risk entailed by masturbation was articulated around the spectres of venereal disease, syphilis, crimes
against the person, physical and psychical impotence, sexual
neuroses, infant mortality and uncontrollable fertility.[114]

During the first three decades of the twentieth century a national debate with sharply defined differences was established. As well as early differences between educationalists and medical doctors, another important schism that ran through discourse on this subject was the lay/Catholic divide. Lay sex reformers, who often supported national eugenic campaigns, argued for the introduction of compulsory sex education in schools.[115] Liberal thinkers, without adopting necessarily an anticlerical stance, argued for a consensus position, and advocated sex education in schools with the parents' permission.[116] The most conservative Catholics wished to limit sexual pedagogy (understood as 'education for chastity') to the domestic environment, leaving it up to the initiative of parents to choose the best way forward, often guided by the priest.[117] Certain sectors of the workers' movement, such as the anarchists, demanded communal sex education which would also serve as a critique of bourgeois society.[118] This intricate debate has been examined elsewhere;[119] for now, the most important aspect is to discuss how this new 'communicative' method was to act upon 'homosexuality'.

It must be stated first of all that, as in medicine generally, the prevention of homosexuality was not the primordial task of sex education. Since its establishment in the eighteenth century in Germany, the 'pedagogization' of sex was initially concerned with the extirpation of onanism.[120] The centrality of onanism was maintained in pedagogical texts on sexuality in Spain in the first two decades of the twentieth century but would lose its primacy in the decades to come.[121] From the beginning of the twentieth century, those sex education texts which drew specifically on eugenics were more concerned with the transmission of sexual diseases (particularly syphilis). Sexual diseases were variously associated with visits to brothels,[122] uncontrolled fertility,[123] the havoc wrought by pornography and piquant literature (*sicalipsis*),[124] and with the general category of the sexual aberrations. From a eugenic standpoint, it was believed that all these problems inhered in the 'stock' or the population, thus contributing to a decline of the 'race'.

Masturbation continued to be considered a problem but its status as an agent in the cause of multiple disorders gradually declined. By the 1920s and 1930s, masturbation began to be accepted as a normal practice as sexuality developed, even though its persistence into adult life was frowned upon. It is in this period that, together with the risks entailed by venereal disease,[125] the sexual perversions and, in particular, homosexuality move to centre stage.[126]

This increasing concern with respect to homoeroticism in the literature of sex education also had something to do with the actual dynamics of the educational strategy. The first texts, especially those closest to Catholic appeals for chastity, sought to control the sexual impulse.[127] Gradually, as psychoanalytic texts and endocrinological arguments became more common a dual strategy was embraced: education in order to sublimate the sexual instinct[128] and education in order to promote sexual differentiation.[129] The second of these two strategies, held particularly dear by Marañón, was extremely influential in the burgeoning corpus of sex-related literature published from the late 1920s up to the Civil War.[130] In order to achieve adequate sexual differentiation as a goal of the sex education literature it was necessary to manage or even suppress the 'intersexual states' and to promote in young boys the development of physical and psychic virility. From this perspective, homosexuality became one of the main enemies to be combatted by sex education.

NOTES

1 F. Ortega, *Genealogias da Amizade* (São Paulo: Iluminuras, 2002), pp. 53–62.

2 The monastic rules of the Visigothic period in Spain contained similar prohibitions. Rule 16 of the *Regla de San Fructuoso* states: 'No deben acostarse dos en un mismo lecho; ni a ninguno se le permitirá dormir fuera de su propio dormitorio. Entre las camas debe haber una separación de un codo, para evitar los incentivos de la pasión, si están próximos los cuerpos. Ninguno hablará a otro en la oscuridad, ni se acercará en manera alguna un joven a la cama de otro después de completas' [Two [men] should not retire to the same bed. Neither should it be allowed that anyone sleep outside his own dormitory. Beds should be at arm's length in order to prevent the incentives of passion if bodies are close together. No-one will speak to another in darkness and no youth will approach the bed of another after compline] (Santos Padres Españoles, *Reglas Monásticas de la España Visigoda* [Madrid: BAC, 1971], p. 155). As Foucault has demonstrated, the *askesis* of the monastery replaced the relationship of friendship between master and disciple, a characteristic of the *paideia* and *askesis* of ancient Greece, by a relationship of obedience between monk and his superior. Friendships between monks were frowned

upon (F. Ortega, *Amizade e Estética da Existência em Foucault* [Rio de Janeiro: Graal, 1999], p. 125). On the concern over homoeroticism in early monasticism see C. Espejo Muriel, *El Deseo Negado. Aspectos de la problemática homosexual en la vida monástica (siglos III–VI d.C.)* (Granada: Pub. Universidad de Granada, 1991). On precautions and interdictions in the Counter-Reformation, see J. L. Flandrin, *La Moral Sexual en Occidente* (Barcelona: Granica, 1984), pp. 284–6 and F. Vázquez García and A. Moreno Mengíbar, *Sexo y Razón. Una Genealogía de la Moral Sexual en España (siglos XVI–XX)* (Madrid: Akal, 1997), pp. 92–3.

3   E. Goffman, *Asylums: essays on the social situation of mental patients and other inmates* (Garden City, NY: Doubleday, 1961), pp. 1–124.

4   J. B. Seoane Cegarra, 'La Pasión y la Norma. Una Genealogía de la Moral Sexual Infantil en España (1800–1920)' (unpublished Ph.D. thesis, University of Cadiz, Cadiz, 2001), 216.

5   J. Donzelot, *The Policing of Families* (London: Hutchinson, 1979), pp. 9–47; J. Varela and F. Álvarez-Uría, *Arqueología de la Escuela* (La Piqueta: Madrid, 1991), pp. 220–4.

6   R. Cleminson and E. Amezúa, 'Spain: the political and social context of sex reform in the late nineteenth and early twentieth centuries', in F. X. Eder, L. Hall and G. Hekma (eds), *Sexual Cultures in Europe. National Histories* (Manchester: Manchester University Press, 1999), pp. 173–96.

7   V. Suárez Casañ, *Conocimientos para la Vida Privada*, vol. VI, *La Pederastia* (Barcelona: Casa Editorial Maucci, 20th edition, 1910), pp. 25–6.

8   The idea that pederastic initiation takes place from a masturbatory basis acquired in schools frequented by children of the upper classes held sway between the latter years of the nineteenth century and the Civil War. Ballesteros, a pedagogical figure close to the Institución Libre de la Enseñanza, warned that schools were dangerous places: 'Este es el camino que lleva fatalmente al autoerotismo, y en muchos casos a la perversidad sexual. Sobre todo en los colegios que frecuenta la clase más elevada de la sociedad, y, desde luego, en todos los que tienen internado' [This is the route that leads directly towards auto-eroticism and in many cases to sexual perversity. Above all in those schools frequented by the society's upper classes and in boarding schools]. See A. Ballesteros, 'Sobre educación sexual', *Revista de Pedagogía*, 84 (1928), 536–52 (538).

9   Suárez Casañ, *La Pederastia*, p. 25.

10 J. de Letamendi, *Curso de Clínica General*, 2 vols, (Madrid: Imp. de los Sucesores de Cuesta, 1894), vol. II, p. 126.

11 In 1908 Madrid possessed 135 state schools and 311 private Catholic ones. Even in the state schools, the teaching of the catechism and religion were obligatory. See P. Conard, 'Sexualité et Anticléricalisme (Madrid, 1910)', *Hispania. Revista Española de Historia*, 117 (1971), 103–34 (113).

12 De Letamendi, *Curso*, vol. II, p. 123. In C. Bernaldo de Quirós and

J. M. Llanas Aguilaniedo, *La Mala Vida en Madrid. Estudio psicosoci-ológico con dibujos y fotografías del natural* (Madrid: B. Rodríguez Sierra, 1901) several cases of sexual inversion are described. One of them, 'La Tonta del Rastro', showed signs of precocious mysticism: 'hasta los catorce años estuvo en un colegio dirigido por sacerdote; juegos místicos (altarcitos, bautizos, etc. . .)' [up to the age of fourteen he was in a school directed by priests; mystical games (little altars, baptisms, etc. . . .)] (p. 264).

13   G. González Carreño, *La Educación Sexual* (Madrid: Sáinz de Labera Hermanos Ed., 1910), p. 45.

14   González Carreño, *La Educación Sexual*, p. 371.

15   R. Forns, *Higiene. Breves apuntes de las lecciones dadas en el curso de 1908 a 1909* (Madrid: Biblioteca de la Revista de Especialidades Médicas, 1915), p. 321.

16   C. Juarros, *Normas de Educación Sexual y Física* (Madrid: Renacimiento, 1925), p. 40.

17   One of the first to comment on Freud's work in Spain, Dr Fernández Sanz, considered nevertheless that abstinence was perfectly tolerable without negative consequences for health in normal individuals. See E. Fernández Sanz, 'Sobre Educación Sexual. Su importancia para la profilaxia de las psicosis y psiconeurosis', *El Siglo Médico*, 62 (1915), 386–9 (389).

18   F. Bravo y Moreno, *Exposición de un caso clínico médico-legal de psicopatía homo-sexual* (Santander: Tip. El Cantábrico, 1903), pamphlet, pp. 11; F. Bravo y Moreno, 'Exposición de un caso clínico médico-legal de psicopatía homo-sexual', in *Actes du XIC Congrès International de Médecine*, publiés sous la direction de Ms. le Dr. Fernández-Caro. Section d'Hygiène, Épidémiologie et Science Sanitaire Technique (Madrid: Imp. de J. Sastre, 1904), pp. 96–102.

19   Bravo y Moreno, 'Exposición', p. 102.

20   Two other references, in this case fictional, to priests who abused children can be found in R. Pérez de Ayala, *A.M.D.G.* (Madrid: Editorial Pueyo, 1931 [1910]), pp. 164–5, a novel whose publication caused a considerable degree of scandal at the time (Conard, 'Sexualité', pp. 103–4). The second case is mentioned in the porno-graphic story written by Francisco Bullón, *Colegiales Adorables* (1930). The main character in the text is Padre Canuto who used the confessional in order to have sexual relations with his flock. His initiation, however, took place when he was a novice at the seminary where he was placed in charge of a group of small children. With them he used to play a 'game' which ended when the priest 'empujaba su implacable ariete dentro de sus redondos traseros carnosos' [forced his unstoppable tool into their round fleshy behinds] (S. Haliczer, *Sexualidad en el Confesionario. Un Sacramento Profanado* [Madrid: Siglo XXI, 1998], see the section 'Solicitación y Confesión en la imaginación Anticlerical', pp. 255–85 [270]).

21   P. Ariès and G. Duby (eds), *Historia de la Vida Privada*, vol. IV, *De la Revolución Industrial a la Primera Guerra Mundial* (Madrid: Taurus, 1989), pp. 594–5.

[22] J. P. Aron and R. Kempf, *La Bourgeoisie, le Sexe et l'Honneur* (Brussels: Ed. Complexe, 1984), p. 48.

[23] J. Danet, *Discours Juridique et Perversions Sexuelles (XIXᵉ et XXᵉ siècles)* (Nantes: Université de Nantes, 1977), p. 25.

[24] J. del Moral y Pérez Aloe, *El Estado y la Prostitución* (Madrid: Casa Editorial de Felipe G. Rojas, 1913), p. 84.

[25] L. Jiménez de Asúa and J. Antón Oncea, *Derecho Penal conforme al Código de 1928*, vol. II, *Parte Especial* (Madrid: Reus, 1929), p. 348.

[26] Article 555 of the 1848 Penal Code read as follows: 'El que abusare deshonestamente de persona de uno u otro sexo, concurriendo cualquiera de las circunstancias expresadas en el artículo anterior, será castigado, según la gravedad del hecho, con la pena de prisión menor o la correccional' [He who commits a crime against decency with a person of either sex, under the circumstances outlined in the previous article [where the parameters of rape are described], will be punished, depending on the seriousness of the crime, by a prison sentence of up to six years or confined to a correctional prison]. The 1870 Code (in Article 454) retains the same wording although the prison terms are different.

[27] We refer here to a paragraph added to Article 556 of the 1848 Code, which refers to sexual activity with minors. It reads: 'Cualquier otro abuso deshonesto cometido por las mismas personas y en iguales circunstancias, será castigado con prisión correccional' [Any other form of abuse committed by the same persons and under the same circumstances [these included anyone in authority over the abused person such as priest, domestic servant, tutor or master] will be confined to a correctional prison]. The 1870 Code retains this wording (in Article 458) but the punishment differs.

[28] 'El que, habitualmente o con escándalo, cometiere actos contrarios al pudor con personas del mismo sexo será castigado con multa de 1000 a 10.000 pesetas e inhabilitación especial para cargos públicos de seis a doce años' [Whoever habitually or with public scandal, commits acts against public morality with persons of the same sex will be submitted to a fine of 1,000 to 10,000 pesetas and will not be allowed to perform any kind of public role for six to twelve years].

[29] Jiménez de Asúa and Antón Oneca, *Derecho Penal*, vol. II, p. 352.

[30] A. Retana, *Los Extravíos de Tony (confesiones amorales de un colegial ingenuo)* (Madrid: Biblioteca Hispania, 1919).

[31] Retana, *Los Extravíos*, p. 174.

[32] Retana, *Los Extravíos*, pp. 236–7.

[33] Letamendi, *Curso*, vol. II, p. 111.

[34] C. Juarros, *La Sexualidad Encadenada. Ejemplos y Consejos* (Madrid: Mundo Latino, 1931), p. 166.

[35] A. D'Halmar, *Pasión y Muerte del Cura Deusto* (Madrid: Editora Internacional, 1924). Pedro Miguel and Padre Deusto call each other 'my friend' ('amigo') and 'my great friend' ('amigote', almost 'my love').

[36] De Letamendi, *Curso*, vol. II, p. 128.

[37] A. Martín de Lucenay, *Homosexualidad* (Madrid: Editorial Fénix, 1933), p. 17.

38 J. Bugallo Sánchez, *La Higiene Sexual en las Escuelas* (Madrid: Morata, 1930), pp. 58–9.

39 Bugallo Sánchez, *La Higiene Sexual*, p. 30.

40 J. de Eleizegui, *La Sexualidad Infantil (Normas de Educación)* (Madrid: Unión Poligráfica S.A., 1934), p. 164.

41 G. Marañón, *Ensayos sobre la Vida Sexual* (Madrid: Espasa Calpe, 1969 [1926]), p. 147.

42 Marañón, *Ensayos*, p. 151.

43 Eleizegui, *La Sexualidad Infantil*, p. 106.

44 G. Rodríguez Lafora, *La Educación Sexual y la reforma de la moral sexual* (Madrid: Publicaciones de la Revista de Pedagogía, 1933), p. 25, argued against the use of corporal punishment because in some children and adults it excited sexual pleasure.

45 Marañón, Freud and Havelock Ellis are the authors most cited by doctors and educational experts who wrote about sex education in Spain from 1926–36. In general, an eclectic approach is adopted, combining reference to hereditary factors, environmental elements and the activation of innate predispositions by environmental circumstances. Examples of this ambivalent eclecticism include Rodríguez Lafora, *La Educación Sexual*, p. 24, and, Eleizegui, *La Sexualidad Infantil*, p. 104.

46 De Letamendi, *Curso*, vol. II, p. 120.

47 A. Piga, *Higiene de la Pubertad* (Toledo: Imp. de la Vda. e Hijos de J. Peláez, 1910), p. 20.

48 G. Marañón, 'La vida sexual en España', *El Siglo Médico*, 76 (1925), pp. 577–80 (580).

49 Marañón, 'La vida sexual', p. 580. It is also in Seville, with its mixture of Moorish sensuality and Catholic Baroque flavours, that most of the action in Augusto D'Halmar's *Pasión y Muerte del Cura Deusto* takes place.

50 Juarros, *La Sexualidad Encadenada*, p. 163.

51 P. Mata, *Tratado de Medicina y Cirugía Legal Teórica y Práctica*, IV vols, (Madrid: Bailly-Baillière, 1874), vol. I, p. 485; T. Yáñez, *Lecciones de Medicina Legal y Toxicología* (Madrid: Librería de Saturnino Calleja, 1878), p. 333. Curiously, Mata in his *Vademécum de Medicina y Cirugía Legal* (Madrid: Imp. Calle de Padilla, 1844), vol. II, p. 70, mentions schools, prisons, ships and barracks but does not refer to day or boarding schools. It is possible that the increased interest in pederasty that Mata displays in his 1874 *Tratado de Medicina* responds to the publication of the works of Casper and Tardieu in the 1850s.

52 M. Foucault, *The History of Sexuality*, vol. I, *An Introduction* (Harmondsworth: Penguin, 1990), pp. 104–5.

53 Seoane, 'La Pasión'.

54 F. M. Koch, *Venus Sexual: tratado de las enfermedades que resultan de los excesos sexuales, hábitos solitarios* . . . (Madrid: Imp. El Resumen, 1903), p. 53, wrote 'Respecto a la denominación de vicio solitario, tampoco es más justa, ya que la masturbación no solo se ejecuta por sí sola, sino que se verifica en común' [With respect to the term solitary vice,

this is not more correct since masturbation is not performed alone but rather with others].

55   J. Giné y Partagás, *Curso Elemental de Higiene Privada y Pública* (Barcelona: Librería de Juan Bastinos e Hijo, 1871), p. 546. Francisco Javier Santero, professor of public hygiene in the Faculty of Medicine, Madrid, reproduced literally these words in his *Elementos de Higiene Privada y Pública* (Madrid: El Cosmos Editorial, 1885), vol. I, pp. 409–10. The figure of the school masturbator would have a long life. Between the latter years of the nineteenth century and the first years of the twentieth, he would be considered to be a degenerate: 'En la segunda infancia, en las escuelas, entre los pensionados de los colegios, cunde la acción contagiante del niño masturbador. Los nerviosos, los histéricos, los predispuestos a las neurosis por herencia, son sus casos escogidos' [In second childhood, in schools, amongst boarders, the contagious activity of the masturbator spreads. The nervous, the hysterical, those predisposed to neurosis through inheritance, are his chosen victims]. (J. M. Zapatero, *Pedagogía Sexual. Lo que se debe saber* [Barcelona: F. Isart S. en C. Editores, 1922], p. 129).

56   B. Alcina, *Tratado de Higiene Privada y Pública* (Cadiz: José Vidas, 1882), vol. I, p. 513.

57   De Letamendi, *Curso*, vol. II, p. 126, wrote that 'Entre mujeres, entre mozos recién púberes el riesgo de transgresión sexual de la pura amistad a la homoerastia es mayor que entre hombres ya hechos' [Amongst women, amongst boys who are just emerging out of puberty and even amongst children, the risk of sexual transgression from pure friendship to homoerastia is greater than among grown men].

58   Both quotations from J. M. Escuder, *Locos y Anómalos* (Madrid: Establecimiento Tip. Sucesores de Rivadeneyra, 1895), p. 176.

59   Escuder, *Locos*, p. 177, wrote 'Siendo hombres según la ley, claro está que donde un maricón de estos se introduce, colegio, cuartel, cofradía, convento o sociedad masculina, ha de ser un foco de depravación, de corrupción, de deshonra. Oprobio de la especie humana, malean a los que con ellos se relacionan' [Being men according to the law, it is clear that wherever a *maricón* appears in a school, in a barracks, religious association, convent or any male society, he will be a centre of depravity, of corruption, of dishonour. The opprobrium of human kind, they pervert those with whom they come into contact].

60   Koch wrote that it was in schools where this 'asqueroso vicio' [disgusting vice] was perpetrated. This resulted in 'niños delgados, tísicos, con grandes ojeras' [emaciated, consumptive children with large bags under their eyes]. (Koch, *Venus Sexual*, p. 59).

61   González Carreño, one of the first authors to publish on sex education in Spain, offers many details on the initiation of masturbatory practice amongst schoolchildren. He believed that the main source for this practice was the boarding school. However, he argued that the healthiest boarding schools were the religious ones (González

Carreño, *La Educación Sexual*, p. 28). Without proposing a causal link, González Carreño did suggest that there was a certain 'juxtaposition' between school masturbation and the 'beginnings of aberrations' (p. 340). The same link can be seen in C. Bayo, *Higiene Sexual del Soltero* (Madrid: Librería de Antonio Rubiños, 1919 [1902]), pp. 116–17.

[62] Retana, *Los Extravíos de Tony*, p. 24.

[63] Retana, *Los Extravíos de Tony*, pp. 73–4.

[64] Retana, *Los Extravíos de Tony*, p. 294.

[65] Retana, *Los Extravíos de Tony*, pp. 188–9.

[66] 'The *Capricious Romans* are hailed with protests by the public. Some would ask, But are they Roman men or women?' (Retana, *Los Extravíos de Tony*, p. 223).

[67] Retana, *Los Extravíos de Tony*, pp. 267–8.

[68] A. Lorulot, 'Perversiones y desviaciones del instinto sexual. VIII. El homosexualismo', *Iniciales*, 8 (1932), reproduced in R. Cleminson, *Anarquismo y Homosexualidad. Antología de artículos de La Revista Blanca, Generación Consciente, Estudios e Iniciales (1924–1935)* (Madrid: Huerga y Murcia, 1995), pp. 75–83 (p. 80) wrote 'Es cierto que la pederastia ha progresado enormemente en Francia y en España después de la guerra. (Téngase en cuenta que hablo de la *pederastia*, no del *uranismo*). Es uno de los frutos de la decadencia general' [It is true that pederasty has progressed enormously in France and Spain since the war [the First World War]. (Remember that I am talking about *pederasty*, not *Uranism*). It is one of the fruits of general decadence].

[69] The Italian anarchist Camillo Berneri published two articles in the *Revista Blanca* in April and June 1928 on the subject of sexuality and schools (see C. Berneri, 'La degeneración sexual en las escuelas', *La Revista Blanca*, 118 (1928), and, 'El contagio moral en el ambiente escolar', *La Revista Blanca*, 122 (1928), reproduced in Cleminson, *Anarquismo*, pp. 51–5 and 57–68, respectively.

[70] Ariès & Duby, *Historia*, pp.168–73; Seoane, 'La Pasión', 418–24.

[71] R. V. Krafft-Ebing, *Psicopatía Sexual. Estudio Médico-Legal para uso de Médicos y Juristas* (Buenos Aires: El Ateneo, 1955 [1886]), with a foreword by Dr Moll and introduced by Dr Pierre Janet, p. 497.

[72] A. Forel, *La Cuestión Sexual expuesta a los adultos ilustrados* (Madrid: Bailly-Baillière, 1912), pp. 356–8.

[73] E. Régis, *Tratado de Psiquiatría* (Madrid: Imp. Saturnino Calleja Fernández, 1911), p. 109.

[74] A. Vigouroux and P. Juquelier, *El Contagio Mental* (Madrid: Daniel Jorro Ed., 1914), pp. 258–9.

[75] H. Ellis, *Estudios de Psicología Sexual*, vol. II, *La Inversión Sexual* (Madrid: Hijos de Reus, 1913), pp. 171–2.

[76] S. Freud, 'Contribuciones al Simposio sobre la Masturbación', in *Obras Completas*, vol. II (Madrid: Biblioteca Nueva, 1973 [1912]), p. 1703.

[77] Freud, 'Contribuciones', pp. 1706–9. Fernández Sanz, one of the first to discuss Freud in Spain, believed that masturbation and mere

mental pleasure ('psychic onanism'), on substituting immediate contact with imagined contact, gave rise to 'aberraciones pasionales de orden sexual' [passionate aberrations of a sexual order]. These would in turn play a role in the development of psychoses and psychoneuroses (Fernández Sanz, 'Sobre Educación Sexual', p. 388). Ángel Garma, the first in Spain to construct a broadly accepted psychoanalytic orthodoxy, however, disagreed. For Garma, 'si se le prohibe la masturbación, amenazándole con toda clase de castigos, el niño se seguirá masturbando secretamente; pero esta masturbación irá acompañada de sentimientos de culpabilidad, y, por lo tanto, de remordimientos y de neurosis' [if masturbation is prohibited by all kinds of threats, the child will continue to masturbate but in secret. But this masturbation will be accompanied by guilt feelings and, therefore, by remorse and neurosis]. See A. Garma, 'Psicología de la aclaración de la sexualidad en la infancia', *Revista de Escuelas Normales*, 103 (1934), 98–103 (100).

78 G. Rodríguez Lafora, *Los Niños Mentalmente Anormales* (Madrid: Ed. de la Lectura, 1917), pp. 430–1.

79 Lafora alluded to the presence in schools of 'muchachos lascivos y relajados que presumen de listos y conocedores de la cuestión sexual y que encuentran un deleite en interrogar e instruir grosera e indecentemente a los menores y a los recién ingresados' [lascivious lax boys who pretend to know about the sexual question and who take much delight in questioning and teaching those younger and recently arrived in the most vulgar and indecent manner], in G. Rodríguez Lafora, *La Educación Sexual*, p. 31.

80 Rodríguez Lafora, *La Educación Sexual*, p. 24.

81 Lafora wrote in his *La Educación Sexual*, p. 48, that 'Un problema importante de la pubertad es la "madurez sexual precoz" o precocidad sexual, derivada de complejos endocrinos y de factores hereditarios' [One important problem in puberty is 'precocious sexual maturity' or sexual precociousness. This results from endocrinological complexes or hereditary factors]. The relationship between masturbation and sexual precocity can also be seen in J. M. Escalante, *Iniciación en la Vida Sexual* (Barcelona: Librería Ameller, 1932), p. 99.

82 Lafora in his *Los Niños Mentalmente Anormales* takes a path midway between environmental theories (Freud, Binet, Garnier and Féré) and innate theories (Hirschfeld, Römer and Näcke) on the genesis of homosexuality. Lafora mentions the possibility of child suicide (*La Educación Sexual*, pp. 82–3), which for many authors was connected to the expression of homosexuality. One of the tropes of representation of homosexuals as victims is their tragic end, often associated with solitude and impossible love, leading to suicide (see F. Eribon, *Réflexions sur la Question Gay* (Paris: Fayard, 1999), pp. 62–3; R. Llamas, *Teoría Torcida. Prejuicios y discursos en torno a la 'homosexualidad'* (Madrid: Siglo XXI, 1998), pp. 154–64). This much is present in Spanish literature of the time as in *El Ángel de Sodoma* (1928), *Pasión y Muerte del Cura Deusto* (1924) and *Sortilegio*, an unpublished work attributed to María Martínez Sierra, but performed in Buenos Aires

in 1930 and 1942 (P. W. O'Connor, *Mito y realidad de una dramaturga española: María Martínez Sierra* (Logroño: Gobierno de la Rioja, 2003), pp. 165–76). Manuel Azaña in his *El Jardín de los Frailes* discusses in a section with the title 'El Jovencito Ahorcado en el Colegio' [The Young College Man Found Hanging], the case of a companion who took his own life on discovering his sexual inversion: 'sentía una pasión inmoral, que minaba el decoro de la familia' [he felt an immoral passion, which undermined the decorousness of the family], in M. Azaña, *El Jardín de los Frailes*, in *Obras Completas*, vol. I (Madrid: Ed. Giner, 1990), pp. 457–8.

83   This same kind of eclecticism, in which hereditary and congenital tendencies were mixed with environmental influences, was common amongst sex educationalists. In other cases, we see a division of tasks whereby the surgeon or doctor is to intervene in cases of organic anomaly or congenital perversion. The pedagogue has to channel, by means of a 'benéfico influjo educativo' [beneficent educational influence] the normal course of sexual differentiation (see, for example, Ballesteros, 'Sobre educación sexual', p. 543; D. Barnés, *La Psicología de la Adolescencia como base para su educación* (Madrid: Editorial Páez-Bolsa, 1930), p. 153; Eleizegui, *La Sexualidad Infantil*, pp. 16–17).

84   C. Juarros, *Psiquiatría Forense* (Madrid: Imp. de Antonio Marzo, 1914), p. 24; C. Juarros, *La Psiquiatría del médico general* (Madrid: Imp. Ruiz Hermanos, 1919), p. 10.

85   'Another mechanism in the arrival at [the state of] homosexuality is the creation of irregular erogenous zones. For example, anal ones in men', wrote Juarros, *Normas*, p. 64.

86   C. Juarros, *Normas*, pp. 63–4; C. Juarros, *Los Horizontes de la Psicoanálisis* (Madrid: Mundo Latino, 1928), p. 75.

87   Juarros, *Los Horizontes*, p. 75.

88   C. Juarros, *El Amor en España. Características Masculinas* (Madrid: Ed. Páez, 1927), p. 89.

89   The unrepentant masturbator and the incipient invert share timidity and the vice of an excessive 'hanging on to the mother's skirts'. Such a practice betrays in both individuals a lack of manhood, lack of willpower, passivity and effeminacy. On the timidity of the masturbator in nineteenth-century Spanish hygiene, see Seoane, 'La Pasión', pp. 114–15. For the twentieth century, note Rodríguez, *Educación Sexual*, p. 36: 'El niño reposado y al que le guste almacenar cacharritos, que es una tranquilidad para su madre, no tiene verdadero sexo varonil; en la lucha que se mantiene en el interior de su organismo está venciendo el "eterno femenino"' [The peaceful boy who likes to store items away, who is bliss for the mother, is not in possession of the true masculine sex. In the battle waged in the interior of his organism, the 'eternal feminine' is winning] and Martín de Lucenay, *Homosexualidad*, p. 16: 'En estas condiciones transcurren algunos años, diciéndose de estos niños que gustan de "estar pegados a las faldas"' [Some years pass under these conditions, in which it is said

that those boys like to 'hold on to their mother's skirts']. Marañón, for his part, associated homosexuality with timidity. See Marañón, *Ensayos*, p. 159.

90 Juarros, *El Amor*, p. 105. Masturbation was seen to favour a lack of interest in the other sex, according to Bugallo, *La Higiene Sexual*: 'suele tener gran trascendencia patológica si se prolonga demasiado o si no se la vigila convenientemente, porque puede derivar hacia la homosexualidad' [it usually has grave pathological consequences if it is prolonged in time or if it is not managed correctly, because it may drift towards homosexuality] (p. 46). Oliver Brachfeld, Professor at the Instituto Psicotécnico de Barcelona, had studied in depth the adolescent sex surgeries that were inaugurated under the Weimar Republic and considered that the most irredeemable form of onanism was the one that prevented the subject from developing ties with the other sex. The individual contented himself with the '"*faute de mieux*" of masturbation' and was stuck down by the most absolute 'passivity' when it came to approaching the other sex (O. Brachfeld, 'Los Consultorios Juveniles: principios y resultados', *Revista de Pedagogía*, 155 (1934), 502–8 (507)).

91 Juarros, *El Amor*, p. 36.

92 Juarros, *El Amor*, pp. 34–9.

93 Juarros, *Normas*, p. 34.

94 This criticism was also present amongst Spanish psychiatrists of the first third of the twentieth century. César Juarros in 'Escuela y Hogar', *El Siglo Médico*, 65 (1918), 302–3, noted that 'el régimen de escuela considerado como procedimiento exclusivo presenta también gravísimos inconvenientes, que es forzoso cortar si no queremos que subsista la ineducación ambiente que lleva a España a la catástrofe' [the regime in schools as the only component [of education] also entails serious consequences, which it is necessary to forestall if we do not wish to see the persistence of the reigning lack of education that is driving Spain towards catastrophe] (p. 303).

95 P. F. Monlau, *Elementos de Higiene Pública* (Barcelona: Imp. de P. Riera, 1846), p. 475.

96 Seoane, 'La Pasión', 205–7.

97 Seoane, 'La Pasión', 203–9.

98 P. M. Alonso Marañón, 'Notas sobre la Higiene como materia de Enseñanza Oficial en el siglo XIX', *Historia de la Educación*, 6 (1987), 22–41; R. Ballester and E. Perdiguero, 'Salud e Instrucción Primaria en el ideario regeneracionista de la Institución Libre de Enseñanza', *Dynamis*, 18 (1998), 25–50; E. Rodríguez Ocaña, 'Una Medicina para la Infancia', in J. M. Borrás Llop (ed.), *Historia de la Infancia en la España Contemporánea 1843–1936* (Madrid: Ministerio de Trabajo y Asuntos Sociales/Fundación Germán Sánchez Ruipérez, 1996), pp. 149–69 (149–52); Seoane, 'La Pasión', 293–6; A. Terrón Bañuelos, 'La higiene escolar: un campo de conocimiento disputado', *Áreas. Revista de Ciencias Sociales*, 20 (2000), 73–94 (83–91).

99 Ballester and Perdiguero, 'Salud e Instrucción Primaria'.

[100] V. Cacho Vío, *La Institución Libre de Enseñanza* (Madrid: Rialp, 1962), p. 211.

[101] Ballester and Perdiguero, 'Salud e Instrucción Primaria', 42–4; I. Palacios Lis, 'Cuestión social y educación: un modelo de regeneracionismo educativo', *Historia de la Educación*, 4 (1985), 305–19 (311–14).

[102] Cossío cited in Ballester and Perdiguero, 'Salud e Instrucción Primaria', 28.

[103] González Carreño, *La Educación Sexual*, pp. 283–90. The connection between excessive intellectualism and sexual depravation is a topic which persists well into the twentieth century amongst sex educators. For example, see L. Huerta, *Eugénica, Maternología y Puericultura. Ensayo de un estudio sobre el cultivo de la especie humana por las leyes biológicas* (Madrid: Imprenta de Fontanet, 1918), p. 318, and, Juarros, *Normas*, pp. 52–3.

[104] The idea that the channelling of the instinct took place within the process of character formation would be another well rehearsed topic among sex educators. See in this sense De Eleizegui, *La Sexualidad Infantil*, p. 146; Rodríguez, *Educación Sexual*, p. 31; E. Masip, 'Enseñanza, respecto de las funciones sexuales, que debe darse a los niños desde el punto de vista higiénico de esta función orgánica', in *Actas del Primer Congreso Español de Higiene Escolar* (Madrid: Imp. Vda. Fco. Badía, 1912), pp. 173–82 (p. 175).

[105] F. Giner de los Ríos, 'El estudio higiénico de la Infancia en el Congreso de Londres', in *Obras Completas de Francisco Giner de los Ríos*, vol. XVI, *Ensayos menores sobre Educación y Enseñanza* (Madrid: Imprenta Julio Lozano, 1927 [1889]), pp. 177–229; F. Giner de los Ríos, 'La educación de los niños según Krafft-Ebing', in *Obras Completas de Francisco Giner de los Ríos*, vol. XVI, *Ensayos menores sobre Educación y Enseñanza* (Madrid: Imprenta Julio Lozano, 1927 [1896]), pp. 231–5.

[106] Giner de los Ríos, 'La educación de los niños según Krafft-Ebing', p. 232.

[107] 'La coacción de la clase cesa allí; los muchachos obran con entera libertad . . . el egoísmo y el sentimentalismo, la debilidad y la afeminación tienen que desaparecer' [The coercion of the classroom ends there. The children act with complete freedom . . . egotism and sentimentality, weakness and effeminacy have to disappear', wrote F. Giner de los Ríos, 'Juegos Corporales' (Informe leído en el Congreso de Profesores de Gimnasia, Zurich, 1885), in *Obras Completas de Francisco Giner de los Ríos*, vol. XVI, *Ensayos menores sobre Educación y Enseñanza* (Madrid: Imprenta Julio Lozano, 1927 [1885]), p. 281. F. Salazar Quintana in his *Elementos de Higiene* (Madrid: Librería de Hernando y Compañía, 1896), p. 52, observed that 'la gimnasia higiénica, con o sin aparatos, preserva el desarreglo de la inervación, los males de la vida sedentaria . . .; es además un gran preservativo de las preocupaciones lúbricas, que en la adolescencia son muy perjudiciales' [hygienic gymnastics, with or without equipment, protects against the dissolution of enervation, the ill effects of sedentary

life . . . It is also sound protection against lubricious thoughts, which in adolescence are extremely dangerous]. This emphasis on gymnastics as a means to prevent sexual precociousness was a common element among sex educators (see, for example, Ballesteros, 'Sobre educación sexual', p. 542; Fernández Sanz, 'Sobre Educación Sexual', p. 389). On the history of gymnastics and physical education in the Restoration years see A. Martínez Navarro, 'Anotaciones a la Historia de la Educación Física Española en el Siglo XIX', *Historia de la Educación*, 2 (1983), 153–64; A. Martínez Navarro, 'El Escultismo en el Marco de la Educación Física: su implantación en España', in Various Authors, *La Educación en la España Contemporánea. Cuestiones Históricas* (Madrid: SM, 1985), pp. 151–63.

[108] J. M. Bernal Martínez, 'De las escuelas al aire libre a las aulas de la Naturaleza', *Áreas. Revista de Ciencias Sociales* 20 (2000), 171–82.

[109] M. Pereyra, 'Educación, Salud y Filantropía: el origen de las colonias escolares de vacaciones en España', *Historia de la Educación*, 1 (1982), 145–68. Sex education texts published in Spain between the years 1910 and 1936 would constantly refer to an idyllic form of sex education in primary schools which would take place in the open air while observing plants and animals under the guidance of the master (Vázquez García and Moreno Mengíbar, *Sexo y Razón*, pp. 146–7).

[110] One of the first articles written about sex education to be published by the ILE argued that coeducation was a means of preventing against 'o por lo menos, reducir a un mínimo, el terrible peligro del homosexualismo' [or at least reducing to a minimum, the terrible danger of homosexualism], opined A. Moll, 'La Educación Sexual', *Boletín de la Institución Libre de Enseñanza*, 33 (1909), 294–6 (296).

[111] The idea that coeducation could effeminize boys and virilize women often appeared in pedagogical literature in the mid nineteenth century (see Seoane, 'La Pasión', 216–17). Hygienists believed that one of the main causes of masturbation was 'la promiscuidad de sexos en los juegos y en las reuniones' [the promiscuity of the sexes in games and in meetings] – see P. F. Monlau, *Higiene del Matrimonio o El Libro de los Casados*) (Madrid: Imp. De Rivadeneyra, 1865 [1853]), p. 567. The effeminacy thesis is likewise defended by those averse to coeducation during the Second Republic (see F. Blanco Nájera, *Coeducación y Educación Sexual* (Madrid: Manuales *Studium* de Cultura Religiosa, 1935), p. 54). The minister of public education of the first government of the Republic approved a law in 1931 that prescribed coeducation in primary schools but it was revoked under right-wing rule in 1934. It appears that the law was, in any case, not observed or was sidestepped in many cases, according to Rodríguez Lafora, *La Educación Sexual*, pp. 46–7. At the end of the 1920s there existed in Spain more than 10,000 mixed schools as well as many colleges and universities (according to Ballesteros, 'Sobre educación sexual', 542–3). Most of those in favour of coeducation also defended general coeducation as part of their programme (examples can be seen in E. Madrazo, *Cultivo de la Especie Humana. Herencia y Educación*

(Santander: Imp. Blanchard y Arce, 1904), p. 304; Rodríguez Lafora, *Los Niños*, p. 545).

[112] Forns, *Higiene*, p. 166.

[113] An example of this is Gumersindo de Azcárate, discussed in F. Vázquez García and A. Moreno Mengíbar, 'Genealogía de la educación sexual en España. De la pedagogía infantil a la crisis del Estado del Bienestar', *Revista de Educación*, 309 (1996), 67–94 (77–8).

[114] Vázquez García and Moreno Mengíbar, *Sexo y Razón*, pp. 131–2; F. Vázquez García, 'Gobierno de la infancia y educación sexual (España 1900–1936)', *Cahiers Alfred Binet*, 661 (1999), 33–48 (45–6).

[115] See, in addition to many of those already mentioned, the works by L. Huerta, *La Educación Sexual del Niño y del Adolescente* (Madrid: Instituto Samper, 1930); 'Pedagogía y Eugénica', in E. Noguera and L. Huerta (eds), *Genética, Eugenesia y Pedagogía Sexual. Libro de las Primeras Jornadas Eugénicas Españolas* (Madrid: Morata, 1934), pp. 150–69, and, 'La eugenesia y la preparación del maestro', *Revista de Pedagogía*, 151 (1934), 296–301. See also J. Noguera, *Moral, Eugenesia y Derecho* (Madrid: Morata, 1930) and Q. Saldaña, *Siete Ensayos de Sociología Sexual* (Madrid: Ed. Mundo Latino, 1930).

[116] See, for example, Ballesteros, 'Sobre educación sexual'; Bugallo, *La Higiene Sexual*; Marañón, *Ensayos sobre la Vida Sexual.*

[117] A. Manjón, *El Pensamiento de Ave María. Tercera Parte. Modos de enseñar* (Granada: Imprenta-Escuela del Ave María, 1902); R. P. Ruiz Amado, *La Educación de la Castidad* (Barcelona: Imp. Ibérica, 1908); S. Aznar, 'Prólogo', in S. Stall, *Lo que debe saber el Niño* (Madrid: Bailly-Baillière e Hijos, 1910), pp. 1–13; González Carreño, *La Educación Sexual*; S. Salete Larrea, *Verdadera Explicación de la Concupiscencia* (Barcelona, 1912); Blanco Nájera, *Coeducación.*

[118] See, for example, I. Puente, 'Necesidad de la iniciación sexual', *Estudios*, 98 (1931), 6–7. In October 1934, the review *Estudios* created a new monthly section on 'Eugenesia y moral sexual'. The first article to appear under this rubric was F. Martí Ibáñez, 'Nueva moral sexual', *Estudios*, 134 (1934), 13–14.

[119] Vázquez García, 'Gobierno'; Seoane, 'La Pasión', 375–430.

[120] Vázquez García and Moreno Mengíbar, 'Genealogía', 73.

[121] Some establish a causal relationship between masturbation and organic weakness, thus facilitating the onset of tuberculosis. See V. H., 'La Higiene y la Enseñanza', *Revista de Medicina y Cirugía*, 94 (1909), 359–64 (363), and, Fernández Sanz, 'Sobre Educación Sexual', p. 388. Still at the beginning of the twentieth century numerous tracts were published on the supposed health risks entailed by masturbation (e.g. D. Carbonell, *El Onanismo. Su Prehistoria, su Historia, sus Causas y sus Consecuencias* (Caracas, 1907), discussed in an anonymous review of the book in *Revista Iberoamericana de Ciencias Médicas*, XIX (1902), 223–4). The inaugural text, so to speak, of the campaign in favour of sex education, *Lo que debe saber el niño*, was translated into Spanish in 1907 and one of its prime objectives was to prevent the practice of onanism (Seoane, 'La Pasión', 375–9). It could be argued that there was a revitalization of

the anti-onanism campaign during the first decade of the twentieth century (Seoane, 'La Pasión', 390–4).

[122] See Madrazo, *Cultivo*, pp. 307–17; Huerta, *Eugénica*, pp. 149–50; Huerta, *La Educación Sexual*, pp. 32–3. The best analysis of the texts and campaigns from the sex education point of view on the subject of the prevention of venereal disease can be found in R. Castejón Bolea, *Moral Sexual y Enfermedad: la medicina española frente al peligro venéreo (1868–1936)* (Granada: Universidad de Granada/Instituto Alicantino de Cultura Juan Gil-Albert, 2001).

[123] Huerta, 'Pedagogía y Eugénica', p. 169; Huerta, 'La eugenesia y la preparación del maestro', 301. On the relationship between the debate on sex education and the birth control controversy in Spain from 1900 to 1936, see Vázquez García, 'Gobierno', 47.

[124] Huerta, *Eugénica*, pp. 194–5; Huerta, *La Educación Sexual*, p. 33. On the concerns with respect to pornography and the corruption of children, see Seoane, 'La Pasión', 361–74.

[125] E. Mañueco Villapadierna, 'Profilaxia personal de las enfermedades venéreas', *El Siglo Médico*, 66 (1919), 1074–6; Zapatero, *Pedagogía Sexual*, pp. 131–48; D. Sánchez de Rivera y Moset, *Lo Sexual (peligros y consecuencias de los vicios y enfermedades sexuales)* (Madrid: Imp. Helénica, c.1925), pp. 83–127; Juarros, *El Amor en España*, pp. 105–6; L. Jiménez de Asúa, *La Lucha contra el Delito de Contagio Venéreo* (Madrid: Ed. Caro Raggio, 1925), pp. 149–63; A. Calmette, 'Educación sexual de los niños y de los púberes', *Boletín de la Inspección Provincial de Sanidad de Sevilla* (15 October 1927), 31–8; Noguera, *Moral*, pp. 96–7, 101; Rodríguez, *Educación Sexual*, pp. 38–9; Rodríguez Lafora, *La Educación Sexual*, pp. 13–15, 86–8.

[126] A. Fernández Martín, Review of Hermann Rohleder, *Fisiología Sexual, Psicología Sexual y Filosofía Sexual*, *El Siglo Médico*, 68 (1921), 1290; Juarros, *Normas*, p. 34; Jiménez de Asúa, *La Lucha*, p. 152; Bugallo, *La Higiene Sexual*, pp. 39–43; Noguera, *Moral*, pp. 96–7; Huerta, *La Educación Sexual*, p. 55; Barnés, *La Psicología*, p. 175; Rodríguez, *Educación Sexual*, pp. 57–61; Escalante, *Iniciación*, p. 169; Rodríguez Lafora, *La Educación Sexual*, pp. 40, 110; R. Contreras Pazo, 'La educación de los sexos', *Revista de Escuelas Normales*, 101 (1934), 45–6 (46); Eleizegui, *La Sexualidad Infantil*, pp. 104, 190–5.

[127] 'Es indispensable que la escuela realice la educación sexual, apoyándose en la educación moral y religiosa, sin extremar la nota en ningún sentido, limitándose tan sólo a desarrollar en el individuo la facultad de dominar el impulso sexual, hasta que sea oportuna la legitimación de ese acto' [It is indispensable that the school undertakes sex education, based on moral and religious education, without entering into excesses but limiting its activity to develop the individual's ability to control the sexual impulse until the time when that act finds its opportune and legitimate moment], wrote Masip, 'Enseñanza', 177. On the arsenal of ascetic resources produced by the 'education for chastity' movement, see Seoane, 'La Pasión', 375–400.

[128] Fernández Sanz, 'Sobre Educación Sexual', 387.

[129] An early formulation of this would be: 'la principal regla de Pedagogía sexual es evitar la primera ocasión, el primer contacto de los goces excitants adultos, educando la virilidad' [the principal rule of sexual pedagogy is to prevent the first time, the first contact with adult pleasures, by educating virility], by Zapatero, *Pedagogía Sexual*, p. 28.

[130] Huerta places Marañón in the arcade of the most important scientific figures: 'Marañón es nuestro Darwin. Un Darwin *muy siglo XX*' [Marañón is our Darwin. A *very twentieth-century* Darwin], he wrote in 'El marañonismo y la intersexualidad', *Estudios*, 69 (1929), 9–12 (9).

Chapter Five

'In Search of Men': *Regeneracionismo* and the Crisis of Masculinity (1898–1936)

Introduction

It is now widely acknowledged that European societies in their transition from the nineteenth to the twentieth centuries were assailed with profound doubts with respect to notions of decline and decadence. More recently, historians have noted that another facet of this turn of the century crisis was that centred on masculinity, a set of values and practices that seemed to be under threat from a constellation of processes which placed in jeopardy the strict division between the sexes and the genders.[1] Amongst these processes, the emergence of the feminist movement, the growing visibility of homosexuality in the big cities, a supposed weakening of the will and the enervation of modern, busy city life, the growth of the sexological sciences and the effects of literary aestheticism and the 'decadent' poets and writers are all important. National identity was viewed as being shorn up by masculine values which were equated with bravery, sacrifice, strength and willpower; any decline in these values was understood as an attack on the substance of the nation.

Our principal aim in this chapter is to trace how this crisis in masculinity made its appearance in essays which were written around the years of the 'Disaster', the loss of the remnants of the

Spanish empire, in the form of Cuba, Puerto Rico and the Philippines. The legacy of this loss of the colonies as loss of national pride and male vigour was to last beyond the Civil War well into Francoism and beyond. For some time now, the 'biopolitical' aspects of the Regenerationist movement in its attempt to order the population between the Restoration and the Second Republic have been studied. Social medicine, psychiatry and educational measures all fit into this broad process of disciplining the population in order to sift out and prevent foci of 'degeneration'.[2] The gendered aspects of this process, however, are much less well known.[3] In order to analyse this question, firstly we will explore the gendered content of some of the foundational texts of regenerationism written by Costa, Picavea, Mallada, Isern, Morote, Altamira and Ganivet. As a second step, we will show how the general context allowed for the explanation of decline as viewed from the trope of masculinity, and the parallels and differences with respect to other European countries will be traced. Thirdly, we will illustrate how this discourse was perpetuated in the 1920s at the time of the Spanish defeats in the war in Morocco and beyond, into the post-Civil War period. Finally, the concerns about the loss of masculinity and virile values will be traced in the anticlericalism of the late nineteenth and early twentieth centuries. Throughout, the relation between the loss of masculinity, national decline, and the threat of homosexuality will be examined.

The Decadence of Spain and the Decline of Masculinity

The expression of masculinity that appears in texts in the years surrounding the 'Disaster' correspond most closely to that embraced by the educated middle classes, rich in cultural and technical capital. This form of masculinity is counterposed to that of the 'decadent' bourgeoisie and aristocratic classes, classes depicted as being characterized by indolence, inertia and laziness, far from the dynamism and modernism of the nobility of other European countries. The Spanish landowning classes and aristocracy are depicted as having frittered away their wealth and time in the pursuit of pleasure and decadence. The result is the corruption of even its youngest representatives:

No es la torpe cobardía de evitar peligros personales, casi siempre
imaginarios, lo que retiene en la Corte y en las grandes capitales a
los más acaudalados terratenientes; es la torpe cobardía, disipada y
sedienta de vanas y divertidas novedades . . . En esa torpe cobardía
hay muchas debilidades que notar, por algunas de las cuales el sexo
fuerte sometido a los caprichos del débil, sea éste representado por
impúdicas cortesanas, carcoma y ruina de grandes haciendas, o por
virtuosas señoras.[4]

[It is not the lack of valour before possible personal danger, which
is almost always imaginary, that holds sway in the wealthiest
landowners in the Court and in the cities. It is the dissipated lack of
valour, hungry for the enjoyment of vain and new diversions [that
holds sway] . . . In this lack of valour there are many weaknesses to
be noted, by means of which the stronger sex is submitted to the
caprices of the weaker one, in the form of vulgar courtesans, the
cancer and ruin of large estates, or in the form of virtuous ladies.]

Mallada, who was opposed to compulsory military service,
recalled that the payment of a certain sum deprived the army of
'millares de individuos que distan mucho de presenter las formas
hercúleas y el vigoroso brazo de los famosos guerreros de la
antigüedad' [thousands of individuals who are far from presenting the Herculean forms and the vigorous forearm of the ancient
warriors].[5]

One could cite many more references from regenerationist
literature which depict the upper classes as victims of a lack of
vigour,[6] dissolution,[7] passivity,[8] and their attraction to the city and
its pleasures.[9] The weakness and degeneration of the upper
classes is always contrasted with the muscular healthiness of the
working classes.[10] The innate energies of the latter, however, are
corroded by poverty, squalor and brutality, factors which in turn
are seen to be derived from poor government and the decadent
elites.

The understanding of masculinity as expressed in regenerationist texts can be seen, therefore, to hinge on two basic interpretations. On the one hand, decadence is seen as the result of a
general process of 'devirilization' and effeminization of the population. On the other, the 'ills of the nation' are represented as the
result of a battle between the powers of masculinity and the
weaknesses of femininity. The solution to such a state of affairs is
predicated on the restoration of masculinity over and above
feminine values.

These dual interpretations are to be found in many examples. In Joaquín Costa's *Colectivismo Agrario en España*, the decline of the nation is expressed as the inversion of gender roles:

> Hace algunos años, cuando más enardecida la guerra, dije de España que era una nación unisexual, compuesta de dieciocho millones de mujeres. Cuando ahora vuelvo la vista atrás y abarco en una mirada las cosas horrendas, inverosímiles, sucedidas en estos cuatro años . . . comprendo el agravio que hice a las mujeres con aquella calificación. No: España no es una nación unisexual; es una nación sin sexo. No es una nación de mujeres, es una nación de eunucos.[11]

> [Some years ago, when war was being waged, I commented that Spain was a unisexual nation, made up of eighteen million women. Now, when I look back and I see what terrible, unbelievable things have come to pass in the last four years . . . I comprehend the injustice I perpetrated against womankind with this notion. No. Spain is not a unisexual nation; it is a sexless nation. It is not a nation of women; it is a nation of eunuchs.]

For his part, Macías Picavea connected effeminacy with the excessive centralization of the Spanish state. Madrid in his understanding would be a feverous city 'porque todos los asuntos del país tienen que ser despachados en ella. Existe un desequilibrio entre la agitación capitalina y la parálisis de las provincias' [because all matters of state must be dispatched there. There is an imbalance between the activity of the capital and the paralysis of the provinces]. Madrid, like Paris, is the 'brain' of the nation, but both are 'neurotic, degenerate' brains, overexcited by frenetic activity and therefore weakened in spirit. The decadence of the provinces was equated by Picavea to feminine qualities and a 'falta de salud mental, de virilidad afectiva' [lack of mental health, and male sensibility].[12] The city, as emblem of modernity, speed and rapid reactions, becomes the source of nervous stress, weakness and the undermining of virility.[13]

Mallada, who as we have already seen equated the Spanish aristocracy with the 'weaker sex', now views the Spanish crisis in general as one of a crisis of masculinity. In his *Los Males de la Patria* (1890) it is deemed certain that 'el pueblo español posee menor virilidad en el presente que en otros tiempos pasados' [the Spanish people possess less virility than in former times].[14] This situation arises in part, he argues, from the poorer racial stock in

Spain in comparison to the Anglo-Saxon and Slavic races that possess more 'vital energy' than their Latin counterparts. But the main reason for the inferiority of the Spanish lies in historico-geographical causes such as poor food, the cruel climate of the mountainous areas and the infelicitous racial mixes with invaders.[15]

The accusation of effeminacy is also evoked by these writers when they discuss what they see as another specifically Spanish trait: the tendency to gossip. This 'chismografía feminista y camarillesca' [feminine gossiping in groups], Picavea suggests, produces a 'voluptuosa vibración de los nervios' [voluptuous tingling of the nerves], similar to that experienced by decadent morphine users. This is contrasted to the natural repugnance that a healthy man feels in the face of gossip which 'le abruma, le asfixia' [overwhelms him, suffocates him].[16] Mallada criticizes 'la falta de virilidad, o sea la cobardía, que lleva aprejada consigo la maledicencia' [the lack of virility, or rather the cowardice, that accompanies evil gossiping].[17] Finally, Altamira relates the propensity to gossip with the 'carencia de estimación de lo propio' [lack of self-worth] that washes over the nation with its debilitating effects.[18]

In the light of this brief survey, two main points can be made. Firstly, the concern with gender inversion as national decline is a one-way process. The problem is always the loss of masculinity in men and not the masculinization of women. While references can be found in this literature to the deficient educational resources available to women, in particular the poor upbringing of the daughters of economically well off families, there is no mention of any decline in specifically feminine values.[19] In this sense, Spain may well contrast with discourse on national decline in other European countries such as England, France and Germany, where concerns about the masculinization of women are present from earlier on, often formulated in response to the rise of the feminist movement. In Spain, such concerns would be voiced later, in the 1920s, in the work of Gregorio Marañón and Roberto Nóvoa Santos, for example. Despite this, it would perhaps be unwise to relate the lack of this discourse to the weaknesses of feminism in Spain at the turn of the century. In France too, feminism was weak at this time, but this did not prevent the articulation of fears with respect to the loss of femininity.[20]

What is to be found in regenerationist texts is the suggestion that women, being less prone to decline and degeneracy than the Spanish male could constitute a hope for the resurrection of the nation. The Spanish woman is described as 'la admirable, la santa madre española, que conserva todos los atributos de tal por no haberse contaminado por las corruptoras costumbres' [the admirable, saintly Spanish mother, who conserves all her values because she has resisted contamination by the prevailing habits of corruption]. This pristine figure has not managed to attain the excessive luxuries enjoyed by other women and she will remain faithful to womanly values. She will not succumb to the 'voto tan frecuente en las madres (especialmente en la burguesía) francesas del único hijo, de reducir la familia a un solo vástago' [desire so frequent in French mothers (especially in the bourgeoisie) to have a single child, to reduce the family to one birth], a practice that is viewed as 'non-Spanish'.[21]

This optimism as expressed by Morote with respect to the maintenance of Spanish women's prolific natalism, is contrasted with the situation across the Pyrenees. In France, the 'birth strike' would be one of the main causes of Gallic decadence.[22] In Spain, however, decline is not associated with the drop in the birth rate.[23] This contrast with France allows us to introduce a second observation. In France, the decline in the birth rate and the increasing blurring of gender differences were often put down to the proliferation of the 'sexual perversions'.[24] In particular, homosexual relations were viewed as a threat to the recuperation of a vigorous birth rate which, in turn, was supposed to halt any national decline. In Spanish regenerationist thought, however, the sexual 'deviations' occupy little space: the prime matter for concern is gender inversion or lack of clarity between the sexes. In Chapter Two we saw how many Spanish doctors viewed homosexuality as a 'foreign vice'. Of more immediate concern amongst doctors and regenerationists, however, was the broad notion of 'effeminacy' in males. This quality was associated with passivity, with a lack of vital energy, with an excess of sensibility and bohemian lifestyles in the cities.[25]

The 'decadent poet' was often evoked as someone to be decried. Ramiro de Maeztu contrasts the poet with the stature of the energetic intellectual that Spain needed: '¡basta de Tenorios y Cyranos! . . . Las mujeres prefieren los hombres bien nutridos a los *golfos* escuálidos – y a los poetas decadentes' [Enough of

Tenorios and Cyranos! ... Our women prefer healthy men to weakling layabouts and to decadent poets].[26] For his part, Altamira recommended that the male youth undertook 'useful work' and a 'serious undertaking' instead of 'wailing lyricism' and the 'delusions of erotic delirium' which could be found in the doctrines and the literature of the modernist generations.[27] Instead of this weak modernism, it was necessary to regenerate education itself and allow the universities to 'crear generaciones de ánimo viril, que no se apoquen ante las dificultades comunes a todos los pueblos' [forge generations of virile will, which do not cower in the face of those difficulties faced by all nations].[28]

In Damián Isern's work, *Del Desastre Nacional y sus Causas* (1899), the influence of French degenerationist thought is evident in his allusions to sexual inversion. Isern relies on a topos often used in Europe at the time in order to express the decline of the nation. The decadence of ancient Rome and Greece is invoked to condemn both *molitie* and homosexuality, which in turn are seen to have occasioned such a decline in the first place: 'degeneradas aquellas ciudades en las cuales reviven por modo especial los vicios de la decadencia de Grecia y Roma y, en especial, el estetismo' [degenerate are those cities which rekindle the decadent vices of Greece and Rome and, above all, aestheticism].[29] This swipe at aestheticism was two-pronged. On the one hand, it allowed Isern to criticize those viewed as 'aesthetes' or 'dandies' such as Oscar Wilde and Robert de Montesquiou, associated in Spain with literary modernism, and on the other, he could attack the 'sexual invert', of effeminate manners who was increasingly visible in European *fin de siècle* cities.[30] What was thought as repugnant here was not so much actual homosexuality, as sexual practices between people of the same sex, but a much broader set of properties, which implied the reversal of roles between the sexes, including passivity, transvestism and effeminacy.[31] Homosexuality is contrasted with heterosexuality but 'inversion' and 'aestheticism' are contrasted with masculinity, whose crisis, linked to the phenomenon of national decline, was what concerned the Spanish regenerationists.

A Displaced Rhetoric

The lamentations for 'lost manhood', seen as a cause and a consequence of the decline of the nation, are not limited to a few sporadic mentions in regenerationist thought. To some degree, the whole of the oeuvre which accompanied the 'Disaster' is permeated by this concern. Regenerationist thought can be seen, at least in part, as a paean to lost masculinity. But above all, the fundamental crisis of the nation is rooted in inactivity, in 'abulia'. This is not something which is located in the province of one class; it is a general and widespread cause of decay. Regeneration-ists used a variety of terms to express this idea. While 'apathy' was used by Mallada, 'abulia' by Ganivet and Altamira, 'laziness' and 'indolence' by Mallada, 'weakness' by Altamira and 'general paralysis' by Morote, Maeztu and Picavea, all coincided that feminine 'passivity' expressed by Maeztu was opposed to 'will-power', 'character' and 'energy', all values associated with mascu-linity.[32]

The reasons behind this lack of willpower varied according to the author. Some believed that it was a constitutional characteris-tic of Latin races, reinforced by specific Spanish circumstances.[33] Others, retaining an essentialist explanation, recognized the ambivalent inheritance supplied by Spain's links to Africa: a strong and positive independent spirit dogged by an 'instinto de discordia, de desunión, de separatismo' [instinct of discord, of disunity, of separatism],[34] which had been triumphant in the historical arena. Some viewed passivity as rooted in Spanish history itself. Original Spanish virtues may have been tainted by a 'cuerpo extraño' [foreign body]. In this sense, Macías Picavea introduced the idea of 'Austracism' to describe the imperial designs introduced by the Germanic races and the 'monomanía teológica y teocrática' [theological and theocratic monomania] of the Habsburg dynasty, which made the country embark on an ill-advised series of adventures of conquest. Spain's energies were thus dissipated and its constitution fatally weakened.

Despite this, not one of the regenerationist writers sees this end result as part of an irreversible historical process. What history has done, can be undone. In this sense, regenerationist thought is opposed to Darwinian inevitability as expressed in Lord Salis-bury's famous speech on 'dying nations' in May 1898. According to this thesis, the weakest nations, which would include the former powers of Spain and the Ottoman Empire, would be unable to adapt themselves to the new prevailing circumstances and would, hence, perish.[35]

The notion of masculinity articulated by these regenerationist writers, drawn from the professional and intellectual bourgeoisie, contrasts clearly with that which they attributed to the old decadent nobility and, by extension, to the whole of the nation. Virility, in this new formulation, is not seen as the aggressive and intermittent force employed by the warlike aristocracy, dismissing hard work both intellectual and manual. Neither is it linked to inheritance or blood ties. Instead it is a biological and psychological quality based on the values of self-control, foresight, discipline and knowledge. This is a modern form of masculinity which tries to maintain some of the old aristocratic values such as asceticism, stoicism in the face of adversity, noble generosity, dignity, and strength of character. It tries to combine all these with the new bourgeois values of self restraint, pride in one's work, the values of knowledge for knowledge's sake, morality and civic sensibility.[36] The regenerationists speak of an outmoded masculinity, 'a puro de tanto pelear, de sangre depauperada, de nervios agotados, de inteligencia yerma' [of the fighting man, of impoverished blood, of exhausted nerves, of barren intellect],[37] as dead and gone. The 'new man' will rise, phoenix-like, from the ashes of the old.

One of the principal motifs that regenerationist writers would have recourse to for the materialization of this new man would be, in accordance with Costa's exhortation of 'escuela y despensa', the provision of fully costed education. But once more, we come up against an antagonism between what were understood as the female and the male principles in education. The former would embrace a purely intellectual mode of instruction, which was seen to overstimulate comprehension, while the latter would emphasize the strengthening of the will and would have more to do with morality and religion. Intellectual education is not denied, however; the regenerationists were concerned about the cultivation of sentiment at the expense of practical knowledge. This asymmetry between 'education' and 'instruction' was, in the psychiatric language of the times, postulated as a disease known as 'neurasthenia' that was to become common in the period.[38] Neurasthenia was a condition characterized by nervous overexcitement which would result in fatigue and loss of intellectual and bodily powers. It was increasingly associated with particular lifestyles, such as those of bohemians and poets, but also with anarchists and intellectuals. Mut denounced 'Esos jóvenes viciosos, desaplicados y holgazanes' [These lazy and indolent young people of both sexes], 'esos juerguistas, derrochadores' [those late-night drinkers and party-goers], as useless for society. Those who lived for the latest fashion, 'esclavos de sus tiranías, con el ala del sombrero levantada por la parte anterior, aun cuando haga un sol canicular; con pantalón bien arremangado aunque no haya barro' [slaves of its caprices, whose hats are cocked up from behind, despite the midday heat; with rolled up trousers even though there is not a speck of mud], formed the 'inmensa falange de asténicos' [huge phalanx of pale-faced individuals].[39]

'Neurasthenia' is also a pathology which affects 'los que trabajan mucho intelectualmente' [those who engage in much intellectual work], including poets and students,[40] and 'esos bohemios melenudos, hipersensibles, que mueren jóvenes debido a su vicio' [those long-haired hypersensitive bohemians who die young as a result of their vices].[41] It brings with it weakness, enervation and thus provokes feminization, as several hygienists were to argue: 'un hombre perezoso, entregado al vicio o enervado por la profesión sedentaria, se afemina con facilidad' [a lazy man, absorbed by vice or enervated by sedentary occupations, becomes effeminate with great ease].[42] For this same reason, neurasthenia is associated with the rapid and busy lifestyle of the big city, although towns and villages are not exempt from such a plague.[43] With respect to sexuality, César Juarros was to argue that overexcitation of the mind and a too vivid imagination could arise from masturbatory practices.[44] A surplus of undirected intelligence led to 'la lujuria, y con ella a las aberraciones sexuales y a la homoerastia' [luxurious behaviour, and to the sexual aberrations and homoerastia].[45] A direct relationship is thus constructed between an excess in refinement, sharp intelligence and erotic interest in those of the same sex. Such an equation anticipates the debate which would come at the end of the 1920s on the subject of the relationship between genius and homosexuality.

Against this dissipation of intellect, regenerationists advocated a form of education that would rely on energy, will and discipline. Altamira spoke of an education of will that would heal the defects present in the national psyche and that would make up 'ciudadanos en quienes vibre el sentimiento de la disciplina social y del amor a la patria, y sea claro y enérgico el concepto de la

convivencia social' [citizens in whom social discipline and love of
the *patria* would hold strong and in whom there would be a clear
and energetic notion of conviviality].[46] Morote also alluded to the
need to create 'national energy' and advocated a form of education that would 'cultivar la paciencia, . . . dominar los propios
impulsos, . . . consultar con la razón tranquila la conducta que
debemos seguir' [cultivate patience, . . . would control one's own
impulsiveness, . . . would rely on one's calm rationality to determine the way to proceed].[47] Finally, Matías Picavea proclaimed:
'¡La disciplina! ¡Hay que resucitar la santa, entonadora, espiritual
disciplina . . . Donde quiera en Europa se conserva; ¡sólo en
España se ha hecho de ella tabla rasa, hasta el monstruoso
absurdo de haber llegado a su total, absoluta, rotunda anulación!'
[Discipline! We have to resuscitate strong, spiritual and abnegated
discipline . . . Throughout Europe this has been preserved; it is
only in Spain that it has been reduced to almost nothing, made to
appear as a monstrous, absolute and total negation of its former
self!].[48]

The anti-intellectualism of this pedagogical proposal is confirmed when we examine the importance awarded to physical
education. This was emphasized by Costa, especially: 'educación
física en interés mismo de la intelectual y de todo el individuo,
porque el hombre no vive sólo de abstracciones' [physical education for the benefit of intellectual education and for the individual as a whole, because man does not live by abstractions
alone'.][49] The regenerationists, as we have pointed out, understood the lack of energy and virility that characterized Spanish
culture as something to do with the 'flojedad de cuerpo' [weak-
ness of body] which, in Mallada's words, was at the heart of
'national apathy'.[50] Luis Morote considered that 'en la educación
física estará el remedio de ese mal' [physical education will be the
remedy for this illness] and he was to praise highly the pedagogical work of Francisco Giner de los Ríos.[51] The Institución Libre de
Enseñanza (1876), the incarnation of the regenerationist educa-
tive spirit, considered that physical education was of prime importance. This included gymnastics, sports, excursions into the
countryside and the establishment of educational camps or colonies. In physical play, Giner de los Ríos pointed out, 'los muchachos obran con entera libertad' [pupils enjoy complete freedom];
'el egoísmo y el sentimentalismo, la debilidad y la afeminación

tienen que desaparecer' [egotism, sentimentality, weakness and effeminacy must disappear].[52]

The dichotomy between male and female present in a number of scenarios illustrated above did not refer only to human faculties such as activity/passivity, reason/sentiment, strength/weakness, or to attitudes such as chauvinism/patriotism, words/deeds, to professions (technician/writer, engineer/lawyer), or to practices (education as opposed to instruction). It also took on a geographical significance. Differences were inscribed between north and south and between centre and periphery. The North could be Europe and the South Africa, as in Costa's *Política Quirúrgica* (1905) where the necessary Europeanization of Spain was contrasted with Spain's colonies in black Africa: 'España pedía a sus gobiernos europeización, y los gobiernos han contestado africanizándola' [Spain demanded from its governments Europeanization and our governments gave us Africanization].[53] The same concern is seen in Matías Picavea who compares the dejected situation of the rural Spaniard with that of the 'African hordes'.[54]

Africa, like the Orient and in contrast to Europe, is a symbol in turn of the century Europe of the reign of passion and sentiment over and above reason, of the predominance of the feminine over the masculine.[55] But Luis Morote believed that this could be overcome through education. Japan would be an example of the triumph of education above sentiment: 'que de ser un pueblo de civilización asiática decadente, se ha trocado en un pueblo de civilización europea joven, robusta, sana, maravillosamente progresiva' [from being a decadent Asian people, it has become a young European civilization, robust, healthy and marvellously progressive].[56]

For Ramiro de Maeztu, the north/south divide is expressed alongside the periphery/centre contrast. On the one hand, this materialized as a difference between the hard-working north of Spain, with its Basque and Catalan industrialists and the centre and south, the land of administrators, *latifundistas* and *caciques*.[57] On the other hand, ills arose from the dissonance between the coast ('en la hora actual toda la costa se ha modernizado económicamente' [the whole coast is now modernized in the economic sense]) and the *meseta* ('Castilla, despoblada por mil guerras, arruinada por la usura y por el fisco, atrasada porque en ella perviven las odiosas leyendas de los tiempos muertos' [Castile, bled by a thousand wars, ruined by usury and its tax burden, held back by its odious legends from moribund times]).[58] But this antithesis between active and passive spaces is not merely present in Spain's geography. It also makes its presence felt in the spheres of sociability and socialization. There are places where the race decays and becomes degenerate, where the national vices of verbosity, flamenco dancing, laziness, drunkenness and excess such as the casino, the bar and the bordello thrive.[59]

But who should lead the nation out of this mire? Regenerationist writers coincided in the need for a strong, charismatic leader who personified precisely the qualities that had been absent in Spain's governments to date. This figure would not necessarily be a dictator; while Mallada and Macías Picavea did point to this solution, others such as Costa and Altamira opted for a democratic regime of some variety. What was necessary, all admitted, was a figure in whom all the qualities of a new virility coincided. The third chapter of Costa's *Política Quirúrgica* is entitled 'En Busca de Hombres' [In Search of Men]. These men would be exemplars in whose 'venas corra sangre caliente, que levanten a España del cieno de Sedán' [veins there runs hot blood, who can raise Spain up from the mire of Sedan].[60] This man must act with conviction, with iron strength, 'blandiendo su maza de hierro para limpiar la tierra de monstruos' [brandishing his iron hammer to rid this land of monstrosities].

This kind of virile politician was scarce in Spain at the time, the regenerationists argued. The type of political figure that triumphed was the upstart, the voluble and effeminate politician who sold himself to the highest bidder and who became the puppet of the *caciques*. The failure of these politicians, corrupted and effeminate, appears to have surpassed the boundaries of the genre of the political essay. In a *costumbrista* novel of 1885, published five years before Mallada's *Los Males de la Patria*, the inadequate effeminate politician made his appearance in Ángel María Segovia's suggestively and captivatingly entitled novel *Los Maricones*.

This rather extraordinary text, published under the pseudonym 'K. Arbbón de Kock', was not, despite first appearances, an erotic or indecent publication. The author invited the potential reader to open 'sin desconfianza este libro y llévale a tu casa sin temor a la curiosidad de las mujeres. Esta obra pueden leerla tu madre, tu esposa y tus hijas' [this book with no mistrust and take it home without fearing the curiosity of your womenfolk. Your mother, your wife and your daughters can all read this book].[61] In this text the word *maricón* is not used to signify 'homosexual' but rather is used to suggest weakness, indecisiveness, and effeminacy. It signifies deviation with respect to gendered characteristics and not sexual object choice. He who is a disgrace to his sex, who lacks manliness, is a *maricón*.

The backdrop of this novel is the political scene of the period between Isabel's reign and the beginning of the Restoration. The context, therefore, is the corrupt political period of the *turno pacífico*, characterized by the rule of the *caciques*. This *caciquismo*, the author proclaims, is the 'esencia del más grosero egoísmo personal' [outgrowth of the most vulgar form of personal ambition].[62] Such a system contaminates and ends up destroying even the most intimate of social relations, including privacy, matrimony, family and friendship ties.

For his story Segovia uses the Cervantine device of the lost manuscript. The fictional author of this manuscript is one Pedro Sopeña – the alter ego of the story's protagonist – whose misfortune in politics resulted in his and his family's decline into poverty. Sopeña is found after an unsuccessful suicide attempt and his wife hands Segovia the manuscript of the novel. Segovia vows to publish it in order to raise the Sopeña family out of its misfortunes.

Los Maricones relates the triumph of vice and corruption in public life. Segovia's subject is the decline of the virile and upright politician and the rise of the self-serving, womanizing political figure such as the protagonist Bardales in a period of political hypocrisy: 'la época a la que vamos refiriéndonos, 1870, era la más a propósito para abrirse paso un tipo como Bardales: la revolución entraba en el periodo de delirio, los hombres de Estado luchaban entre sí como rameras, y hacían falta maricones que atizasen la tea de la discordia' [the year that we refer to, 1870, was ideal for the emergence of a figure such as Bardales: the revolution was in a moment of delirium, statesmen grappled with one another like whores and all that was needed were some *maricones* to light the fires of discord].[63] The first of the figures to be presented is Pablo Peláez, the son of an influential member of the Liberal Party. Peláez is of Aragonese stock, and is the heroic defender of his convictions to the degree of having to suffer exile.

He is 'uno de esos liberales a toda prueba, cuya raza va extin-
guiéndose' [one of those liberals worth his salt, whose race is
gradually becoming extinct].[64]

But Peláez is a political failure. After having fought for political
liberties and his return from exile, he places himself in the service
of Miguel Recencio, a dissident minister of the provisional government after the 1868 revolution. Peláez is the editor of a
newspaper, *El Centinela Avanzado*, which campaigns for the rebel
minister, and runs to his aid when his former allies desert him
and he spends his copious inheritance in maintaining the newspaper. Thanks to Peláez's support, Recencio gradually recovers
his former glory and becomes prime minister. However, he
dismisses his few supporters who helped him in his hour of need
and takes on his former adversaries. Pablo Peláez is obliged to
close the newspaper and, disillusioned and bankrupt, with his
family in tatters, his inheritance is gone.

The story of Peláez stands for the fate of all honest virile
politicians ('hombres serios, varoniles, denodados, verdaderos
amantes de la patria y de la libertad' [serious, manly, daring, true
lovers of the *patria* and of freedom]), and is contrasted with the
sea of opportunistic, corrupt politicians referred to as 'maricones'. Amongst these are the ugly Juan Becerril, a shop assistant
who has become a landlord, who is totally dominated by his wife,
and Juan Bardales, the former owner of the *Centinela*, who is
prepared to sell the newspaper to the highest bidder. There is also
the figure of Policarpo Moaré ['moiré' in English], 'vistoso y fino
como el tejido que lleva su nombre ... veleidoso, inconstante
como una mujer coqueta' [showy and refined as the cloth that
bears his name ... capricious and inconstant as a flirtatious
woman].[65] Finally, we have Miguel Recencio himself who is
described as not having had sufficient 'virilidad para proceder
como hombre denodado, y contesta a las nobles palabras de
Pablo, como contesta la mujerzuela: con arranques de femenil
soberbia' [virility to allow him to proceed with valour and who
replies to Pablo's noble words just as any harpy may with bursts of
feminine pride].[66]

Segovia emphasizes the very real comparisons to be made
between his fiction and reality in Spain, 'un país regido por
politiquillos sin pudor, charlatanes de oficio, intrigantuelos de
baja estofa, ignorantes enfatuados' [a country ruled by shameless

politicians, charlatans, the lowliest intriguers, infatuated ignoramuses].[67] Cánovas, however, the architect of the politics of the Restoration, 'es un hombre enérgico, brioso. Emprende las más arduas empresas con fe, con intrepidez; acomete los obstáculos, los arrolla y triunfa. En suma; es un hombre' [is an energetic man, full of brio. He undertakes the most arduous of tasks with faith, without wavering. He takes on obstacles, defeats them and triumphs over them. In a word, he is a man].[68] A kind of social law is then imputed. In Spain, when a virile politician emerges, he is accompanied by his shadow, the effeminate corrupt politician: 'en la misma nave, cuyo capitán es Cánovas del Castillo, un contramaestre como Fernández Villaverde. Junto a lo grande, lo pequeño . . . junto al hombre vigoroso, la mujerzuela vengativa; junto al esforzado marino . . . el afeminado y rabiosuelo contramaestre' [in the same ship captained by Cánovas del Castillo, there is the quartermaster Fernández Villaverde. Alongside the great, the miserable . . . alongside the vigorous man, the vengeful woman; alongside the hard-working seaman . . . the effeminate, unmanly quartermaster].[69]

The use of the word 'maricón' to describe the degenerate politician appears at the end of the novel, once Pablo Peláez has entered the realms of despair:

> Por la imaginación de Pablo cruzaban sin cesar las sombras de estos hombres, y no acertaba a darles el calificativo que merecían, hasta que en el colmo de la exaltación se le ocurrió llamarles maricones. ¿Qué nombre más adecuado? Si la calidad natural del hombre es la entereza, el denuedo, la intrepidez; la propiedad del maricón, es el enervamiento, la procacidad, la astucia, el disimulo, la soberbia. Su tendencia a los hábitos femeniles se manifiesta siempre según su posición. Si mandan son déspotas; si obedecen humildes; odian la honradez y temen la franqueza; por eso no quieren a su lado hombres de corazón varonil. Quieren ductilidad, no firmeza; hipocresía, no lealtad; esclavos viles, no amigos dignos.[70]

> [In Pablo's imagination, the shadows of these men were constantly present. He could not think of a word to describe them adequately until in a moment of exaltation the word 'maricón' occurred to him. What could be a better description? If the natural qualities of men are uprightness, daringness, intrepidness, the properties of the *maricón* are enervation, shamelessness, a manipulative nature and pride. Their tendency towards feminine habits is always

manifest in whatever position they hold. If they rule they are
despotic. If they obey they are timid. They hate honour and fear
frankness; this is why they do not want men with virile hearts at
their side. They want ductility, not firmness; hypocrisy, not loyalty;
they are vile slaves and not worthy men.]

Discretion and the hiding of one's emotions used by real
inverts in the face of stigma and insult are transposed on to the
maricón in Segovia's story and made into essential qualities. These
qualities are marshalled into a critique of the politicians of the
day and it is this set of metaphorical transpositions that bring
Segovia's account into the fold of regenerationist writings. But the
'discretion' of the invert, the duplicity of one's remarks and
actions, and the membership of clandestine associations, all characteristics ascribed to the Jew, will have a long life, well into the
years beyond the Civil War.

The Impotent Male, Colonial War and Loss of Manhood

If the dual rhetoric of the nation in decline and lost masculinity
was felt especially strongly when the last outposts of the Empire
were lost, its echo would last much longer. A first example of the
persistence of the metaphor of loss were the comments and
analysis which resulted from the disaster of Annual (1921), the
battle lost to the Rif in the Protectorate of Morocco, and which
was to propel the advent of the Primo de Rivera dictatorship. The
control that Spain held over this part of North Africa as a result of
the European sharing out of the continent at the beginning of the
twentieth century did not precisely make Spain a colonizing
nation in the traditional sense. Spain's role was limited to certain
questions of law and order and the military pacification of the
area, a part of Africa in constant unrest against the European
presence. This military adventure had already produced important defeats for the Spanish notably that of the Barranco del Lobo
in 1909, and public opposition to military recruitment for the war
was extensive and often violent. The pacification of the region was
short-lived and in 1921 the Rif led by Abd-el-Krim took control of
the whole area under Spanish supervision up to the gates of
Melilla.

The reactions to this latest military disaster reflected many of
the arguments made in the years leading up to and beyond 1898.

The whole imaginary of Spain as an effeminate nation came to the fore once more. One article by César Juarros, published in 1922 under the title 'Morocco the Perverse', described the war as a feminine campaign, whose narcotic effects ended up debilitating Spanish troops. The invisibility of the enemy, the ambushes, and the astute methods of the Rif all made for a struggle imbued with feminine values, of softness and deceit. Juarros was to ask: '¿por qué resulta tan delicada, tan enfermiza el alma de la guerra de Marruecos?; ¿por qué huele tanto a mujer?' [why is the soul of the Moroccan war so delicate, so sickly? Why does it smell so of woman?] The skirmishes with the local population smelt of 'aliento de ramera, a perversión y decadencia' [whores' breath, perversion and decadence]. Indeed, it was a war with little public support and of dubious moral justification. It was a war in which 'el militar no tiene atmósfera de héroe, sino de víctima' [the soldier has no aura of heroism but of victimhood].[71]

There was no lack, however, of legionnaires and regular soldiers who enrolled in this war. Juarros put this seductive aspect of the war down to the unreality of the enemy and the disorientation afforded by the tireless sun. The European association between the seductive woman and the Orient once again makes its appearance in the Moroccan war ('¿vas percibiendo, lector, de dónde procede el encanto brujo de perversión y de decadencia de los combates de Marruecos?' [Dear reader, do you now realize from where the seductive enchantment of perversion and decadence in the wars of Morocco stem?]). In the battles waged in Morocco there is a mixture of anaesthetizing pleasure and androgynous ambiguity: 'todo ello, exquisito cual la piel de algunos hombres femeninos de adolescente, suena como sonaría un curso de Religión explicado por la "Maja Desnuda" de Goya' [everything about it, is as exquisite as the flesh of a feminine adolescent male; it sounds how the strains of a course on religion would if recounted by Goya's 'Maja Desnuda'].[72]

A different tone is detected in the writing of Dr Aguado Marinoni, a member of the Institute of Social Medicine, even though the motif of abulia to explain the defeat in Africa and the degeneration of the race are invoked. Marinoni echoes the desires for reform and energy present in the regenerationist writers. When discussing the causes of the Moroccan defeat Marinoni returns to the language of 1898. He speaks of the 'degeneration of the race' (high infant mortality, poor physical and spiritual development as evidenced by the state of the conscripts, a proliferation of 'raquíticos, tuberculosos, sifilíticos, intoxicados, dispépticos, imbéciles, histéricos e impulsivos' [syphilitics, dyspeptics, imbeciles, hysterics, and others affected by tuberculosis, beriberi, various intoxications, and nervous impulsions]).[73] The rate of illiteracy is high, land goes to waste through the indolence of landlords and Spain is plagued by useless lawmakers, 'false patriotism', 'cowardice', and the inability to make decisions even amongst the most able of Spaniards. Spain seems to have been bled dry, her vitality having been wasted in the imperial age.[74] Spain was a nation incapable of engaging in any colonizing undertaking: '¿Qué vitalidad, qué cultura, qué riqueza pública, qué autoridad, qué prestigio vamos a llevar a Marruecos si no lo tenemos en casa?' [What kind of vitality, culture, riches, what authority and prestige are we going to take to Morocco if we have none at home?][75]

Once again, following Costa's dictum, 'in search of men', the presence of 'real men' is sought. These men are the very substrate of the nation; they will raise the nation from its degenerative state: 'Hay que legislar para hombres, educar hombres, conducir hombres, no seres imaginarios; hombres son los que han de realizar las empresas, y a los caracteres intrínsicos de estos hombres hay que atenerse para el desarrollo de las mismas'.[76] [We must legislate for men, educate men, and lead men and not imaginary beings. It is men who will undertake the necessary tasks and it is the intrinsic character of these men that must be attended to in order to undertake these tasks.]

This manliness was placed in jeopardy by many factors in the colonial territories and in Spain itself. At the same time as the Moroccan crisis Spanish doctors were renewing their interest in a form of pathology connected to the loss of masculinity: 'psychic impotence'. Throughout the nineteenth century, male impotence had been explained by doctors as a result of the drain on energy that arose from onanism, spermatorrhea and 'involuntary seminal loss'.[77] In the passage from the nineteenth to the twentieth century the emphasis shifted and the aetiology of impotence was lodged in the neurasthenia camp. It resulted, from now on, from overexcitation of the nervous system, something derived in many cases from masturbation itself, from a degenerative trait or from the practice of unsatisfactory sexual relations such as *coitus interruptus* and other 'fraudulent' practices.

Thus, around 1910, 'psychic impotence' was born. Unlike previous forms of impotence, there were no physical lesions to be detected or dysfunctions in the sexual organs. The *potential coeundi* declined because of a psychic mechanism. The imagination, instead of exciting the nervous centres that entailed sexual excitement, inhibited erection in the male. The very representation of impotence became the cause of such impotence.[78]

In all of the medical accounts presented at the time there was a common factor in psychic impotence. Somehow in the patient there had been a critical loss of masculinity. The syphilis expert Juan de Azúa, the urologist Ángel Pulido and the psychiatrists César Juarros and Gonzalo Rodríguez Lafora argued that a cluster of causes could be named ranging from onanism, shyness in relations with women, an unsatisfactory experience with a prostitute, the homosexual tendencies inherent in childhood mutual masturbation, a failed marriage and suicidal desires. In all events, the cures offered by quacks and charlatans were to be resisted[79] and the advice contained in 'pseudo-scientific' medical literature was to be questioned.[80]

Initially, psychic impotence was not seen as hard to cure. Juan de Azúa argued that it was possible to cure it by means of positive suggestion and recommended that the patient undertake sleep therapy.[81] But more obstinate cases began to appear. For these, a huge range of therapies appeared including suggestion, doses of electrical current, hydrotherapy and hypnosis.[82] Pulido, shortly before the rise of the endocrinological sciences, led in Spain by Marañón, mentioned the usefulness of glandular therapies, from injections of gonadal tissue through to hormonal treatment, procedures that would also be held to be useful as 'cures' for homosexuality.[83] Pulido believed that these treatments, as complimentary somatic therapies, were compatible with psychoanalysis. He also mentioned other psychological forms of treatment such as hypnosis, automatic handwriting and oral association.

Juarros, however, believed that psychic impotence was never merely psychic and he continued to proclaim that masturbation in the infant and adolescent was a primordial cause.[84] In this way, he repeated the arguments of other authors such as Wallace, Moll, Gibson, Wiley and Löwenfeld, and followed the same line of reasoning that Pulido and others from a more sexological perspective had displayed.[85] Frequent onanism, together with incomplete sexual experiences, generated a species of hyperaestesia, congestion in the prostate and urethra resulting in the inability to perform coitus and hence impotence. For this reason, Juarros believed that psychic impotence was 'frecuentísima en España. Acaso por tratarse de un país donde abundan los casos de masturbación conservados después de la adolescencia' [extremely frequent in Spain. This may well be because Spain is a country where there is an abundance of cases of masturbation carried over from adolescence].[86] In such cases, an old remedy from the times of Lallemand was recommended: the introduction of a little silver nitrate in the lower part of the urethra by means of an exploratory syringe.[87]

In addition, Juarros believed that psychic impotence was a symptom of mental illness, that is, the result of a lesion in the nervous system (hysteria, psychasthenia or paranoia). Of course, this somatization of mental illness in fact contradicted the very psychic elements of the disease itself. Rodríguez Lafora argued against Juarros's conceptualization of this illness as an individual complaint; for Rodríguez Lafora psychic impotence was part of a collective threat, with a statistical probability. To use the terms offered by Castel,[88] Lafora did not view this illness as part of an individual problem to be resolved in each individual case, but rather as a question of 'risk management'. In Lafora's case, psychiatry concurred with the prophylactic model of mental hygiene and became an instrument in the control of popula-tions.[89] For this reason, Lafora emphasized the high degree of correlation between impotence and the suicide rate:

> El problema, a pesar de su importancia para la felicidad individual y para la propagación de la especie, está aún poco estudiado, conformándose la mayoría de los libros con decir que es una forma de neurastenia, y aconsejando tratamientos medicamentosos y autosugestivos que sólo alguna vez dan un resultado práctico. Y sin embargo, cada hombre prematuramente impotente es el centro de una tragedia de amor. Los suicidios en los días que anteceden o que siguen al matrimonio, van aumentando de día en día.[90]

> [This problem, despite its importance in terms of individual happiness and for the reproduction of the species, has hardly been studied. The vast majority of texts are content with declaring that it is a form of neurasthenia and they advise treatment with medicines and autosuggestion which only once in a while obtain any practical effect. Rather, any man who suffers from premature impotence is

an individual in the heart of an amorous tragedy. Suicides in the days immediately before matrimony or just after it are on the increase.]

In turn, the proliferation of impotent individuals was connected to the increasing tendency of late nuptials. This artificial delay in the practising of sexual relations would entail, according to this schema, the rise in cases of impotence. In Spain, the situation was particularly serious, where the husband-to-be would often leave home in search of work to marry on his return. When he finally returned, many years later, 'cae en la cuenta de que quizá no sea ya capaz a los cuarenta años de cumplir bien sus deberes matrimoniales; hace un ensayo, a veces el primero, y el fracaso lo pone en situación desesperada' [he realizes that perhaps at the age of forty he is not capable of fulfilling his matrimonial duties. He tries, perhaps for the first time, and his failure brings desperation].[91]

Lafora regarded the majority of cases of impotence as psychic conditions, even though they would have some relation with organic processes. Impotence, in reality, was not actually an illness; it was a symptom of a much broader set of illnesses.[92] Lafora's characteristic eclecticism rejected purely organic explanations as well as purely psychological ones, such as those found in the Freudian school. The relative importance of psychological and somatic factors depended on the type of pathological state. Lafora argued that there were three principal types: a congenital predisposition; an acquired predisposition from the first years of childhood; and an acquired predisposition from later years. In the first two cases at least, the subject's impotence points towards an incomplete form of masculinity.

Those whose impotence resulted from congenital psychic predisposition displayed a weakness from birth in their nervous system. In later childhood, this fragility would be manifest in 'pasividad en los juegos, falta de vivacidad, tendencias femeninas y una especial precocidad sexual sin ir acompañada de un desarrollo proporcional de los genitales' [passivity in games, a lack of vivaciousness, feminine tendencies and a particular sexual precociousness without the accompanying genital development]. During adolescence, these subjects displayed gestures that 'se parecen a los del hombre dentro de cierto afeminamiento' [were similar to those of the grown up man, within certain effeminate parameters].[93]

In the case of impotence acquired in the first years of childhood, the explanation was seen to lie in the developmental stages of sexuality first elucidated by Freud. Psychic impotence was the result of the fixation of the libido in the incestuous phase. This subconscious desire for the mother was repressed and the individual would be unable to establish sexual relations with individuals of the 'opposite' sex. In due course, sexual desire could be channelled towards other members of the family (such as a sister, cousin or aunt) or towards members of the same sex, giving rise to latent homosexuality. Together with this 'incestuous timidity', which gave rise to impotence, Lafora emphasized the role of the 'castration complex'. The child's fear of being punished for his desire towards the mother would create the type of anxiety characteristic of those who suffered from psychic impotence.

But Lafora was not satisfied with mere psychoanalytic explanations which privileged environmental causes of impotence. To complete the picture, biologistic accounts were required. Those individuals who were incapable of getting over the oedipal stage of the instinct, of adapting to the conflicts of adult sexual life, would suffer from 'cierta disposición hipogenital atenuada que causa esa deficiencia compensadora del instinto genital ante vivencias de la primera infancia' [a weakened hypogenital disposition caused by the compensation for the lack of genital instinct which arose from experiences in early childhood]. There existed a congenital tendency towards the fixation of the libido, an impulse that could remain dormant as long as 'adequate sexual education' was practised.[94]

Amongst these psychically generated forms of impotence arising in early childhood appeared latent homosexuality. This came about in individuals who lacked sexual differentiation.[95] This form of impotence was also known as 'female identification' as those affected by it showed 'tendencias femeninas derivadas de su constitución' [feminine tendencies derived from their constitution], as well as an intense 'adhesión a la madre' [attachment to the mother]. Lafora associates impotence with the inversion of the sexual instinct in these individuals who are unaware of their homosexuality:

Muchos son marcadamente narcisistas y visten con femenina coquetería y esmero. Si llegan a tener contacto sexual con mujeres consiste sólo en masturbación mutua, en cunilingus o excitación del clítoris con la lengua y otras prácticas perversas en las cuales el sujeto siente el orgasmo cuando consigue producírselo a su compañera, lo que no altera sus fantasías femeninas. En el trato social con las mujeres se comportan casi como rivales de ellas.[96]

[Many are clearly narcissistic and dress in a coquettish and extremely careful feminine manner. If they achieve sexual contact with women this is only in the form of mutual masturbation, cunnilingus, or the excitation of the clitoris with the tongue, and other perverse practices in which the subject experiences orgasm only when he manages to induce the same in his partner. His feminine fantasies remain intact and in his social intercourse with women he behaves almost as their rival.]

In this way the Madrid psychiatrist established a clear relationship between impotence as a result of latent homosexuality and a lack of virility. If manliness is demonstrated in combat – and by extension by the 'struggle for life', as Marañón would say – one element in this form of psychical impotence is feminine fearfulness, their cowardice on the battlefield. For this reason, Lafora argued that the First World War served as a means to illustrate how common this latent homosexuality actually was.[97]

In a nation where, according to Juarros and Lafora, impotence had become an endemic condition, the result was a lack of vigour and decisiveness and Spain's elimination as a world power. The symbolic relationship between the loss of virility and the weakening of the national soul, so characteristic of the regenerationist writers, made its reappearance in the 1920s in the context of discussions of impotence. At the same time, fears of weak masculinity were reinforced by another factor that the literature of the Disaster had barely touched upon: the 'virilization' of women and the new types of subjectivity afforded by feminism.

Anticlericalism and Sexual Impropriety

Similar kinds of rhetorics on decay and decline, resulting from a loss of manhood and the increase in effeminacy, can be seen to have operated in the sphere of anticlericalism, a broad and powerful set of motifs that were especially present in the early years of the nineteenth century and the first three decades of the twentieth. Although the anticlerical imaginary goes back in Spain to the medieval and early modern periods,[98] anticlericalism as a set of rationalized political discourses and practices, including speeches, pamphlets, novels, newspapers, theatrical works, medical treatises, cartoons, educational reforms and the disentailments, is much more recent.

Spanish anticlericalism, as a key element in the 'governmentality' of the population in Foucauldian terms, dates from the end of Absolutism to the end of the Civil War, that is from 1833 to 1939.[99] The defence of this particular ideology was made from a number of perspectives ranging from Krausist Catholics through to republican positivists but all coincided in their vision of the Church as the principal obstacle blocking the creation of a modern nation or, in the case of anarchism and some strands of socialism, the emancipation of the oppressed.

According to this anticlerical logic, the advent of a self-regulating market, the freedom of the press, the establishment of a constitutional regime, the separation of the public and private sphere, the expansion of the cities and of salaried work, the progress of science and the arts, amongst many other 'modern' features, were all held back by the recalcitrant power of the Church.

If the priesthood was the incarnation of all that was opposed to the imaginary national community, which was in turn identified with a strong dose of virility, it comes as no surprise to see that the Church was identified with the triumph of a weak, effeminate character, duplicity and deceit and unbalanced sexuality.

There were perhaps two principal elements in this formulation of anticlericalism at the time. Firstly, the influence exerted by the priesthood over women, in particular those who belonged to the bourgeois and upper classes. Secondly, there was the question of the 'sexual aberrations' which were seen to derive from the vow of chastity taken by priests and from their isolation from the rest of society. Along with this, there often went the accusation of pederasty with young boys and amongst priests themselves.

The first question – the influence of Catholicism over women – is expressed in naturalist and realist literature and in some sectors of the Restoration press. The defeat of Carlism, as an alternative clerical politics, added to the slow disappearance of Church properties during Isabel's reign, merely bolstered the claims of anticlerical propaganda in the 1860s. But at the same time, the Church managed to consolidate its influence in charity work and in education. This step was, in part, guaranteed by the cooperation between Church and women of the upper classes. The participation of women through the Women's Guilds and charity and religious associations, supported the Church's expansion of influence during the Cánovas years of government.

By means of this association, the priest as confessor, spiritual director or participant in charity campaigns, found himself placed in close cooperation with women of social esteem from the upper classes. In this way, influence could be exerted over the course of politics in the country. All that was seen to be the virile expression of a modern political spirit was effectively co-opted by these alliances.[100] According to the anticlericalists, then, superstition and religious charity became the opponents of utilitarianism and scientific criteria in the relentless march towards modernity.

The priest and the devout bourgeois or upper-class woman was the butt of satire and criticism in many novels of the period. While seduction was hinted at, or expressed openly, this did not necessarily lead to anything sexual. The confessional was understood to be an important element in the priest's control and manipulation of these women. This was one of the principal themes of *Le Prêtre, la femme et la famille* by Jules Michelet (1845) translated into Spanish in 1908 as *El Cura, la Mujer y el Confesionario*.[101] Another of the many novels that illustrates this issue is Leopoldo Alas's *La Regenta* (1884–5). By means of the confession of the protagonist, Ana Ozores, the most intimate details of her life are laid bare to Fermín de Pas, resulting in the priest's complete domination of her existence from that point on.[102]

Another source of opposition to the influence of the confessional in daily existence is that of radical naturalism. A number of authors fall into this category including López Bago, A. Sawa, J. Zahonero, E. Sánchez Seña, R. Vega Armentero and E. A. Flores. Part of the success enjoyed by this group of authors in the 1880s was without doubt due to the anticlerical elements present in their work. Some of their work was published in offprints inserted in anticlerical publications such as *El Motín, Las Dominicales del Libre Pensamiento, Satanás* and *¡Verán Ustedes!*,[103] providing a strange but potent fusion between the reporting of the 'dark deeds' of the clergy and their incorporation into novelistic form.

Such an offensive against the priesthood was to a large degree facilitated by a law on the freedom of the press passed in 1883.

Other works, such as *Mi Mujer y el Cura. Confidencias de un aldeano* by J. Zahonero (*c.*1888) and, especially, *El Confesionario (Satiriasis)* by López Bago (1885), lay bare the mechanisms by which women were inveigled into the priest's literal or metaphorical arms. In *El Confesionario*, López Bago describes how the attractive Padre Román manages to exert a tyranny over the Marquesa Gertrudis by manipulating the latter's desire for penitence. A million 'reales' are thus obtained from Gertrudis which Román proposes to use to climb the ecclesiastic ladder. But, in addition to Román's ambition, is a burning desire which takes Gertrudis as its centre point. Román, in order to impede any impropriety with the marquesa, finds himself having recourse to a prostitute.[104]

López Bago illustrates how pernicious the use of the confession becomes in the hands of the priesthood. In particular, the inquisitorial methods use by priests to enforce the Sixth Commandment does little more than excite adolescents' curiosity, leading to an unhealthy interest in matters sexual. Amongst the possible undesirable consequences of this morbid interest the author relates the activities of a paedophile priest, who took advantage of his position to engage in reprobate acts.[105]

The negative influence exerted by the priest on family women would, in this way, go further than perverting matrimonial harmony to affect the morality of the children and, in particular, the family's daughters. Young boys and girls would be encouraged to enter the religious orders with unfortunate results and disasters untold in years to come.[106]

In the 1930s we see a similar phenomenon. The confessor is equated with a seducer in the case of *Colegios Adorables* (1930) by Francisco Bullón and Segismundo Pey Ordeix's *Sor Sicalipsis* (1931). Bullón narrates how Padre Canuto utilizes the confessions of the young girls in his charge to extort sexual favours.[107] It emerges in the novel that Canuto, while training to become a priest, began his sexual life by ritually practising anal sex with a group of boys in his charge. In the second novel, Pey Ordeix recounts the story of an adolescent girl who falls in love with her confessor. The priest in this account manages to convince the young girl to join a convent, where he exercises the most complete power over her.[108]

From the evidence presented here, anticlerical discourse only rarely made reference to paedophilic or pederastic practices. But the trope of masculinity, and therefore national integrity, were both affected by the corrosion of gender differences as derived from the spiritual care which particularly women received. Virility, identified with the male prerogative of control in the domestic sphere, was subverted by priestly outsiders who converted husbands into the playthings of their wives and who disrupted the privacy of the home and the public sphere.

However, the depiction of sex between men or between adults and minors was to make its appearance in the context of another aspect of anticlerical discourse: that related to celibacy and to the cloistering of monks and nuns. The vow of chastity was criticized by anticlericals as a betrayal of the biopolitical injunction to renew the population. This particular element in Spain can be traced back to the Enlightenment. On the one hand, drawing on the Galenic and Hippocratic traditions, it was believed that the retention of semen entailed multiple illnesses. On the other hand, the population was considered to be the principal source of power that a nation possessed; an excessive number of religious establishments were seen, in contrast, as a source of demographic debility.[109]

Throughout the nineteenth century, hygienists gave voice to this kind of criticism of perpetual chastity, effectively coming out in support of a quantitative model for human sexuality. Hygienists believed that excessive use of the genital organs as well as their lack of use was detrimental to overall health and demographic vitality. Masturbation, frequent coition and lifelong chastity ran contrary to the balance of the organism and resulted in impotence, sterility and various mental disorders, according to the hygienists.[110]

In the work of Sales Mayo, *La Condesita* (1866), the representation of one of the characters, a priest, conforms exactly with the images conjured up by medical doctors with respect to the consequences wrought by chastity. Vicario is the protagonist of this account, a priest who is sent to a provincial parish accompanied by Irene, his sister who at times helped the priest in his offices. Suddenly, Vicario experiences ardent desires for the woman on reading some missives sent to her by a lover. Tempted by this incestuous relationship, the priest finally decides to 'renovar su juramento sacerdotal de inviolable castidad' [renew his religious vows of inviolable chastity].[111] But after her marriage to her suitor, Irene experiences sensual desires which she manages to drown in the pleasures of eating and drinking during the day and, at night-time, by mortifying herself, sleeping barefoot on one occasion on a bench outside the parish church. She soon falls victim to hysterical spasms which prevent her from resting and she begins to decline visibly.

While the undesirable consequences of chastity were portrayed at length in the 1880s and 1890s, at the beginning of the twentieth century links between sexual abstinence and the 'sexual aberrations' were reconsidered in the light of the dissemination of the psychopathology of the 'perversions'.[112] In degenerate individuals or those organically predisposed, long periods of chastity resulted in 'attacks' of sexual perversity. This framework, based on similar tenets to that explaining epilepsy, also viewed the lack of contact with the other sex, a characteristic of religious institutions, particularly convents, as a major factor in the production of the sexual 'perversions'. The combination of chastity and isolation would be particularly dangerous in the case of spiritual directors and ecclesiasts charged with the education of youth.[113]

It is in this context, as we suggested in Chapter Four, that the figure of the perverse priest makes his entry.[114] He is responsible, according to many texts of the time, for pederastic practices amongst his pupils and for the 'ruin of the race'. In the previous chapter, this was discussed in the context of the corruption of minors; here we present a synthesis of the principal elements which made up the association between the priesthood and perverse sexuality. The perverse priest is a figure that emerges in novels,[115] psychiatric case studies,[116] in journalistic accounts,[117] and in legal and criminological reports.[118] The perverse priest, corrupter of children and emblem of the past, is presented as the antipathy of the new, secular modern Spain which places faith in the youth as a force for the renewal of a tired national spirit.

A number of real life controversies and scandals arose at the beginning of the twentieth century riding on the wave of criticism of celibate life and in the light of the science of the sexual 'perversions'. In part, such concerns are voiced in the context of the demographic consequences of celibacy. Also present is the ongoing polemic over coeducation and the regime in convents and boarding schools, as well as the pedagogical discussions on the advantages and disadvantages of chastity.[119] The sex reformers of the 1920s and 1930s (Huerta, Marañón, Juarros and Lafora, for example) considered sexual abstinence to be unnatural and pathogenic. Despite some sex reformers' defence of youthful continence in sexual relations, to be broken only once the marriage vows were taken, other saw chastity as an unhealthy product of repressive sex education. Such a stance was often taken from a psychoanalytic perspective whereby repression was understood to be a source of neurosis and perversion; it became the task of sex education to reveal these dangers.[120]

Despite these negative images of the priest, laced with pathologizing references and at times rather lurid accounts the truth of which was perhaps to be questioned, one book was to provide a rather novel and compassionate account of the relations between clergy and youth. *Pasión y Muerte del Cura Deusto* (1924),[121] written by the Uruguayan diplomat Augusto D'Halmar, was in effect an attempt to humanize and aestheticize the impossible passion between the *padre* Deusto, a Basque priest in his thirties who had recently arrived in Seville, and Pedro Miguel, 'El Aceitunita', a Gypsy choir boy of pre-adolescent beauty. The novel has been considered 'one of the most important examples of orientalist literature characteristic of the nineteenth century', despite having been published in the twentieth century.[122]

There is no question that the Occident/Orient or North/South divide is a driving force in the novel. Pedro Miguel, the son of a Gypsy mother and Jewish father, of 'linajes sin patria' [lineages with no country],[123] constitutes the incarnation of oriental sensuality and the female principle. Deusto, on the other hand, is described as a 'man of the North', robust but refined.[124] This notion is carried through with respect to the religiosity of the Andalusian south and that of the North. In the North, the liturgy enjoys greater importance and mortification is deemed less crucial; in the South, there is an air of 'Moorish tolerance',[125] where an aesthetics of renunciation and self-control characteristic of 'an iron race' are dominant.[126] Andalusia and the Basque Country are presented as the 'two poles of our character'.[127] On the one hand there is a certain feminine softness and sensuality which breaks down strict divisions between the sexes; on the other a virile and rigorous principle remains.

The central emphasis of the novel is placed upon the decay of these rigid differences and the transgression of limits. A brief synopsis of the novel will illustrate how these elements are depicted. Deusto, on his arrival in Seville, is captivated by the beauty of the boy and offers to house him in the priest's home. The boy sings as a member of the choir at first but, given his excellent performance, is shortly promoted to altar boy. This favouritism causes a certain amount of comment amongst the parishioners and the devout who are jealous of the amount of attention afforded to the boy. Deusto is entranced by the virginal innocence of Pedro Miguel and he comes to consider the relationship as a kind of substitute for the ones he missed during his time in the seminary. Throughout the novel, there are few open references to any bodily contact and, where there is, this comes from the boy rather than from the adult. A hand is furtively squeezed by the altar,[128] some kisses are proffered to the priest when he is bedridden;[129] these are acts that often cause discomfort in Deusto.[130]

Barely an adolescent, Pedro Miguel comes into contact with a group of people who are the antithesis of the protected world of the church. Amongst the figures inhabiting this world are a painter of Jewish origin, a famous bullfighter, a flamenco singer, and a famous but somewhat ambiguous Sevillian artist, Giraldo Alcázar. Alcázar is depicted as a dandy-like figure, a Sevillian Dorian Gray who lives in a *ménage à trois* with his secretary and the latter's wife. The young Gypsy makes contact with this circle via another painter, Sem Rubí. Rubí manages to convince Deusto to allow the altar boy to pose nude in his studio in order to capture Pedro Miguel's ephebic beauty.

Pedro Miguel, finally, deserts the priest and goes to live in the company of this assortment of artistic figures. His talents as a flamenco singer surprise all present and he embarks on an affair with one of the accompanists, while a poet openly flirts with him. Meanwhile, Deusto sinks into the most abject despair. He believes that the boy has been taken by force and he tries to get him back by disguising himself and frequenting places of ill repute, populated by bullfighters, flamenco singers and prostitutes.

After a suicide attempt, exhausted by tavern life and his flamenco labours, Pedro Miguel decides to return to Deusto, ignoring his brother's attempt to carve out an artistic vocation for him. He is now a young man and has lost his virginal candour. But life with the priest is not to be as expected. It is full of tension and their knowing glances betray a distance that is irrecoverable: 'Lo nuestro no tiene solución en esta tierra' [what is between us knows no solution on this earth], the young man pronounces.[131] Their clandestine relationship makes things worse: 'porque esa vuelta clandestina al hogar de adopción tenía algo, a la vez, de rapto y de secuestro. El cura vasco, amparador de un menor, contra su propia familia, se colocaba fuera de la ley y la afrontaba. Una tal noticia, transpirando hasta un diario anticlerical, bastaría para motivar la opinión pública y cubrirle de oprobio' [because that secretive return to his adoptive home was something akin to a forced stay or even a kidnapping. The Basque priest, by providing refuge to a minor, against the wishes of his own family, was placed outside and against the law. The news of this, if published in the pages of an anticlerical newspaper, would be sufficient to incite public opinion and to cover him in shame].[132]

Given the impossible situation, the boy flees once more. Deusto manages to catch up with him on the railway station platform, as he boarded a train destined for Madrid. Pedro Miguel proposes that the priest boards the train with him and leaves his Seville life behind to begin afresh. When the boy asks: '¿has sabido nunca cómo yo te quiero?' [have you ever realized how much I love you?] Deusto pushes him aside and declares: 'ahora lo sé, y, por piedad no lo digas, ¡también he visto claro en mí!' [I know now, and, for pity's sake say it not, for I have seen the same in myself!] After this declaration the priest wanders dreamily towards the head of the train ('marchaba hacia el Norte, el Norte donde viniera' [he walked towards the North, the North from whence he came]) and descends to the tracks.[133] The train pulls away and crushes the priest under its iron frame.[134]

Throughout the novel limits and borders are fused and disappear: Pedro Miguel states on one occasion 'usted sabe como yo que hemos tocado el límite' [you know just as well as I do that we are going beyond any limits] in the affair.[135] They are up against the differences between Occident and Orient, between North and South, at the limits of what curtails the eroticism of religion, between promiscuity and abstinence,[136] the love of the father and the love of the lover.[137] Indeed, these are the limits between the sacred and the profane and, in the final analysis, between life and death. The South and the Orient blur differences and make things indistinct. The boy's voice becomes androgynous and 'indecisa como si participara de los dos sexos' [indecisive, as if it were of both sexes];[138] he is 'ya no pueril y todavía no viril' [no longer a youth but not yet a man].[139] He wanders and knows no country in his 'vagabond instinct' and is ambivalent in his relationship as a young boy with the older priest.[140]

This play with borders and limits is reminiscent of some of George Bataille's work, particularly his *Histoire de l'œil*, set, as it happens, in a famous chapel in Seville. In the novel written by D'Halmar, the love between the priest and the ephebic choir boy transcends any moral condemnation, despite the suicide of the priest at the end, and refuses any clinical diagnosis. The relationship between the two, on the one hand the priest, an emblem of the obscurantist past, and the boy, representing the future of the race, a prodigy of modernity and progress, serves as an enticement towards the impossible dissolution of all difference.

NOTES

[1]   A. Maugue, *L'Identité Masculine en Crise au Tournant du Siècle* (Paris: Rivages-Histoire, 1987); R. Nye, *Masculinity and Male Codes of Honor in Modern France* (New York/Oxford: Oxford University Press, 1993), pp. 72–9; E. Badinter, *La Identidad Masculina* (Madrid: Alianza Editorial, 1993), pp. 29–38; G. Mosse, *The Image of Man. The Creation of Modern Masculinity* (New York/Oxford: Oxford University Press, 1996), pp. 77–106.

[2]   F. Álvarez-Uría, *Miserables y locos: Medicina mental y Orden social en la España del siglo XIX* (Barcelona: Tusquets, 1983), pp. 158–68; R. Campos Marín, 'La teoría de la degeneración y la clínica psiquiátrica en la España de la Restauración', *Dynamis*, 19 (1999), 429–56; R. Campos Marín, 'La Teoría de la Degeneración y la Profesionalización de la Psiquiatría en España (1876–1920)', *Asclepio*, 51, 1 (1999), 185–203.

[3]   Some aspects of the gendered and sexualized discourse of *regeneracionismo* were examined in R. Cleminson, 'En torno a *Sexualidad*: "desviación sexual", raza y la construcción de la nación', *Reverso: Revista de estudios lesbianos, gays, bisexuales, transexuales, transgénero . . .*, 3 (2000), 41–8.

[4]   L. Mallada, *Los Males de la Patria y la Futura Revolución Española* (Madrid: Alianza Editorial, 1994 [1890]), pp. 49–50.

[5]   L. Mallada, *La Futura Revolución Española y otros escritos regeneracionistas* (Madrid: Biblioteca Nueva, 1998 [1897]), p. 316.

[6]   J. Costa, *Oligarquía y Caciquismo* (Madrid: Ed. de la Revista del Trabajo, 1975 [1901]), p. 224.

[7]   R. de Maeztu, *Hacia otra España* (Madrid: Biblioteca Nueva, 1997 [1899]), p. 173.

[8]   R. Altamira, *Psicología del Pueblo Español* (Madrid: Biblioteca Nueva, 1997 [1902]), p. 141.

9   R. Macías Picavea, *El Problema Nacional* (Madrid: Biblioteca Nueva, 1996 [1899]), p. 123.

10   Mallada, *Los Males de la Patria*, p. 193.

11   J. Costa, *Colectivismo Agrario en España*, cited in E. Tierno Galván, 'Costa y el Regeneracionismo', in *Escritos (1950–1960)* (Madrid: Tecnos, 1971), pp. 369–1079 (p. 462). Costa, in his *Política Quirúrgica* (1905), when discussing the Zaragoza martyrs of the Revolution of 1868, wrote 'siguen abochornándonos con el recuerdo de su virilidad y de su fe' [their virility still provides discomfort for our memories]. See J. Costa, *Política Quirúrgica* (Madrid: Biblioteca Costa, 1914 [1902]), p. 39.

12   Macías Picavea, *El Problema Nacional*, pp. 301–2.

13   Mosse, *The Image of Man*, pp. 82–3.

14   Mallada, *Los Males de la Patria*, p. 37.

15   Mallada, *Los Males de la Patria*, p. 38. The poor diet of the middle classes is discussed in Mallada, *La Futura Revolución*, p. 323.

16   Macías Picavea, *El Problema Nacional*, pp. 178–9.

17   Mallada, *Los Males de la Patria*, p. 156.

18   Altamira, *Psicología*, pp. 146–7.

19   This is true of the essays written around the time of the 'Disaster', but in naturalist novels and some medical sources, as was pointed out in Chapter Two, women who led lives of luxury and pleasure were depicted as a dangerous force for the differentiation between the sexes. Recently, Shubert has shown how women bullfighters were vilified in the press at the end of the nineteenth century (A. Shubert, *Death and Money in the Afternoon. A History of the Spanish Bullfight* [Oxford: Oxford University Press, 1999], pp. 100–4).

20   Mosse, *The Image of Man*, p. 104.

21   L. Morote, *La Moral de la Derrota* (Madrid: Biblioteca Nueva, 1997 [1900]), p. 250.

22   This situation was commented upon in the Spanish medical press. See, for example, J. Rochard, 'Causas de la Disminución de los Nacimientos en Francia', *El Siglo Médico*, 32 (1885), 145–50; Anon., 'Los célibes en Francia', *El Siglo Médico*, 32 (1885), 650.

23   The first expression of birth control propaganda in Spain was that organized by L. Bulffi and his anarchist review *Salud y Fuerza*, 1904–1914. See M. Nash, 'El Neomalthusianismo Anarquista y los Conocimientos Populares sobre el Control de la Natalidad en España', in M. Nash (ed.), *Presencia y Protagonismo. Aspectos de la Historia de la Mujer* (Madrid: Ediciones del Serbal, 1984), pp. 307–40; R. Álvarez Peláez, 'La Mujer Española y el Control de la Natalidad en los Comienzos del siglo XX', *Asclepio* 42, 2 (1990), 175–200; R. Cleminson, *Anarchism, Science and Sex: Eugenics in Eastern Spain, 1900–1937* (Oxford: Peter Lang, 2000), pp. 109–56. Anarchists and socialists defended a different kind of masculinity from the one described here. Theirs was an internationalist, virile masculinity, whose aim was solidarity but also, at least on paper, one which professed equality between the sexes. The fertility rate only started to decrease in Spain at the beginning of the twentieth century, affecting

the birth rate quite abruptly in the 1930s. See F. Dopico, 'Ganando espacios de libertad. La mujer en los comienzos de la transición democrática en España', in G. Duby and M. Perrot (eds), *Historia de las Mujeres*, vol. IV, *El Siglo XIX* (Madrid: Taurus: 2000), pp. 597–611.

[24] R. Nye, 'Sex Difference and Male Homosexuality in French Medical Discourse, 1830–1930', *Bulletin of the History of Medicine*, 63, 1 (1989), 32–51; Nye, *Masculinity*, pp. 98–126.

[25] See A. Mira, 'Modernistas, dandis y pederastas: articulaciones de la homosexualidad en la "edad de plata"', *Journal of Iberian and Latin American Studies*, 7, 1 (2001), 63–75.

[26] De Maeztu, *Hacia otra España*, p. 222.

[27] Altamira, *Psicología*, p. 198.

[28] Altamira, *Psicología*, p. 191.

[29] D. Isern, *Del Desastre Nacional y sus Causas* (Madrid: Imprenta de la Viuda de M. Minuesa de los Ríos, 1899), pp. 75–6.

[30] Mira, 'Modernistas', pp. 64–5; Mosse, *The Image of Man*, pp. 86–8. Robert de Montesquiou (1855–1921) is the less well known of the two figures, having lived a dandified life in Paris accompanied by the Peruvian Gabriel Yturri for twenty years, alongside whom he was buried on his death. See the entry 'Count Robert de Montesquiou-Fezensac' by Robert Aldrich in R. Aldrich and G. Wotherspoon (eds), *Who's Who in Gay and Lesbian History From Antiquity to World War II* (Routledge: London/New York, 2001), pp. 317–18.

[31] G. Chauncey, 'From Sexual Inversion to Homosexuality: The Changing Medical Conceptualization of Female "Deviance"', in K. Peiss, C. Simmons and R. A. Padgug (eds), *Passion and Power: Sexuality in History* (Philadelphia: Temple University Press, 1989 [1982/3]), pp. 87–117; D. M. Halperin, 'How to do the History of Homosexuality', *GLQ: Gay and Lesbian Quarterly*, 6, 1 (2000), 87–121 (103–9).

[32] Mosse, *The Image of Man*, pp. 22–7.

[33] Mallada, *La Futura Revolución*, pp. 295–6.

[34] Morote, *La Moral*, p. 113.

[35] R. de la Torre, 'La prensa madrileña y el discurso de Lord Salisbury sobre las "naciones moribundas"' (Londres, Albert Hall, 4 mayo 1898)', *Cuadernos de Historia Moderna y Contemporánea*, 6 (1985), 163–80.

[36] For similar processes elsewhere, see Mosse, *The Image of Man*, pp. 20–4; Nye, *Masculinity*, pp. 8–10.

[37] Morote, *La Moral*, p. 152.

[38] Two descriptions of neurasthenia can be found in A. Mut, 'Los Neurasténicos', *Revista Ibero-Americana de Ciencias Médicas*, 16 (1906), 213–19, and, J. Martínez Valverde, *Guía del Diagnóstico de las Enfermedades Mentales* (Barcelona: Hijos de Espasa Editores, 1899), pp. 212–13.

[39] Mut, 'Los Neurasténicos', 218.

[40] R. Serret, 'Neurastenia sifilítica', *El Siglo Médico*, 40 (1893), 793–5 (794).

[41] D. Sánchez de Rivera y Moset, *Lo Sexual (peligros y consecuencias de los vicios y enfermedades sexuales)* (Madrid: Imp. Helénica, c.1925), p. 95.

J. Labanyi, *Gender and Modernization in the Spanish Realist Novel* (Oxford: Oxford University Press, 2000), pp. 133–5, places the increased interest in neurasthenia in Restoration novels in the context of fears over the loss of masculinity associated with the growth of the big city and increased consumerism.

[42] F. Salazar y Quintana, *Elementos de Higiene* (Madrid: Librería de Hernando y Compañía, 1896), p. 40.

[43] T. Valera y Jiménez, 'La neurastenia en los pueblos', *El Siglo Médico*, 49 (1902), 517–18.

[44] C. Juarros, 'Diagnóstico de las neurastenias', *Revista Médica de Sevilla*, (30 November 1911), 289–96 (294).

[45] R. Forns, *Higiene. Breves apuntes de las lecciones dadas en el curso de 1908 a 1909* (Madrid: Biblioteca de la Revista de Especialidades Médicas, 1915), p. 166.

[46] Altamira, *Psicología*, p. 195.

[47] Morote, *La Moral*, p. 247.

[48] Macías Picavea, *El Problema*, p. 284.

[49] J. Costa, *Maestro, Escuela y Patria (notas pedagógicas)* (Madrid: Biblioteca Costa, 1916), vol. X, p. 135.

[50] Mallada, *La Futura Revolución*, p. 295.

[51] Morote, *La Moral*, p. 251.

[52] F. Giner de los Ríos, 'Juegos Corporales' (Informe leído en el Congreso de Profesores de Gimnasia, Zurich, 1885), in *Obras Completas de Francisco Giner de los Ríos*, vol. XVI, *Ensayos menores sobre Educación y Enseñanza* (Madrid: Imprenta Julio Lozano, 1927), p. 281. On the connections between the ILE and the advocacy of physical education, see A. Martínez Navarro, 'Anotaciones a la Historia de la Educación Física Española en el Siglo XIX', *Historia de la Educación*, 2 (1983), 153–64, and, R. Ballester and E. Perdiguero, 'Salud e Instrucción Primaria en el ideario regeneracionista de la Institución Libre de Enseñanza', *Dynamis*, 18 (1998), 25–50. On the relationship between physical education, the introduction of gymnastics in school and regenerationism, see A. Martínez Navarro, 'El Escultismo en el Marco de la Educación Física: su implantación en España', in Various Authors, *La Educación en la España Contemporánea. Cuestiones Históricas* (Madrid: SM, 1985), pp. 151–63. On school 'colonies' [colonias], see M. Pereyra, 'Educación, Salud y Filantropía: el origen de las colonias escolares de vacaciones en España', *Historia de la Educación*, 1 (1982), 145–68.

[53] Costa, *Política Quirúrgica*, p. 30.

[54] Macías Picavea, *El Problema Nacional*, p. 123.

[55] E. Said, *Orientalism* (London: Penguin, 2003).

[56] Morote, *La Moral*, p. 243.

[57] De Maeztu, *Hacia otra España*, pp. 195–7.

[58] De Maeztu, *Hacia otra España*, p. 168.

[59] De Maeztu, *Hacia otra España*, p. 165, criticizes the culture of 'género chico' and 'tertulias'; Mallada, *Los Males de la Patria*, p. 199, highlights the antagonism between Sunday school and the bordello;

Macías Picavea, *El Problema Nacional*, discusses the influence of prostitution (p. 105) and 'poor morality and flamenco customs' (p. 119).
Flamenco was associated with national decadence, effeminacy and
racial weakness, and was sometimes evoked to condemn Gypsies. The
pioneer of eugenics in Spain, Dr Madrazo, believed that the Gypsy
came from an 'alma de prehistórico salvaje' [soul of a prehistoric
savage]. See E. Madrazo, *Cultivo de la Especie Humana. Herencia y
Educación* (Santander: Imp. Blanchard y Arce, 1904), p. 104. The
association between laziness and the Gypsy was not evoked when it
came to bullfighting, despite the links between the two. Flamenco
was seen to effeminize because it brought to bear the influence of
Gypsies; bullfighting virilized because it transformed sloth into
energy.

60 Costa, *Política Quirúrgica*, p. 31.
61 A. M. Segovia, *Los Maricones. Novela de Costumbres* (Madrid: Tipografía
Hispano-Americana, 1885), p. 5.
62 Segovia, *Los Maricones*, p. 280.
63 Segovia, *Los Maricones*, p. 73.
64 Segovia, *Los Maricones*, p. 73.
65 Segovia, *Los Maricones*, p. 112.
66 Segovia, *Los Maricones*, p. 170.
67 Segovia, *Los Maricones*, p. 169.
68 Segovia, *Los Maricones*, p. 169.
69 Segovia, *Los Maricones*, p. 170.
70 Segovia, *Los Maricones*, p. 291.
71 All quotations in this paragraph are from C. Juarros, 'Marruecos la
Perversa', *El Siglo Médico*, 69 (1922), 639–40.
72 Both quotations in this paragraph are from Juarros, 'Marruecos',
640.
73 A. Marinoni, 'Medicina Social', *El Siglo Médico*, 68 (1921), 950–73.
74 Marinoni, 'Medicina Social', 972.
75 Marinoni, 'Medicina Social', 973.
76 Marinoni, 'Medicina Social', 972.
77 See, for example, M. Curtis y La Mert, *La Conservación Personal.
Tratado interesante de las causas de la decadencia prematura de la energía
física y mental y demás atributos de la virilidad* (Barcelona: Imp. de
Oliveres Hermanos, 1849), and P. Mata, 'Discurso pronunciado por
el Dr. Mata en la sesión del día 14 de enero de 1860', *El Especialista.
Revista Quincenal de Sifilografía, Oftalmología, Afecciones de la Piel y del
Aparato Genito-Urinario*, 8–13 (1860), 83–199. See also Vázquez García
and Moreno Mengíbar, *Sexo y Razón*, pp. 98–9.
78 J. de Azúa, 'Impotencia psíquica', *El Siglo Médico*, 63 (1916), 338–40
(338); G. Rodríguez Lafora, 'Impotencia sexual masculina de forma
psíquica', *El Siglo Médico*, 75 (1925), 237–40 (239).
79 De Azúa, 'Impotencia psíquica', 340; A. Pulido Martín, 'Algunos
Conceptos Modernos sobre la Potencia Sexual', *El Siglo Médico*, 67
(1920), 977–9 and *El Siglo Médico*, 68 (1921), 8–9.
80 G. Rodríguez Lafora, 'La impotencia masculina y la neurastenia
moral', *El Siglo Médico*, 88 (1931), 541–52 (549).

81   De Azúa, 'Impotencia psíquica', 339–40.
82   Anon, 'Observaciones neurosexuales en el frente', *El Siglo Médico*, 65 (1918), 674.
83   Pulido, 'Algunos Conceptos', *El Siglo Médico*, 67, 977–98.
84   C. Juarros, *El Amor en España. Características Masculinas* (Madrid: Ed. Páez, 1927).
85   Pulido, 'Algunos Conceptos', *El Siglo Médico*, 68, 8. See also A. San de Velilla, *Higiene de los Placeres* (Barcelona: Biblioteca de Iniciación Sexual, *c*.1930), pp. 34–5
86   Juarros cited in Rodríguez Lafora, 'La impotencia masculina', 544.
87   Pulido, 'Algunos Conceptos', 8; San de Velilla, *Higiene*, pp. 34–5.
88   R. Castel, *El Orden Psiquiátrico. La Edad de Oro del Alienismo* (Madrid: La Piqueta, 1980), pp. 294–5.
89   N. Rose, *Governing the Soul: The shaping of the private self* (London: Free Association Books, 1999), pp. 6–7.
90   Rodríguez Lafora, 'Impotencia sexual', 237.
91   Rodríguez Lafora, 'Impotencia sexual', 239.
92   Rodríguez Lafora, 'La impotencia masculina', 541.
93   Both quotations from Rodríguez Lafora, 'La impotencia masculina', 548.
94   Both quotations from Rodríguez Lafora, 'La impotencia masculina', 549.
95   Rodríguez Lafora, 'La impotencia masculina', 551.
96   Rodríguez Lafora, 'La impotencia masculina', 551.
97   Rodríguez Lafora, 'La impotencia masculina', 551. R. Nóvoa Santos, *La Mujer, Nuestro Sexto Sentido y Otros Esbozos* (Madrid: Biblioteca Nueva, 1929), p. 20, observed along the same lines that 'la importancia de los choques emocionales en la aparición de caracteres somáticos y espirituales de tipo femenino, ha sido señalada por Pende y por otros investigadores a raíz de su última conflagración europea. Soldados antes sanos y vigorosos tornándose miedosos, infantiles, con rasgos somáticos y psíquicos propios de la mujer' [the importance of emotional shocks in the appearance of feminoid somatic and spiritual characters has been indicated by Pende and other researchers in the light of the last European conflagration. Formerly healthy and vigorous soldiers became fearful and infantile, with somatic and psychic traits displayed by women].
98   J. Caro Baroja, *Introducción a una Historia Contemporánea del Anticlericalismo Español* (Madrid: Istmo, 1980), pp. 13–106.
99   C. Gordon, 'Governmental Rationality: an introduction', in G. Burchell, C. Gordon and P. Miller (eds), *The Foucault Effect: Studies in Governmentality* (London: Harvester Wheatsheaf, 1991), pp. 1–48 (pp. 2–3).
100 Caro Baroja, *Introducción*, p. 120.
101 S. Haliczer, *Sexualidad en el Confesionario. Un Sacramento Profanado* (Madrid: Siglo XXI, 1998), especially the section 'Solicitación y Confesión en la imaginación Anticlerical', pp. 255–85 (272), and, P. Fernández, *Eduardo López Bago y el Naturalismo Radical* (Amsterdam: Rodopi, 1995), p. 182.

102 Labanyi, *Gender*, p. 235.
103 Popular erotic fiction of the time also depicted raunchy tales of priests and nuns. See Fernández, *Eduardo López Bago*, p. 187.
104 Fernández, *Eduardo López Bago*, pp. 182–3; Haliczer, 'Solicitación', pp. 264–5.
105 Fernández, *Eduardo López Bago*, p. 183.
106 Fernández, *Eduardo López Bago*, p. 186.
107 Fernández, *Eduardo López Bago*, pp. 268–70.
108 Fernández, *Eduardo López Bago*, p. 276.
109 On the medical defence of chastity in Feijoo and on works against celibacy, see Vázquez García and Moreno Mengíbar, *Sexo y Razón*, pp. 97–8, 100–2, respectively. In general, see T. Tarczylo, 'From lascivious erudition to the history of mentalities', in G. S. Rousseau and R. Porter (eds), *Sexual Underworlds of the Enlightenment* (Manchester: Manchester University Press, 1987), pp. 26–41 (35–6).
110 Nye, 'Sex Difference', 34. For the views of contemporary doctors, see M. Hurtado de Mendoza, *Instituciones de Medicina y Cirugía* (Madrid, 1839), vol. I, pp. 101–2; A. Rodríguez Guerra, *El Conservador de la Salud. Manual de Higiene Pública y Privada* (Cadiz: Imprenta de D. José Mª Ruiz, 1846), p. 191; P. F. Monlau, *Elementos de Higiene Privada* (Madrid, 5th edn, 1875), vol. I, p. 350.
111 F. de Sales Mayo, *La Condesita (Memorias de una Doncella)* (Madrid: Oficina Tipográfica del Hospicio, 1870 [1866]), p. 106.
112 E. Madrazo in his *Cultivo de la Especie Humana. Herencia y Educación* (Santander: Imp. Blanchard y Arce, 1904), p. 297, wrote 'De esta suerte, la exageración del sentido de la castidad trae consigo el furo del sensualismo' [In this way, the exaggeration of the sense of chastity brings with it the flames of sensualism]. Another figure, Forns, *Higiene*, p. 167, noted 'la gran mayoría de los individuos a quienes se les imposibilita la fisiológica satisfacción de su apetencia genética, no se someten, y caen en las aberraciones sexuales, en el onanismo, la homoerastia, el amor sáfico y la bestialidad' [the great majority of figures whose physiological satisfaction of the genetic instinct is thwarted, do not control themselves and fall into the sexual aberrations, in onanism, in homoerastia, sapphic love and bestiality]. Even in 1930 J. Noguera, *Moral, Eugenesia y Derecho* (Madrid: Morata, 1930), p. 50, argued that 'La libido es la obra del Genio de la especie, sin la cual ésta no se perpetuaría' [The libido is the work of the Genius of the species, without which the latter would not reproduce]. If the libido was denied, the resulting passions could drive the individual to crime or 'por medio de imaginaciones ardientes la tendencia morbosa a placeres solitarios y *contra natura*' [by means of the ardent imagination the morbid tendency towards solitary pleasures and those *against nature*] would be born.
113 Other pedagogues and popularizers of sex education defended, nevertheless, the compatibility between permanent chastity and good health. See E. Fernández Sanz, 'Sobre Educación Sexual. Su importancia para la profilaxia de las psicosis y psiconeurosis', *El Siglo Médico*, 62 (1915), 386–9, where he notes 'La abstinencia me parece

perfectamente soportable sin detrimento para la salud por los individuos normales y que se cuiden de poner en práctica los medios
auxiliares oportunos de sublimación y derivación' [Abstinence seems
to me to be perfectly compatible with good health without negative
effects in normal individuals who are careful enough to put into
practice the necessary additional means for sublimation and deriva-
tion] (389). See also T. de R. Climent, *Higiene Sexual del Soltero y la
Soltera* (Barcelona: La Vida Literaria, *c.*1910), pp. 20–1, and, Zapatero, *Pedagogía Sexual*, p. 161. Others opted for an intermediate
position. For C. Bayo, *Higiene Sexual del Soltero* (Madrid: Librería de
Antonio Rubiños, 1919 [1902]), p. 116, chastity was fine in balanced
individuals but not in those 'morbidly predisposed'.

[114] Vázquez García and Moreno Mengíbar, *Sexo y Razón*, pp. 255–60.

[115] Brother Echevarría in *A.M.D.G.* (1910) by Pérez de Ayala used to
engage his students in masturbatory practices (see R. Pérez de Ayala,
A.M.D.G. (Madrid: Editorial Pueyo, 1931)). Father Canuto, in Francisco Bullón, *Colegiales Adorables* (1930) also tried to involve children
in sexual practices. See Haliczer, 'Solicitación', p. 270.

[116] See the case of the priest U. L. in F. Bravo y Moreno, *Exposición de un
caso clínico médico-legal de psicopatía homo-sexual* (Santander: Tip. El
Cantábrico, 1903), pamphlet, p. 11; F. Bravo y Moreno, 'Exposición
de un caso clínico médico-legal de psicopatía homo-sexual', in *Actes
du XIC Congrès International de Médecine*, publiés sous la direction de
Ms. le Dr. Fernández-Caro. Section d'Hygiène, Épidémiologie et
Science Sanitaire Technique (Madrid: Imp. de J. Sastre, 1904),
pp. 96–102.

[117] An extensive study on the anticlerical press with this in mind is still to
be undertaken. The case of one member of the Sacred Heart in
Seville, who solicited young boys from pimps in the same city, was
described in *El Aeroplano* in 1912. See F. Vázquez García and A.
Moreno Mengíbar, *Poder y Prostitución en Sevilla. Siglos XIV al XX*
(Seville: Publicaciones Universidad de Sevilla, 1998), vol. II, *La Edad
Contemporánea*, p. 219.

[118] The case of the priest Meliá, implicated in the blackmailing of
homosexuals, and who was murdered in 1898, is mentioned in J. del
Moral y Pérez Aloé, *El Estado y la Prostitución* (Madrid: Casa Editorial
de Felipe G. Rojas, 1913), p. 84, and in C. Bernaldo de Quirós and J.
Mª Llanas Aguilaniedo, *La Mala Vida en Madrid. Estudio psicosociológico
con dibujos y fotografías del natural* (Madrid: B. Rodríguez Sierra,
1901), p. 285.

[119] Azaña, in his *Jardín de los Frailes*, noted in the 1920s that 'ciertas
formas de religiosidad exaltada y duras penitencias y mortifica-
ciones . . . no estaban en lo hondo limpias de fermentos de lujuria'
[certain forms of exalted religiosity, harsh penitence and mortification . . . deep down were not free of the ferments of luxuriousness].
See M. Azaña, *El Jardín de los Frailes* (1921–7) in *Obras Completas*
(Madrid: Ed. Giner, 1990), vol. I, p. 671. C. Juarros, in his *Normas de
Educación Sexual y Física* (Madrid: Renacimiento, 1925), p. 40, wrote
that 'la abstención de la función genital hará que la sexualidad se

troque [*sic*] en misticismo religioso, social, artístico o heroico, o se
convierta en una neurose o se desvíe hacia la perversión sexual ...
Esta y no otra es la razón de la abundancia de síndromes psicone-
orósicos en los conventos' [the abstention of the genital function will
mean that sexuality will turn into religious, social, artistic or heroic
mysticism, or will become a neurosis or will deviate towards sexual
perversion ... This, and only this, is why there is an abundance of
psychoneurotic syndromes in convents].

120 H. F. Delgado, 'El psicoanálisis en la escuela', *El Siglo Médico*, 66
     (1919), 982–3 (983); A. Garma, 'Psicología de la aclaración de la
     sexualidad en la infancia', *Revista de Escuelas Normales*, 103 (1934),
     98–103 (100–1).
121 A. D'Halmar, *Pasión y Muerte del Cura Deusto* (Madrid: Editora Inter-
     nacional, 1924).
122 Mira, 'Modernistas', p. 72.
123 D'Halmar, *Pasión y Muerte*, p. 52.
124 D'Halmar, *Pasión y Muerte*, p. 20.
125 D'Halmar, *Pasión y Muerte*, p. 21.
126 D'Halmar, *Pasión y Muerte*, pp. 54–5.
127 D'Halmar, *Pasión y Muerte*, p. 54.
128 D'Halmar, *Pasión y Muerte*, p. 36.
129 D'Halmar, *Pasión y Muerte*, p. 60.
130 D'Halmar, *Pasión y Muerte*, pp. 122–3.
131 D'Halmar, *Pasión y Muerte*, p. 259.
132 D'Halmar, *Pasión y Muerte*, pp. 246–7.
133 D'Halmar, *Pasión y Muerte*, pp. 282–3.
134 On the role of the train as a symbol of technological development
     that crushes 'deviant' sexuality, see R. Cleminson, 'Male Homosexu-
     ality in Spain: Signposts for a Sociological Analysis', *Paragraph. A
     Journal of Modern Cultural Theory*, 22, 1 (1999), 35–54 (36) but also
     one that permits it in Á. J. Gordo López & R. M. Cleminson, *Techno-
     Sexual Landscapes: Changing Relations Between Technology and Sexuality*
     (London: Free Association Press, 2004), pp. 77–96.
135 D'Halmar, *Pasión y Muerte*, p. 280.
136 D'Halmar, *Pasión y Muerte*, p. 260.
137 D'Halmar, *Pasión y Muerte*, pp. 174–5.
138 D'Halmar, *Pasión y Muerte*, p. 42.
139 D'Halmar, *Pasión y Muerte*, p. 152.
140 D'Halmar, *Pasión y Muerte*, p. 55.

Chapter Six

Homosexual Subcultures in Spain: the Intersection of Medicine, Politics and Identity

Introduction

The purpose of this chapter is to show how some of the discourses analysed in previous chapters impacted on the real lives of homosexual subjects as lived in a variety of scenarios which could be termed 'subcultures'. Although Michel Foucault understood homosexuality from the mid nineteenth century primarily as a medico-legal 'creation', our previous chapters have suggested that other discourses and practices were also productive in the objectification of 'homosexuality'. These other discourses and practices are equally suggestive for an understanding of how homosexuality became a subject for intervention from a much broader range of perspectives and social or professional groups. Medical and legal sources are, then, but a starting point. Indeed, recent studies have questioned the power of medico-legal theories alone to shape sexual identities and discourse about them; this chapter places emphasis on the mutual formation of discourses on homosexuality from medical and legal sources together with discourses arising from other sources, including different types of literature, memoirs and personal accounts.

The chapter begins with a discussion of a number of texts which focused their attention on prostitution and 'vice' in the major Spanish cities. While these texts – some of which have been discussed in Chapters Two and Three for their contribution to the process of medicalization of homosexuality – treated primarily female prostitution, increasingly same-sex prostitution and life-styles became part of their subject matter, often as part of a presentation of pathological types in Spanish cities and the 'social dangerousness' implied by their existence. These texts can be taken to a greater or lesser degree as a reliable depiction of homosexual subcultures, constructed around places of homo-sexual rendezvous and parts of the city most renowned for the relatively high visibility of homosexual life.

Like most of these accounts of prostitution, many of the literary texts discussed in the next section of the chapter were generally part of an educated or 'high cultural' form of discursive production. While a study of homosexuality in literature, or 'homosexual literature' is not the objective of this chapter, some key texts are analysed for their incorporation of literary, legal and medical depictions of homosexuality; they can be viewed as sites where these concerns coincided to produce a truly unique and often contestatory combination for the times.

These 'high cultural' creations are contrasted with the more popular accounts of homosexuality deriving from sources such as cheap novelettes produced in the early twentieth century, the popular culture of the music hall in the 1920s, the regional press and a number of memoirs written by subjects close to, or part of, homosexual subcultures of the period. Some of these texts – in fact, the minority – were written from a first person perspective by individuals who were clearly involved in homosexual subcultures or who lived a homosexual lifestyle in the period of the 1920s and 1930s, the most fecund years for this kind of source material. These first person accounts are extremely important in terms of the articulation of a self-aware homosexual subculture with its own mechanisms for representation and contestation. While nei-ther their extent nor their effects should be exaggerated, a study of the relationship between such accounts and the medical and legal professions is illustrative not only of how medical and legal discourses 'colonized' homosexuality but also how homosexual subjects themselves accepted – or rejected – the terms of refer-ence supplied by these professions.

The final section of the chapter attempts to paint in broad brushstrokes a picture of homosexual subcultures as lived by homosexual subjects themselves in the period 1850–1936. This, necessarily, is a problematic exercise, not least because the materials utilized come from a variety of sources and one cannot suppose that the depiction of homosexuality in such texts concurred with a strict version of 'reality'. The picture painted, here, therefore is a subjective one but rather than being purely descriptive is guided by questions such as: What was the relationship between lived homosexual experience, the law and the agents of law enforcement? How were medical theories of homosexuality received by the public at large and by homosexuals themselves at a particular time? What mechanisms or forms of knowledge did homosexual subjects utilize in order to identify each other?

One of the many difficulties we face when writing about homosexuality is that it is easy to reproduce the contents and meanings of the discourse provided by the sexual and psychiatric sciences. Since homosexuality became a topic for discussion in a markedly different way from the mid nineteenth century, those individuals objectified by these sciences were seen – it may appear tautological to say – primarily as sexual subjects, rather than as human beings that engaged in activities other than those connected to sex. As we know from Foucault and other historians, the mid nineteenth century was a period in which the sexual came to represent the key to a person's mind, body and actions. Sexuality became *the* secret to be explored and discovered as the truth of the person and indeed of society itself.

Our account, therefore, to some degree at least, is bound by the discourses produced, from a variety of sources and perspectives, on homosexuality. Is there any other way of writing this kind of history? Can we write a history of homosexuality without concentrating to such a large degree on the sexuality of the individuals or collectives that we are proposing to study? Clearly, we cannot. Despite this restriction, however, it is necessary to attempt to go beyond these sources, to rethink what we understand by the 'sexual' and not impose our present conceptualization of the sexual on the past. This requires a broader framework for thinking about sexuality which is tailored to the realities of an earlier period. It requires thinking about the limits constructed around 'sexuality' in the past and the wealth of insights that may be afforded by concentrating on silences as well as declarations on or about homosexuality. It also invites thought on the limits of 'homosociality' as a way that people positioned themselves and were positioned with respect to 'homosexuality' in the past.

Male Prostitution in Spanish Cities

As is the case with medical and legal interest in homosexuality, moral concerns with respect to the presence of homosexual prostitution were to spark a considerable amount of interest in broad sectors of society, both from a middle and working-class perspective. In some cases, this interest linked medical and legal attention; male and female prostitutes alike were pathologized and viewed as 'socially dangerous' subjects by a range of experts. With respect to male prostitution as such in Spain there was no actual national legal framework in place for its criminalization. However, the elastic terms of the public scandal laws and local ordinances, such as that of Cadiz of 1889,[1] often constituted a potent resource allowing the authorities to intervene as part of a campaign to control 'vice'.

As in many other countries, the 'white slave trade', male incontinence and general 'immorality' in the cities became a platform from which to launch a medico-moral campaign which intervened, often aggressively, in the behaviour of the general population, particularly in the working class, a population that was seen to be most in need of moral and physical correction. The potent combination of the elements of what Foucault has called 'bio-power' – the discursive and material intervention of the state in the individual and collective body – became united to form a strategy which was utilized by those in power or those who aspired to it, notably doctors and other technical professionals. In Spain, the workings of this bio-power can be seen, for example, in the treatises on the moral character of the population from the mid nineteenth century onwards, through to the regenerationist texts of the latter part of the century which concentrated on the health of the nation and which were, as we have seen in Chapter Five, intensely imbued with class and masculinist motifs. The beginning of the twentieth century saw, accordingly, the publication of a number of texts from different positions – medical, 'anti-vice', pedagogical – which sought to expose degeneracy, crime and vice, particularly with respect to sexuality.

In common with other countries,[2] in Spain the problems of the big city loomed large in these writings. This kind of concern was present in the works of a number of social commentators and public hygiene experts such as Manuel Gil Mestre,[3] Julio Vallmit-jana,[4] and Julián Juderías[5] who focused primarily on the relation-ship between poverty and crime. Prostitution in turn was seen principally as the daughter of poverty and vice, two characteristics that touched working-class populations especially. Rather than merely descriptive of prostitution, however, these texts steadily incorporated the new knowledge afforded by psychiatry and the sexual sciences. In this way, they afforded a transition from a purely moral account through to one which sought the underly-ing causes not now in men's brutal nature or women's weakness but in a cluster of environmental and psychopathic causes as articulated by the new sexual sciences.

In turn, many of the books on crime in the city were imbued with a strong nationalist flavour which responded to authors' desires to acknowledge Spanish problems and to place them in context with those of other countries, thus denying that Spain was unique in suffering this kind of hardship. This is the case of Juderías's 1906 book on poverty and criminality and his later analysis of the 'black legend' in Spain, a book which reads as a nationalist apologia and an exaltation of Spanish culture against foreign misinterpretations.[6] In his 1906 volume on criminality he opens with a clear task in mind: to dispel the clouds of disillusion and pessimism that hang over the national spirit. He writes of 'nuestra ignorancia' and 'nuestra incultura' in comparison with more advanced nations.[7]

Despite the emphasis on poverty as the major cause of prostitu-tion Juderías's study, in terms of its sophistication, surpassed that of the practically contemporary work of Rafael Eslava, head of the Sección de Higiene.[8] Eslava claimed that prostitution in Madrid had two principal causes. These were: the brutality of men in their passions and the organic weakness of women, and prostitution was consequently seen as a result of either biological or moral weaknesses. Juderías, while still acknowledging that poverty was the chief cause of prostitution also incorporated new theories on degeneration and perversion as major factors. His study of a few years later devoted entirely to female prostitution was archetypical of this kind of approach, which combined moral and scientific explanations of poverty in the construction of a discourse around the 'trata de blancas', the white slave trade of women in prostitution.[9]

Degenerationist, psychiatric and sexological thought thus slowly permeated the field of female prostitution. Max Bembo's own 1912 account of the 'mala vida' [low life] in cities such as Barcelona and Madrid incorporated the lessons of the new sexual sciences into the aetiology of prostitution, and argued that prostitution resulted from three primordial causes: degeneration, hereditary factors and what he termed 'reinversion', a state which was derived from the other two causes and which was characterized by the corruption of minors, rape, and scandalous behaviour; a kind of perverted sexual instinct.[10] That this volume was a bridge between the older accounts which focused on vice and the newer ones which adopted psychiatric and sexological premises is suggested by Max Bembo's acknowledgement of his debt to Julio Vallmitjana, author of *Criminalidad típica local.*

Some studies of the period, while taking female prostitution as the principal area of comment, also introduced an analysis of the male variety.[11] At first, the analysis followed similar patterns to those present in texts on female prostitution. 'Vice' was seen as the major cause; only later did the newer psychiatric and sexological theories permeate this kind of thought. Indicative of the earlier type was that written by the medical doctor and former member of the Public Hygiene Commission in Barcelona, Prudencio Sereñana y Partagás. While this author focused primarily on female prostitution in his 1882 study on prostitution in Barcelona, he also dedicated a section of his book to the male variety. He defined this form of male prostitution as pederasty or 'cenydismo',[12] an activity he defined as rare in Barcelona. Sereñana y Partagás, like many other authors of the period, such as Suárez Casañ,[13] began his section on male prostitution with a customary historical excursion on the subject of homosexuality. He discussed the biblical punishment of such practices and the prevalence of male prostitution in Roman society. Amongst the remedies for such practices the author advocated a general clean-up of morals, severe punishment for pimps, and the confinement of pederasts in penitentiaries.

The vigour and indignation with which Sereñana discussed homosexuality were extreme. Wondering whether pederasts belonged to the group of men who had lost all rationality and therefore to those who were mentally ill – 'La aberración del sentido genésico en tan abominables séres nos autoriza á dudar de su integridad mental' [The aberration of the genesic sense in such abominable beings permits us to doubt their mental integrity] – and in the light of his confessed ignorance of psychiatrists' studies on such cases, he argued that it was necessary to intern homosexuals in institutions in order to save civilization. As a step towards such preventive measures, he argued, it was necessary to determine whether the instinct of the pederast obeyed 'psychic disorders'. In the meantime, 'conviene secuestrar tan vergonzosos séres; para lo cual podria [*sic*] recluírseles en algun establecimiento penitenciario, á fin de que por medio del trabajo mecánico y de una prolongada abstencion [*sic*] de sus actos antinaturales, se logra volverlos regenerados al seno de la sociedad' [it is advisable to remove these shameful beings. They could be locked away in some penitentiary establishment, with the aim that through hard work and the prolonged abstention from their anti-natural acts, they can be returned, regenerated, to society].[14] Quite evidently, for this author, homosexuality was synonymous with prostitution; it was caught between 'vice' on the one hand and perverted mental faculties on the other. It was plainly a vice which needed to be curtailed and quarantined.

Actual prostitution where money changed hands, however, existed in a number of places in the capital, according to E. Rodríguez-Solís in his history of prostitution. These corresponded to brothels for 'pederasts' and places of homosexual rendezvous, such as the Prado, the Botanical Garden, the Plaza de Oriente, and Calle Dos de Mayo. In 1870 and 1875, respectively, houses of male prostitution were encountered in the Calle del Calvario and in Horno de la Mata. Here, lower class 'chulos' and thieves ('rateros') were found together with 'elegantes caballeros y elevados personajes' [elegant gentlemen and worthy persons]; the presence of the latter explained the impunity with which the house operated for some time.[15] This mix of classes, as we will see, played an important part in the morphology of homosexual subcultures in late nineteenth and early twentieth-century Spain.

According to some authors, it was not only the mix between classes that was cause for scandal and for the attention of the authorities. Indignation was also caused by the prostitution of minors. This indignation was usually confined to the often forced prostitution of young girls but occasionally male minors were mentioned. Citing Dr. Antonio Navarro Fernández, one lawyer from Madrid, Joaquín del Moral, lamented that the authorities had paid a great deal of attention to the 'trata de blancas', that is to female prostitution, but had left another disgraceful trade untouched: the 'trata de blancos', or the sex trade in young men or boys.[16] This 'asqueroso tráfico' [disgusting traffic] was centred on boys of between ten and fifteen years. It was, apparently, a widespread affair: 'En las principales calles de las grandes poblaciones pululan, por sus aceras, cafés y *tupis*, un número considerable de *golfillos* que se prestan á satisfacer toda clase de vicios contra la naturaleza' [In the main streets of the large cities, on the pavements, in the cafés and drinking establishments, there is a throng of urchins who dedicate themselves to the satisfaction of all kinds of vice against nature].[17] One immediate consequence of such practices was the range of venereal disease suffered by these children; the law, however, could do little without a complaint made by the parent or guardian or without the perpetrator having been caught in flagrante.

The volume written by Joaquín del Moral was one of the most detailed accounts of the subculture of prostitution in Spain at the time. But this text, often combining social comment, new forensic techniques and the insights of psychiatry was by no means unique. Just two years later legal experts Constancio Bernaldo de Quirós and José María Llanas Aguilaniedo published their *La mala vida en Madrid*, helping to forge in Spain a new kind of study which merged anthropology with the new psychiatric sciences. Being inspired no doubt by Sighele's *La mala vita a Roma* published in the mid 1890s,[18] this book included an extensive section on 'sexual inversion' in relation to prostitution, the medical aspects of which were discussed in Chapter Three. With respect to homosexual prostitution, which, the authors argue, flourished alongside the heterosexual variety but 'extra-legally', we are presented with nineteen cases of men arrested on a variety of public scandal charges.[19]

These men are classified according to a schema which included a huge taxonomic range from 'real' inverts through to 'polysexuals', taking in the various permutations of sexual proclivities according to an active/passive divide, and oral, masturbatory and anal sexual activities. Not all of the individuals presented, however, were actually noted to be engaged explicitly in prostitution and the authors' account actually confuses, perhaps deliberately, the exercise of prostitution with homosexual activity per se. This, as we have seen, was not unique in the minds of many psychiatrists and criminologists. The authors, in any case, were keen to emphasize such an association and the link between homosexuality and prostitution is at intervals made explicit. They write, for example, that both innate and acquired inverts engaged in sex for money. While the extent of this phenomenon amongst the lower classes had been exaggerated by Ellis and Symonds, the authors warned, in Spain Uranians could easily pick up men for sex.[20] This probably reflected reality to some degree. We cannot doubt, however, that this association was also a means by which homosexuality in all its manifestations could be vilified and presented as 'socially dangerous'. As the twentieth century wore on this link would become more and more virulently explicit, reaching a height in the mid to late 1920s in reviews such as *Sexualidad*, edited by Dr Antonio Navarro Fernández.

Whether prostitutes or not, many of the individuals were described as 'feminine' or 'effeminate'. Some were known to dress in female clothes when exerting their profession and all had camp female nicknames, such as 'La Rosita de Plata', from Cadiz, or as a reference to their main or only profession as in the case of 'La Florera', originally from Santander. Despite this emphasis on prostitution, however, the authors did admit that many of their subjects did not actually engage in paid sex; some of the nineteen case studies professed that their activity responded not to the desire to earn money but to the seeking of pleasure.

Apart from the obvious inference that Madrid must have been a place where homosexuals congregated either for pleasure or for work – the subjects discussed come from all parts of the country from Murcia to Oviedo – a number of other characteristics of homosexual life at the time can be derived from *La mala vida en Madrid*. Despite the fact that there is no particular insight to be drawn from the variety of professions in which these individuals were engaged (ranging from shop worker, book binder through to cook), there does seem to be a concentration around jobs such as waiters in bars and houses of prostitution, and servants. This may reflect an already established association between houses of prostitution and inverts (see, for example, the ordinance of Cadiz of 1889 referred to above) and between homosexuality and the aristocracy or high middle classes whose servants may have also had to offer sexual favours.

What is striking in the case studies presented is the use of popular slang to designate homosexuals. This slang was indicated by the researchers and, according to the printed accounts, was used by their subjects. For example, in their categorization of 'inverts' Bernaldo de Quirós and Llanas de Aguilaniedo acknowledged that popular terms included 'marica' and 'zape' which correspond to 'real' inverts who were passive in anal sex but active in oral sex, and 'bujarrón' and 'bufo' were used for 'pseudo' inverts who would be active in anal sex but passive in oral practices. Some of these usages appear to have been current in the cases studied. One individual described is recorded as having dismissed his unfaithful lover with the words 'para *marica*, se basta él' [if he wants a *marica*, he can go it alone].[21] Another individual, La Perejilera, was teased as a 'marica' from childhood because of his demeanour, tastes and participation in certain children's games.

Other individuals, in contrast, were noted for their virile disposition; inversion of the sexual instinct did not necessarily coincide with inversion of physical sexual characteristics, it was admitted. The authors note: 'Hay hombres de aspecto varonil entre los homosexuales, que luego en sus maneras y en cuanto se relaciona con su psiquis, muestran claramente el afeminamiento' [There are men of a virile aspect amongst the homosexuals, who later by their mannerisms and with respect to their psychic state show clearly their effeminacy].[22] Bernaldo de Quirós and Llanas Aguilaniedo were also quick to note that effeminacy did not necessary translate into cowardice. There were cases of homicide amongst inverts, showing their 'bravery'.

Many of the motifs elaborated by Bernaldo de Quirós and Llanas Aguilaniedo reappeared in another work, again of extraordinary depth and insight into the homosexual world, this time centred on Barcelona. The association between homosexuality and prostitution, the discussion of active and passive roles, the degree of virility or effeminacy in 'inverts' all appeared in the 1912 account of the 'mala vida' in Barcelona written by Professor Max Bembo. Max Bembo's in-depth account of poverty and vice in Barcelona from the late nineteenth to the early twentieth century drew on many of the same frameworks used by Bernaldo de Quirós and Llanas Aguilaniedo. The book was published within a new range of titles on criminal pedagogy issued by Editorial Maucci in Barcelona and the prologue illustrated the innovations implied by his work. Convinced that it was not just the task of the psychiatrist, the mental doctor (the 'frenópata' or phrenologist is referred to) or the criminologist to examine human degeneracy, abnormality and crime, Max Bembo advanced the pedagogical sciences as a faculty with a fundamental role. Foreshadowing Ortega's comment by two years that the problem of Spain was essentially one of pedagogy,[23] what was required, according to Max Bembo, was a fusion of various new techniques.

The obstacles, however, were not underestimated. Bembo conceded that his book would raise eyebrows. He hoped, however, that its polemical nature would be beneficial to the country's youth as well as to the poor unfortunates whose plight was exposed to the public eye. The task of the book was not to provoke disgust, but compassion: 'a pesar de que el estilo se resienta y la impresión que se saque de su lectura sea penosa, indudablemente brotará del pecho de cada lector más que el odio, la compasión; más que la ira, la misericordia' [despite the fact that its style repels and that the impression gained upon reading it is lamentable, it is without doubt that from the heart of every reader there will spring not hate but compassion, not anger but sympathy].[24]

What is perhaps most extraordinary about this book is the author's engagement with the communities that he described. The study relied in part on interviews of many homosexuals in Barcelona, and it stands as something similar to the anthropological studies or those which described crime communities of the early twentieth century conducted by Margaret Mead or Hayden White. This was an expert's view looking in from the outside but it also 'gave voice' to those that constituted the subject of the book.

Bembo's discussion of male prostitution was confined to a brief but informative appendix at the end of the section he devoted to female prostitution. For the author, male prostitution was present in all major cities, and was made up in part by 'normal' men who sold their bodies like female prostitutes and in part by 'real' homosexuals. The first kind of prostitution, Bembo noted, was extensively described in the works of Tardieu, Chevalier, Moll and Tarnowsky.

Despite the fact that male prostitution was widespread in many European cities, in Barcelona 'Esta prostitución no es numerosa, no es lo suficiente grande y extendida para creerla un problema'

[This form of prostitution is not extensive; it is not sufficiently developed or numerous to be held as a problem].[25] In this sense, Bembo coincided with Sereñana y Partagás and with other later commentators such as Saldaña who understood homosexuality, to some degree at least, as a foreign matter or habit.[26] On the other hand, the general presence and visibility of male homosexuality on the streets of Barcelona was acknowledged by Bembo and seen by other authors who were virulent in their disapproval of homosexuality as a major public problem.[27]

In similar fashion to many other writers who wrote about the same subject in other countries, Bembo conjured up an image of the world of male prostitution that described those thus engaged as men who imitated 'los gritos de las vírgenes, pintándose el rostro, ensortijándose los dedos, cuidando minuciosamente su cuerpo; hacen la carrera; su andar afeminado y sus modales, les hace reconocer bien pronto de todos los viciosos' [the cries of virgins, painted their faces, manicured their fingers, took special care of their appearance and proposed to passers-by. Their effeminate gait and their manners easily identify them amongst all those dedicated to vice].[28] Like other cities more famous for their male prostitutes, continued Bembo, the Barcelona variety was to be found in houses of prostitution, where many such men lived as waiters or domestic servants. In Barcelona there was, he acknowledged, a male homosexual prostitute subculture whose participants used female pseudonyms, derived from famous operas, names of flowers, singers and the like. Bembo assured his readers that the male prostitutes were well known by the police and that many had been arrested on public scandal charges, presumably under the articles of the 1870 Penal Code.

The author also remarked that male prostitutes believed that they were the only real homosexuals in the city. This may be anecdotal but, if true, could betray a rivalry between one type of homosexual and another, or a high degree of fragmentation between different communities. Bembo affirmed that the male prostitute he thus described was very different from the more ubiquitous Uranian; their only point in common was their mutual desire for men. We will return to the question of variety within the homosexual subculture below.

It is possible that Bembo's study shows how much the male homosexual subculture was evolving. One of the many changes that the author noted with respect to the organization and structure of the homosexual community was that, according to his informants, prostitution was no longer a lucrative business. Those he interviewed put this down to the fact that it was so easy for homosexuals to find others, without having to pay. As a result, prostitutes were shunned by all 'real homosexuals'.[29] If this appreciation reflected the real state of affairs at the time it hints at a more extensive and perhaps self-confident subculture than one might have imagined.

In this economy of 'real' and 'other' homosexuals, Max Bembo suggested that there was a direct link between more or less formal prostitution and effeminacy; the latter would be a device utilized by prostitutes for making themselves known to members of the public. It is also possible, however, that the margins between effeminate male homosexuality and 'trade' may well have been blurred and earning a few pesetas for a 'trick' may have been part of working-class homosexual, or 'non-homosexual' life (Chauncey argues this was the case in New York). In any case, actual homosexual prostitution was a minority activity, and not particularly successful at that. What predominated was virile homosexuality, or Uranism: 'Los afeminados sólo pueden medrar en las poblaciones donde el uranismo es reducido. Sin embargo, se ven grandes focos de prostitutos masculinos en algunas capitales del extranjero' [The effeminates can only triumph in places where Uranism is not extensive. However, large groups of male prostitutes can be seen in the capital cities of foreign countries].[30]

Homosexual Literature or Literature with Homosexual Themes

Max Bembo's work is fascinating for its mixture of perspectives: like many of the works examined above, it is written from an outsider's or 'etic' perspective. However, it also incorporates an 'emic' or internal view, from the perspective of homosexual participants. The emphasis in this section is increasingly on the emic; however, as in Bembo's book, the texts discussed were characterized by a large degree of hybridity between both positions.

Like written materials, such as novels and medical treatises, paintings, portraits and cartoons are texts which emerge from a particular context, from conditions of possibility which are constantly shifting in form and degree of explicit reference to the subject in hand. In some cases, these texts are so cautious as to be practically invisible to the outside observer.[31] Through a range of subtleties, nevertheless, a varied discourse is constructed from the 1850s to the late 1930s which speaks of homosexuality however covertly. In this articulation of discourse around homosexuality, silences or near silences can be as evocative as loud speeches.

The nascent or even established homosexual subculture of some cities of the south of Spain has been acknowledged.[32] While the tolerance of cities such as Granada and Cadiz may well have been overplayed,[33] what cannot be denied is the existence of a lively intellectual and artistic culture in Granada based a round the group of friends that included Federico García Lorca, Manuel de Falla and Manuel Angeles Ortiz, amongst others, and in bars and cafés, such as 'El Polinario' in the grounds of the Alhambra.[34]

Within this circle, there were those who articulated a voice which spoke of homosexuality more clearly than others, working between silence and expression. Lorca's own *Sonetos del amor oscuro*, and the work of the Granada-born Arabist Emilio García Gómez are examples of this phenomenon. García Gómez published an anthology of Arab-Andalusian poems in 1930, two of which openly acknowledged same-sex love. In the introduction to the collection, he wrote of some fragments which, more or less openly, alluded to what he called 'Greek love'. This form of homosexual love was placed firmly in the tradition of 'man–adolescent boy' love and referred to the increased beauty afforded by the arrival of the boy's facial hair at the time of adolescence. One eleventh-century poet found in the boy's burgeoning adolescence more reason for his love: 'Pensaba que el bozo haría salir de mí el/ cariño que por él sentía./ Mas yo no vi en el bozo de sus mejillas más que tahalíes que ceñían los sables de/ su mirada' [I thought his first hairs would expel from me/ the affection I felt for him./ But I saw nothing in the down on his cheeks but the pouch that held the daggers of/ his glance].[35]

This more intellectual voicing of same-sex desire was seen in artistic form in others of Lorca's circle. For example, Gabriel Morcillo (renowned for his paintings of ephebes)[36] took up the Arabic theme in his 'Moro', dressed 'effeminately', adorned with grapes and wearing huge earrings. Perhaps such a depiction was reminiscent of travels to Morocco, a land famed as a destination for foreign homosexuals.[37]

This kind of production formed a bridge between those who professed their homosexual desires, those 'in the know' and the broader public. A reverse process, equally indicative of the more general acknowledgement of homosexuality, was constituted by the numerous cartoons which appeared in the periodical press. Cartoons are renowned for their function as a satire on behaviour, ideas or some aspect of identity as perceived by the artist or the publication in which they appear. That homosexuality was an issue in the public consciousness is shown by its many depictions in the satirical and daily press. This expression of homosexuality, in this case made by outside observers, was notably of the more effeminate variety, the traditional and visible butt of satire. In Granada, there appeared on the front page of one local daily a cartoon depicting a conversation between a beefy man who had 'lost' his wife, and an effeminate individual sitting on a park bench. The dialogue below the title, 'The Lost Wife', is as follows: 'Alms, Sir, for I have lost my wife'. The suggestive reply, as the sitting individual coquettishly responds, reads: 'Well now! And haven't they found her yet?'[38]

In other quarters, the references were far more explicit. Retaining the device of the effeminate homosexual, the Barcelona satirical review *L'Esquella de la Torratxa* depicted an effeminate dandy-like male, with prominent eyelashes, painted face and effeminate pose declaring that he was also, presumably like many radical or 'modern' people of the time, in favour of 'free love'.[39] A more ambiguous drawing at the time of the forthcoming elections two years later saw two individuals, one possibly a woman and the other a man, pondering how they would vote; 'as men or as women'.[40]

This form of representation of homosexuality in the early 1930s may well be a testimony to how much the presence of homosexuality had permeated the consciousness of wider society. That 'gender deviance' was the means by which 'homosexuals' were identified confirms that by this time homosexuality was viewed as a mix of gender and sexual non-conformity; something much closer to a kind of 'sexual inversion' which incorporated both. Homosexuality was visible and identifiable in a way not possible just thirty years before.

This visibility was consolidated by several novels and short stories with a homosexual theme that were published in the late 1920s and 1930s. For example, the Chilean author Augusto D'Halmar published the novel, *Pasión y Muerte del Cura Deusto* (1924), about a priest who had fallen in love with a choir boy (see Chapter Five), confirming the association in the popular mentality between pederastic or libidinous clergy and sexual deviance. As in the later novel *El Ángel de Sodoma* by Alfonso Hernández-Catá, death and tragedy were to be the fate of the homosexual protagonist.

The novel by Alfonso Hernández-Catá was one of the first fictional accounts in contemporary Spain to examine the theme of homosexuality.[41] The second edition of this work was underwritten by two major figures of the contemporary Spanish scientific and legal establishment – Gregorio Marañón wrote the book's prologue and Luis Jiménez de Asúa, law professor and architect of the 1931 Republican constitution, contributed the epilogue – and stands as an important indicator of the combined workings of literature, medicine and juridical concerns with respect to the construction of discourse around sexuality. The place of publication and the date of this edition (Valparaíso, Chile, 1929) were not chance events.

Indeed, this second edition came shortly after the attempt by the Primo de Rivera dictatorship in Spain to introduce a new Penal Code in 1928. This new Penal Code included articles which criminalized homosexuality not now as part of an article on public morals but in itself.[42] The novel also coincided with a similar attempt to introduce legislation on homosexuality in Chile at the end of the 1920s, measures to which both Marañón and Jiménez de Asúa made reference in their respective sections in the *Ángel de Sodoma*. The prologue, the novel itself and the epilogue, taken together and considering the moment in which they emerged, represent not only a more humanitarian treatment of male homosexuality but also a medico-legal defence of the right of homosexuals to be free from discrimination or persecution.

The author, Alfonso Hernández-Catá, was born in Aldeadávila (Castile) on 24 June 1885, spent much of his life in the diplomatic profession and was Ambassador to Spain in Havana. He wrote *El Ángel de Sodoma* in Cuba, probably, even though the Madrid house Mundo Latino published the first edition in 1928.[43] The central aspect of the novel is the protagonist's growing realization that he is attracted to other men. José-María Vélez-Gomara, the son of an old and established family of an unnamed once-wealthy coastal city (there are some allusions to Cadiz or perhaps Havana), following the death of his mother and the suicide of his father lives with his two sisters, Amparo and Isabel-Luisa. José-María gradually discovers his attraction to men and the plot slowly unfurls as the young man tries to reconcile himself to his desires. The homosexuality of the eldest son is a cipher for the fall of the Vélez-Gomara household, devoured by the growing seed of hereditary degeneracy in the form of the alcoholism and suicide by car crash of the father, the gender deviance and homosexuality of the son, and the erratic, perhaps hysterical behaviour of one of the sisters.

The contributions made to Hernández-Catá's novel by Marañón and Jiménez de Asúa must be understood within the context of the two professionals' social and political outlook and the development of theories on sexuality emerging during this period. Both Marañón and Jiménez de Asúa were renowned for their oppositional stance towards the Primo de Rivera dictatorship and for their advocacy of a Republic.[44] Even though there were differences in emphasis in each author's piece in the book, this common inheritance united their demand for a more humanitarian and scientific treatment of homosexuality. Even though Marañón would oppose the claims of André Gide in his preface to the second Spanish edition of *Corydon*,[45] discussed below, he believed that any kind of legal imposition against homosexuals was morally unjustified and scientifically misguided. Jiménez de Asúa, as a lawyer, was less averse to seeking legal measures for 'crime' but was clear on the need to decriminalize homosexuality.[46]

Marañón's prologue to the book is a fine example of humanist and Enlightenment writing, which extols the virtues of science and professes opposition to the criminalization of homosexuality. The link between science and literature in Hernández-Catá's book were beneficial since 'arte y ciencia se nutren de la misma substancia' [art and science drink from the same source].[47] In Marañón's view, science should have the last word on the question of 'intersexuality', a stance that we will see repeated in the case of his attention to Gide's work. There had been many pleas for homosexuality to be seen as 'normal' but, he urged, the conclusions of science were quite the opposite.

While homosexuals should not be stoned, burned or imprisoned, it was necessary to stifle the source which gave rise to such proclivities. It was necessary to 'fortificar la diferenciación de los sexos, exaltar la varonía de los hombres y la feminidad de las mujeres' [to strengthen differentiation between the sexes, to exalt the masculinity of men and the femininity of women].[48]

This kind of compassionate, even though ultimately pathologizing analysis was less evident in Jiménez de Asúa's epilogue. He criticised the Chilean and German penal codes for legislating 'a espaldas de la ciencia' [with their backs turned to science]. The proposed Spanish law of 1928 made neither scientific nor legal sense.[49] There was no point in condemning the homosexual to prison; homosexuals should be seen 'como enfermos y no como delincuentes' [as people who are ill and not as delinquents].

He appeared in this text to be less acquainted with the scientific literature on the subject than Marañón, and focused primarily on legal questions. This stance taken by Jiménez de Asúa had featured in his more extensive study of the new Penal Code in a co-authored volume published the same year.[50] In this book, he argued against the qualification of homosexuality and other expressions as 'sexual perversions', declaring that there were instead instances of 'sexual pathology'. These had been classified by a large number of authors and it was unacceptable to think of the homosexual as a delinquent; instead, there were psychic and endocrinological reasons which impelled the subject to act as he did.

The similarity between the thought of Marañón, Jiménez de Asúa and indeed, it appears, Hernández-Catá, shows that amongst some members of the scientific establishment and the literary world there was agreement on the need to profess a more liberal attitude towards the homosexual question. The alliance, however, was fragile and was prone to disintegration. This can be seen in Marañón's and others' rejection of the principal tenets of *Corydon*, authored by André Gide.

Advocacy for a Cause: From Gide to Nin Frías

The kinds of connections forged between literature, medicine and the law by the novel *El Ángel de Sodoma* drew on traditions established in the very late nineteenth century in other European countries and became lasting ones in the history of homosexuality in the West. But not all books that advocated a sympathetic stance on homosexuality were written in the same style as this one. While Hernández-Cata's novel presented a rather pathetic and finally tragic picture of the homosexual trapped between a male body and a female psyche – a kind of intersexual of the type established by Marañón – other authors painted a much more militant and uncompromising figure of the homosexual. Around the late 1920s and early 1930s a number of foreign authors had their works on the subject published in Madrid. These works – we will concentrate on two authors, André Gide and Alberto Nin Frías – oscillated between the demand to view male homosexuality as completely natural (in its most virile form) and, as a kind of tributary of late nineteenth-century apologists' work on homosexuality, the argument that however fragile or deviant homosexuality might be this expression of sexuality was located in the province of the genius and was therefore excusable or even beneficial to society.

As in other countries such as England and the United States – one has only to recall the intense debates and eventual legal intervention with respect to Radclyffe Hall's *The Well of Loneliness* – in Spain the multiply fractured picture of homosexuality in the late 1920s and early 1930s as depicted by Gide and Nin Frías corresponds to an intense discourse and counter-discourse, a 'unity' as Foucault would have it, in the treatment of homosexuality. The intense debates and retrenchment of established positions can also be considered in the light of Bourdieu's notion whereby demarcations between groups may become more sharply defined in an exponential process; when one self-construction takes place, a counter-construction may occur.[51] In this case, one group is constructed as humanitarian, scientific or bestowing of rights; another group advocates what is merely a lifestyle that it perceives as natural for the group it defends. In contrast, those who oppose such reasoning rely upon a particular notion of morality, a defence of 'civilization' coupled to a trans-historical justification.

Corydon, written by André Gide and privately printed in an anonymous limited edition in France in 1914 and later with the author's name in the early 1920s, unleashed controversy in France and was quickly countered by the medical profession in the form of the volume *L'Anti-Corydon* written by Dr François Nazier.[52] The antipathy to Gide's thesis of masculine, superior homosexuality was reflected on the other side of the Pyrenees in the publication of Gregorio Marañón's prologue to the second Spanish edition of 1929 of Gide's work and by the liberal jurist Emilio Donato's own 'Anti-Corydon' published in 1931.[53]

In the second edition of Gide's *Corydon*, Marañón, like Donato as we will see, treated Gide's treatise with the respect that we would expect from the endocrinologist but he was unequivocal in his condemnation of the author's thesis.[54] In the opening section of his 'anti-Socratic' dialogue with an imaginary publisher, Marañón replied to the latter's remark that Gide's book had been misunderstood by many readers and critics. This state of affairs, the publisher noted, would be all the worse in Spain where the level of culture was lower and the level of prudishness higher. Marañón's response was to criticize not the scientific aspects of the book but rather its pretension, as a literary work, to use science as a device to support the original author's argument. Gide had attempted to use a scientific hypothesis in order to open up a debate and to explore what he understood as the field of truth. But Marañón viewed this project as hopeless from the outset. The truth sought by Corydon in the dialogue was not simply false, Marañón argued, but, even worse, it was incapable of being true. It was impossible, Marañón countered, that what was understood as 'abnormal' could with any reason be presented by Corydon in any other light.

The attempt by Gide to present homosexuality of a certain type as 'normal' and 'natural' was of course one of the main objectives of his book; *Corydon* constituted a reasoned Socratic dialogue to prove that point. For Marañón, the desire to present homosexuality as normal was at the heart of the tragedy of Oscar Wilde; he spoke before the court not as his friends advised him, admitting his vice, but from the perspective of his own 'normality'. This loyalty to his own concept of what was acceptable was to be his downfall. The only way in which homosexuality could be thought 'normal', wrote Marañón, was as one expression of 'intersexuality'; nature created many imperfections even though they were 'natural'.

But was the use of moral arguments unacceptable when considering what was natural? Marañón's reply to this question made it clear that human ethics were indeed a factor in the natural evolution of living things as they interacted with environment and the 'internal energies' of life. In articulating this response Marañón resorted, as he often did, to metaphysical and literary devices to justify his faith in science. In so doing, his defence of normality and 'abnormality' as something within the range of natural possibilities was based on an evolutionary notion whereby the useless and the imperfect were rooted out as nature continually advanced. The fact that remains of the other sex were present in each human individual was a state to be surpassed. Not so for Gide, Marañón argued:

> Mas para Corydon es una normalidad final. Para nosotros es una normalidad interina, de ahora. Pasará; del mismo modo que se han acortado los brazos, que en una cierta fase de su evolución llegaban normalmente casi hasta el suelo; como se ha erguido el espinazo; como se ha ampliado la capacidad de nuestra calavera, etc., etc.[55]

> [But for Corydon it is a final normality. For us, it is an intermediate normality, from the present. It will pass, in the same way that our arms have become shorter, from the period of evolution when they normally nearly reached the ground. In the same way, our spine has straightened and the capacity of our brain has increased, etc.].

In order to guard against the fall into homosexuality, especially common at the time of adolescence when the sex instinct was still undetermined, it was the task of the master and the father to keep youth on the right track with a 'báculo viril' [virile staff].[56] The days when homosexuality was acceptable socially, in the time of Pericles and the Renaissance, had gone, never to be resuscitated, and the 'pestilent wound' of homosexuality had been cured. In his increasingly virulent attack on the normality of homosexuality Marañón finally gave thanks for the fact that he was not writing his piece in Castile, but in France. For if he had written the prologue in the birthplace of the Inquisition he may have felt compelled to 'quemar el libro, con la efigie del autor, en el brasero que todo lo purifica' [burn the book, with an effigy of the author, in the fires that purify everything].[57]

Corydon was not only a book of passing interest for Marañón; it engaged and sustained the talents of other commentators who were equally reluctant to accept the French author's thesis. Three further examples will suffice. Dr. San de Velilla, in his rather extravagant book on Sodom and Lesbos, complained that a number of medical doctors, including Marañón, had been 'duped' by what he termed the cynical advocacy of homosexuality by some authors including Gide.[58] San de Velilla dismissed entirely the Gidean thesis. For him the book amounted to nothing more than 'pederastic propaganda', an advocacy of one type of pederastic relationship opposed to homosexuality as effeminacy. The impunity and tolerance with which the book was treated resulted in nothing less than its ascendant popularity.

The reluctance that Gide displayed in publishing his volume was slowly dissolved by 'far too sympathetic' doctors and other supporters, such as Moll, Westphal and Carpenter, who had presented, under the guise of science, the argument that homosexuality was natural. The publication of Corydon had contributed to 'la corrupción de costumbres y el vergonzoso descoco de los homosexuales, a los que la benignidad de las leyes ha dado un peligroso salvoconducto para operar sin reservas' [the corruption of customs and the shameful outlandishness of the homosexuals, to whom the benign law has given a safe pass so they can operate with no compunction].[59] Corydon, according to the doctor, had no saving graces; its value in literary and scientific terms was practically nil. In fact, he continued, the book had only become popular because of the current vogue of homosexuality. This new fashion, which, San de Velilla declared, Marañón had unjustly credited to the infamous trials of Oscar Wilde, was made possible because of the 'scientific' protection that this kind of 'perversion' enjoyed.

Along with the prologue written by Marañón, however, the most reasoned and ostensibly 'objective' account of Corydon was contained in the lengthy essay by the jurist Emilio Donato. In a review of this book in the Siglo Médico, one doctor praised Donato's rebuttal of Gide to the extent of valuing it more highly than Marañón's prologue. Like Marañón, the review's author refused to accept the 'normality' of homosexuality.[60] The doctor

who reviewed Donato's text remarked upon a paradox: the proliferation of studies on sexual problems of the time 'ha ido en
detrimento de su calidad y de su honradez de propósito' [has
taken place in detriment to their quality and the honesty of their
aims].[61] Donato's *Frente a Gide* disproved the 'normality of the
homosexual tendency' and constituted 'una de las pocas obras de
sexología digna de ser leída y meditada' [one of the few works of
sexology worth reading and meditating upon].[62]

The book by Donato, *Homosexualismo (Frente a Gide)*, of more
than 130 pages, can be compared to Marañón's prologue in
respect of its principal argument. Donato also displayed a measure of intellectual respect towards his adversary but was equally
adamant in his condemnation of Gide's argument. Donato
employed a naturalizing framework in order to understand 'pederasty' as an illness, 'una cosa natural porque es algo que se
produce según leyes naturales, por el desarrollo de ciertos
gérmenes naturales, o por funcionamiento irregular de ciertos
órganos también naturales' [something that is natural because it
is produced by natural laws, by the development of certain natural
germs, or by the irregular functioning of certain organs which are
also natural].[63] But Gide, the author noted, wanted to take things
further and advocated a normal form of pederasty, which was not
sick. From this perspective 'La major manera de curar a un
pederasta es convencerle de que su perversión no lo es, que su
enfermedad no es una enfermedad' [The best way of curing a
pederast is to convince him that he is not [ill], that his illness is
not an illness].[64] The rest of Donato's essay was dedicated to
illustrate the falsity of this premise. However, like Marañón and
Jiménez de Asúa, Donato was utterly opposed to legal sanction of
consensual homosexuality. Homosexuality, for Donato, occupied
a 'no man's land' with respect to morality – it was not immoral but
'extramoral'.[65] Like Marañón and Asúa he regarded the 1928
attempt to criminalize homosexuality as 'una de las secreciones
más absurdas del período dictatorial' [one of the most absurd
secretions of the dictatorial period].[66]

An interesting product of Gide's work was the popularization
of the term 'Corydon' to signify 'homosexual'. Perhaps this was
not the case in broad sectors of the population, but in certain
artistic circles there seems to have been some knowledge of this
association. For example, Lorca's friend Rafael Rodríguez Rapún
was to play the part of the fisherman Corydon in the *Burlador de*

Sevilla, a role that, according to his own account, he interpreted quite well, perhaps because he was a 'Corydon' in the proper sense of the word. The reference, to those 'in the know', would be unmistakable.[67]

Despite the *succès de scandale* of Gide's work, we must not let this originally French dimension obscure what was being written in Spanish from a similar perspective just a few years later *contra* medical and legal figures such as Marañón and Donato. Much attention has been devoted to André Gide's *Corydon* but two works in Spanish whose aim was similar to that of Gide have passed practically unnoticed despite a certain level of debate at the time of their publication. Published in 1932 and 1933 respectively, Alberto Nin Frías' *Alexis o el significado del temperamento urano* and his *Homosexualismo creador*, were remarkable for their depth of scholarship and for their powerful plea for homosexual rights.[68]

Nin Frías' elegantly literary *Alexis* was, perhaps even more than Gide's own *Corydon*, a work conscious of the period in which it was written and was prepared to embrace the new times that the author felt allowed for reflection, new ethical considerations and a new set of values. Part of this new order was the analysis of the 'androgynous' tendency, Uranism or 'homogenic love'; an aspect, Nin Frías admitted, that was reflected in Gide's *Corydon*.[69]

However, for Nin Frías, Gide's work was not convincing for one principal reason: the author did not account for his own psychic state and that of individuals who sought his kind of love. There must exist, Nin Frías argued, a profound and deep-rooted reason that obliged not unintelligent or immoral people to follow this path.[70] But the reasons behind this kind of love were perhaps not so different from those adduced by Gide. The core of the argument presented in *Alexis* and extensively elaborated in his *Homosexualismo creador* resides in the assertion that such love, heroic and romantic as it was, could only be present in a select minority or aristocratic group of persons.[71]

The account presented by Nin Frías, despite its attempt to locate homosexual eroticism on a higher plane, as a select disposition, did not manage to save it from prevailing pathological explanatory frameworks. Nin Frías argued for the reader's suspension of belief in the category of pathology for an instant in order to consider the beautiful aspects of homosexual desire. But the author continually had recourse to psychological and medical accounts to do so. Firstly, he claimed, the 'homosexualizing tendency' was of a prenatal origin, guided by the feelings and thought of the mother. Secondly, the deviation responded to the lack of maturity of the sexual appetite of the Uranian, a projection from adolescent times into adulthood.

This unification of biology and psychology was not, as we have seen, uncommon. The Uranian desire did not spring from the practice of the solitary vice in school or from the engagement in sodomy at that age, Nin Frías held. Instead, these practices were elevated by the search for new emotions, the refining of the spirit and the formation of a 'peculiaridad psíquica perfectamente calificada' [perfectly qualified psychic peculiarity].[72] The making of such 'exalted idealists', nevertheless, was a psycho-biological process whose workings were known only to God.[73] Despite naming the large number of scientific and literary supporters of more liberal attitudes towards homosexual love – figures ranging from Lorca to Ingenieros are cited – Nin Frías still talked of illness. If one side of the coin held poetry and beauty, the other hid abnormality, aberration, perversion. Such was the human condition that human grandeur was 'La perla [que] es el producto de una enfermedad' [The pearl [which] is the product of an illness]; behind all things exquisite there lay tragedy.[74]

The relationship between genius and homosexuality had already been mooted in the work of late nineteenth-century apologists of homosexuality and Nin Frías was to develop this argument in his nearly four hundred pages of *Homosexualismo creador*, published one year later. This volume traced a history of primarily male homosexuality, homosociality and male-male friendship from the times of Sodom and Gomorrah in an account that hardly went beyond the end of nineteenth century and, curiously, did not discuss Latin America or Spain.

Why was there no mention of homosexuality in Spain in *Homosexualismo creador*? Was the subject too risky for a Spanish and Latin American audience under such an explicit title? Was it Nin Frías's tactic to discuss homosexuality in other countries, hoping eventually for liberalization in Hispanic countries? This was perhaps why Nin Frías wrapped Hispanic homosexuality in an artistic and literary covering in the form of *Alexis*. He fully acknowledged the hostile environment in which he was working:

En todo el medio hispanoparlante – lo he recorrido personalmente todo él – existe un innato horror al homosexualismo; pero esta postura resulta más bien un fenómeno verbal de patología sexual, que un hecho positivo. Esta reticencia ha retardado enormemente se ocupen los investigadores iberos de este problema médico-legal. Poco o nada de documentado se sabe respecto da las aficiones eróticas de sus artistas o de otras personalidades notables. ¡Felices los países en que los hombres son hombres y las mujeres, mujeres![75]

[In the whole of the Spanish-speaking world – I personally have travelled throughout it – there exists an innate horror of homosexualism. But this posture is in fact a verbal form of sexual pathology, not a real one. This reticence has delayed Iberian researchers' interest in this medico-legal problem enormously. Little or nothing documented is there known of the erotic interests of [Iberia's] artists or other persons of renown. Happy are those countries where men are men and women are women!]

Despite the reticence of researchers and Nin Frías's somewhat guarded approach, at least in *Homosexualismo creador*, the work of this Uruguayan lecturer and literary critic stands on a plane similar to André Gide in respect of his advocacy for the normalization of homosexuality in the Hispanic world.

As is to be expected, Nin Frías' ideas received a hostile reception from a number of sources. We can turn to San de Velilla once again for an uncompromising critique which turned out to be more of an insult than a cool appraisal. San de Velilla wrote of a 'stupid' defence of homosexuality, an 'intolerable' book which provoked 'indignation and revulsion' and of an author who was 'unbalanced'.[76] The doctor attacked one of the central premises of Nin Frías's thesis; that homosexuality was somehow linked to genius. As in his critique of Gide's *Corydon* San de Velilla had not one good word to say of the doctors who had aired the subject in public, outside the confines of the Academy. Under the wing of scientific authority, the 'effeminate voices' of the most daring homosexuals that began by petitioning a more tolerant attitude for their 'unfortunate psychoses' now felt confident enough to look down upon 'normal' love.[77]

The work of individuals like Nin Frías and Hernández-Catá from different literary perspectives and Gregorio Marañón from a scientific position is indicative of the complexities and the multiple alliances formed around the concept of homosexuality in Spain in the late 1920s and early 1930s. It is likely that, of all the years considered here, what was written and discussed in various forums during these few years was of most consequence for the lived experience of homosexuals in Spain. Though it is improbable that most homosexuals would have come across the novel by Hernández-Catá or even the theories of Gregorio Marañón, that there were some reverberations of this kind of work in some quarters of the broad homosexual subculture is, as we have already suggested, undeniable. But if we speak here of 'alliances' between literature, progressive lawmakers and scientists, we cannot say the same of another kind of literature that was not prepared to pact with these elite discourses. Similar in some respects to the arguments offered by some homosexuals, such as Friedländer, who dissented from Magnus Hirschfeld's theories in Germany at the beginning of the twentieth century,[78] in the world of erotic novelettes of the 1920s there emerges a fascinating challenge to both the literary justifications of homosexuality marshalled by Hernández-Catá and the scientific theories espoused by Marañón. We find a satirical and some would say 'frivolous' attack on these positions articulated by the songwriter and erotic novelist Álvaro Retana. It is in Retana that we find some of the earliest 'first person' public accounts of homosexuality which mark their distance from other literary and scientific explanations of homosexuality. Retana, while by no means attaining the sophistication of the argument offered by commentators such as Friedländer (such was not his aim), does provide a further insight into another self-construction as part of the exponential process in the articulation of demarcations of discourse around homosexuality.

The short novels, often of a mildly pornographic or piquant nature, written by Álvaro Retana were numerous and daring for the times concerned. He wrote about transvestites and their amours in *Las locas de postín*, about ambiguous and effeminate men in other works, and about the Madrid homosexual subculture in *A Sodoma en tren botijo*.[79] What characterizes Retana is his irreverence: he would attend workers' demonstrations dressed in his silk dressing gown, and he would dismiss the attempts of doctors such as Marañón to 'explain' homosexuality in terms which he believed to be ultimately pathological. While the influence of Retana is debatable in homosexual circles and in the medical literature (Marañón, for instance, does not mention him), his interventions can be understood as a protest against what he perceived as the medicalization of homosexuality in a way which was significant, although different from that of Gide or Nin Frías.

Spurning the medical model, and advocating the 'naturalness' of homosexuality, Retana coincided with some other homosexuals in the early twentieth century (and many who came later) who questioned the implicitly pathological representation of homosexuality articulated by progressive doctors such as Magnus Hirschfeld and Gregorio Marañón. Despite the many differences between Retana and Hirschfeld's detractors such as Friedländer, what these individuals held in common was a position which advocated the separation of homosexual desire and practice from medical attention. Indeed, they argued that homosexuality was not an illness, thus combating the authority of the experts of the medical faculty. This was a bold move for it was an attempt to shift the whole linguistic and epistemological debate, creating a challenge that went beyond the authorizing strategies of medical science and 'do-gooders' who advocated 'tolerance' for homosexuality while at the same time proposing measures that would limit its expression.

Retana's *Las locas de postín* depicts a world of aristocratic transvestites and homosexuality which probably reflected some of his own experiences in the Madrid of the 1920s. This work relates a train journey whose destination was Barcelona. Álvaro, the protagonist, meets two of his admirers, Tito and Graciela, who are twins. They become friends, even though Álvaro prefers the male youth. The outcome of the novel is not a happy one, however. The girl becomes a sexual plaything of the rich and her brother commits suicide in a police cell. A similar but more daring approach is taken in Retana's *El Infierno de la voluptuosidad* in which a young, somewhat effeminate, aristocrat embarks on a voyage of decadent seduction of both sexes. Death once more seals the end of the novel.[80]

Some of the same motifs are carried through in another of Retana's literary productions, *A Sodoma en tren botijo*, which is an explicit depiction of the homosexual world of the early 1930s. Retana's prologue to his work makes reference to how he fell foul of the dictatorship in the 1920s, having been charged with being 'an immoral writer'. The somewhat famous case resulted in five months in prison and a fine. Despite this, Retana was to boast that he was 'el primer novelista del mundo que ha ingresado en la cárcel acusado de voluptuoso' [the first novelist in the world to have been sent to prison accused of being voluptuous].[81]

The novel is remarkable in a number of senses. Retana casts satirical aspersions on censorship by professing that his depiction of the behaviour of his characters is not one that he approves; whoever loves vice and danger will end up dying by them, he remarks. It would therefore be impossible to overestimate the dangers for inexperienced and naive youth posed by the wiles of the 'third sex'.[82] This tongue-in-cheek introduction is followed by the story of Nemesio, an upper-class youth from Almería, who decides to leave his provincial birthplace to go to Madrid. Here, he enters into contact with the world of aristocratic homosexuality, of parties and cocktail drinks; a world in which men have 'queridos' as well as 'queridas', there is talk of men who are 'in the know', 'that way' and of those who belong to the third sex.

This short novel is indicative of the world of aristocratic homosexuality that existed in some parts of Spain, in particular Madrid, in the early part of the century. It is illustrative also of the slang of the homosexual world, the use of feminine terms attested by doctors and lawyers such as Bernaldo de Quirós and Llanas Aguilaniedo, and a certain self-awareness of homosexual subjects that was only intermittently recorded in psychiatric and legal discourse.

The self-awareness, or articulation of discourse in the first person, was consolidated in Retana's later critique of the novel *El Ángel de Sodoma*, written by Hernández-Catá. In his *La Ola Verde* (1931), he criticized Hernandez-Catá for showing a 'perfecto desconocimiento psicológico o de una preconcebida mala fe, pues solamente a Hernández-Catá que, o no sabe nada o lo sabe todo, se le puede ocurrir hacernos creer que un hombre, al descubrir en sí tendencias homosexuales, se arroje tranquilamente al mar' [perfect incomprehension of psychology or a measure of preconceived bad faith, since it can only occur to Hernández-Catá, who either knows everything about the subject or nothing, to try to make us believe that a man, on finding out that he has homosexual tendencies, throws himself nonchalantly into the sea].[83] Despite the inaccuracy here (the protagonist actually threw himself under a train), Retana declared that if all homosexuals were to do the same, given their numbers, 'estarían las regiones submarinas más frecuentadas que la Exposición de Barcelona' [the sea's waters would be more frequently visited than the Barcelona Exhibition].[85] Retana clearly moved in circles where the expression of sexual unorthodoxy was common. His homosexual subculture of Madrid was but one facet of this variegated world. The morphology and characteristics of this subculture occupy us next.

The Existence of Subcultures: Homosexual Life in the Years 1850–1936

The treatment of male prostitution and homosexuality in literary works and cultural production provides an insight into the culture of the time, its constraints and the possibility of a homosexual discourse adopted in first person accounts. But what was homosexual life actually like in Spain? What were the specific daily practices of male homosexuals and what relation did these have with the articulation of a 'subculture'? Once more, it is important not to overestimate the extent and openness of any such subculture. Despite this, a number of sources point to the ongoing – albeit changing – existence of a variety of subcultural forms constructed around 'homosexuality' in the period concerned. On occasion, these overlapped; at other times they were radically dissimilar or were even eschewed by one another. Social class, degrees of effeminacy, the level of open acknowledgement of homosexuality or its hidden nature, are all factors that must be taken into account to understand homosexual expression in the period.

Most likely of a high-class nature were the late nineteenth-century homosexual balls and dances in the major cities such as Barcelona and Madrid. These dances apparently took place relatively openly. In 1879, for example, in the dance hall 'El Ramillete', in Alameda Street in Madrid, on the last day of Carnival, 'más de cien sodomitas con elegantes trajes y ricas joyas' [more than one hundred sodomites in elegant dress and sumptuous jewels] could be counted.[85] However, this dance culture appears to have been rather short-lived. Max Bembo noted that by the early twentieth century these balls were things of the past. What was once a rich homosexual life in Barcelona appears to have declined by the early twentieth century: 'Yo no he podido encontrar en el homosexualismo barcelonés las apariencias que tenía muchos años atrás; las fiestas en que se celebraban los bautizos de

un homosexual; los bailes escandalosísimos; las fiestas sardana-
pálicas, vergüenza de una ciudad' [I have not been able to find
amongst Barcelona homosexuals the aspects that were found
years ago – the parties in which the baptism of a homosexual was
celebrated, the scandalous dances, the fiestas characteristic of
Sardanapalus, a disgrace for the city].[86] This was possibly, Bembo
noted, as a result of the public scandal laws, whose effect had
been the withdrawal of homosexuals from the streets and the
reliance on small groups of friends for socializing.

During this same period of 'scandalous dances' there were
more discrete forms of homosexual life which revolved around
private clubs and societies of interested parties. Perhaps the
'homosexual baptisms' that Max Bembo referred to were what
Teodoro Yáñez described in 1884. 'Some years ago', Yáñez noted,
in the Madrid square Herradores, there was a huge scandal.
Neighbours saw that 'suspicious types' frequented an address;
because the times were full of political conspiracies (the author
may have been referring to the turbulent times of the 1860s
revolution or the period around the First Republic) the authorities were placed on alert. One night, the authorities surprised
those in the house in 'full assembly'. In reality, there was no
political plot being hatched but 'Era un club de pederastas;
entraban aquellos individuos, se desnudaban, poniéndose otras
ropas parecidas á las de las mujeres, y se dedicaban á su ejercicio'
[It was a pederasts' club. These people entered, undressed, put
on clothes similar to those of women, and got on with their
business]. Some days, newcomers were admitted and underwent
an initiation ceremony: 'y despues [*sic*] de acreditar que no
habían conocido varon [*sic*] con dos testigos, se les ponía una
túnica blanca y una corona de azahar, y se les paseaba por el
recinto, haciendo luego uno de ellos la primera introduccion
[*sic*]' [and after verifying that they had not been with a man by
means of two witnesses, they dressed them in a white tunic and
orange blossom crown, and led them around the place, and one
of [the assembled] made the first introduction].[87]

It is likely that these 'baptisms' were what Bernaldo de Quirós
and Llanas Aguilaniedo also referred to. There were other dimensions to these cultural practices, however, which invoked marriage
and birth. Similar to some of the practices of the 'Mollies' in
eighteenth-century London,[88] they are worth referring to in
detail:

La ceremonia del *partorio* es complicada y variable en cada caso. Celébranse en lugares de reunión, algunos de los cuales se han hecho famosos. Aparece un uranista en traje femenino, con el vientre abultado, andando penosamente. El supuesto médico y la reunión de amigos, deudos y familiares, alarmados, oblíganle a tenderse en el lecho, prodíganle toda clase de cuidados, refrescan con paños mojados su frente y sienes, sobreviniendo, al fin, tras una larga brega simulada, y en medio de grandes alaridos, el alumbramiento del muñeco, que es inmediatamente presentado al oficioso senado de expectantes. La más viva alegría se pinta en las caras; corre el vino a raudales, y el suspirado desenfreno hace al fin su aparición entre la grotesca turba.[89]

[The 'birth' ceremony is complicated and varies from case to case. It takes place in certain meeting places, some of which have become famous. A Uranian appears in female dress, with a distended midriff, walking with difficulty. The supposed doctor and the assembled friends, acquaintances and family, in a state of alarm, make him lie on the bed, administer him all kinds of comforts, refresh his brow and forehead with moistened cloths. After a long pretend struggle, at last, among great cries, the doll is born and is immediately displayed to the officious assembly of expectant persons. The greatest happiness is painted upon their faces, the wine flows free and the long awaited release at last makes its appearance among the grotesque crowd.]

The authors remark that similar to this kind of ceremony were the weddings and baptisms in which 'palpita una ironía dolorosa contra la Naturaleza' [a painful irony is brought alive against nature]. Here, money, luxury and the final orgy flow freely.[90] Perhaps a similar kind of secret society was that recounted by Rodríguez Solís. Referring to the novel by Francisco Sales Mayo, *La Condesita*,[91] the author presents the society of 'San Guiñolé', an upper-class or at least economically well-off group of men and women who frequented the Casino, Círculo Mercantil and the Opera and who treated one another with excessive affection and in tones full of insinuations. These 'guiñolistas' followed Sappho and Cain in their unions between women and between men, Rodríguez-Solís wrote. There appears to have been a broader underlying aim in these circles; Sales Mayo also alludes to how young men, hardly of school-leaving age, took up the most important posts in public offices. In the best seats of the theatre a 'multitude' of young men were 'almibarados en melosa plática con hombres serios al parecer, y con viejos relamidos' [sweetly engaged in sickly talk with seemingly serious men, and with elegant old men]. They were all 'guiñolistas'.[92]

Of a different physiognomy and cultural extraction were the music halls and cabarets of the 1920s in major cities such as Madrid and Barcelona. Several testimonies and interpretations point to the gender play that these places afforded. San de Velilla, predictably enough, denigrated the atmosphere to be breathed in these locales: 'las bellas de nuestros *music-halls* y cafés cantantes son reemplazadas por adolescentes que cantan y bailan procurando excitar lascivos deseos, que luego aplacan con ayuntamientos anormales' [the beauties of music halls and dancing venues are replaced by adolescents who sing and dance, trying to excite lascivious desires, which they later placate with abnormal embraces].[93] These establishments became renowned in the 1920s as part of the spirit of eroticism that swept the country known at the time as 'sicalipsis'. The levels of prostitution and general 'immorality' in these places was to spark off a number of morality campaigns in the early twentieth century such as those led or supported by figures of national importance including Maeztu, Unamuno and Canalejas.[94]

The atmosphere of the 'cafés cantantes' and small theatres also catered for transvestite spectaculars and suggestive lyrics, written by, amongst others, Álvaro Retana. Retana, in addition to the novelettes we have discussed, was the author of the famous *cuplé* (music hall song) 'Tardes del Ritz' which was premiered in 1923 by the transvestite Edmond de Bries.[95] Rather than places with a specifically homosexual reputation, the 'cafés cantantes' and the like were suggestive of all kinds of erotic waywardness. Other commercial establishments, however, had more of a reputation for their homosexual clientele. Bars were the most obvious of these. While the 'Polinario' in the Calle Real de la Alhambra in Granada was no doubt an untypical establishment, several bars and cafés in other places were renowned for the presence of homosexuals. Still in Andalusia, a small bar in San Fernando (Cadiz) enjoyed the tunes of a homosexual piano player[96] and the Madrid establishments the 'Café de Levante' and the 'Café del Vapor' were the respective haunts of aristocratic homosexual Antonio Hoyos y Vinent and Pedro de Répide, 'un homosexual tranquilo . . . [que] olía a perfume barato y se empolvaba la cara' [a peaceful homosexual . . . [who] smelt of cheap perfume and who powdered his face].[97] In Barcelona, cafés of this nature and

music halls where prostitution was practised were centred on the
Barri Xinès, in the heart of the city.[98] Cartoons of the time suggest
the availability of aging male prostitutes in this quarter.[99]

The protagonists of these different worlds did at times overlap.
If urinals were one place where workers and bosses met according
to Gide,[100] some bars too were renowned for their class mix, in
networks of informal prostitution, often between older richer
men and working-class youths. Once more, Rodríguez Solís notes
that in two Madrid streets in the 1870s petty criminals and
working-class youths ('chulos') were found in the company of
elegant gentlemen and high-class individuals. It was, Rodríguez
Solís, remarks, the social position of the latter that explained the
impunity with which they operated.[101]

The fact that few cases had been brought to court against
homosexuals and those which had were thrown out meant that,
for the public at large, homosexuality was something intrinsic to
the aristocracy.[102] This association between homosexuality and
aristocracy was not new, however. In Spain Marañón had hinted at
such an interpretation in his prologue to Bloch's 1924 volume on
contemporary sexual life;[103] in other countries homosexuality was
known as the 'aristocratic vice'. The aristocracy, Marañón noted,
was used to travelling, used 'exotic' languages, dressed differently,
and in the Spanish case was imbued with a cosmopolitanism
which extended to sexual life. This kind of association was
confirmed in the figure of Don Juan, as we have seen in Chapter
Three, and in other literary personages such as the Marqués de
Bradomín, notably in *Estío*, by Valle-Inclán. But these were not just
literary associations. There is plenty of evidence to show that a
homosexual subculture had been present around aristocratic
figures for some time. Attention was drawn to such individuals on
the basis of the existence of the excessively effeminate male, those
who liked to dress in exquisite clothes or those who lead a
luxurious but somewhat secretive life, manifested in the dandy or
the aesthete.[104]

In this sense, Alan Sinfield has argued that there was a 'pre-'
and 'post-' Oscar Wilde period, a faultline at which effeminacy
and dandyesque characteristics came to signify some form of
sexual 'deviance'.[105] In this process, aspects of Wilde's and others'
characters such as fine dress, green carnations and such like, were
'resignified' to betray homosexuality. Similar associations are true
in the Spanish case, although there was no resounding legal

prosecution such as that of Oscar Wilde. In Seville, for example, the partial unmasking of an individual described as 'un sodomita, invertido o esteta' [a sodomite, invert or aesthete] was to cause, according to the periodical in which the story first made headlines, a public commotion. This individual was supposed to be a corruptor of minors, being able to fulfil his desires in houses of prostitution in the city. That the person in question, whom the paper refused to name outright, was a member of the Casino de Labradores, professed Catholicism and was married, was sufficient to fulfil the requisites associated with prostitution, homosexuality and the upper class.[106]

Possibly the most concrete real-life representation of this type was Antonio de Hoyos y Vinent; 'el aristócrata de americana, zapato de tacón alto y monóculo, frecuentaba el Café Levante, donde coqueteaba con torerillos. Por sus salones pasaban jovencitos de los bajos fondos y gente de la alta sociedad en busca de emociones perversas' [the aristocrat dressed in a jacket, high heels and monocle, frequented the Café Levante, where he would flirt with the young bullfighters. Throughout the venue low-life youngsters and men of high society would pass in search of perverse emotions].[107] Hoyos would search for young working-class males for sex, often lured his way by his 'intérprete y celestina [el] inseparable Luisito Pomés, ese chico bonito . . . de cara cuidada como una señorita y sin el cual el aristocrático sordo no podría hacer sus conquistas' [interpreter and go-between [the] inseparable Luisito Pomés, that beautiful boy . . . of delicate facial features like a young lady without whom the deaf aristocrat was incapable of making his conquests].[108] Hoyos was renowned for his decadent lifestyle and for his appetite for new experiences. It is certain that it was he that Luis Buñuel described in his autobiography *My Last Breath*. Buñuel encountered Hoyos in a Madrid tram and was given a small amount of money in exchange for his agreement to meet up the following day. Needless to say, Buñuel failed to keep his part of the bargain.[109]

If the tram was one place to make contact, there were many others in the city. Intrinsic to homosexual life in European urban places from the late medieval period onwards, and especially from modern times, were sites where men met for sexual purposes. Authors in Spain recorded such places, as we have seen. Suárez Casañ, for example, in a short section on Barcelona, after having discussed Paris, Rome and Naples, acknowledged the existence of certain areas of the city frequented by 'pederasts'. He noted that there existed 'paseos oscuros y solitarios durante la noche, en los cuales, á merced de las sombras, se cometen las mayores torpezas' [dark, solitary alleyways in the night, where, protected by the shadows, the greatest of disgraceful acts would be committed].[110] The general public, he wrote, was aware of these places and should be more vociferous in its campaign against pederasty: 'El honrado vecindario barcelonés debiera protestar enérgicamente y pedir que se atajasen ciertos abusos que todos conocen' [The honourable Barcelona public should protest energetically and demand that certain well-known abuses be curtailed]. So well known were these places that people tried not to pass by them at night. But this was no remedy in itself. What was needed was a concerted campaign by the authorities to root out such activities. Electric lights ought to be installed 'que auyentaran [*sic*] con sus rayos á esos nocturnos pajarracos, enemigos de la moralidad' [to scare off these nightbirds, enemies of morality, with their beams]. Unfortunately, Suárez Casañ does not tell us where these places were in Barcelona.

More comprehensive in a number of respects but equally evasive in terms of explicit location was Bembo. According to this author, the abundance of 'Uranians' (he also talks of effeminates, pedicates, cynadae, fellators, 'pacientes', adolescents, twins, pederasts and inverts) in Barcelona was such that one could talk of a 'third sex', despite the difficulties in setting their precise number. The Uranians interviewed by Bembo spoke of numbers between 6,000 and 30,000, including those who were undeclared, incognito, or 'suspect'. Such a quantity placed Barcelona in second place after Madrid and before Seville for its homosexual population.

Bembo identified a number of generic places in Barcelona where homosexuals could be found. His list included: cinemas, theatres, the street, public baths, churches, crowds, urinals and trams.[111] Unfortunately he does not name these places specifically, averring that, in the case of cinemas, while there are many which enjoy such a reputation 'No digo sus nombres para no hacer el caldo gordo a la inversión sexual' [I will not mention their names so as not to promote sexual inversion].[112] However, he remarks that the Paralelo was the main area for these establishments, but since the economic crisis in the cinema trade, interest has passed to the city centre. Sexual acts, the author assured us, occured within these locales.

With respect to the theatres, premieres were the occasions most prolifically attended by Uranians. Bembo recounted that once, when accompanied by a Uranian, the latter managed to count one hundred and fifty of his type on one premiere night. Other encounters took place in the street, where money often changed hands. Urinals were another place for meetings and where the adolescent was introduced to the homosexual world. Despite a campaign some years previously by upstanding women of the city to demolish urinals (which was ridiculed by the press), this was one of the principal places for 'la crápula homosexual' [homosexual licentiousness], and homosexual acts in urinals 'pudieran llenar todo un volumen' [could fill a whole volume].[113]

Parks and gardens, again unsurprisingly, provided another refuge for homosexual activity. More privacy was to be obtained in the hills which Bembo describes as similar to those of Montserrat. It is possible that the author here was referring to Monjuïc, still a popular cruising ground. Such is the presence of homosexuals in these public spaces that 'Ya no es el Parque el sitio de los enamorados: lo es el de los homosexuales' [the parks are no longer the place for lovers, but for homosexuals instead], as if homosexuals do not 'make love' but merely pursue sex.[114]

Like the medical doctors we have reviewed, the Barcelona public, at least according to Bembo, was clearly capable of identifying at least some homosexuals. Somewhat ironically, Bembo denied that homosexuals could recognize one another with a mere glance, proceeding himself to identify the most effeminate homosexual. This type, however, was so rare in the city that 'ni vale la pena de preocuparse de él' [it is not even worth bothering about].[115] The majority, the author assured his reader, were masculine and many effeminates tried to hide their traits.

Despite the availability of sexual relations in the places mentioned, Bembo was keen to assert that most of Barcelona's homosexuals did not engage in such practices. This may have been due to a sense of shame, prudishness or in a bid for respectability on their part. The majority homosexual lifestyle, according to the author, was different from that led by those who frequent parks, cinemas and baths: 'Se limitan a uno o dos amantes escogidos entre sus amigos o compañeros de estudio o

trabajo. Existen en Barcelona gran número de parejas homosexuales que pasan completamente desapercibidas, . . . que al parecer
viven felices y que no se meten con nadie' [They limit themselves
to one or two lovers chosen amongst their friends, study- or
work-mates. In Barcelona, there is a large number of homosexual
couples who are not even noticed, . . . and who, it would seem, *live
happily* and do not disturb anyone].[116] This did not mean that
homosexuals were invisible, however. Far from it; with a good
guide 'queda uno asombradísimo al ver surgir homosexuales por
todas partes, donde antes parecía que no habían de encontrarse'
[one would be surprised to see homosexuals pop up everyewhere
and in places where there did not seem to be any]. This more
intimate and restrained homosexual lifestyle meant, the author
tells us, that most homosexuals were 'virile', individualist, did not
congregate in large groups and, because of their Catalan sensibilities, were married, had children and lived discretely.[117]

While the image of a rather extensive and, perhaps, relatively
trouble-free homosexual lifestyle may have been the case for some
Barcelona homosexuals, the aggression suffered by many cannot
be minimized. Amongst these was doubtless the potential for
blackmail. This was something that Bembo was to criticize
severely. Known as the 'ronda ful' or simply 'la ful', individuals
posing as police would surprise homosexuals in urinals or parks
and would extort a payment in exchange for their silence.[118] This
practice was confirmed by others at the time. Madrid homosexuals were to fall victim to the same phenomenon and many were
the scandals caused by homosexuals and their persecutors.[119] In
the case of Barcelona at least, however, Bembo recorded that few
homosexuals fell victim to these blackmailers' wiles; the latter
were well known and only foreigners or those not from the city
would succumb.[120]

Crime, as we have noted throughout this study, was associated
to homosexuality in a number of contexts and became a long-
lasting fellow traveller. While the Franco period was undoubtedly
the worst for homosexuals there were a few cases before this time
that resulted in prosecution, usually under the public scandal
laws.[121] In the Republican period, for example, three cases that
went to the Supreme Court can be mentioned. In chronological
order, the first case related how one male individual had fondled
another in a theatre, an action that resulted in a fight. Despite the

individual concerned being absolved of the crime in a lesser court, the Supreme Tribunal's decision was to impose Article 616 of the Penal Code on the prisoner. In passing, it is worth noting that the individual was known to the police 'as an invert', which presupposed his recidivism.[122]

The second case heard by the Supreme Court revised the opinion of the Oviedo criminal court, qualifying an individual's crime not as one of public scandal but of abuse of minors. The case concerned the introduction of the man's penis into the mouth of a boy who at the time was less than twelve years old. The perpetrator in question was charged under Article 453 of the 1870 Penal Code, equivalent to Article 431 of the new Code.[123]

The military Code, however, was more stringent than the civil. According to Article 298 of the Military Code of Justice, the crime of 'abusos deshonestos' was recorded when the integrity of a male person was violated by the attempt, whether taken to fruition or not, to perform some kind of sexual act with a person of the same sex. Both participants would be judged under this legislation which drew on a sentence from December 1896. In the case concerned, it was recorded that the two individuals had discussed homosexual acts; no opposition to the touching of genitalia had been made and therefore both could be condemned.[124]

It remains clear that the homosexual 'subculture' in Spain was polymorphous and was criss-crossed by class, different types of sexual practice, sometimes payment for sex, and by the different spheres (literature, dance halls, bars, public places) in which homosexuals could be seen. The term 'subculture' is overflowed by these different manifestations of homosexuality and cannot possibly contain its different expressions or the schisms existent in its varied forms. But 'homosexuality', wherever it was and by whomever it was articulated, was not a series of unconnected worlds, as Chauncey has cogently argued in the case of New York. We have seen how and where different classes met; we have seen how men looking for homosexual sex congregated in particular places and we have noted how from at least the mid nineteenth century there were specific cultural forms, such as dances, initiation ceremonies or 'marriages' that homosexuals entertained.

The morphology of this homosexual subculture and the views from the outside and those from within changed over time. After an initial subculture which emerged, or continued to be present around small groups of pederasts who had their own meetings and dances in the mid nineteenth century, there followed the growth of this phenomenon into a much more extensive and well known publicly visible presence with large scale extravagant dances. Afterwards, such dances went into decline and there was a certain 'going underground' at the beginning of the twentieth century. The particularly effeminate and visible male prostitution of the late nineteenth and very early twentieth century was not so evident by the 1920s. This is acknowledged by outside observers such as Bembo and, if we are to trust his sources, by homosexual prostitutes themselves. As the century wore on, observers such as Bembo and Lucenay would remark that it was becoming increasingly difficult to identify homosexuals because they looked like 'normal' people. If it is true that there was a 'virilization' of homosexuality why was this so? Or, in reality, was such virilization a product of the medical and legal gaze; perhaps these experts had concentrated initially on the obvious *maricas* and effeminates to turn later to the realization that homosexuals were a much more diverse breed?

There may be a number of responses to these questions. Firstly, it is possible that in reality there took place a process of virilization of male homosexuality for reasons of taste, anonymity or the desire to evade the attention of the public or the police. Secondly, perhaps as the 1920s wore on, with the emergence of an increased fluidity between the sexes, in the light of the challenges provided by feminism and the 'New Woman', there was shift in gender signifiers. If women could become more 'virile' in their clothing and aspirations, masculinity also underwent a change and slowly re-set its position relative to femininity. A possible reaction of male homosexuals towards this encroachment of women into the field of masculinity was a hardening of masculinity itself. Third, the acknowledgement of the virilization of male homosexuality was made principally by progressive texts such as those written by Bembo, Lucenay and even Marañón. The depiction of some homosexuals as 'normal' people invited a less condemnatory stance. Needless to say, however, this still left many practising homosexuals 'out in the cold'. Those who were 'effeminate' or who powdered and painted their faces were the victims of more extreme vilification such as that voiced by the review *Sexualidad* as the levels of anxiety caused by visible homosexuality, particularly in its this form, intensified in the mid 1920s.

Despite this conjecture, what remains certain is that from the early 1930s a more 'politicized' and self-confident expression of homosexuality emerged in the form of literary and artistic expression as well as in the lived experience of homosexuals themselves. That one fictional character remarked 'La gente ya no se asusta de nada desde que hay República' [People are not shocked by anything since the Republic's been in][125] is a testimony to an aura of greater liberties that the new political and social regime afforded. That this was to be short-lived was a tragedy for progressive Spain in general and for homosexual life in particular.

NOTES

[1] This regulation included an article that expressly prohibited the presence of 'inverts' in brothels, even as servants. Such a rule must have coincided with the extensive presence of male homosexuals in such establishments, attending not only, one presumes, to general serving matters but also to clients' sexual demands. See A. Moreno Mengíbar and F. Vázquez García, *Crónica de una Marginación. Historia de la Prostitución en Andalucía desde el siglo XV hasta la Actualidad* (Cadiz: BAAL, 1999), p. 177.

[2] See, for example, the work of Nordau and Simmel in Germany, and the Chicago School in the United States.

[3] M. Gil Maestre, *La criminalidad en Barcelona y en las grandes poblaciones* (Barcelona: Tipografía de Leodegario Obradors, 1886); M. Gil Maestre, *Los malhechores de Madrid* (Gerona: Imp. y Lib. de Paciano Torres, 1889).

[4] J. Vallmitjana, *Criminalidad típica local* (Barcelona: Tip. 'L'Avenç', 1910).

[5] J. Juderías, *La miseria y la criminalidad en las grandes ciudades de Europa y América* (Madrid: Publicaciones de la Revista Penitenciaria, 1906).

[6] J. Juderías, *La leyenda negra: estudios acerca del concepto de España en el extranjero* (Barcelona: Araluce, 1917).

[7] Juderías, *La miseria*, p. 5.

[8] R. Eslava, *La prostitución en Madrid. Apuntes por un estudio sociológico* (Madrid: Vicente Rico, 1900).

[9] J. Juderías, *La trata de blancas. Estudio acerca de este problema en España y en el Extranjero* (Madrid: Sociedad Española de Higiene, 1911). At the time of writing Juderías was Secretary of the Patronato Real para la Represión de la Trata de Blancas.

[10] Max-Bembo, *La mala vida en Barcelona. Anormalidad, miseria y vicio* (Barcelona: Maucci, 1912), pp. 194–7. The author's name was hyphenated in the original, but we have deleted this hyphen in the main text assuming it was the publisher's error.

[11] The sexologist Iwan Bloch noted that E. A. Duchesne discussed male

prostitution in his *De la prostitution dans la ville d'Alger depuis la conquête* (Paris: J. B. Baillière/Garnier Frères, 1853), and thus introduced a new term. See I. Bloch, *La vida sexual contemporánea* (Madrid/Berlín/Buenos Aires: Editora Internacional, 1924), vol. I, p. 439. Duchesne has a section in this book on 'Sodomie ou prostitution mâle', pp. 35–55, in which these practices were seen as inherent in the 'Arabs' and 'Turks'. The edition consulted was a microfilm of the 1853 text (New Haven, 1975) from the original in New York Public Library. A later study which documented 'Prostitution antiphysique' was F. Carlier, *Études de pathologie sociale: Les deux prostitutions* (Paris: E. Dentu, 1887), pp. 271–514. Carlier's text discusses the different types of 'pederasts', blackmail, and male prostitution houses at home and abroad.

12 P. Sereñana y Partagás, *La prostitución en la ciudad de Barcelona* (Barcelona: Imprenta de los sucesores de Ramírez y Cª, 1882), pp. 125–6. The term *cenydismo* comes from the Greek *kinaidos* or *cinaedus*, meaning an effeminate trait, possibly related to homosexuality. See J. J. Winkler, *The Constraints of Desire: The Anthropology of Sex and Gender in Ancient Greece* (New York/London: Routledge, 1990), *passim.*

13 For example, in his text on prostitution, *La prostitución* (Barcelona: Maucci, 10th edn, 1895), Suárez Casañ writes extensive sections on male prostitution from biblical times through to the present. Generally within a framework that saw 'vice' as the cause of prostitution (public dances, lascivious customs and libertinage, for example, are named to account for it) all the vices of pagan times were to be found in the present. Suárez Casañ, however, makes no specific mention of male prostitution in Spain.

14 Both quotations are taken from Sereñana y Partagás, *La prostitución*, p. 215. His 'pre-psychiatric' thought and his referral to homosexuality as a possible aberration of 'rational thought' place him on the cusp between nineteenth-century mental hygienic thought and later psychiatric frameworks.

15 E. Rodríguez-Solís, *Historia de la prostitución en España y en América* (Madrid: Biblioteca Nueva, c.1921 [1899]), p. 242. It is interesting to note that C. Bernaldo de Quirós and J. Mª Llanas Aguilaniedo in *La mala vida en Madrid* (Madrid: B. Rodríguez Sierra, 1901), discussed below, record the cruising activities of 'Uranians'. These are centred on the Plaza Mayor, the Puerta del Sol and the Calle de Sevilla in Madrid. In these places, the authors note, 'los uranistas de todas categorías hacen *la carrera*, una carrera doble en que el íncubo busca al súcubo y éste a aquél . . . a veces con equivocaciones involuntarias de funestas o grotescas consecuencias' [Uranians of all types try to pick up, a double act in which the incubus looks for the succubus and vice versa . . . sometimes with attendant errors of grave or grotesque consequences] (p. 274).

16 J. del Moral, *El estado y la prostitución* (Madrid: Felipe G. Rojas, 1913),

p. 83. Bernaldo de Quirós and Llanas also discussed the phenomenon of young delinquents or 'micos' who sometimes prostituted themselves (p. 184).

[17] Del Moral, *El estado y la prostitución*, p. 82. The presence of 'street urchins' or *golfillos* is noted in social literary works such as those by José Mas, *Hampa y miseria* (Madrid: Saez Hermanos, 1923).

[18] Compare also the work of Argentinian criminologist E. Gómez, *La mala vida en Buenos Aires* (Buenos Aires: Juan Roldan, 1908), discussed in J. Salessi, 'The Argentine Dissemination of Homosexuality, 1890–1914', *Journal of the History of Homosexuality*, 4, 3 (1994), 337–68.

[19] The discussion in the paragraphs that follow refers to Bernaldo de Quirós and Llanas Aguilaniedo, *La mala vida en Madrid*, pp. 247–75.

[20] Bernaldo de Quirós and Llanas Aguilaniedo, *La mala vida en Madrid*, p. 266.

[21] Bernaldo de Quirós and Llanas Aguilaniedo, *La mala vida en Madrid*, p. 257.

[22] Bernaldo de Quirós and Llanas Aguilaniedo, *La mala vida en Madrid*, p. 268.

[23] J. Ortega y Gasset, 'Vieja y Nueva Política', from the text of a conference given at the Teatro de la Comedia on 23 March 1914, in *Obras de José Ortega y Gasset* (Madrid: Espasa Calpe, 1936), pp. 83–120.

[24] Max-Bembo, *La mala vida en Barcelona*, p. 14.

[25] Max-Bembo, *La mala vida en Barcelona*, p. 249.

[26] Sereñana y Partagás, *La prostitución*, p. 125, and Q. Saldaña, *La Sexología (Ensayos)* (Madrid: Mundo Latino, 1930), p. 117.

[27] V. Suárez Casañ, *La pederastia* (Barcelona: Centro Editorial, c.1905), pp. 54–5.

[28] Max-Bembo, *La mala vida en Barcelona*, p. 249.

[29] Max-Bembo, *La mala vida en Barcelona*, p. 250.

[30] Max-Bembo, *La mala vida en Barcelona*, p. 251.

[31] Daniel Eisenberg has observed that the work by G. Martínez Sierra, *Granada (Guía emocional)*, published in Paris by Garnier-Hermanos, even though textual references are made to the woman traveller, was in fact written with the homosexual in mind. The evidence presented, however, seems to be rather scant. See 'Una temprana guía *gay*: *Granada (Guía emocional)*, de Gregorio Martínez Sierra (1911)', *http://users.ipfw.edu/JEHLE/deisenbe/Other_Hispanic_Topics/Guiagay.htm*

[32] A. Martín de Lucenay, *Homosexualidad* (Madrid: Editorial Fénix, 1933), p. 28.

[33] José Luis Vila-San-Juan wrote in 1975 that highly Catholic and conservative Andalusian society was particularly averse to homosexuality and that at the time of writing 'despite Freud, Marañón and López Ibor' the term 'homosexual' was still seen as an insult. See J. L. Vila-San-Juan, *García Lorca, asesinado: toda la verdad* (Barcelona: Planeta, 1975), pp. 242–3.

[34] The literature on Lorca is, of course, extensive. For these questions see I. Gibson, *La represión nacionalista de Granada en 1936 y la muerte de Federico García Lorca* (Paris: Ruedo Ibérico, 1971) and I. Gibson, *Federico García Lorca. 1. De Fuente Vaqueros a Nueva York* (Barcelona:

Grijalbo, 1985). Antonina Rodrigo discusses the bar 'El Polinario' in *Memoria de Granada: Manuel Angeles Ortiz & Federico García Lorca* (Granada: Diputación Provincial de Granada, 1993), pp. 149–63.

35 Abenraxic de Masila, 'El bozo', in E. García Gómez, *Poemas arábigoandaluces* (Madrid: Editorial Plutarco, 1930), p. 119.

36 Gibson, *La represión nacionalista*, pp. 148–9.

37 R. Aldrich, *The Seduction of the Mediterranean: Writing, Art and Homosexual Fantasy* (London/New York: Routledge, 1993).

38 *El Noticiero Granadino*, 9124 (1932), 1.

39 The caption read 'Ai, *zí, zenyors*. Jo també *zóc* partidari de l'amor lliure . . . !', *L'Esquella de la Torratxa*, 20 November 1931, p. 755.

40 The caption read 'Com votarem, nosaltres? Com a homes? Com a dones?', *L'Esquella de la Torratxa*, 2832, 13 October 1933, p. 661. Another drawing of the period proclaimed the dangers of increased railway travel in terms of the 'undesirables' it would bring. See 'El que portaran els enllaços ferroviaris a Barcelona', *L'Esquella de la Torratxa*, 2821, 28 July 1933, pp. 472–3. Amongst the many groups of people represented, including blacks, prostitutes, nudists and escaped prisoners were 'Els Ricarditos' whose symbol was a searching eye and whose members were well dressed and gender-ambivalent. It is possible that the eye was a motif carried forward from the 'Guiñolistas', discussed below.

41 The edition consulted is H. [*sic*] Hernández-Catá, *El Ángel de Sodoma* (Valparaíso: 'El Callao', n.d. [1929]). A preliminary discussion of the novel's significance for the history of homosexuality in Spain is made in F. Vázquez García and R. Cleminson, 'Democracia y culturas sexuales: La irrupción de la homosexualidad en la escena política española', *Er. Revista de Filosofía*, 32 (2003), pp. 129–66 (pp. 135–140). A more extensive treatment is R. Cleminson, 'Medicine, the Novel and Homosexuality in Spain', in A. Carling (ed.), *Globalization and Identity: Development and Integration in a Changing World* (London: I.B. Tauris, 2006), pp. 201–20, from which this section draws extensively.

42 For the text of the Code see E. Barriobero y Herrán, *Los delitos sexuales en las viejas leyes españolas* (Madrid: Mundo Latino, 1930), pp. 182–3, 197, 200. For an extensive discussion of the legal treatment of homosexuality in Spain with emphasis on the modern and contemporary periods see V. Domínguez Lorén, *Los homosexuales frente a la ley. Los juristas opinan* (Barcelona: Plaza y Janés, 1977).

43 Further details are found in A. Mira, *Para Entendernos: diccionario de cultura homosexual, gay y lésbica* (Barcelona: Ediciones de la Tempestad, 1999), pp. 74–5.

44 Both were members of the Liga de Educación Social; they were associated with the Federación Universitaria Escolar and Marañón was a founder member of the intellectual alliance the Agrupación Al Servicio de la República. See S. Ben-Ami, *The Origins of the Second Republic in Spain* (Oxford: Oxford University Press, 1978), pp. 37–42.

45 G. Marañón, 'Diálogo antisocrático sobre *Corydon*' (1929), in *Obras Completas* (Madrid: Espasa-Calpe, 1968), vol. I, pp. 465–72.

46 Despite opposing the Primo de Rivera Code, he did provide the legal

architecture of the 1933 Law of 'Vagos y Maleantes' which allowed for a certain criminalization of homosexual activities, somewhat paradoxically since it was introduced under the more liberal Second Republic. See A. García Valdés, *Historia y presente de la homosexualidad* (Madrid: Akal, 1981), p. 121.

47   G. Marañón, 'Prólogo', in Hernández-Catá, *El Ángel de Sodoma*, p. 13.
48   Marañón, 'Prólogo', in Hernández-Catá, *El Ángel de Sodoma*, p. 17.
49   Hernández-Catá, *El Ángel de Sodoma*, p. 89.
50   L. Jiménez de Asúa and J. Antón Oneca, *Derecho Penal conforme al Código de 1928* (Madrid: Editorial Reus, 1929), vol. II, pp. 243–53. Here, his acquaintanceship with the medical theories was much more extensive and he cites, amongst others, Krafft-Ebing and Garnier.
51   P. Bourdieu, *Language and Symbolic Power* (Cambridge: Polity Press, 1991), p. 130.
52   F. Nazier, *L'Anti-Corydon, essai sur l'inversion sexuelle* (Paris: Éditions du Siècle, 1924).
53   E. Donato, *Homosexualismo (Frente a Gide)* (Madrid: Morata, 1931).
54   A. Gide, *Corydon* (Madrid: Oriente, 2nd edn, 1929). The prologue, 'Diálogo antisocrático sobre Corydon', is reproduced in G. Marañón, *Obras Completas* (Madrid: Espasa-Calpe, 1968), vol. I, pp. 465–72. The third edition, also published by Oriente, held the title *Corydon, la novela del amor que no puede decir su nombre*, according to I. Gibson, *Federico García Lorca. 2. De Nueva York a Fuente Grande* (Barcelona: Grijalbo, 1987), p. 262 (note).
55   Marañón, 'Diálogo', p. 468.
56   Marañón, 'Diálogo', p. 471.
57   Marañón, 'Diálogo', p. 472.
58   A. San de Velilla, *Sodoma y Lesbos Modernos: Pederastas y Safistas, estudiados en la clínica, en los libros y en la historia* (Barcelona: Carlos Ameller, 1932), pp. 24 ff. on Marañón and pp. 108–11 on Gide.
59   San de Velilla, *Sodoma y Lesbos Modernos*, p. 110. In a footnote on that page, San de Velilla remarks that if the increase in literacy rates amongst Spaniards was to continue in this vein, one would be obliged to lament their new reading habits.
60   Dr T. B., review of Donato, *Homosexualismo (Frente a Gide)*, *El Siglo Médico*, 88 (1931), 468–9.
61   Dr T. B., review of Donato, *Homosexualismo*, p. 468.
62   Dr T. B., review of Donato, *Homosexualismo*, p. 469.
63   Donato, *Homosexualismo*, p. 8.
64   Donato, *Homosexualismo*, p. 9.
65   Donato, *Homosexualismo*, p. 127.
66   Donato, *Homosexualismo*, p. 128.
67   Gibson, *Federico García Lorca. 2. De Nueva York a Fuente Grande*, pp. 261–2.
68   A. Nin Frías, *Alexis*; (Madrid: Morata, 1932) *Homosexualismo creador* (Madrid: Morata, 1933).
69   Nin Frías, *Alexis*, p. 14.
70   Nin Frías, *Alexis*, p. 15.
71   Nin Frías, *Alexis*, p. 20. This association between the aristocracy and

homosexuality was common and has been discussed, for example, in A. Mira, 'Modernistas, dandis y pederastas: articulaciones de la homosexualidad en "la edad de plata"', *Journal of Iberian and Latin American Studies*, 7, 1 (2001), 63–75.

[72] Nin Frías, *Alexis*, p. 36.

[73] Nin Frías, *Alexis*, p. 48.

[74] Nin Frías, *Alexis*, pp. 189–90.

[75] Nin Frías, *Alexis*, p. 179.

[76] San de Velilla, *Sodoma y Lesbos Modernas*, pp. 112–13.

[77] San de Velilla, *Sodoma y Lesbos Modernas*, p. 115.

[78] On the political differences in Germany with respect to notions of manliness, medicalization of homosexuality and the role of Friedländer see H. Oosterhuis and H. Kennedy (eds), *Homosexuality and Male Bonding in Pre-Nazi Germany* (New York: Harrington Park Press, 1991).

[79] Á. Retana, *A Sodoma en tren botijo* (Madrid: Imp. Saez Hermanos, 1933).

[80] Both novels are related in L. A. de Villena, 'Álvaro Retana, en el abanico de la "novela galante-decadente"', *Turia. Revista Cultural*, 21–22 (1992), 19–28 (26–7).

[81] Cited in L. Litvak, *Antología de la novela corta erótica española de entreguerras. 1918–1936* (Madrid: Taurus, 1993), p. 54.

[82] Retana, *A Sodoma en tren botijo*, p. 5.

[83] Á. Retana, *La Ola Verde. Crítica frívola* (Barcelona: Ed. Jasón, 1931), p. 297. For another contemporary analysis of Hernández-Cata's book see José Balseiro, 'Un libro de Hernádez-Catá *Bulletin of Spanish Studies* 6, 22 (1929), 60–63.

[84] Retana, *La Ola Verde*, p. 297.

[85] Rodríguez-Solís, *Historia de la prostitución*, p. 243. Bernaldo de Quirós and Llanas Aguilaniedo also refer to the 'sociedad de baile', 'El Ramillete' where Uranians gathered. Subsequently, they gathered in the Liceo Rius and other theatres. See Bernaldo de Quirós and Llanas Aguilaniedo, *La mala vida en Madrid*, 1901 edition, p. 265.

[86] Max-Bembo, *La mala vida en Barcelona*, pp. 51–2.

[87] T. Yáñez, *Elementos de Medicina Legal* (Madrid: Imprenta de Enrique Rubiños, 1884), p. 323.

[88] R. Trumbach, 'The Birth of the Queen: Sodomy and the Emergence of Gender Equality in Modern Culture, 1660–1750', in M. B. Duberman, M. Vicinus and G. Chauncey (eds), *Hidden From History: Reclaiming the Lesbian and Gay Past* (Harmondsworth: Penguin, 1991), pp. 129–40; R. Norton, *Mother Clap's Molly House: The Gay Subculture in England 1700–1830* (London: GMP, 1992).

[89] Bernaldo de Quirós and Llanas Aguilaniedo, *La mala vida en Madrid*, (1901 edition) p. 273.

[90] Bernaldo de Quirós and Llanas Aguilaniedo, *La mala vida en Madrid* (1901 edition), p. 273.

[91] F. de Sales Mayo, *La Condesita (Memorias de una doncella)* (Madrid: Oficina Tipográfica del Hospicio, 3rd edn, 1870).

[92] Rodríguez-Solís, *Historia de la prostitución*, pp. 241–2.

93 San de Velilla, *Sodoma y Lesbos Modernos*, p. 140.
94 S. Salaün, 'Apogeo y decadencia de la sicalipsis', in M. Díaz-Diocaretz and I. M. Zavala (eds), *Discurso erótico y discurso transgresor en la cultura peninsular, siglos XI al XX* (Madrid: Ediciones Tuero, 1992), pp. 129–53. See also the introduction to Litvak, *Antología*, pp. 11–79.
95 De Villena, 'Álvaro Retana', p. 24.
96 J. Casado Montado, *Memorias de un mal nacido* (San Fernando: The Author, 2nd edn, 1989), p. 73.
97 Litvak, *Antología*, p. 16.
98 Martín de Lucenay, *Homosexualidad*, p. 28.
99 One cartoon on the subject of what the New Year will bring shows the mayor Cambó honouring his 'old friendships'. An older man, dressed in skirt and wearing high heels, drags the politician by the coat-tails into his lair. Cambó looks on desirously and the caption reads 'En Cambó fará honor a les seves antigues amistats' (Cambó will honour his old friendships). It is likely that the imaginary scene takes place in the 'Chinese Quarter'. See *L'Esquella de la Torratxa*, 2740 (1932), 8–9.
100 Juan Vicente Aliaga, 'Háblame, cuerpo. Una aproximación a la obra, de Pepe Espaliú', *http://www.accpar.org/numero1/aliaga.htm*
101 Rodríguez-Solís, *Historia de la prostitución*, p. 242.
102 Max-Bembo, *La mala vida en Barcelona*, p. 43.
103 Marañón's 'Prólogo', in Bloch, *La vida sexual contemporánea*, pp. v–xvi (p. x).
104 See Mira, 'Modernistas', pp. 63–75.
105 A. Sinfield, *The Wilde Century: Effeminacy, Oscar Wilde and the Queer Moment* (London: Cassell, 1994), pp. 3–4. On Wilde in Spain, see L. E. Davis, 'Oscar Wilde in Spain', *Comparative Literature*, 35 (1973), 136–152; R. A. Cardwell, 'Oscar Wilde and Spain: Medicine, Morals, Religion and Aesthetics in the *Fin de Siglo*', in F. Bonaddio & X. de Ros, *Crossing Fields in Modern Spanish Culture* (Oxford: University of Oxford, 2003), pp. 35–53. It is interesting to note that Frank Harris' *Oscar Wilde: his life and confessions*, 2 vols., (New York: The Author, 1916) was published in Spain by Biblioteca Nueva (Madrid) in 1928 and translated by Ricardo Baeza as *Vida y Confesiones de Oscar Wilde*. The 'Prólogo' (pp. 5–17) by Baeza does not duck the issue of Wilde's homosexuality, which is referred to as 'su anomalía sexual' [his sexual anomaly], 'la tal peculiaridad sexual' [this sexual peculiarity], 'la *nefanda* acusación' [the accusation not to speak its name] (p. 8).
106 *El Aeroplano*, 3 May 1912. See F. Vázquez García & A. Moreno Mengíbar, *Poder y Prostitución en Sevilla. Siglos XVI al XX* (Seville: Publicaciones Universidad de Sevilla, 1998), vol. II, *Edad Contemporánea*, p. 219.
107 Litvak, *Antología*, p. 16.
108 C. González Ruano, cited in Vázquez G. and Cleminson, 'Democracia y cultura sexuales', 162.
109 Luis Buñuel, *My Last Breath* (London: Vintage, 1994, trans. Abigail Israel), p. 147, where Hoyos was described as one of the only four 'official' pederasts in Madrid. Buñuel also relates the story of a group

of men in San Sebastián who ventured out of doors without their hats and were attacked for being *maricones* (p. 85). Such an incident recalls that related by Bernaldo de Quirós and Llanas Aguilaniedo, *La Mala Vida en Madrid*, p. 283, in which a bald woman was mistaken for a pederast and nearly stoned to death.

110 All quotations in this paragraph from Suárez Casañ, *La pederastia*, p. 55.

111 Max-Bembo, *La mala vida en Barcelona*, p. 46.

112 Max-Bembo, *La mala vida en Barcelona*, p. 46.

113 Max-Bembo, *La mala vida en Barcelona*, p. 48.

114 Max-Bembo, *La mala vida en Barcelona*, p. 50.

115 Max-Bembo, *La mala vida en Barcelona*, p. 45.

116 Max-Bembo, *La mala vida en Barcelona*, p. 51.

117 Max-Bembo, *La mala vida en Barcelona*, p. 52.

118 Max-Bembo, *La mala vida en Barcelona*, p. 59.

119 Del Moral, *El estado y la prostitución*, pp. 84–5. Del Moral called this phenomenon the 'ronda del ful'. This practice apparently continued into Francoism, according to the former police officer Mauricio Carlavilla del Barrio. See his *Sodomitas* (Madrid: Nos, 1956), pp. 127–36, where he discusses the 'policía "ful"' and the case of an ostensibly non-homosexual man caught up in the same trap.

120 Max-Bembo, *La mala vida en Barcelona*, p. 59.

121 The following information is taken from the *Repertorio de Jurisprudencia del Tribunal Supremo* (Pamplona: Aranzadi, 1945). The various indices were searched under titles such as 'Escándalo público', which contained sub-sections on 'Homosexualismo', 'Corrupción de menores' and 'Abusos deshonestos'. The latter were heterosexual crimes usually against children and matters associated with prostitution. The military index was also searched. While 'Homosexualismo' had several entries for the years from 1954 onwards, the first two cases discussed here were entered under 'Escándalo público'. The third case discussed here was heard by a military tribunal.

122 Case 231, 4 April 1930, 'Escándalo público', *Repertorio de Jurisprudencia. Años 1930–1* (Pamplona: Aranzadi, 1945), p. 96.

123 Case 664, 17 April 1934, 'Abusos deshonestos', *Repertorio de Jurisprudencia. Año 1934* (Pamplona: Aranzadi, 1945), p. 324.

124 Case 2035, 10 October 1935, 'Abusos deshonestos', *Repertorio de Jurisprudencia. Año 1935*, (Pamplona: Aranzadi, 1945), pp. 890–1.

125 Retana, *A Sodoma en tren botijo*, p. 8.

Chapter Seven

Conclusion

Over the course of this study, we have followed the processes which led to the construction of male homosexuality in Spain between 1850 and 1939 as an area of social, political and medical concern. Chapters Two and Three discussed how different expressions of the medical sciences colonized homosexuality and made it into a subject for a variety of interventions in the legal, medical and psychiatric fields. In Chapter Four we saw how these medical sciences and other areas of expert knowledge, particularly pedagogy and sexology, contributed to articulating the risks seen to be inherent in childhood with respect to the loss of gender differentiation, the presence of certain sexual practices and the spectre of same-sex sexuality in schools and in daily life. An element common to all these forms of expert knowledge was the concern over the loss of virility, which in turn was seen to be intimately connected to national decline described in Chapter Five. That homosexuality was a matter for broad-based concern and consternation was proven by what commentators saw as an increasingly visible homosexual subculture, discussed in Chapter Six. This subculture was more than just a figment of the imagination of sexologists, psychiatrists and nationalist pundits; through the use of a variety of sources from criminology, literature, medicine and a wide range of reviews the broad brushstrokes of the presence of homosexuals throughout the period covered by this book have been painted.

An objective present throughout this book has been to show the degree to which Spain was really different with respect to discourse on homosexuality and homosexual lifestyles from that of other countries. In conclusion, we point to some comparisons and some differences between Spain and other countries and indicate a number of future venues for further research.

A first question relates to the medicalization process. In countries such as Germany,[1] England,[2] or the United States,[3] the construction of the 'invert', and later the 'homosexual' as a special type of pathological subject, was related to the existence of a legal framework that punished sexual acts between males. In these countries, the rise of psychopathological theories of homosexuality was related to the aim of naturalizing homosexuality as something 'deviant' but not necessarily worthy of punishment or persecution as such.

In France, Spain and Italy, however, a different legal tradition had been in force since the late eighteenth or early nineteenth century. This liberal legislative framework did not punish homosexual acts between consenting adults in private.[4] Despite this, the lack of reproductive potential of homosexual acts was increasingly seen in France in the late nineteenth century as a threat to the health and vigour of the nation.[5] Homosexuality was linked both to an internal threat that meant that human stocks were not renewed, as well as to an external threat that spelled military defeat. For some commentators, France's military defeat by Prussia in 1870 served to prove this point. From the 1880s,[6] the highly moral and condemnatory tone of many French psychiatric studies on 'sexual perversions' was in some sense a response to what commentators believed was a discernible decline in the strength of the nation and the existence of a worryingly low birth rate.[7]

In contrast, in Spain such overt legal condemnation would only be visible in the twentieth century, in the Penal Code of 1928.[8] The lateness of any explicit legal measures against homosexuality in Spain does not mean, however, that medical doctors and legal experts had not discussed the issue beforehand. From the mid nineteenth century, texts from a variety of perspectives (legal medicine, medical hygiene, venereal medicine, criminology, psychiatry, pathology and sexology) discussed the moral, medical and legal aspects of homosexuality, often drawing their analysis, taxonomies and suggested aetiologies from French and German studies.

However, the new terminology afforded by these theories did not simply replace old concepts and vocabulary. The divides between the pure and impure, the natural and unnatural and active and passive sexuality, linked in turn to old moral and theological accounts, did not disappear once the new division between normal and pathological was articulated. Instead, as we have seen, a mixture between the new (categories such as 'psychic hermaphroditism', 'Uranism', 'inversion', 'homosexuality') and the old formed a complex and polysemic picture where the old was reinterpreted and 'resignified' in the light of the new.[9]

This tendency may well have been due to the lack of influence of medical science in Spanish society at the time, which, even though it was equipped with a whole new stock of terms to describe Spanish sexual life, entered general and public awareness somewhat later than some other European countries. The new technical language of sexuality only gained some influence in restricted sectors of the professional bourgeoisie. Later on, the scientific urge amongst workers' movements would disseminate such knowledge amongst an avid but relatively specialized working-class readership. In general terms, a complex kind of interrelationship was forged between ecclesiastical and scientific authorities, with the former maintaining an extremely strong influence throughout the period studied here.[10] The result of this transaction was that amongst Spanish medical doctors two kinds of language are to be detected: on the one hand, that of the moral-theological tradition and on the other that of the new psychopathology of sexual perversions. It is as though medical doctors combined two kinds of *habitus*, with all the imaginable combinations of the two, which would lead them to a combination of classificatory schemas born of their new knowledge and those deriving from a 'pre-scientific' historical past.[11]

One point of tension between these traditions was to be seen in 1928, when as a response to the proposed criminalization of same-sex acts, sex reformers such as the lawyer Luis Jiménez de Asúa, the medical doctor Gregorio Marañón and the writer Alfonso Hernández-Catá collided head on with the position held by the Catholic Church. Despite this, in general, scientific morality did not fully 'excuse' homosexuality; rather it stigmatized it as an illness or anomaly instead of a vice or sin, arguing that it should not, in most cases, be punished.[12]

We have talked of a 'truncated' process of medicalization in order to describe what was a relative rather than 'complete' degree of pathologization of homosexuality in Spain. 'Truncated', however, does not stand for 'failed'. Instead, the 'dissemination', in Salessi's words,[13] of ideas on homosexuality was multifaceted and responded to certain characteristics of the medical and social habitus at the time. In Spain, we do not see the rather seamless journey of the sodomitical act ending up at the 'homosexual person' that Foucault and some of his followers have suggested for other countries. While the intermediate figure of the 'invert', as suggested by Chauncey,[14] may have preceded or even aided in the 'creation' of the 'homosexual' the same cannot necessarily be said for Spain. In Spain there coexisted a number of timescales and old and new discourses on the subject. This took place not only amongst those writers who did not hold eminent scientific positions or who were less well known but also with respect to renowned specialist figures such as Bernaldo de Quirós or Rodríguez Lafora. The invert primarily denoted gender deviance well into the twentieth century in Spain.

The consequences of this coexistence of multiple and, at times, contradictory discourses may be considered to be twofold. First, it shows how medical discourse does not merely colonize broader discourse on a phenomenon but that, to a large degree, it relies on the wider discourse in order to reach its own conclusions which it then presents as 'scientific'.[15] Secondly, it shows that it is necessary to revise Foucault's model of the 'medicalization of homosexuality', a model that has become (against Foucault's intentions) canonical in the hands of many historians.[16] It is possible that the concentration on the sexual history of north-western European countries, where the consolidation of the new psychiatric categories was fairly rapid and decisive, has con-structed a too clear line of progression from sodomite to homo-sexual via the invert. The Spanish case, however, emphasizes the many fissures and breaks in this pattern. This, together with the contemporaneous existence of different categories, makes a uni-tary and progressive reading impossible.

In Spain, the language used by experts in order to describe same-sex sexuality between men thus modernizing their descrip-tions of such practices, is largely drawn from foreign work on the subject. French, German and Italian sources are the principal ones, with a steady increase in interest in Germanic materials from the 1920s onwards. In this way, French degenerationist thought and Italian positivism were gradually displaced by Kraepelin's psychopathology and the psychoanalysis of Freud and Adler. In the 1920s, a further current which was considered to be largely 'home-grown', was forged by Gregorio Marañón, in Luis

Huerta's words, the 'our Darwin' [Marañón es nuestro Darwin].[17] Marañón's understanding of 'intersexuality' placed sexual inversion firmly in the science of endocrinology and the internal secretions. Homosexuality, in the light of this theory, was reconceptualized as a failure in the differentiation process between the two sexes, but it was also naturalized as an ontogenetic and phylogenetic characteristic of the human species.

Marañón's theory was extremely influential and the period from the 1920s up to the Civil War was characterized by an especially eclectic mixture of notions on the genesis of homosexuality drawn from organicist psychopathology, psychoanalysis and endocrinology.[18] Such a degree of eclecticism appears to be characteristic of Spanish science as a whole and, more specifically, of Spanish medical theories of sexuality.

A second issue worthy of note is the relationship between the social construction of masculinity and that of national identity. This question was discussed in Chapter Five. A crisis of masculinity related to perceived national decline in the *fin de siècle* and in the ensuing years across many countries of Europe is, in the light of the many studies on the subject, now unquestionable.[19] In Spain, this situation came to be of heightened interest around 1898, the year of the loss of most of the remaining colonies established from the late fifteenth century onwards. The diffuse movement of *regeneracionismo* was an obvious response to both these concerns, amongst many others. Rather than an ideology or *Weltanschauung*, regenerationism is best thought of as a technique of government based on certain premises by which social, political and economic problems, underdevelopment and conflicts between classes and interest groups would be resolved. As we have seen, one of the remedies for the decline of the nation was a reinforcement of masculinity, virility and willpower. At the same time as these concerns were articulated, various specialized fields such as criminal anthropology, legal medicine, the press and the forces of law and order signalled the ever-growing visibility of inverts in Spanish cities as a manifestation of the loss of virility that the Spanish nation appeared to be suffering.

The same coming together of concerns – that of the blurring of gender divisions and a feeling of national decline – was evident in other western European countries, although each displayed somewhat different modalities. In Britain,[20] and in the United States,[21] such concerns were intrinsically linked to the alarm that the feminist and suffragette movements provoked, seen by many as one further notch in the decline of the embattled hierarchy of the sexes and clear, demarcated sex roles.[22]

In France, a slightly different scenario was produced.[23] Here the concern was not about feminism per se, but instead about the declining birth rate, which was held to be a sign of declining virility and national vigour. This concern with respect to feminism and the loss of the cardinal points of gender differences characterized Germany too during the same period, as did the concern over depopulation, but, again, like France, the principal threats seemed to lie in other quarters.[24] In Germany, those who were deemed 'outsiders', such as Jews, inverts and the mentally ill, were portrayed as sapping the 'race' of its vitality and virility.[25] The cultural cosmopolitanism and the vitality of cities such as Berlin and Vienna was seen by many to encapsulate the very opposite of Germanic values; frivolity was contrasted with hard work and effeminacy with the values of blood and soil.

In Italy, Catholic conservatives lamented the loss of the traditional values that bound its people together in 'harmony' and 'solidarity'; two values supposedly destroyed by urban growth and economic modernization. Despite the fact that this was essentially restricted to some geographical regions, particularly the North, its destructive potential was considered to be at the root of the military defeat in Ethiopia in 1896.[26] Increased sexual 'immorality' and the blurring of gender roles were viewed as yet other signs of the general pervading loss of traditional values. Many saw the Great War as an opportunity to regenerate the country and to recuperate lost social and sexual orders.[27] The triumph of fascism in the 1920s can be interpreted as the victory of a movement whose objectives included the restoration of strict gender roles and the reinstatement of Rome's warlike virility.[28]

But in Spain, the nexus established between the loss of gender distinctions and the feeling of national decline did not draw on any demographic disaster or the threat of outsiders. Nor did it rely on a particularly audible vilification, at least until the 1920s, of the feminist movement. Any invocation of a glorious past was not a predominant element of this period, as it would be under Francoism. Instead, the main concern was related to national failing, the lack of will to accomplish reform, the upper classes' devotion to slothfulness and a culture of consumption and pleasure. Together with the ignorance of, and the dangers presented by a militant working class, all these elements combined to produce a lamentable moral, social, hygienic and political picture.

The prostration of the forces of national vigour was metaphorically represented as a loss of virility. The greater visibility of inverts was just one element that confirmed this diagnosis. The collective organism was seen to be under attack by the combined forces of luxury, crime and the sexual perversions. But this notion was not confined to the Catholic or reactionary Right. The notion of the priest as pervert triumphed in certain sectors of liberal and republican politics.[29] The anticlerical imaginary of the times constructed the priest as an enemy of national unity and modernity and associated him with retrograde Catholic nationalisms such as Carlism. In similar fashion, in working-class political and trade union circles, the capitalist exploiter was often seen to be allied with the sexual pervert. The class enemy, converted in a 'biological enemy',[30] was a force unleashed to undermine the worker's resolve and the formation of revolutionary consciousness.

There is, therefore, an element of connection between those movements that aspired to the construction of new modern identities and social structures (the nation for the regenerationists, the emancipated working class for political parties and unions) and the demand for greater or restored virility. The nation and the proletariat are 'imagined' as fraternal communities composed of active, vigorous and resistant males.[31] In Spain, in the decade of the twenties, the rejection of male effeminacy was accompanied by what was perceived as a process of the masculinization of women, in the context of feminism and the 'New Woman'. The reassertion of gender differences enlisted a potent supporter in the figure of Marañón whose treatises on the sexual life and the roles to be fulfilled by each sex struck a chord amongst the Spanish intelligentsia in the 1920s and 1930s and went beyond any ideological divide.

A third point of comparison and contrast between Spain and other countries concerns the issue of male friendship and homosociality amongst children and youth as a cause of sexual inversion and their relationship with the subculture and identities forged by inverts themselves. How was sexual inversion acquired? What kind of cultural world did inverts inhabit? Such questions were at the heart of Chapters Five and Six.

As we have already shown, the history of homosexuality is inseparable from the history of male friendship. Although in Spain male friendship was not imbued with the same values of fraternity present in student circles in Germany and Britain[32] (the *Residencia de Estudiantes* is a possible exception), what was common to all these societies was the desire to expunge any traces of eroticism between males. Hygienists and educators joined forces to recommend the separation of the sexes in schools in the nineteenth century in order to prevent, among other aspects, the virilization of girls and the effeminization of boys. The school, despite these measures, was still considered to be a source of sexual danger which had to be managed by new techniques.

In this context, the question of mutual and solo masturbation in schools makes its appearance. By the end of the nineteenth century, hygienists had already declared that such a practice not only ruined the health of youth but that it could be a seed bed for the development of sexual inversion. At the same time, the relationship between master and pupil, and between tutor and tutored, came under scrutiny. Child pederasty and the initiatory perversions of adults was another topic for concern. The nexus between 'perverted' priests and cloistered education was seized upon by anticlerical propagandists to discredit religious education and religious values in general. In this sense, the Spanish case coincides with what took place in France and Italy during the same period.

Another question emerged in the early twentieth century that was contemporaneous to the 'anti-masturbatory crusade' and the immoral consequences of religious education. This was the notion of 'childhood in danger' as a result of poor social conditions and the deleterious effects of living a 'street life'. Children, generally of a working-class background, often succumbed to the wiles of pimps and grown men in search of illicit pleasures and were enrolled in prostitution. Parental neglect, the promiscuity of the home, poverty, incest and early sexual initiation on the part of brothers, sisters or parents, could drive the child into pederastic prostitution.

Both these elements – concern about homoeroticism in the school environment and child prostitution – were also present in the broader European panorama. During the last quarter of the nineteenth century legislative measures and propaganda campaigns in both the Catholic and Protestant world increased markedly. The aim of these measures was to prevent the corruption of 'innocent' childhood, opposition to pornography, incest and venereal disease and the creation of the conditions whereby the sexual perversions, uncontrolled fertility and ruined childhood years could be prevented.

A key element in this campaign of prevention was the inauguration of a new set of techniques grouped under the rubric of 'sex education'. Beginning in the early twentieth century, the aim of this intervention was to act against masturbation, disease amongst children, and particularly homosexuality. This offensive came earlier and expired sooner in Protestant countries as the German[33] and English cases illustrate.[34] Although faced with opposition from the Catholic Church, sex education flourished in the countries of southern Europe, in France, Italy and Spain.[35]

At the same time, as we have noted, the presence of homoerotic subcultures became increasingly visible in European capitals. Spain was not different in this sense and the existence of parks, taverns, cafés, public urinals, masked balls, 'marriage' and transvestism has been documented in Madrid and Barcelona. This subculture dates at the very least from the 1860s and enjoyed increased vitality in the early years of the twentieth century. The presence of homosexual circles, such as 'Els Ricarditos', dance halls ('El Ramillete') and upper-class associations such as the 'San Guiñolé' testify to a broad and diverse homosexual 'scene'. On the other hand, homosexual prostitution in down town bars and cafés where gentlemen, working-class boys, thieves and bohemians were found to be rubbing shoulders provided another facet of this variegated life.

This very special microcosm came under the punitive eye of the Primo de Rivera regime in the late 1920s but flowered once more, and with renewed strength, under the Second Republic. The lack of sources does not permit as clear a picture of this subculture as one may like, but the general ambience of its rituals, spaces of sociability and connectivity can be reconstructed. Despite this vitality, it would appear that these spaces in Madrid and Barcelona did not attain the legendary aura of those of Berlin, Paris or New York at the same time.

This subcultural world, with the odd exception, was not accompanied by a first person voice (at least in the historical evidence we have come by) comparable to that of Ulrichs, Hirschfeld or Friedländer in Germany, Symonds, Wilde, Pater or Carpenter in

England or Gide and Proust in France. There was, nevertheless, a form of literary expression that emerged in the 1920s that reflected the aesthetic nature and the victim status of the sexual invert in essays, plays and works of fiction. These works often questioned the association between the invert and criminality, even though they tended to accept rather unquestionably the new pathologizing, if naturalizing theories of psychiatry and the sexual sciences.

The invert appeared in these accounts as a tragic, suffering and ultimately failed (or even suicidal) personage destined to self-destruction. The novel by Hernández-Catá, *El Ángel de Sodoma* (1928), and María Martínez Sierra's *Sortilegio* (first performed in Argentina in 1930) expressed this trope of the homosexual as victim and of homosexuality as death and disease. In both cases, the work finishes with the suicide of the homosexual protagonist.

Of a more ambivalent nature are the works by Nin Frías (*Alexis o el significado del temperamento urano*, 1932, and *Homosexualismo Creador*, 1933) and the novel by Augusto d'Halmar (*Pasión y Muerte del Cura Deusto*, 1924). The first two exalt Socratic love and adolescent eros and have much in common with Gide. In these texts, the 'Uranian temperament' is seen as a gift which is reserved for an aristocratic minority, something held by those of heightened intellect or the genius. At the same time, Nin Frías acknowledges that such a sensibility is an anomaly, a kind of lack of sexual maturity, of permanent adolescence and fate which leads to misfortune. D'Halmar's work is different in that it recreates an idealized expression of love between a Basque priest and a Gypsy choir boy, drawn on the canvas of a Seville bathed in Oriental light and sensuality. The Socratic love of the novel is praised and exalted but its tragic end is inescapable. The priest, as he feverishly searches for his lost love, is killed by the very train that carries his *enamorado* out of reach, a leitmotif of separation, disconnection and death.

An obvious example of a first person voice in Spain during the period concerned is that of Álvaro Retana. This novelist and nightbird of twenties Madrid makes light of the identarian essentialism forged by scientific figures such as Marañón as a means of defending homosexuality against the curse of the law. Retana rejects the medical model, which pathologizes and naturalizes the homosexual simultaneously, and he favours looser terms such as 'those in the know' ('los que entienden') and the 'Third Sex'. At the same time (Retana is no theorist of homosexuality; his views will have come from observation and practice), he, in his *Mi novia y mi novio* for example, advocates an unstable form of bisexuality. His novels question, in playful and irreverent terms, any essentialization of homosexuality through biology or psychiatry.

Is Retana, in this way, a kind of precursor of today's 'queer theory'? Rather than this, what we see in this author is the literary form of a tradition that viewed sex between men as a practice rather than an identity. This so-called 'Mediterranean model' of sexuality, used to describe a millenary experience practised throughout the countries bordering on the Mare Nostrum, is a form of sexuality where relations between youths and older men, considered along the active/passive divide, take preference over any strong expression of identity.

This Mediterranean model, which recently has been advocated by intellectuals such as Alberto Cardín and Juan Goytisolo,[36] is to be contrasted with the dominant identarian model in the German and Anglo-Saxon world. It would appear to be a model that predominates also in most Latin American countries as a combination of limited tolerance and persistent 'closet' sexuality.

In the Spain of the 1920s and 1930s, it is interesting to note that perhaps the strongest first person voices were articulated from the shores of Latin America. It is no doubt significant that most of the authors just mentioned were not of Spanish nationality or were Spaniards living abroad. Hernández-Catá, while born in Castile, lived in Cuba and published his novel in Chile. Nin Frías and D'Halmer were Uruguayan and had strong links with Latin America. In part, this relationship existed as an expression of the close intellectual and literary ties between Spain and Latin America at the time. Uniting both worlds was the attempt to decriminalize same-sex acts in private amongst consenting adults. But it also shows, as many commentators lamented, how difficult it was to raise questions of sexuality in Spain, and especially with respect to the much maligned practice of homosexuality.

Whatever the case, the existence of a Mediterranean model which overflows its own boundaries to connect both sides of the Atlantic, imbued with its own discursive characteristics, suggests an alternative to the identarian model prevalent in north western European countries and the United States. It also, equally importantly, forces us to reconsider the dominant models of historical analysis present in Lesbian and Gay and Queer Studies. The significance of this interpretation has been signalled already in a number of publications.[37] Research into the historical expression of a particular Mediterranean case, Spain, and the recovery of lost memories consigned to dust and discrimination under Francoism constitute two objectives of this book. We hope that it will inspire further work into the many uncharted territories of homosexual life in Spain in the present and in the past.

NOTES

[1]   See M. Herzer, *Magnus Hirschfeld: Leben und Werk eines jüdischen, schwulen und sozialistischen Sexologen* (Frankfurt: Campus, 1992); H. Oosterhuis, 'Medical Science and the Modernisation of Sexuality', in F. X. Eder, L. Hall and G. Hekma (eds), *Sexual Cultures in Europe. National Histories* (Manchester: Manchester University Press, 1999), pp. 221–41 (p. 230); F. X. Eder, 'Sexual Cultures in Germany and Austria, 1700–2000', in Eder *et al.* (eds), *Sexual Cultures in Europe. National Histories*, pp. 138–72 (pp. 156–9).

[2]   The process took place somewhat later in England. See J. Weeks, *Coming Out: Homosexual Politics in Britain, from the Nineteenth Century to the Present* (London: Quartet Books, 1977), pp. 23–32; L. Hall, 'Sexual Cultures in Britain: some persisting themes', in Eder *et al.* (eds), *Sexual Cultures in Europe. National Histories*, pp. 38–42; I. D. Crozier, 'Taking Prisoners: Havelock Ellis, Sigmund Freud and the Construction of Homosexuality, 1897–1951', *Social History of Medicine*, 13, 3 (2000), 447–66; I. D. Crozier, 'The Medical Construction of Homosexuality and its relation to the Law in Nineteenth-Century England', *Medical History*, 45 (2001), 61–82.

[3]   G. Chauncey, 'From Sexual Inversion to Homosexuality: The Changing Medical Conceptualization of Female "Deviance"', in K. Peiss, C. Simmons and R. A. Padgug (eds), *Passion and Power: Sexuality in History* (Philadelphia: Temple University Press, 1989 [1982/3]), pp. 87–117; G. Chauncey, *Gay New York* (London: Flamingo, 1994); B. Hansen, 'American Physicians' "Discovery" of Homosexuals, 1880–1900: A New Diagnosis in a Changing Society', in C. E. Rosenberg and J. Golden (eds), *Framing Disease: studies in cultural history* (New Brunswick: Rutgers University Press, 1992), pp. 104–33.

[4]   This does not mean, however, that homosexual acts were never punished. One interpretation of the notion of 'dishonest abuse' could lead to their sanction. For the situation in France, which was similar, see R. Nye, *Masculinity and Male Codes of Honor in Modern France* (New York/Oxford: Oxford University Press, 1993), pp. 106–7.

[5]   R. Nye, 'Sex Difference and Male Homosexuality in French Medical Discourse, 1830–1930', *Bulletin of the History of Medicine*, 63, 1 (1989), 32–51 (32–3); Nye, *Masculinity*, pp. 98–123; R. Nye, 'Sex and sexuality

in France since 1800', in Eder *et al.*, *Sexual Cultures in Europe. National Histories*, pp. 91–113 (pp. 96–7); C. J. Dean, *The Frail Social Body. Pornography, Homosexuality and Other Fantasies in Interwar France* (Berkeley: University of California Press, 2000), p. 132.

6   Nye has argued that in France medical understandings of the sexual invert did not follow the same steps as in Germany. While in this country, there was a steady passage from an anatomical understanding to a psychological one, in France the same linear process did not take place. See Nye, *Masculinity*, pp. 103–6, and, Nye, 'Sex and sexuality', pp. 96–7. On the condemnatory nature of French medicine with respect to homosexuality, see Nye, *Masculinity*, pp. 106–7.

7   The Italian case, while sharing many peculiarities with Spain, has much in common with French realities. In the first instance, for example, there was a powerful autochthonous discourse on criminology (Lombrosian positivism), which stigmatized homosexuals and considered them to be innate criminals who resulted from the atavistic return of primitive hermaphroditism (B. P. F. Wanrooij, 'Italy: sexuality, morality and public authority', in Eder *et al.*, *Sexual Cultures in Europe. National Histories*, pp. 114–37 (p. 123)). Secondly, the experience of the First World War reinforced the rejection of any practice that blurred gender divisions. Such behaviours were considered to undermine fertility and virility, fundamental for military might, and were thus considered antipatriotic (Wanrooij, 'Italy', pp. 124–5). Thirdly, fascist pro natalism (D. Horn, *Social Bodies. Science, Reproduction and Italian Modernity* [Princeton, Princeton University Press, 1994]) and machismo (B. Spackman, *Fascist Virilities: Rhetoric, Ideology and Social Fantasy in Italy* [Minneapolis: Minnesota University Press, 1996]) encouraged the repression of homosexuality, although not by legal measures (B. P. F. Wanrooij, *Storia del Pudore. La Questione Sessuale in Italia, 1860–1940* [Venice: Marsilio Editori, 1990], p. 212).

8   In Italy, preliminary considerations for the Penal Code of 1930, drawn up by Rocco, entertained the possibility of punishing homosexuality. In the event, and in contrast to the Spanish Code of 1928, this possibility was thrown out. It was believed that the explicit inclusion of such a clause would soil the image of the new, strong, masculine Italy (Wanrooij, *Storia*, p. 212). On the Penal Code of 1930 as a compromise between classical liberal law and the new positivist theses of 'social defence', see Horn, *Social Bodies*, pp. 33–4.

9   A similar process occurred in Argentina during the last decades of the nineteenth century. However, the active/passive or insertive/receptive divide was a much more widespread notion in Argentina, and in many other Latin American countries, than in Spain. See J. Salessi, 'The Argentine Dissemination of Homosexuality, 1890–1914', *Journal of the History of Homosexuality*, 4, 3 (1994), 337–68 (350–1).

10   R. Cleminson and E. Amezúa, 'Spain: the political and social context of sex reform in the late nineteenth and early twentieth centuries', in F. X. Eder, L. Hall and G. Hekma (eds), *Sexual Cultures in Europe.*

National Histories (Manchester: Manchester University Press, 1999), pp. 173–96 (pp. 177–8).

11   The idea of a non-unitary *habitus* is expressed in Bourdieu (P. Bourdieu and A. Sayad, *Le Déracinement. La crise de l'agriculture traditionelle en Algérie* [Paris: Minuit, 1964], pp. 68–70) but its theoretical elaboration is found in B. Lahire, *L'Homme Pluriel. Les ressorts de l'action* (Paris: Nathan, 1998), pp. 27–35. This theoretical *bricolage* may well have differed across the media in which doctors expressed their ideas, such as articles, conferences, university expositions and popular sexological publications.

12   In France and in Italy lay discourse in general followed the same path in issues of social morality. See, respectively, L. Boltanski, *Puericultura y Moral de Clase* (Laia: Barcelona, 1974), p. 23, and, Wanrooij, *Storia*, pp. 14–15, 31.

13   Salessi, 'The Argentine Dissemination'.

14   Chauncey, 'From Sexual Inversion'.

15   Chauncey, 'From Sexual Inversion', pp. 87–9; H. Oosterhuis, 'Medical Science and the Modernisation of Sexuality', in Eder *et al.*, *Sexual Cultures in Europe. National Histories*, pp. 221–41 (p. 222).

16   E. K. Sedgwick, *Epistemology of the Closet* (New York/London: Harvester Wheatsheaf, 1991), pp. 44–8; D. M. Halperin, 'How to do the History of Homosexuality', *GLQ: Gay and Lesbian Quarterly*, 6, 1 (2000), 87–121.

17   L. Huerta, 'El marañonismo y la intersexualidad', *Estudios*, 69 (1929), 9–12 (9).

18   This eclecticism obliges us to revise some of Foucault's ideas such as the opposition between degenerationist ideas, associated with eugenics and racism, and psychoanalysis, as a rupture with hereditarianism. See M. Foucault, *The History of Sexuality*, vol. I, *An Introduction* (Harmondsworth: Penguin, 1990), pp. 118–19. While Foucault recognizes that the medicine of the perversions and eugenics were enabled to be 'merged' together 'for the theory of "degenerescence" made it possible for them to perpetually refer back to one another' (118), and despite the idea that 'the series composed of perversion-heredity-degenerescence formed the solid nucleus of the new technologies of sex' (118), psychiatry at the end of the nineteenth century 'would be hard to comprehend if one did not see the rupture it brought about in the great system of degenerescence' (119). Further, Foucault argues that psychiatry 'sought to free it [the sexual instinct] from its ties with heredity, and hence from eugenics and the various racisms' (119). The eclecticism of Spanish psychiatry, combining Freudian concepts with degenerationist thought, goes some way towards questioning the universality of the incompatibility between diverse elements advanced by Foucault. See also F. Vázquez García and A. Moreno Mengíbar, *Sexo y Razón. Una Genealogía de la Moral Sexual en España (siglos XVI–XX)* (Madrid: Akal, 1997), pp. 162–3.

19   Two examples, amongst many, are Nye, *Masculinity*, p. 125, and

G. Mosse, *The Image of Man. The Creation of Modern Masculinity* (New York/Oxford: Oxford University Press, 1996), pp. 77–8.

[20] Weeks, *Coming Out*, pp. 96–100; Mosse, *The Image of Man*, pp. 104–5.

[21] E. Badinter, *XY: On Masculine Identity* (New York: Columbia University Press, 1995, trans. Lydia Davis), pp. 13–20.

[22] An example of the power of feminist movements is the rapidity and successfulness with which the issue of the abolition of prostitution, as opposed to its regulation, made its mark in both countries. See J. R. Walkowitz, *Prostitution and Victorian Society. Women, Class and the State* (Cambridge: Cambridge University Press, 1980) and R. Rosen, *The Lost Sisterhood. Prostitution in America, 1900–1918* (Baltimore: The Johns Hopkins University Press, 1982).

[23] Nye, *Masculinity*, pp. 72–97.

[24] On the 'feminist threat', see Badinter, *XY: On Masculine Identity*, pp. 13–20 and on depopulation see F. X. Eder, 'Sexual Cultures in Germany and Austria, 1700–2000', in Eder *et al.*, *Sexual Cultures in Europe. National Histories*, pp. 138–72 (pp. 159–64).

[25] Mosse, *The Image of Man*, pp. 56–76.

[26] Wanrooij, *Storia*, p. 58.

[27] Wanrooij, 'Italy', p. 124.

[28] Wanrooij, *Storia*, p. 211.

[29] The same anticlerical imaginary which attributed perverse sexuality to priests and hysteria to nuns can be seen in France (Nye, 'Sex Differences', 38–9) and in Italy (Wanrooij, *Storia*, pp. 64–8.)

[30] M. Foucault, *Genealogía del racismo* (Madrid: La Piqueta, 1992), pp. 271–2.

[31] G. Mosse, *Sessualitá e Nazionalismo. Mentalitá Borghese e Rispettabilitá* (Bari: Laterza, 1984), p. 86.

[32] G. Mosse, *Sessualitá*, pp. 73–91.

[33] L. D. H. Sauerteig, 'Sex Education in Germany from the eighteenth to the twentieth century', in Eder *et al.*, *Sexual Cultures in Europe. National Histories*, pp. 9–33.

[34] Weeks, *Coming Out*, pp. 151–5; R. Porter and L. Hall, *The Facts of Life. The Creation of Sexual Knowledge in Britain, 1650–1950* (New Haven/ London: Yale University Press, 1995).

[35] On France, see J. Donzelot, *The Policing of Families* (London: Hutchinson, 1979), and M. L. Stewart, 'Science is always chaste: sex education and sexual initiation in France, 1880s–1930s', *Journal of Contemporary History*, 32, 3 (1997), 381–94. On Italy, see Wanrooij, *Storia*, pp. 69–77, 160–70; G. Rifelli and C. Ziglio, *Per una storia dell'educazione sessuale (1870–1920)* (Scandicci: La Nuova Italia, 1991). On Spain, see F. Vázquez García and A. Moreno Mengíbar, 'Genealogía de la educación sexual en España. De la pedagogía ilustrada a la crisis del Estado del Bienestar', *Revista de Educación*, 309 (1996), 67–94; F. Vázquez García, 'Gobierno de la infancia y educación sexual (España 1900–1936)', *Cahiers Alfred Binet*, 661, 4 (1999), 33–48; J. B. Seoane Cegarra, 'La Pasión y la Norma. Una Genealogía de la Moral Sexual Infantil en España (1800–1920)' (unpublished Ph.D. thesis, University of Cadiz, Cadiz, 2001).

[36] A. Mira, 'Laws of silence: homosexual identity and visibility in contemporary Spanish culture', in B. Jordan and R. Morgan-Tamosunas (eds), *Contemporary Spanish Cultural Studies* (London: Arnold, 2000), pp. 241–50 (p. 242).

[37] Salessi, 'The Argentine Dissemination', 338; Mira, 'Laws of silence', pp. 244–6; F. Garza, *Quemando mariposas. Sodomía e imperio en Andalucía y México, siglos XVI–XVII* (Barcelona: Laertes, 2002), pp. 48–9.

Bibliography

Anon., 'Los exhibicionistas', *El Siglo Médico* (1877), 429–30

Anon., 'Noticias', *El Siglo Médico*, 32 (1885), 92

Anon., 'Los célibes en Francia', *El Siglo Médico*, 32 (1885), 650

Anon., 'Observaciones neurosexuales en el frente', *El Siglo Médico*, 65 (1918), 674

Anon., 'Un caso de hermafrodismo', *La Medicina Ibera*, 135, (1920), 181

Anon., 'Los hermafroditas', *La Medicina Ibera*, 395 (1925), 564–5

Abenraxic de Masila, 'El bozo', in E. García Gómez, *Poemas arábigoandaluces* (Madrid: Editorial Plutarco, 1930), p. 119

Adler, A., *El Problema del Homosexualismo y otros estudios sexuales* (Barcelona, Apolo, 1936)

Agote, L., 'Neuropatología. Nuevo método gráfico para fijar la herencia', *Revista Iberoamericana de Ciencias Médicas*, 7 (1902), 402–7

Alberich, J., *Del Támesis al Guadalquivir. Antología de Viajeros Ingleses en la Sevilla del siglo XIX* (Seville: Publicaciones de la Universidad de Sevilla, 1976)

Alcina, B., *Tratado de Higiene Privada y Pública* (Cadiz: José Vidas, 1882)

Aldrich, R., *The Seduction of the Mediterranean: Writing, Art and Homosexual Fantasy* (London/New York: Routledge, 1993)

Aliaga, J. V. and J. M. G. Cortés (eds), *Identidad y diferencia: sobre la cultura gay en España* (Barcelona/Madrid: Egales, 1997)

Alonso Marañón, P. M., 'Notas sobre la Higiene como materia de Enseñanza Oficial en el siglo XIX', *Historia de la Educación*, 6 (1987), 22–41

Altamira, R., *Psicología del Pueblo Español* (Madrid: Biblioteca Nueva, 1902)

Álvarez Junco, J., *Mater Dolorosa. La idea de España en el siglo XIX* (Madrid: Taurus, 2001)

Álvarez Peláez, R., 'Introducción al estudio de la eugenesia española (1900–1936)', *Quipu*, 2, 1 (1985), 95–122

Álvarez Peláez, R., 'El Instituto de Medicina Social: primeros intentos de institucionalizar la eugenesia', *Asclepio*, 40 (1988), 343–58

Álvarez Peláez, R., 'Origen y desarrollo de la eugenesia en España', in J. M. Sánchez Ron (ed.), *Ciencia y Sociedad en España. De la Ilustración a la Guerra Civil* (Madrid: Ed. El Arquero/CSIC, 1988), pp. 178–204

Álvarez Peláez, R. and R. Huertas García-Alejo, *¿Criminales o locos? Dos peritajes psiquiátricos del Dr. Gonzalo Rodríguez Lafora* (Madrid: CSIC, 1987)

Álvarez Peláez, R., 'La Mujer Española y el Control de la Natalidad en los Comienzos del siglo XX', *Asclepio*, 42, 2 (1990), 175–200

Álvarez-Uría, F., *Miserables y locos: medicina mental y orden social en la España del siglo XIX* (Barcelona: Tusquets, 1983)

Amezúa, E., 'Cien años de temática sexual en España: 1850–1950. Repertorio y análisis. Contribución al estudio de materiales para una historia de la sexología', *Revista de Sexología*, 48 (1991), 1–197

Amezúa, E., 'Los hijos de Don Santiago: paseo por el casco antiguo de nuestra sexología', *Revista de Sexología*, 59–60 (1993), 1–281

Anon., 'Teoría Psicoanalítica de Freud. Sesión del día 23 de abril. Academia Médico-Quirúrgica de Madrid', *El Siglo Médico*, 64 (1917), 320–1

Aranguren, J. L., *Moral y Sociedad. La Moral Española en el siglo XIX* (Madrid: Taurus, 1982)

Ariès, P. and G. Duby (eds), *Historia de la Vida Privada*, vol. IV, *De la Revolución Industrial a la Primera Guerra Mundial* (Madrid: Taurus, 1989)

Arnalte, A., *Redada de Violetas: La represión de los homosexuales durante el franquismo* (Madrid: La Esfera de los Libros, 2003)

Aron, J. P. and R. Kempf, *La Bourgeoisie, le Sexe et l'Honneur* (Brussels: Ed. Complexe, 1984)

Arteaga, J. F., 'Cuerpo extraño en el recto', *El Siglo Médico*, 49 (1902), 59

Association du Mariage Chrétien, *La Iglesia y la Educación Sexual: manual para los padres y educadores* (Barcelona, Liturgia Española, 1932)

Azaña, M., *El Jardín de los Frailes*, in *Obras Completas*, vol. I (Madrid: Ed. Giner, 1990), pp. 457–8

Badinter, E., *XY: On Masculine Identity* (New York: Columbia University Press, 1995, trans. Lydia Davis)

Ballester, R. and E. Balaguer, 'La infancia como valor y como problema en las luchas sanitarias de principios de siglo en España', *Dynamis*, 15 (1995), 177–92

Ballester, R. & E. Perdiguero, 'Salud e Instrucción Primaria en el ideario regeneracionista de la Institución Libre de Enseñanza', *Dynamis*, 18 (1998), 25–50

Balseiro, J. A., 'Un libro de Hernández-Catá', *Bulletin of Spanish Studies*, 6, 22 (1929), 60–3

Barnés, D., *La Educación de la Adolescencia* (Barcelona: Labor, 1930)

Barnés, D., *La Psicología de la Adolescencia como base para su educación* (Madrid: Editorial Páez-Bolsa, 1930)

Barriobero y Herrán, E., *Los delitos sexuales en las viejas leyes españolas* (Madrid: Mundo Latino, 1930)

Bataille, G., *L'Érotisme*, in *Oeuvres Complètes*, vol. X (Paris: Gallimard, 1987)

Bayo, C., *Higiene Sexual del Soltero* (Madrid: Librería de Antonio Rubiños, 1902)

Bembo, M., *La mala vida en Barcelona. Anormalidad, miseria y vicio* (Barcelona: Maucci, 1912)

Ben-Ami, S., *The Origins of the Second Republic in Spain* (Oxford: Oxford University Press, 1978)

Bernal Martínez, J. M., 'De las escuelas al aire libre a las aulas de la Naturaleza', *Áreas. Revista de Ciencias Sociales,* 20 (2000), 171–82

Bernaldo de Quirós, C., 'Delincuentes que escriben', *Revista Iberoamericana de Ciencias Médicas,* 4 (1900), 509–12

Bernaldo de Quirós, C., *Criminología de los delitos de sangre en España* (Madrid: Editorial Internacional, 1906)

Bernaldo de Quirós, C. and J. Mª Llanas Aguilaniedo, *La mala vida en Madrid* (Madrid: B. Rodríguez Sierra, 1901)

Berneri, C., 'La degeneración sexual en las escuelas', *La Revista Blanca,* 118 (1928), reproduced in R. Cleminson, *Anarquismo y Homosexualidad. Antología de artículos de la Revista Blanca, Generación Consciente, Estudios e Iniciales (1924–1937)* (Madrid: Huerga y Fierro, 1995), pp. 51–5

Berneri, C., 'El contagio moral en el ambiente escolar', *La Revista Blanca,* 122 (1928), reproduced in R. Cleminson, *Anarquismo y Homosexualidad. Antología de artículos de la Revista Blanca, Generación Consciente, Estudios e Iniciales (1924–1937)* (Madrid: Huerga y Fierro, 1995), pp. 57–68

Birken, L., *Consuming Desire. Sexual Science and the Emergence of a Culture of Abundance, 1871–1914* (Ithaca/London: Cornell University Press, 1987)

Blanco Nájera, F., *Coeducación y Educación Sexual* (Madrid: Manuales *Studium* de Cultura Religiosa, 1935)

Bloch, I., *La vida sexual contemporánea* (Madrid/Berlín/Buenos Aires: Editora Internacional, 1924)

Boltanski, L., *Puericultura y Moral de Clase* (Laia: Barcelona, 1974)

Borderies-Guereña, J., 'Niños y niñas en familia', in J. M. Borrás Llop (ed.), *Historia de la Infancia en la España Contemporánea 1843–1936* (Madrid: Ministerio de Trabajo y Asuntos Sociales/Fundación Germán Sánchez Ruipérez, 1996), pp. 21–66

Borrás Llop, J. M. (ed), *Historia de la Infancia en la España Contemporánea 1843–1936* (Madrid: Ministerio de Trabajo y Asuntos Sociales/ Fundación Germán Sánchez Ruipérez, 1996)

Bourdieu, P., *Language and Symbolic Power* (Cambridge: Polity Press, 1991)

Bourdieu, P. and A. Sayad, *Le Déracinement. La crise de l'agriculture traditionelle en Algérie* (Paris: Minuit, 1964)

Brachfeld, O., 'Crítica de las teorías sexuales del Dr. Marañón', *El Siglo Médico,* 4081 (1932), 214–21

Brachfeld, O., 'Los Consultorios Juveniles: principios y resultados', *Revista de Pedagogía,* 155 (1934), 502–8

Brachfeld, O., *El problema del homosexualismo* (Barcelona: Apolo, 1936)

Braudel, F., *The Mediterranean and the Mediterranean world in the age of Philip II,* 2 vols (London: Collins, 1972–3)

Bravo y Moreno, F., *Exposición de un caso clínico médico-legal de psicopatía homo-sexual* (Santander: Tip. El Cantábrico, 1903), pamphlet, 11 pp.

Bravo y Moreno, F., 'Exposición de un caso clínico médico-legal de psicopatía homo-sexual', in *Actes du XIC Congrès International de Médecine,* publiés sous la direction de Ms. le Dr. Fernández-Caro.

Section d'Hygiène, Épidémiologie et Science Sanitaire Technique (Madrid: Imp. De J. Sastre, 1904), pp. 96–102

Briand, J., J. Bouis and J. L. Casper, *Manual Completo de Medicina Legal y Toxicología*, 2 vols (Madrid: Moya y Plaza, 1872)

Bugallo Sánchez, J., *La Higiene Sexual en las Escuelas* (Madrid: Morata, 1930)

Bumke, O., *Tratado de las enfermedades mentales* (Barcelona: Francisco Seix, 1920)

Buñuel, L., *My Last Breath* (London: Vintage, 1994, trans. Abigail Israel)

Burke, P., *The French Historical Revolution: The Annales School, 1929–89* (Cambridge: Polity, 1990)

Butler, J., *Excitable Speech. A Politics of the Performative* (New York: Routledge, 1997)

Buxán, X. M., (ed.), *ConCiencia de un singular deseo* (Barcelona: Laertes, 1997)

Cacho Vío, V., *La Institución Libre de Enseñanza* (Madrid: Rialp, 1962)

Calmette, A., 'Educación sexual de los niños y de los púberes', *Boletín de la Inspección Provincial de Sanidad de Sevilla* (15 October 1927), 31–8

Campillo, A., 'Foucault y Derrida: historia de un debate sobre la historia', in *La Invención del Sujeto* (Madrid: Biblioteca Nueva, 2001), pp. 109–48

Campoamor, C., *Mi pecado mortal: el voto femenino y yo* (Seville: Instituto Andaluz de la Mujer, 2001 [1936])

Campos Marín, R., 'La sociedad enferma: higiene y moral en España en la segunda mitad del siglo XIX y principios del XX', *Hispania*, 191, 3 (1995), 1093–112

Campos Marín, R., 'Higiene mental y peligrosidad social en España (1920–1936)', *Asclepio*, 49, 1 (1997), 39–59

Campos Marín, R., 'La teoría de la degeneración y la clínica psiquiátrica en la España de la Restauración', *Dynamis*, 19 (1999), 429–56

Campos Marín, R., 'La teoría de la degeneración y la profesionalización de la psiquiatría en España (1876–1920)', *Asclepio*, 51(1), 1999, 185–203

Canguilhem, G., *Le Normal et le Pathologique* (Paris: PUF, 1966)

Canguilhem, G., *et al.*, *Du Développement à l'évolution au XIX siècle* (Paris: PUF, 1985)

Cansinos-Assens, R., *Ética y Estética de los Sexos* (Madrid: Biblioteca Júcar, 1973 [1920])

Carbonell, D., *El Onanismo. Su Prehistoria, su Historia, sus Causas y sus Consecuencias* (Caracas: 1907)

Cardwell, R. A., 'Oscar Wilde and Spain: Medicine, Morals, Religion and Aesthetics in the *Fin de Siglo*', in F. Bonaddio and X. de Ros, *Crossing Fields in Modern Spanish Culture* (Oxford: University of Oxford, 2003), pp. 35–53

Carlavilla del Barrio, M., *Sodomitas* (Madrid: Editorial Nos, 1956)

Carlier, F., *Études de Pathologie Sociale. Les Deux Prositutions* (Paris: E. Dentu, 1887)

Caro Baroja, J., *Introducción a una Historia Contemporánea del Anticlericalismo Español* (Madrid: Istmo, 1980)

Carpintero, H., 'Influencias germánicas en la psicología española', in J. de Salas and D. Briesemeister (eds), *Las influencias de las culturas académicas alemana y española desde 1898 hasta 1936* (Madrid/ Frankfurt: Ibero-americana/Vervuert, 2000), pp. 223–37

Carrasco, R., *Inquisición y represión sexual en Valencia. Historia de los sodomitas (1565–1785)* (Barcelona: Laertes, 1985)

Casado Montado, J., *Memorias de un mal nacido* (San Fernando: The Author, 2nd edn, 1989)

Castejón Bolea, R., *Moral Sexual y Enfermedad: la medicina española frente al peligro venéreo (1868–1936)* (Granada: Universidad de Granada/ Instituto Alicantino de Cultura Juan Gil-Albert, 2001)

Castel, R., *El Orden Psiquiátrico. La Edad de Oro del Alienismo* (Madrid: La Piqueta, 1980)

Castilla del Pino, C., *La cultura bajo el franquismo* (Barcelona: Ediciones del Bolsillo, 1977)

Chauncey, G., 'Christian Brotherhood or Sexual Perversion? Homosexual Identities and the Construction of Sexual Boundaries in the World War One Era', *Journal of Social History*, 19 (1985), 189–211

Chauncey, G., 'From Sexual Inversion to Homosexuality: The Changing Medical Conceptualization of Female "Deviance"', in K. Peiss, C. Simmons and R. Padgug (eds), *Passion and Power: Sexuality in History* (Philadelphia: Temple University Press, 1989), pp. 87–117

Chauncey, G., *Gay New York: The Making of the Gay Male World, 1890–1940* (London: Flamingo, 1995)

Cleminson, R., *Anarquismo y Homosexualidad. Antología de artículos de la Revista Blanca, Generación Consciente, Estudios e Iniciales (1924–1937)* (Madrid: Huerga y Fierro, 1995)

Cleminson, R., 'Male Homosexuality in Contemporary Spain: Signposts for a Sociological Analysis', *Paragraph: A Journal of Modern Critical Theory*, 22, 1 (1999), 35–54

Cleminson, R., 'The Review *Sexualidad* (1925–28), Social Hygiene and the Pathologisation of Male Homosexuality in Spain', *Journal of Iberian and Latin American Studies*, 6, 2 (2000), 119–29

Cleminson, R., 'En torno a *Sexualidad*: "desviación sexual", raza y la construcción de la nación', *Reverso*, 3 (2000), 41–8

Cleminson, R., *Anarchism, Science and Sex: Eugenics in Eastern Spain, 1900–1937* (Oxford: Peter Lang, 2000)

Cleminson, R., 'El libro *Homosexualidad* del Dr. Martín de Lucenay: Entre el conocimiento científico y la recepción pública de la ciencia sexológica en España a principios del siglo XX', *Hispania. Revista Española de Historia*, 218 (2004), 961–86

Cleminson, R. M., 'The Significance of the "Fairy" for the Cultural Archaeology of Same-Sex Male Desire in Spain, 1850–1930', *Sexualities*, 7, 4 (2004), 412–29

Cleminson, R., 'Medicine, the Novel and Homosexuality in Spain', in A. Carling (ed.), *Globalization and Identity: Development and Integration in a Changing World* (London: I.B. Tauris, 2006), pp. 201–20

Cleminson, R. and E. Amezúa, 'Spain: the political and social context of sex reform in the late nineteenth and early twentieth centuries', in F.

X. Eder, L. Hall and G. Hekma (eds), *Sexual Cultures in Europe. National Histories* (Manchester, Manchester University Press, 1999), pp. 173–96

Cleminson, R. and R. M. Medina Doménech, '¿Mujer u hombre? Hermafroditismo, tecnologías médicas e identificación de sexo en España, 1860–1925', *Dynamis*, 24 (2004), 53–91

Cleminson, R. and F. Vázquez García, '"Los Invisibles": Hacia una historia de la homosexualidad masculina en España, 1840–2000', *International Journal of Iberian Studies*, 13, 3 (2000), 167–81

Climent, T. de R., *Higiene Sexual del Soltero y la Soltera* (Barcelona: La Vida Literaria, c. 1910)

Comelles, J. M., *La Razón y la Sinrazón. Asistencia psiquiátrica y desarrollo del Estado en la España contemporánea* (Barcelona: PPU, 1988)

Comenge, L., *Generación y Crianza ó higiene de la familia* (Barcelona: José Espasa, Editor, n.d.)

Conard, P., 'Sexualité et Anticlericalisme (Madrid, 1910)', *Hispania. Revista Española de Historia*, 117 (1971), 103–34

Contreras Pazo, R., 'La educación de los sexos', *Revista de Escuelas Normales*, 101 (1934), 45–6

Corbin, A., *Le Miasme et la Jonquille. L'odorat et l'imaginaire sociale, XVIIIe–XIXe siècles* (Paris: Flammarion, 1986)

Costa, J., 'Intervención' in *Actas de las Sesiones* (Madrid: Hernando, 1882), pp. 137–8

Costa, J., *Política Quirúrgica* (Madrid: Biblioteca Costa, 1914 [1902])

Costa, J., *Oligarquía y Caciquismo* (Madrid: Ed. de la Revista del Trabajo, 1975 [1901])

Costa, J., *Maestro, Escuela y Patria (notas pedagógicas)* (Madrid: Biblioteca Costa, 1916)

Criado y Aguilar, F., 'Refutación de las teorías de la intersexualidad', *El Siglo Médico*, 4085 (1932), 321–5

Criado y Aguilar, F., 'Refutación de las teorías de la intersexualidad', *El Siglo Médico*, 4090 (1932), 457–63

Crozier, I. D., 'Taking Prisoners: Havelock Ellis, Sigmund Freud and the Construction of Homosexuality, 1897–1951', *Social History of Medicine*, 13, 3 (2000), 447–66

Crozier, I. D., 'The Medical Construction of Homosexuality and its relation to the Law in Nineteenth-Century England', *Medical History*, 45 (2001), 61–82

Cubí i Soler, M., *Sistema Completo de Frenología* (Barcelona: Don Juan Oliveres Impresor, 1846)

Curtis y La Mert, M., *La Conservación Personal. Tratado interesante de las causas de la decadencia prematura de la energía física y mental y demás atributos de la virilidad* (Barcelona: Imp. de Oliveres Hermanos, 1849)

Dall'Orto, G., '"Socratic Love" as a Disguise for Same-Sex Love in the Italian Renaissance', in K. Gerard and G. Hekma (eds), *The Pursuit of Sodomy: Male Homosexuality in Renaissance and Enlightenment Europe* (New York/London: Harrington Park Press, 1989), pp. 33–65

Danet, J., *Discours Juridique et Perversions Sexuelles (XIXe et XXe siècles)* (Nantes: Université de Nantes, 1977)

Davidson, A. I., 'Sex and the emergence of the family', *Critical Inquiry*, 14 (1987), 16–48

Davis, L. E., 'Oscar Wilde in Spain', *Comparative Literature*, 35 (1973), 136–52

De Azúa, J., 'Impotencia psíquica', *El Siglo Médico*, 63 (1916), 338–40

De Eleizegui, J., *La Sexualidad Infantil (Normas de Educación)* (Madrid: Unión Poligráfica S.A., 1934)

De Fluvià, A., 'El movimiento homosexual en el estado español', in J. R. Enríquez (ed.), *El homosexual ante la sociedad enferma* (Barcelona: Tusquets, 1978), pp. 149–67

De La Pascua Sánchez, M. J., '¿Hombres vueltos del revés? Una historia sobre la construcción de la identidad sexual en el siglo XVIII', in M. J. de la Pascua, M. del Rosario García-Doncel and G. Espigado (eds), *Mujer y deseo* (Cadiz: Universidad de Cádiz, 2004), pp. 431–44

De La Torre, R., 'La prensa madrileña y el discurso del Lord Salisbury sobre las "naciones moribundas" (Londres, Albert Hall, 4 mayo 1898)', *Cuadernos de Historia Moderna y Contemporánea*, 6 (1985), 163–80

De Letamendi, J., *Curso de Clínica General*, 2 vols (Madrid: Imp. de los Sucesores de Cuesta, 1894)

De Maeztu, R., *Hacia otra España* (Madrid: Biblioteca Nueva, 1997 (1899))

Del Moral y Pérez Aloe, J., *El estado y la prostitución* (Madrid: Felipe G. Rojas, 1913)

De Sales Mayo, F., *La Condesita (Memorias de una doncella)* (Madrid: Oficina Tipográfica del Hospicio, 3rd edn, 1870)

De Tapia, E., *Tratado del Juicio Criminal* (Valencia: Imp. de Ildefonso Mompié, 1829)

Del Toro, C., *La Luz y la Pintura* (Cadiz: Real Academia de Bellas Artes de Cádiz, 1894)

Del Toro, C., *La Luz y la Pintura*, 2 vols (Cadiz: Real Academia de Bellas Artes de Cádiz, 1901)

De Villena, L. A., 'Álvaro Retana, en el abanico de la "novela galante-decadente"', *Turia. Revista Cultural*, 21–22 (1992), 19–28

Dean, C., *The Frail Social Body: Pornography, Homosexuality, and Other Fantasies in Interwar France* (Berkeley/Los Angeles/London: University of California Press, 2000)

Deleuze, G., 'The Rise of the Social', foreword to J. Donzelot, *The Policing of Families* (Baltimore/London: Johns Hopkins University Press, 1997), pp. ix–xvii

Delgado, H. F., 'El psicoanálisis en la escuela', *El Siglo Médico*, 66 (1919), 982–3

Delumeau, J., *El Miedo en Occidente (siglos XIV–XVIII)* (Madrid: Taurus, 1989)

Derrida, J., 'Firma, acontecimiento, contexto', in *Márgenes de la Filosofía* (Madrid: Cátedra, 1998), pp. 347–72

D'Halmar, A., *Pasión y Muerte del Cura Deusto* (Madrid: Editora Internacional, 1924)

Diamond, I. and L. Quinby (eds), *Feminism & Foucault: Reflections on Resistance* (Boston: Northeastern University Press, 1988)

Dieguez, A., 'El problema de la nosografía en la obra psiquiátrica de J. Giné y Partagás', *Asclepio*, 50, 1 (1998), 199–222

Dolsa y Ramón, L., 'Contribución al estudio de la hebefrenia', *Revista de Ciencias Médicas de Barcelona*, 15, 11 (1899), 401–3

Domínguez Lorén, V., *Los homosexuales frente a la ley. Los juristas opinan* (Barcelona: Plaza y Janés, 1977)

Donato, E., *Homosexualismo (Frente a Gide)* (Madrid: Morata, 1931)

Donzelot, J., *The Policing of Families* (London: Hutchinson, 1979)

Dopico, F., 'Ganando espacios de libertad. La mujer en los comienzos de la transición democrática en España', in G. Duby and M. Perrot (eds), *Historia de las Mujeres*, vol. IV, *El Siglo XIX* (Madrid: Taurus, 2000), pp. 597–611

Dreger, A. D., 'Hermaphrodites in Love: The Truth of the Gonads', in V. A. Rosario (ed), *Science and Homosexualities* (New York/London: Routledge, 1997), pp. 46–66

Dreger, A. D., *Hermaphrodites and the Medical Invention of Sex* (Cambridge, Mass./London: Harvard University Press, 1998)

Duchesne, E. A., *De la prostitution dans la ville d'Alger depuis la conquête* (Paris: J. B. Baillière/Garnier Frères, 1853)

Eder, F. X., 'Sexual Cultures in Germany and Austria, 1700–2000', in F. X. Eder, L. Hall and G. Hekma (eds), *Sexual Cultures in Europe. National Histories* (Manchester: Manchester University Press, 1999), pp. 138–72

Eder, F. X., L. Hall and G. Hekma (eds), *Sexual Cultures in Europe. National Histories* (Manchester: Manchester University Press, 1999)

Eder, F. X., L. Hall and G. Hekma (eds), *Sexual Cultures in Europe. Themes in Sexuality* (Manchester: Manchester University Press, 1999)

Ellis, H., *Estudios de Psicología Sexual*, vol. II, *La Inversión Sexual* (Madrid: Hijos de Reus, 1913)

Enguix Grau, B., *Poder y deseo: La homosexualidad masculina en Valencia* (Valencia: Edicions Alfons del Magnànim/Generalitat Valenciana, 1996)

Enríquez, J. R., (ed.), *El homosexual ante la sociedad enferma* (Barcelona: Tusquets, 1978)

Eribon, D., *Réflexions sur la question gay* (Paris: Fayard, 1999)

Escalante, J. M., *Iniciación en la Vida Sexual* (Barcelona: Librería Ameller, 1932)

Escuder, J. M., *Locos y Anómalos* (Madrid: Establecimiento Tip. Sucesores de Rivadeneyra, 1895)

Eslava, R., *La prostitución en Madrid. Apuntes por un estudio sociológico* (Madrid: Vicente Rico, 1900)

Espejo Muriel, C., *El Deseo Negado. Aspectos de la problemática homosexual en la vida monástica (siglos III–VI d.C.)* (Granada: Pub. Universidad de Granada, 1991)

Esquirol, E., *Des Maladies Mentales*, 2 vols (Paris: J. B. Baillière Ed., 1838)

Faderman, L., *Surpassing the Love of Men* (London: The Women's Press, 1991)

Fausto-Sterling, A., *Sexing the Body: Gender politics and the construction of sexuality* (New York: Basic Books, 2000)

Fernández, P., *Eduardo López Bago y el Naturalismo Radical* (Amsterdam: Rodopi, 1995)

Fernández, P., 'Moral y *scientia sexualis* en el siglo XIX. El eros negro de la novela naturalista', *Analecta Malacitana*, 11 (1997), 192–4

Fernández, P., '*Scientia sexualis* y el saber psiquiátrico en la novela naturalista decimonónica', *Asclepio*, 49, 1 (1997), 227–44

Fernández Martín, A., Review of Hermann Rohleder, *Fisiología Sexual, Psicología Sexual y Filosofía Sexual, El Siglo Médico*, 68 (1921), 1290

Fernández Sanz, E., *Histerismo. Teoría y clínica* (Madrid: Librería de Francisco Beltrán, 1914)

Fernández Sanz, E., 'Sobre Educación Sexual. Su importancia para la profilaxia de las psicosis y psiconeurosis', *El Siglo Médico*, 62 (1915), 386–9

Fernández Sanz, E., 'Observaciones polémicas sobre psico-análisis', *Archivos de Medicina, Cirugía y Especialidades*, 154 (1924), 311–18

Fernández Sanz, E., 'Algunas derivaciones eugénicas del problema sexual', *El Siglo Médico*, 75 (1925), 525–9

Fernández Sanz, E., 'Nupcialidad, Natalidad y Eugenesia', *El Siglo Médico*, 75 (1925), 213–17

Fernández Soria, J. M. and A. Mayordomo Pérez, 'Perspectiva histórica de la protección a la infancia en España', *Historia de la Educación*, 36 (1984), 191–213

Flandrin, J. L., *La Moral Sexual en Occidente* (Barcelona: Granica, 1984)

Forel, A., *La Cuestión Sexual expuesta a los adultos ilustrados* (Madrid: Bailly-Baillière, 1912)

Forns, R., *Higiene. Breves apuntes de las lecciones dadas en el curso de 1908 a 1909* (Madrid: Biblioteca de la Revista de Especialidades Médicas, 1915)

Foucault, M., 'L'évolution de la notion d'individu dangereux dans la psychiatrie légale', *Déviance et Société*, 5 (1981), 403–22

Foucault, M., *The History of Sexuality*, vol. I, *An Introduction* (Harmondsworth: Penguin, 1990, trans. Robert Hurley)

Foucault, M., *Genealogía del racismo* (Madrid: La Piqueta, 1992)

Foucault, M., *Los Anormales. Curso del Collège de France (1974–1975)* (Madrid: Akal Universitaria, 2001)

Foucault, M., *El orden del discurso* (Barcelona: Tusquets, 2002)

Freud, S., 'Contribuciones al Simposio sobre la Masturbación', in *Obras Completas*, vol. II (Madrid: Biblioteca Nueva, 1973 [1912]), p. 1703

Fuentes, P., 'Modos de vida y relaciones sociales', in P. Fuentes, *En clave gay* (Madrid: Egales, 2001), pp. 55–87

Galcerán, A., 'Ensayo de clasificación anatomo-patológica de las vesanias', *El Siglo Médico*, 36 (1889), 407–9, 470–2, 486–9

Galera, A., *Ciencia y Delincuencia. El determinismo antropológico en la España del siglo XIX* (Seville: CSIC, 1991)

García Gómez, E., *Poemas arábigoandaluces* (Madrid: Editorial Plutarco, 1930)

García Piñeiro, R., 'Actitudes sociales en la Asturias de postguerra', in J. López Álvarez and C. Lombardía Fernández (eds), *Valentín Vega: Fotógrafo de calle (1941–1951)* (Gijón: Ayuntamiento, 2001), pp. 73–165

García Valdés, A., *Historia y presente de la homosexualidad* (Madrid: Akal, 1981)

Garma, A., 'Psicología de la aclaración de la sexualidad en la infancia', *Revista de Escuelas Normales*, 103 (1934), 98–103

Garrido y Escuín, V., *La Cárcel o el Manicomio. Estudio Médico-Legal sobre la Locura* (Madrid: Casa Editorial de D. José Mª Faquineto, 1888)

Garza, F., *Quemando mariposas. Sodomía e imperio en Andalucía y México, siglos XVI–XVII* (Barcelona: Laertes, 2002, trans. Lluís Salvador)

Gerard, K. and G. Hekma (eds), *The Pursuit of Sodomy: Male Homosexuality in Renaissance and Enlightenment Europe* (New York/London: Harrington Park Press, 1989)

Gibson, I., *La represión nacionalista de Granada en 1936 y la muerte de Federico García Lorca* (Paris: Ruedo Ibérico, 1971)

Gibson, I., *Federico García Lorca. 1. De Fuente Vaqueros a Nueva York* (Barcelona: Grijalbo, 1985)

Gibson, I., *Federico García Lorca. 2. De Nueva York a Fuente Grande* (Barcelona: Grijalbo, 1987)

Gide, A., *Corydon* (Madrid: Oriente, 2nd edn, 1929)

Gil Maestre, M., *La criminalidad en Barcelona y en las grandes poblaciones* (Barcelona: Tipografía de Leodegario Obradors, 1886)

Gil Maestre, M., *Los malhechores de Madrid* (Gerona: Imp. y Lib. de Paciano Torres, 1889)

Giné y Partagás, J., *Curso Elemental de Higiene Privada y Pública* (Barcelona: Librería de Juan Bastinos e Hijo, 1871)

Giné y Partagás, J., *Tratado Teórico-práctico de Frenopatología* (Madrid: Moya y Plaza Libreros Editores, 1876)

Giner de los Ríos, F., '"Juegos Corporales" (Informe leído en el Congreso de Profesores de Gimnasia, Zurich, 1885)', in *Obras Completas de Francisco Giner de los Ríos*, vol. XVI, *Ensayos menores sobre Educación y Enseñanza* (Madrid: Imprenta Julio Lozano, 1927 [1885]), p. 281

Giner de los Ríos, F., 'La nerviosidad y la educación según el Dr. Pelman', in *Obras Completas de Francisco Giner de los Ríos*, vol. XVI, *Ensayos sobre Educación y Enseñanza* (Madrid: Imprenta Julio Lozano, 1927 [1889]), pp. 221–2, 228

Giner de los Ríos, F., 'El estudio higiénico de la Infancia en el Congreso de Londres', in *Obras Completas de Francisco Giner de los Ríos*, vol. XVI, *Ensayos menores sobre Educación y Enseñanza* (Madrid: Imprenta Julio Lozano, 1927 [1889]), pp. 177–229

Giner de los Ríos, F., 'La educación de los niños según Krafft-Ebing', in *Obras Completas de Francisco Giner de los Ríos*, vol. XVI, *Ensayos menores sobre Educación y Enseñanza* (Madrid: Imprenta Julio Lozano, 1927 [1896]), pp. 231–5

Giner de los Ríos, F., *Ensayos* (Madrid: Alianza Editorial, 1973 [1902])

Glick, T., 'El impacto del psicoanálisis en la psiquiatría española de entreguerras', in J. M. Sánchez Ron (ed.), *Ciencia y Sociedad en*

España. De la Ilustración a la Guerra Civil (Madrid: Ed. El Arquero/ CSIC, 1988), pp. 204–21

Glick T. F., 'La "idea nueva": ciencia, política y republicanismo', in B. Ciplijauskaité and C. Maurer (eds), *La voluntad de humanismo: Homenaje a Juan Marichal* (Barcelona: Anthropos, 1990), pp. 57–90

Glick, T. F., 'Marañón, Intersexuality and the Biological Construction of Gender in 1920s Spain', *Cronos*, 8 (1) (2005), 121–37

Goffman, E., *Asylums: essays on the social situation of mental patients and other inmates* (Garden City, NY: Doubleday, 1961)

Goldsborough Serrat, A., *Imagen Humana y Literaria de Gregorio Martínez Sierra* (Madrid: Gráficas Cóndor, 1965)

Gómez, E., *La mala vida en Buenos Aires* (Buenos Aires: Juan Roldan, 1908)

Gómez Ocaña, J., *El sexo, el hominismo y la natalidad* (Madrid: Editorial Saturnino Calleja, 1919)

Gómez Sebastián, F., 'El homosexualismo', *Sexualidad*, 43 (1926), 2–3

González Duro, E., *Historia de la Locura en España*, vol. III, *Del Reformismo del siglo XIX al Franquismo* (Madrid: Ediciones Temas de Hoy, 1996)

González de Samano, M. and A. Francés, 'Dictamen acerca de un presunto atentado de sodomía presentado al juzgado de 1ª instancia de la ciudad de Alfaro', *Boletín de Medicina, Cirugía y Farmacia*, 1 (1846), 231–2

Gordon, C., 'Governmental Rationality: an introduction', in G. Burchell, C. Gordon and P. Miller (eds), *The Foucault Effect: Studies in Governmentality* (London: Harvester Wheatsheaf, 1991), pp. 1–48

Graham, H. and J. Labanyi, 'Culture and Modernity: The Case of Spain', in H. Graham and J. Labanyi (eds), *Spanish Cultural Studies* (Oxford: Oxford University Press, 1995), pp. 1–19

Greenberg, D. F., *The Construction of Homosexuality* (Chicago/London: University of Chicago Press, 1988)

Grosz, E., *Volatile Bodies: Towards a corporeal feminism* (Bloomington: Indiana University Press, 1994)

Guasch, O., *La sociedad rosa* (Barcelona: Anagrama, 1991)

Haan, P., *Nos Ancêtres les Pervers* (Paris: Olivier Orban, 1979)

Hacking, I., 'Five parables', in R. Rorty, J. B. Schneewind and Q. Skinner (eds), *Philosophy in history: essays on the historiography of philosophy* (Cambridge: Cambridge University Press, 1984), pp. 103–124

Hacking, I., 'Making Up People', in E. Stein (ed), *Forms of desire: sexual orientation and the social constructionist controversy* (New York/London: Routledge, 1992), pp. 69–88

Haliczer, S., *Sexualidad en el Confesionario. Un Sacramento Profanado* (Madrid: Siglo XXI, 1998)

Hall, L., 'Sexual Cultures in Britain: some persisting themes', in F. X. Eder, L. Hall and G. Hekma (eds), *Sexual Cultures in Europe. National Histories* (Manchester: Manchester University Press, 1999), pp. 38–42

Hall, R., *The Well of Loneliness* (Paris: Pegasus Press, 1928)

Halperin, D. M., *One Hundred Years of Homosexuality and Other Essays on Greek Love* (New York: Routledge, 1990)

Halperin, D., 'How to do the History of Homosexuality', *GLQ: A Journal of Lesbian and Gay Studies*, 6, 1 (2000), 87–124

Hansen, B., 'American Physicians' "Discovery" of Homosexuals, 1880–1900: A New Diagnosis in a Changing Society', in C. E. Rosenberg and J. Golden (eds), *Framing Disease: studies in cultural history* (New Brunswick: Rutgers University Press, 1992), pp. 104–33

Harris, F., *Oscar Wilde: his life and confessions*, 2 vols (New York: The Author, 1916)

Harris, F., *Vida y Confesiones de Oscar Wilde* (Madrid: Biblioteca Nueva 1928, trans. Ricardo Baeza)

Hauser, P., *Madrid desde el punto de vista Médico-Social*, 2 vols (Madrid: Editora Nacional, 1979)

Hekma, G., 'Same-sex relations among men in Europe, 1700–1990', in F. X. Eder, L. Hall and G. Hekma (eds), *Sexual Cultures in Europe. Themes in Sexuality* (Manchester: Manchester University Press, 1999), pp. 79–103

Hernández-Catá, H. [A.], *El Ángel de Sodoma* (Valparaíso: 'El Callao', 1929)

Herrera Rodríguez, F., 'Un acercamiento a la obra de Federico Rubio y Galí (1827–1902)', *Revista de la Historia de El Puerto*, 29 (2002), 63–88

Herzer, M., *Magnus Hirschfeld: Leben und Werk eines jüdischen, schwulen und sozialistischen Sexologen* (Frankfurt: Campus, 1992)

Herzog, D., 'Hubris and Hypocrisy, Incitement and Disavowal: Sexuality and German Fascism', *Journal of the History of Sexuality*, 11, 1/2 (2002), 3–21

Hildegart, *El problema sexual tratado por una mujer española* (Madrid: Morata, 1931)

Hobsbawm, E., *Age of Extremes: The Short Twentieth Century, 1914–1991* (London: Michael Joseph, 1994)

Horn, D., *Social Bodies. Science, Reproduction and Italian Modernity* (Princeton, Princeton University Press, 1994)

Huerta, L., *Eugénica, Maternología y Puericultura. Ensayo de un estudio sobre el cultivo de la especie humana por las leyes biológicas* (Madrid: Imprenta de Fontanet, 1918)

Huerta, L., 'El marañonismo y la intersexualidad', *Estudios*, 69 (1929), 9–12

Huerta, L., *La Educación Sexual del Niño y del Adolescente* (Madrid: Instituto Samper, 1930)

Huerta, L., 'Pedagogía y Eugénica', in E. Noguera and L. Huerta (eds), *Genética, Eugenesia y Pedagogía Sexual. Libro de las Primeras Jornadas Eugénicas Españolas* (Madrid: Morata, 1934), pp. 150–69

Huerta, L., 'La eugenesia y la preparación del maestro', *Revista de Pedagogía*, 151 (1934), 296–301

Huertas García-Alejo, R., *Orfila. Saber y Poder Médico* (Madrid: CSIC, 1988)

Huertas García-Alejo, R., 'El concepto de "perversión sexual" en la medicina positivista', *Asclepio*, 42, 2 (1990), 89–100

Huertas García-Alejo, R., 'Niños degenerados. Medicina Mental y regeneracionismo en la España del cambio de siglo', *Dynamis*, 18 (1998), 157–79

Hurtado de Mendoza, M., *Instituciones de Medicina y Cirugía* (Madrid, 1839)

Hurtado de Mendoza, M., *Vocabulario Médico-Quirúrgico* (Madrid: Boix, 1840)

Isern, D., *Del Desastre Nacional y sus Causas* (Madrid: Imprenta de la Viuda de M. Minuesa de los Ríos, 1899)

Jiménez de Asúa, L., *La Lucha contra el Delito de Contagio Venéreo* (Madrid: Ed. Caro Raggio, 1925)

Jiménez de Asúa, L., *Valor de la psicología profunda (Psicoanálisis y psicología individual) en ciencias penales* (Madrid: Editorial Reus, 1935)

Jiménez de Asúa, L. and J. Antón Oneca, *Derecho Penal conforme al Código de 1928* (Madrid: Editorial Reus, 1929)

Juarros, C., 'Diagnóstico de las neurastenias', *Revista Médica de Sevilla*, 30 November 1911, 289–96

Juarros, C., *Psiquiatría forense* (Madrid: Imprenta de Antonio Marzo, 1914)

Juarros, C., 'Escuela y Hogar', *El Siglo Médico*, 65 (1918), 302–3

Juarros, C., *La Psiquiatría del médico general* (Madrid: Ruiz, Hermanos, 1919)

Juarros, C., 'Marruecos la Perversa', *El Siglo Médico*, 69 (1922), 639–40

Juarros, C., *Educación de Niños Anormales. Ponencia Oficial del III Congreso Nacional de Pediatría* (Madrid: Torrent y Cía, 1925)

Juarros, C., *Normas de Educación Sexual y Física* (Madrid: Renacimiento, 1925)

Juarros, C., *El Amor en España. Características Masculinas* (Madrid: Ed. Páez, 1927)

Juarros, C., *Los Horizontes de la Psicoanálisis* (Madrid: Mundo Latino, 1928)

Juarros, C., *La Sexualidad Encadenada. Ejemplos y Consejos* (Madrid: Mundo Latino, 1931)

Juderías, J., *La miseria y la criminalidad en las grandes ciudades de Europa y América* (Madrid: Publicaciones de la Revista Penitenciaria, 1906)

Juderías, J., *La trata de blancas. Estudio acerca de este problema en España y en el Extranjero* (Madrid: Sociedad Española de Higiene, 1911)

Juderías, J., *La leyenda negra: estudios acerca del concepto de España en el extranjero* (Barcelona: Araluce, 1917)

Katz, J. N., *The Invention of Heterosexuality* (New York: Penguin, 1995)

Koch, F. M., *Venus Sexual: tratado de las enfermedades que resultan de los excesos sexuales, hábitos solitarios . . .* (Madrid: Imp. El Resumen, 1903)

Krafft-Ebing, R. V., *Psicopatía Sexual. Estudio Médico-Legal para uso de Médicos y Juristas* (Buenos Aires: El Ateneo, 1955 [1886])

Labanyi, J., *Gender and Modernization in the Spanish Realist Novel* (Oxford: Oxford University Press, 2000)

Lahire, B., *L'Homme Pluriel. Les ressorts de l'action* (Paris: Nathan, 1998)

Lamo de Espinosa, E., *Delitos sin Víctimas. Orden social y ambivalencia moral* (Madrid: Alianza, 1989)

Lanteri-Laura, G., *Lecture des Perversions. Histoire de leur appropriation médicale* (Paris: Masson, 1979)

Laqueur, T., *Making sex: body and gender from the Greeks to Freud* (Cambridge, Mass./London: Harvard University Press, 1990)

Litvak, L., *Antología de la novela corta erótica española de entreguerras. 1918–1936* (Madrid: Taurus, 1993)

Llamas, R., *Teoría torcida. Prejuicios y discursos en torno a «la homosexualidad»* (Madrid: Siglo XXI, 1998)

Llamas, R. and F. Vidarte, *Homografías* (Madrid: Espasa Calpe, 1999)

López Ibor, J. J., *Lo vivo y lo muerte del Psicoanálisis* (Barcelona: Luis Miracle, 1936)

Lorulot, A., 'Perversiones y desviaciones del instinto sexual. VIII. El homosexualismo', *Iniciales*, 8 (1932), reproduced in R. Cleminson, *Anarquismo y Homosexualidad. Antología de artículos de La Revista Blanca, Generación Consciente, Estudios e Iniciales (1924–1935)* (Madrid: Huerga y Murcia, 1995), pp. 75–83

McIntosh, M., 'The Homosexual Role', *Social Problems*, 16 (1968), 182–92

McLaren, A., 'National responses to sexual perversions: the case of transvestism', in F. X. Eder, L. Hall and G. Hekma (eds), *Sexual Cultures in Europe. Themes in Sexuality* (Manchester: Manchester University Press, 1999), pp. 121–38

McNay, L., *Foucault and Feminism: Power, Gender and the Self* (Cambridge: Polity, 1992)

Macías Picavea, R., *El Problema Nacional* (Madrid: Biblioteca Nueva, 1996 [1899])

Madrazo, E., *Cultivo de la Especie Humana. Herencia y Educación* (Santander: Blanchard y Arce, 1904)

Magnan, V., 'Consideraciones generales sobre la locura', *El Siglo Médico*, 34 (1887), 104–6, 118–20

Magnien, B., 'Cultura urbana', in S. Salaün and S. Serrano (eds), *1900 en España* (Madrid: Espasa Calpe, 1991), pp. 107–30

Manjón, A., *El Pensamiento de Ave María. Tercera Parte. Modos de enseñar* (Granada: Imprenta-Escuela del Ave María, 1902)

Mañueco Villapadierna, E., 'Profilaxia personal de las enfermedades venéreas', *El Siglo Médico*, 66 (1919), 1074–6

Marañón, G., *La doctrina de las secreciones internas* (Madrid: Corona, 1918)

Marañón, G., 'Prólogo' to I. Bloch, *La vida sexual contemporánea*, 2 vols (Madrid: Editora Internacional, 1924), vol. I, pp. v–xvi

Marañón, G., 'La vida sexual en España', *El Siglo Médico*, 76 (1925), 577–80

Marañón, G., 'La educación sexual y la diferenciación sexual', *Generación Consciente*, 31 (1926), 15–18 and *Generación Consciente*, 32 (1926), 42–5

Marañón, G., 'Nuevas ideas sobre el problema de la intersexualidad y sobre la cronología de los sexo', *Estudios*, 70 (1929), 17–23 and *Estudios*, 71 (1929), 24–31

Marañón, G., 'Prólogo', in Hernández-Catá, *El Ángel de Sodoma* (Valparaíso: 'El Callao', 1929), pp. 9–19

Marañón, G., 'Acerca del problema de la intersexualidad', *El Siglo Médico*, 4082 (1932), 243–7

Marañón, G., 'La endocrinología y la ciencia penal', prologue in Q. Saldaña, *Nueva criminología* (Madrid: M. Aguilar, 1936), pp. 7–18

Marañón, G., 'Psicopatología del donjuanismo', reproduced in *Obras Completas*, vol. III, *Conferencias* (Madrid: Espasa-Calpe, 1967), pp. 75–93

Marañón, G., 'Diálogo antisocrático sobre *Corydon*' (1929), in *Obras Completas* (Madrid: Espasa-Calpe, 1968), vol. I, pp. 465–72

Marañón, G., 'Notas para la biología de Don Juan', in *Obras Completas*, vol. IV, *Artículos y otros trabajos* (Madrid: Espasa-Calpe, 1968), pp. 75–93 (original 1924)

Marañón, G., *Ensayos sobre la Vida Sexual* (Madrid: Espasa Calpe, 1969 [1926])

Marañón, G., 'Nuevas ideas sobre el problema de la intersexualidad y sobre la cronología de los sexos', in *Obras Completas*, vol. IV (Madrid: Espasa-Calpe, 1976), pp. 165–83 (original 1928)

Marañón, G., *La evolución de la sexualidad y los estados intersexuales*, in *Obras Completas*, vol. VIII (Madrid Espasa-Calpe, 1972), pp. 499–710

Marinoni, A., 'Medicina Social', *El Siglo Médico*, 68 (1921), 950–73

Maristany, L., *El Gabinete del Doctor Lombroso (Delincuencia y fin de siglo en España)* (Barcelona: Anagrama, 1973)

Maristany, L., 'Introducción', in C. Bernaldo de Quirós and J. Mª Llanas Aguilaniedo, *La Mala Vida en Madrid. Estudio psicosociológico con dibujos y fotografías del natural* (Huesca: Instituto de Estudios Altoaragoneses/Egido Editorial, 1998 [1901]), XXXIII–LVIII

Martí Ibáñez, F., 'Consideraciones sobre el homosexualismo', *Estudios*, 145 (1935), 3–6

Martí Ibáñez, F., 'Nueva moral sexual', *Estudios*, 134 (1934), 13–14

Martín de Lucenay, A., *Homosexualidad* (Madrid: Editorial Fénix, 1933)

Martínez Navarro, A., 'Anotaciones a la Historia de la Educación Física Española en el Siglo XIX', *Historia de la Educación*, 2 (1983), 153–64

Martínez Navarro, A., 'El Escultismo en el Marco de la Educación Física: su implantación en España', in Various Authors, *La Educación en la España Contemporánea. Cuestiones Históricas* (Madrid: SM, 1985), pp. 151–63

Martínez Sierra, G., *Granada (Guía emocional)* (Paris: Garnier-Hermanos, 1911)

Martínez Pérez, J., 'Sexualidad y Orden Social: la visión médica en la España del primer tercio del siglo XIX', *Asclepio*, 42 (1990), 119–35.

Martínez Valverde, J., *Guía del Diagnóstico de las Enfermedades Mentales* (Barcelona: Hijos de Espasa Editores, 1899)

Mas, J., *Hampa y miseria* (Madrid: Saez Hermanos, 1923)

Masip, E., 'Enseñanza, respecto de las funciones sexuales, que debe darse a los niños desde el punto de vista higiénico de esta función orgánica', in *Actas del Primer Congreso Español de Higiene Escolar* (Madrid: Imp. Vda. Fco. Badía, 1912), pp. 173–82

Mata, P., *Vademécum de Medicina y Cirugía Legal* (Madrid: Imp. Calle de Padilla, 1844)

Mata, P., *Tratado de Medicina y Cirugía Legal* (Paris: Bailly-Baillière, 1846)

Mata, P., 'Discurso pronunciado por el Dr. Mata en la sesión del día 14 de enero de 1860', *El Especialista*. *Revista Quincenal de Sifilografía, Oftalmología, Afecciones de la Piel y del Aparato Genito-Urinario*, 8–13 (1860), 83–199

Mata, P., *De la Libertad Moral o Libre Albedrío* (Madrid: Imp. Carlos Bailly Baillière, 1868)

Mata, P., *Tratado de Medicina y Cirugía Legal Teórica y Práctica*, 4 vols (Madrid: Bailly-Baillière, 5th edn, 1874)

Maugue, A., *L'Identité Masculine en Crise au Tournant du Siècle* (Paris: Rivages-Histoire, 1987)

Mestre, T., *Introducción al estudio de la psicología positiva* (Madrid: Bailly-Baillière é Hijos, 1905)

Mestre, M. V. and H. Carpintero, 'Enrique Fernández Sanz y la introducción de las ideas de Freud en España', *Historia de la Psicología*, 4, 1 (1983), 69–84

Mestre; V., & H. Carpintero, 'Unas notas sobre la entrada de Jung en España', *Historia de la Psicología*, 10, 1–4 (1989), 139–48

Micheler, S., 'Homophobic Propaganda and the Denunciation of Same-Sex-Desiring Men under National Socialism', *Journal of the History of Sexuality*, 11, 1/2 (2002), 95–130

Mira, A. (ed.), *Para entendernos* (Barcelona: Llibres de l'Index, 1999)

Mira, A., 'Modernistas, dandis y pederastas: articulaciones de la homosexualidad en la "edad de plata"', *Journal of Iberian and Latin American Studies*, 7, 1 (2001), 63–75

Mira, A., 'Laws of silence: homosexual identity and visibility in contemporary Spanish culture', in B. Jordan and R. Morgan-Tamosunas (eds), *Contemporary Spanish Cultural Studies* (London: Arnold, 2000), pp. 241–50

Mira, A., *De Sodoma a Chueca: Una historia cultural de la homosexualidad en España en el siglo XX* (Barcelona/Madrid: Egales, 2004)

Moll, A., 'La Educación Sexual', in the *Boletín de la Institución Libre de Enseñanza*, 33 (1909), 294–6

Monlau, P. F., *Elementos de Higiene Pública* (Barcelona: Imp. de P. Riera, 1846)

Monlau, P. F., *Higiene del Matrimonio o El Libro de los Casados* (Madrid: Imp. M. Rivadeneyra, 1865 [1853])

Monlau, P. F., 'Primera lección de higiene pública y epidemológica', *El Siglo Médico*, 14 (1869), 422–3

Moreno y Díaz-Prieto, C., 'Homosexualismo', *Sexualidad*, 96 (1925), 9

Moreno Mengíbar, A. and F. Vázquez García, *Crónica de una Marginación. Historia de la Prostitución en Andalucía desde el siglo XV hasta la Actualidad* (Cadiz: BAAL, 1999)

Morote, L., *La Moral de la Derrota* (Madrid: Biblioteca Nueva, 1997 [1900])

Mosse, G., *Sessualitá e Nazionalismo. Mentalitá Borghese e Rispettabilitá* (Bari: Laterza, 1984)

Mosse, G., *The Image of Man. The Creation of Modern Masculinity* (New York/Oxford: Oxford University Press, 1996)

Mott, L., and A. Assunção, 'Love's Labors Lost: Five Letters from a Seventeenth-Century Portuguese Sodomite', in K. Gerard and G. Hekma (eds), *The Pursuit of Sodomy: Male Homosexuality in Renaissance and Enlightenment Europe* (New York/London: Harrington Park Press, 1989), pp. 91–101

Moya, G., *Gonzalo R. Lafora. Medicina y Cultura en una España en Crisis* (Madrid: Universidad Autónoma de Madrid, 1986)

Muchembled, R., *L'invention de l'Homme Moderne. Culture et sensibilités en France du XVe au XVIIIe siècle* (Paris: Fayard, 1987)

Muñoz López, P., *Sangre, Amor e Interés. La Familia en la España de la Restauración* (Madrid: Marcial Pons/UAM Ediciones, 2001)

Mut, A., 'Los Neurasténicos', *Revista Ibero-Americana de Ciencias Médicas*, 16 (1906), 213–19

Nash, M., 'El Neomalthusianismo Anarquista y los Conocimientos Populares sobre el Control de la Natalidad en España', in M. Nash (ed.), *Presencia y Protagonismo. Aspectos de la Historia de la Mujer* (Madrid: Ediciones del Serbal, 1984), pp. 307–40

Nash, M., *Defying Male Civilization: Women in the Spanish Civil War* (Denver: Arden Press, 1995)

Nash, M., 'Género y ciudadanía', *Ayer*, 20 (1995), 241–58

Navarro Fernández, A., *La prostitución en la villa de Madrid* (Madrid: Ricardo Rojas, 1909)

Navarro Fernández, A., 'Depravación', *Sexualidad*, 3 (1925), 1–2

Navarro Fernández, A., 'Delincuencia sexual', *Sexualidad*, 46 (1926), 1–2

Nazier, F., *L'Anti-Corydon, essai sur l'inversion sexuelle* (Paris: Éditions du Siècle, 1924)

Nin Frías, A., *Alexis o el significado del temperamento urano* (Madrid: Morata, 1932)

Nin Frías, A., *Homosexualismo creador* (Madrid: Morata, 1933)

Noguera, J., *Moral, Eugenesia y Derecho* (Madrid: Morata, 1930)

Norton, R., *Mother Clap's Molly House: The Gay Subculture in England 1700–1830* (London: Gay Men's Press, 1992)

Norton, R., *The Myth of the Modern Homosexual: Queer history and the search for cultural unity* (London: Routledge, 1997)

Nóvoa Santos, R., *Manual de patología general*, 3 vols (Santiago de Compostela: Tipografía El Eco de Santiago, 1916–19)

Nóvoa Santos, R., *La Mujer, Nuestro Sexto Sentido y Otros Esbozos* (Madrid: Biblioteca Nueva, 1929)

Nye, R., 'Sex Difference and Male Homosexuality in French Medical Discourse, 1830–1930', *Bulletin of the History of Medicine*, 63, 1 (1989), 32–51

Nye, R., *Masculinity and Male Codes of Honor in Modern France* (New York/Oxford: Oxford University Press, 1993)

Nye, R., 'Sex and sexuality in France since 1800', in F. X. Eder, L. Hall and G. Hekma (eds), *Sexual Cultures in Europe. National Histories* (Manchester: Manchester University Press, 1999), pp. 91–113

O' Connor, P. W., *Gregorio and María Martínez Sierra* (Boston: Twayne Pub., 1977)

Olmeda, F., *El látigo y la pluma: homosexuales en la España de Franco* (Madrid: Oberon, 2004)

Oosterhuis, H. and H. Kennedy (eds), *Homosexuality and Male Bonding in Pre-Nazi Germany* (New York: Harrington Park Press, 1991)

Oosterhuis, H., 'Medical Science and the Modernisation of Sexuality', in F. X. Eder, L. Hall and G. Hekma (eds), *Sexual Cultures in Europe. National Histories* (Manchester: Manchester University Press, 1999), pp. 221–41

Oosterhuis, H., *Stepchildren of Nature: Krafft-Ebing, Psychiatry, and the Making of Sexual Identity* (Chicago/London: University of Chicago Press, 2000)

Orfila, M., *Tratado de Medicina Legal* (Madrid: Imp. de D. José M² Alonso, 1847)

Orozco Acuaviva, A., 'El doctor Don Cayetano Del Toro Quartiellers', *Archivo Iberoamericano de Historia de la Medicina y Antropología Médica,* 14 (1972), 261–84

Ortega, F., *Amizade e Estética da Existência em Foucault* (Rio de Janeiro: Graal, 1999)

Ortega, F., *Genealogias da Amizade* (São Paulo: Iluminuras, 2002)

Ortega y Gasset, J., 'Vieja y Nueva Política', in *Obras de José Ortega y Gasset* (Madrid: Espasa Calpe, 1936), pp. 83–120

Ortiz, T., 'El discurso médico sobre las mujeres en la España del primer tercio del siglo veinte', in M. T. López Beltrán (ed.), *Las mujeres en Andalucía. Actas del 2º encuentro interdisciplinar de estudios de la mujer en Andalucía,* vol. I (Málaga: Diputación Provincial de Málaga, 1993), pp. 107–38

Ots Esquerdo, V., 'Inversión sexual intelectiva sistemática', *El Siglo Médico,* 39 (1892), 664–98

Oudshoorn, N., 'Endocrinologists and the conceptualization of sex. 1920–1940', *Journal of the History of Biology,* 23, 2 (1990), 163–86

Palacios Lis, I., 'Cuestión social y educación: un modelo de regeneracionismo educativo', *Historia de la Educación,* 4 (1985), 305–19

Peiró, J. M. and H. Carpintero, 'Historia de la psicología en España a través de sus revistas especializadas', *Historia de la Psicología,* 2, 2 (1981), 143–81

Peiró, P. M. and J. Rodrigo, *Elementos de Medicina y Cirugía Legal arreglados a la Legislación Española* (Madrid: Imp. de la Compañía General de Impresores y Libreros, 1841)

Penn, D., 'Queer: Theorizing Politics and History', *Radical History Review,* 62 (1995), 24–42

Peratoner, A., *Los Peligros del Amor, de la lujuria y del libertinaje en el hombre y en la mujer* (Barcelona: Establecimiento Editorial de José Miret, 1874)

Pereyra, M., 'Educación, Salud y Filantropía: el origen de las colonias escolares de vacaciones en España', *Historia de la Educación,* 1 (1982), 145–68

Pérez de Ayala, R., *A.M.D.G.* (Madrid: Editorial Pueyo, 1931)

Pick, D., *Faces of Degeneration: A European disorder, c.1848–c.1914* (Cambridge: Cambridge University Press, 1989)

Piga, A., *Higiene de la Pubertad* (Toledo: Imp. de la Vda. e Hijos de J. Peláez, 1910)

Plumed Domingo, J. J., and A. Rey González, 'La introducción de las ideas degeneracionistas en la España del siglo XIX. Aspectos conceptuales', *Frenia. Revista de Historia de la Psiquiatría*, 2, 1 (2002), 31–48

Plumwood, V., *Feminism and the Mastery of Nature* (London/New York: Routledge, 1993)

Porter, R. and L. Hall, *The Facts of Life. The Creation of Sexual Knowledge in Britain, 1650–1950* (New Haven/London: Yale University Press, 1995)

Preciado, B., *Manifiesto contra-sexual: Prácticas subversivas de identidad sexual* (Madrid: Opera Prima, 2002)

Puente, I., 'Necesidad de la iniciación sexual', *Estudios*, 98 (1931), 6–7

Pulido Martín, A., 'Algunos conceptos modernos sobre la potencia sexual', *El Siglo Médico*, 3498 (1920), 977–9

Ramón y Cajal, S., 'Prólogo de la edición española', in E. Bleuler, *Tratado de psiquiatría* (Madrid: Calpe, 1924)

Régis, E., *Tratado de Psiquiatría* (Madrid: Saturnino Calleja Fernández, 1911)

Reher, D. S., *La Familia en España. Pasado y presente* (Madrid: Alianza Universidad, 1996)

Retana, Á., *Los Extravíos de Tony (confesiones inmorales de un colegial ingenuo)* (Madrid: Biblioteca Hispania, 1919)

Retana, Á., *La Ola Verde. Crítica frívola* (Barcelona: Ed. Jasón, 1931)

Retana, Á., *A Sodoma en tren botijo* (Madrid: Imp. Saez Hermanos, 1933)

Rey González, A. M., *Estudios médico-sociales sobre marginados en la España del siglo XIX* (Madrid: Ministerio de Sanidad y Consumo, 1990)

Richards, M., *A Time of Silence: civil war and the culture of repression in Franco's Spain* (Cambridge: Cambridge University Press, 1998)

Richards, M., 'Spanish Psychiatry c.1900–1945: Constitutional Theory, Eugenics, and the Nation', *Bulletin of Spanish Studies*, 81, 6 (2004), 823–48

Rifelli, G. and C. Ziglio, *Per una storia dell'educazione sessuale (1870–1920)* (Scandicci: La Nuova Italia, 1991)

Rochard, J., 'Causas de la Disminución de los Nacimientos en Francia', *El Siglo Médico*, 32 (1885), 145–50

Rocke, M., *Forbidden Friendships: Homosexuality and Male Culture in Renaissance Florence* (New York/Oxford: Oxford University Press, 1996)

Rodrigo, A., *Memoria de Granada: Manuel Angeles Ortiz & Federico García Lorca* (Granada: Diputación Provincial de Granada, 1993)

Rodríguez Guerra, A., *El Conservador de la Salud. Manual de Higiene Pública y Privada* (Cadiz: Imprenta de D. José Mª Ruiz, 1846)

Rodríguez Lafora, G., *Los Niños Mentalmente Anormales* (Madrid: Ed. de la Lectura, 1917)

Rodríguez Lafora, G., 'Consideraciones sobre el mecanismo genético de las psicosis paranoides', *El Siglo Médico*, 68 (1921), 1201–5

Rodríguez Lafora, G., 'Impotencia sexual masculina de forma psíquica', *El Siglo Médico*, 75 (1925), 237–40

Rodríguez Lafora, G., 'La impotencia masculina y la neurastenia moral', *El Siglo Médico*, 88 (1931), 541–52

Rodríguez Lafora, G., *La Educación Sexual y la reforma de la moral sexual* (Madrid: Publicaciones de la Revista de Pedagogía, 1933)

Rodríguez Lafora, G., 'La psicología de Don Juan', in *Don Juan, Los milagros y otros ensayos*, (Madrid: Alianza, 1975 [1927]), pp. 7–44

Rodríguez Ocaña, E., *La Constitución de la Medicina Social como Disciplina en España (1882–1923)* (Madrid: Ministerio de Sanidad y Consumo, 1987)

Rodríguez Ocaña, E., 'Una Medicina para la Infancia', in J. M. Borrás Llop (ed.), *Historia de la Infancia en la España Contemporánea 1843–1936* (Madrid: Ministerio de Trabajo y Asuntos Sociales/Fundación Germán Sánchez Ruipérez, 1996), pp. 149–69

Rodríguez-Solís, E., *Historia de la prostitución en España y en América* (Madrid: Biblioteca Nueva, c.1921 [1899])

Roger, H., 'Psicoanálisis y concepto sexual freudiano de las psiconeurosis', *Archivos de Medicina, Cirugía y Especialidades*, 141 (1924), 277–300

Rojo Prieto, C., 'Paralelos entre los niños de las altas esferas sociales y los niños pobres', *El Siglo Médico*, 42 (1895), 532–53

Rosario, V. A., *The Erotic Imagination: French Histories of Perversity* (New York/Oxford: Oxford University Press, 1997)

Rosen, R., *The Lost Sisterhood. Prostitution in America, 1900–1918* (Baltimore: The Johns Hopkins University Press, 1982)

Ruiz Amado, R. P., *La Educación de la Castidad* (Barcelona: Imp. Ibérica, 1908)

Russett, C. E., *Sexual Science: The Victorian Construction of Womanhood* (Cambridge, Mass.: Harvard University Press, 1989)

Said, E., *Orientalism* (London: Penguin, 2003)

Salaün, S., 'Apogeo y decadencia de la sicalipsis', in M. Díaz-Diocaretz and I. M. Zavala (eds), *Discurso erótico y discurso transgresor en la cultura peninsular, siglos XI al XX* (Madrid: Ediciones Tuero, 1992), pp. 129–53

Salazar Quintana, F., *Elementos de Higiene* (Madrid: Librería de Hernando y Compañía, 1896)

Saldaña, Q., *La Sexología (Ensayos)* (Madrid: Mundo Latino, 1930)

Saldaña, Q., *Siete Ensayos de Sociología Sexual* (Madrid: Mundo Latino, 1930)

Saldaña, Q., *Nueva criminología* (Madrid: M. Aguilar, 1936)

Salessi, J., 'The Argentine Dissemination of Homosexuality, 1890–1914', *Journal of the History of Homosexuality*, 4, 3 (1994), 337–68

Salete Larrea, S., *Verdadera Explicación de la Concupiscencia* (Barcelona, 1912)

Salillas, R., *La Vida Penal en España* (Madrid: Imp. de la Revista de Legislación, 1888)

Samblás Tilve, P., 'César Juarros y el *Tratamiento de la Morfinomanía*: ¿cura u ortopedia?', *Frenia. Revista de Historia de la Psiquiatría*, 2, 1 (2002), 123–37

San de Velilla, A., *Sodoma y Lesbos Modernos: Pederastas y Safistas, estudiados en la clínica, en los libros y en la historia* (Barcelona: Carlos Ameller, 1932)

Sánchez Herrero, A., 'Un caso de imbecilidad avanzada', *El Siglo Médico*, 57 (1910), 774–5

Sánchez de Rivera y Moset, D., *Lo Sexual (peligros y consecuencias de los vicios y enfermedades sexuales)* (Madrid: Imp. Helénica, c.1925)

Sanchis Banús, J., *Estudio Médico-Social del Niño Golfo* (Madrid: Tip. Excelsior, 1916)

Sanchis-Banús, J., 'La cuestión del psicoanálisis', *Archivos de Medicina, Cirugía y Especialidades*, 150 (1924), 136–42

Sanfeliú, L., *Juego de damas. Aproximación histórica al homoerotismo femenino* (Málaga: Universidad, 1996)

Santero, F. J., *Elementos de Higiene Privada y Pública* (Madrid: El Cosmos Editorial, 1885)

Santos Padres Españoles, *Reglas Monásticas de la España Visigoda* (Madrid: BAC, 1971)

Sauerteig, L. D. H., 'Sex Education in Germany from the eighteenth to the twentieth century', in F. X. Eder, L. Hall and G. Hekma (eds), *Sexual Cultures in Europe. National Histories* (Manchester: Manchester University Press, 1999), pp. 9–33

Sawicki, J., *Disciplining Foucault: Feminism, Power, and the Body* (New York/London: Routledge, 1991)

Searle, J. R., *The Construction of Social Reality* (Harmondsworth: Penguin, 1996)

Sedgwick, E. K., *Between Men: English Literature and Male Homosocial Desire* (New York: Columbia University Press, 1985)

Sedgwick, E. K., *Epistemology of the Closet* (New York/London: Harvester Wheatsheaf, 1991)

Segovia, A. M., *Los Maricones. Novela de Costumbres* (Madrid: Tipografía Hispano-Americana, 1885)

Seoane Cegarra, J. B., 'La Pasión y la Norma. Una Genealogía de la Moral Sexual Infantil en España (1800–1920)' (unpublished Ph.D. thesis, University of Cadiz, Cadiz, 2001)

Sereñana y Partagás, P., *La prostitución en la ciudad de Barcelona* (Barcelona: Imprenta de los sucesores de Ramírez y Cª, 1882)

Serret, R., 'Neurastenia sifilítica', *El Siglo Médico*, 40 (1893), 793–5

Shubert, A., *Death and Money in the Afternoon. A History of the Spanish Bullfight* (Oxford: Oxford University Press, 1999)

Sinfield, A., *The Wilde Century: Effeminacy, Oscar Wilde and the Queer Moment* (London: Cassell, 1994)

Spackman, B., *Fascist Virilities: Rhetoric, Ideology and Social Fantasy in Italy* (Minneapolis: Minnesota University Press, 1996)

Stein, E. (ed.), *Forms of desire: sexual orientation and the social constructionist controversy* (New York/London: Routledge, 1992)

Stewart, M. L., 'Science is always chaste: sex education and sexual initiation in France, 1880s–1930s', *Journal of Contemporary History*, 32, 3 (1997), 381–94

Strozier, R. M., *Foucault, Subjectivity, and Identity: Historical Constructions of Subject and Self* (Detroit: Wayne State University Press, 2002)

Suárez Casañ, V., *La prostitución* (Barcelona: Maucci, 10th edn, 1895)

Suárez Casañ, V., *La pederastia* (Barcelona: Centro Editorial, *c.*1905), Suárez Casañ, V., *Conocimientos para la Vida Privada*, vol. VI, *La Pederastia* (Barcelona: Casa Editorial Maucci, 20th edn, 1910)

Suárez Casañ, V., *Conocimientos para la Vida Privada*, vol. IX, *El Amor Lesbio* (Barcelona: Casa Editorial Maucci, 20th edn, 1910)

Tarczylo, T., 'From lascivious erudition to the history of mentalities', in G. S. Rousseau amd R. Porter (eds), *Sexual Underworlds of the Enlightenment* (Manchester: Manchester University Press, 1987), pp. 26–41

Tardieu, A., *Estudio médico-forense de los atentados contra la honestidad* (Madrid: Manuel Álvarez, 1863, trans. N. López Bustamente and J. de Querejazu y Hartzensbuch)

T. B., review of Donato, *Homosexualismo (Frente a Gide)*, *El Siglo Médico*, 88 (1931), 468–9

Terrón Bañuelos, A., 'La higiene escolar: un campo de conocimiento disputado', *Áreas. Revista de Ciencias Sociales*, 20 (2000), 73–94

Terry, J., 'Theorizing Deviant Historiography', *Differences: A Journal of Feminist Cultural Studies*, 3, 2 (1991), 55–74

Teruel, B., *Elogio y nostalgia de Gregorio Marañón* (Barcelona: Barca, 1961)

Tierno Galván, E., 'Costa y el Regeneracionismo', in *Escritos (1950–1960)* (Madrid: Tecnos, 1971), pp. 369–1079

Tomás y Valiente, F., 'El Crimen y Pecado contra natura', in F. Tomás y Valiente, *et al.*, (eds), *Sexo Barroco y Otras Transgresiones Premodernas* (Madrid: Alianza Universidad, 1990), pp. 37–8

Torres, R., *Víctimas de la Victoria* (Madrid: Oberon, 2002)

Tort, P., *La Raison Classificatoire* (Paris: Aubier Montaigne, 1989)

Trinidad Fernández, P., *La Defensa Social. Cárcel y Delincuencia en España (siglos XVIII–XX)* (Madrid: Alianza Universidad, 1991)

Trinidad Fernández, P., 'La Infancia Delincuente y Abandonada', in Borrás Llop (ed.), *Historia de la Infancia*, pp. 461–521

Trumbach, R., 'Sodomitical subcultures, sodomitical roles and the Gender Revolution of the Eighteenth Century', in R. P. Maccubin (ed.), *'Tis Nature's Fault: Unauthorized Sexuality during the Enlightenment* (Cambridge: Cambridge University Press, 1985), pp. 117–18

Trumbach, R., 'The Birth of the Queen: Sodomy and the Emergence of Gender Equality in Modern Culture, 1660–1750', in M. B. Duberman, M. Vicinus and G. Chauncey (eds), *Hidden From History: Reclaiming the Lesbian and Gay Past* (Harmondsworth: Penguin, 1991), pp. 129–40

Trumbach, R., *Sex and the Gender Revolution*, vol. I, *Heterosexuality and the Third Gender in Enlightenment London* (Chicago/London: University of Chicago Press, 1998)

V. H., 'La Higiene y la Enseñanza', *Revista de Medicina y Cirugía*, 94 (1909), 359–64

Valentí Vivó, I., *Tratado de Antropología Médica y Jurídica* (Barcelona: Imp. de Jaime Jepús Roviralta, 1889)

Valentí Vivó, I., *La Sanidad Social y los Obreros (Ensayo Antropológico)* (1905), cited in E. Rodríguez Ocaña, *La Constitución de la Medicina Social como Disciplina en España (1882–1923)* (Madrid: Ministerio de Sanidad y Consumo, 1987), pp. 59–82

Vallmitjana, J., *Criminalidad típica local* (Barcelona: Tip. 'L'Avenç', 1910)

Varela, J. and F. Álvarez-Uría, *El Cura Galeote Asesino del Obispo de Madrid-Alcalá* (Madrid: La Piqueta, 1979)

Varela, J. and F. Álvarez-Uría, *Arqueología de la Escuela* (Madrid: La Piqueta, 1991)

Vázquez García, F., 'Ninfomanía y construcción simbólica de la femineidad (España siglos XVIII–XIX)', in C. Canterla (ed.), *VII Encuentro de la Ilustración al Romanticismo. La Mujer en los siglos XVIII y XIX* (Cadiz: Universidad de Cádiz, 1994), pp. 125–35

Vázquez García, F., 'La imposible fusión. Claves para una genealogía del cuerpo andrógino', in D. Romero de Solís, J. B. Díaz-Urmeneta Muñoz and J. López-Lloret (eds), *Variaciones sobre el cuerpo* (Seville: Universidad de Sevilla, 1999), pp. 217–35

Vázquez García, F., 'Gobierno de la infancia y educación sexual (España 1900–1936)', *Cahiers Alfred Binet*, 661, 4 (1999), 33–48

Vázquez García, F., 'El Discurso Médico y la Invención del Homosexual (España 1840–1915)', *Asclepio*, 53, 2 (2001), 159–78

Vázquez García, F. and R. Cleminson, 'Democracia y culturas sexuales: La irrupción de la homosexualidad en la escena política española', *Er. Revista de Filosofía*, 32, (2003), pp. 129–66

Vázquez García, F. and A. Moreno Mengíbar, 'Genealogía de la educación sexual en España. De la pedagogía ilustrada a la crisis del Estado del Bienestar', *Revista de Educación*, 309 (1996), 67–94

Vázquez García, F. and A. Moreno Mengíbar, *Sexo y Razón. Una Genealogía de la Moral Sexual en España (siglos XVI–XX)* (Madrid: Akal, 1997)

Vázquez García, F. and A. Moreno Mengíbar, *Poder y Prostitución en Sevilla. Siglos XVI al XX*, 2 vols (Seville: Publicaciones Universidad de Sevilla, 1998)

Vázquez García, F. and A. Moreno Mengíbar, 'La Sexualidad Vergonzante', in I. Morant (ed.), *Historia de las Mujeres en España y América Latina. Del Siglo XIX a los umbrales del XX*, vol. III (Madrid: Cátedra 2006), pp. 207–33

Vigoroux, A. & P. Juquelier, *El Contagio Mental* (Madrid: Daniel Jorro Ed., 1914)

Vila-San-Juan, J. L., *García Lorca, asesinado: toda la verdad* (Barcelona: Planeta, 1975)

Viñuales, O., *Lesbofobia* (Barcelona: Bellaterra, 2002)

Walkowitz, J. R., *Prostitution and Victorian Society. Women, Class and the State* (Cambridge: Cambridge University Press, 1980)

Wanrooij, B. P. F., *Storia del Pudore. La Questione Sessuale in Italia, 1860–1940* (Venice: Marsilio Editori, 1990)

Wanrooij, B. P. F., 'Italy: sexuality, morality and public authority', in F. X. Eder, L. Hall and G. Hekma (eds), *Sexual Cultures in Europe. National Histories* (Manchester: Manchester University Press, 1999), pp. 114–37

Warner, M., *Fear of a Queer Planet: Queer Politics and Social Theory* (Minneapolis/London: University of Minnesota Press, 1993)

Weeks, J., *Coming Out: Homosexual Politics in Britain, from the Nineteenth Century to the Present* (London: Quartet, 1977)

Weeks, J., 'The "Homosexual Role" After 30 Years: An Appreciation of Mary McIntosh', *Sexualities*, 1, 2 (1998), 131–52

Williams, C. A., *Roman Homosexuality: Ideologies of Masculinity in Classical Antiquity* (New York/Oxford: Oxford University Press, 1999)

Winkler, J. J., *The Constraints of Desire: The Anthropology of Sex and Gender in Ancient Greece* New York/London: Routledge, 1990)

Wright, S, 'Gregorio Marañón and "The Cult of Sex": Effeminacy and Intersexuality in "The Psychopathology of Don Juan" (1924)', *Bulletin of Spanish Studies*, 81, 6 (2004), 717–38

Yáñez, T., *Lecciones de Medicina Legal y Toxicología* (Madrid: Librería de Saturnino Calleja, 1878)

Yáñez, T., *Elementos de Medicina Legal* (Madrid: Imprenta de Enrique Rubiños, 1884)

Yela, M., 'La psicología española', in E. Quiñones, F. Tortosa & H. Carpintero (eds), *Historia de la psicología; textos y comentarios* (Madrid: Tecnos, 1993), pp. 593–603

Zapatero, J. M., *Pedagogía Sexual.Lo que se debe saber* (Barcelona: F. Isart S. en C. Editores, 1922)

Websites

Aliaga, J. V., 'Háblame, cuerpo. Una aproximación a la obra de Pepe Espaliú', *http://www.accpar.org/numero1/aliaga.htm* (21/12/06)

Eisenberg, D., 'Una temprana guía *gay*: *Granada (Guía emocional)*, de Gregorio Martínez Sierra (1911)', *http://users.ipfw.edu/JEHLE/deisenbe/Other_Hispanic_Topics/Guiagay.htm.* (21/12/06)

Index